SECURITY POLITICS IN THE GULF MONARCHIES

COLUMBIA STUDIES IN MIDDLE EAST POLITICS

COLUMBIA STUDIES IN MIDDLE EAST POLITICS

Marc Lynch, Series Editor

Columbia Studies in Middle East Politics presents academically rigorous, well-written, relevant, and accessible books on the rapidly transforming politics of the Middle East for an interested academic and policy audience.

The Arab Uprisings Explained: New Contentious Politics in the Middle East,
edited by Marc Lynch

Sectarian Politics in the Gulf: From the Iraq War to the Arab Uprisings,
Frederic M. Wehrey

From Resilience to Revolution: How Foreign Interventions Destabilize the Middle East,
Sean L. Yom

Protection amid Chaos: The Creation of Property Rights in Palestinian Refugee Camps,
Nadya Hajj

Religious Statecraft: The Politics of Islam in Iran, Mohammad Ayatollahi Tabaar

Local Politics in Jordan and Morocco: Strategies of Centralization and Decentralization,
Janine A. Clark

Jordan and the Arab Uprisings: Regime Survival and Politics beyond the State,
Curtis Ryan

Friend or Foe: Militia Intelligence and Ethnic Violence in the Lebanese Civil War,
Nils Hägerdal

Lumbering State, Restless Society: Egypt in the Modern Era,
Nathan J. Brown, Shimaa Hatab,
and Amr Adly

Classless Politics: Islamist Movements, the Left, and Authoritarian Legacies in Egypt,
Hersham Sallam

SECURITY POLITICS IN THE GULF MONARCHIES

CONTINUITY AMID CHANGE

DAVID B. ROBERTS

Columbia University Press
New York

Columbia University Press
Publishers Since 1893
New York   Chichester, West Sussex
cup.columbia.edu

Library of Congress Cataloging-in-Publication Data
Names: Roberts, David B. (David Bryn), author.
Title: Security politics in the Gulf monarchies : continuity amid change /
David B. Roberts.
Description: New York : Columbia University Press, [2023] | Series:
Columbia studies in Middle East politics | Includes bibliographical
references and index.
Identifiers: LCCN 2022035544 | ISBN 9780231205245 (hardback) |
ISBN 9780231205252 (trade paperback) | ISBN 9780231555913 (ebook)
Subjects: LCSH: Security, International—Persian Gulf Region. | Persian
Gulf Region—Foreign relations. | Persian Gulf Region—Strategic
aspects. | Persian Gulf Region—Politics and government.
Classification: LCC JZ6009.P35 R63 2023 | DDC
327.1/160958—dc23/eng/20221110
LC record available at https://lccn.loc.gov/2022035544

Cover design: Milenda Nan Ok Lee
Cover photo: Arts Illustrated Studios © Shutterstock

FOR FINNY

CONTENTS

ACKNOWLEDGMENTS

W riting a book, for me at least, is a difficult process. I really wouldn't recommend it under almost any circumstances. However, if you insist on doing so, make sure that you are couched firmly amid a range of helpful friends, colleagues, and family who make the process bearable.

When it comes to the subject matter itself, there is just no substitute for endless discussions in classrooms, coffee shops, corridors, malls, souqs, ministries, and military bases, as well as at conferences and on Zoom, Teams, Skype, Google Hangouts, Signal, WhatsApp, and, indeed, over the phone. I must thank a litany of people, including Abdullah Baabood, Adel Hamaizia, Andreas Krieg, Becca Wasser, Cinzia Bianco, Courtney Freer, Eleanor Gillespie, Emile Hokayem, Gerd Nonneman, Jamie Ingram, Jared Koch, Justin Alexander, Karen Young, Kristian Coates Ulrichsen, Kristin Diwan Smith, Matteo Legrenzi, Mehran Kamrava, Michael Stephens, Mari Luomi, Miroslav Zafirov, Mohammed Abdel-Haq, Simon Henderson, Steven Wright, and Toby Dodge. I offer a particular note of thanks to David Des Roches for his patience and willingness to indulge myriad questions about the nuts and bolts of Gulf security. Similarly, I am most grateful to those colleagues—David Des Roches, Kristian Coates Ulrichsen, Mari Luomi, Courtney Freer, Ash Rossiter, and Jim Krane—who spared their time to read through drafts of the manuscript, offering valuable insight and correctives.

I am still in the debt of the Royal United Services Institute for Defence and Security Studies (RUSI)—Jonathan Eyal and Michael Clarke—for appointing me as director of their Gulf office back in the day, which started this (seeming) obsession with the region.

In terms of friends and colleagues from the Gulf itself, I shall not do you the disservice of thanking you here, but I'm quite sure you know who you are. Many Gulf friends have guided me for over a decade now, and I'm genuinely grateful. I am also indebted to some of my more recent Gulf students who have often gone above and beyond with their time, expertise, and hospitality: *shukran jazeelan.*

As for the writing process, it's plainly a horror. But colleagues at King's have helped in myriad ways. I am most grateful to the cofounding members of the Gulshan Strategic Studies Group (GSSG)—Andy Corbett, Cathy Scott, Alex Wilson, Alex Gould, Bence Nemeth, Stefan Schilling, and Matt Uttley—for their discussions and distractions. Moreover, I must offer a particular note of thanks to Bence Nemeth for his willingness to endure countless discussions about the book's structure, themes, and plenty besides. I would also like to thank Amanda Chisholm for launching and running regular writing sprints for all and sundry during lockdown. This offered important structure and focus. Sincere thanks also go to Marc Lynch and to Caelyn Cobb at Columbia for their patience and encouragement, and the production team at KGL for their fastidious and diligent work.

The opportunity to lecture about the Gulf proved to be a highly enjoyable opportunity to refine my arguments and ideas. It's true what they say—teaching a subject really does make you streamline and clarify your thoughts. Many thanks to various classes at the Royal College for Defence Studies (RCDS) and at the UK Defence Academy. Moreover, I am grateful for Sciences Po asking me to author various Gulf- and Middle East–focused MA and BA courses. It has been a pleasure to teach such super-smart students. Similarly, the time spent discussing the work of my wonderful cohort of PhD students has been both enjoyable and frequently insightful—many thanks to Ahlam, Ali, Hessa, Juhaina, and Sara.

As for my family, I am ever grateful for their support. *Merci* to the wonderful French contingent, and *mòran taing* to the Scots lot. Otherwise, I owe, as ever, incalculable thanks to my long-suffering wife for her endless support.

Crouch End
Summer 2022

ABBREVIATIONS

Abu Dhabi Investment Authority (ADIA)
Abu Dhabi Investment Council (ADIC)
American Enterprise Institute (AEI)
Bahraini Defence Force (BDF)
Bahrain Petroleum Company (BAPCO)
Central Command (CENTCOM), United States
Belt and Road Initiative (BRI)
Central Intelligence Agency (CIA), United States
Central Municipal Council (CMC), Qatar
Conference of the Parties (COP)
Council for Economic and Development Affairs (CEDA), Saudi Arabia
Council for Political and Security Affairs (CPSA), Saudi Arabia
Economist Intelligence Unit (EIU)
Food Administration Organization (FAO), United Nations
foreign direct investment (FDI)
gross domestic product (GDP)
Gulf Cooperation Council (GCC)
initial public offering (IPO)
International Monetary Fund (IMF)
international oil company (IOC)
International Petroleum Investment Corporation (IPIC)
international security studies (ISS)

Islamic Front for the Liberation of Bahrain (IFLB)
Islamic State (IS)
Joint Aviation Command (JAC), UAE
Joint Comprehensive Plan of Action (JCPOA)
King Abdullah University of Science and Technology (KAUST)
Kuwait Investment Authority (KIA)
Kuwait Investment Board (KIB)
Kuwait Investment Office (KIO)
Kuwait Liaison Team (KLT)
liquified natural gas (LNG)
Middle East and North Africa (MENA)
Missile Technology Control Regime (MCTR)
North Atlantic Treaty Organization (NATO)
Oman Investment Fund (OIF)
Organization of Petroleum Exporting Countries (OPEC)
People's Democratic Republic of Yemen (PDRY)
per barrel (PB)
Public Investment Fund (PIF), Saudi Arabia
public-private partnership (PPP)
Qatar Investment Authority (QIA)
Qatar National Food Security Programme (QNFSP)
Ras al Khaimah (RAK)
regional security complex (RSC)
Royal Air Force (RAF), United Kingdom
Saudi Arabia National Guard (SANG)
Saudi Arabian Military Industries (SAMI)
Saudi Arabian Monetary Authority (SAMA)
self-sufficiency ratio (SSR)
sovereign wealth fund (SWF)
State General Reserve Fund (SGRF), Oman
United Arab Emirates (UAE)
United Arab Republic (UAR)
United Nations (UN)
value-added tax (VAT)
Yemeni Arab Republic (YAR)

FIGURES

SECURITY POLITICS IN THE GULF MONARCHIES

INTRODUCTION

The historian, like everyone else, is forever trapped in the egocentric predicament, and "presentism" is his original sin.

SCHLESINGER (1990)

A t Blackwell's bookshop in Oxford, the Norrington Room spreads out under Trinity College's lawns next door, and for many years it was listed as the world's largest room selling books. Amid its 160,000 volumes is a corner devoted geographically and thematically to the Arab world, divided into sections focusing on Turkey, Iraq, Iran, political Islam, Israel and Palestine, Edward Said, T. E. Lawrence, and the Middle East. The Gulf monarchies of Kuwait, Saudi Arabia, Bahrain, Oman, Qatar, and the United Arab Emirates (UAE) do not merit a mention even under a collective category such as the Persian Gulf, the Arabian Peninsula, or the Gulf Cooperation Council (GCC). This is a curious omission, given the importance of the Gulf region. Hosting Islam's two holiest places, it is the spiritual center of the Muslim world, with Mecca in Saudi Arabia attracting two-and-a-half-million pilgrims in the annual eight-day Hajj pilgrimage in 2019. The Gulf monarchies supply the world's economy with 23 percent of its oil and 26 percent of its liquefied natural gas (LNG) and, not coincidentally, accommodate an array of military bases vital to U.S. power projection alongside smaller French, British, and

Turkish bases and installations.[1] This hydrocarbon wealth accrued the monarchies approximately $2.3 trillion, accounting for about a third of the world's total sovereign wealth fund (SWF) assets.[2] Although poverty is far from absent in the Gulf monarchies,[3] these states are among the wealthiest on Earth, some of which exert tremendous influence—both positive and negative—worldwide.

Although not bestowed a subsection in the Norrington Room, there is a growing body of literature examining the politics, international relations, political economy, and sociocultural issues of the Gulf region. However, this literature struggles to keep pace with regional changes. According to the Human Development Index from the United Nations (UN), Oman developed more from 1970 to 2010 than any other state in the world.[4] Indeed, the Gulf monarchies transitioned faster than almost anywhere else, moving from the fringes of the world economy a century ago to central spokes today.[5] Swift progress is often conspicuously visible. Photographs of Dubai's central thoroughfare—Shaikh Zayed Road—from as late as 1990 shows it as a strip of tarmac in a dusty desert with a few scattered buildings around. However, today Shaikh Zayed Road is an eight-lane highway thronged with cars and flanked by skyscrapers, with the Burj Khalifa, the world's tallest building looming over all.

The core argument of this book is that despite the epic levels of change experienced by the Gulf monarchies, the underpinning structures and dynamics remain remarkably unchanged. The reason for these continuities stems from how the hydrocarbon industries, and primarily the oil industry, created the primordial soup in which the monarchies emerged in their contemporary forms. The nature of this soup created a paradigm of conditions, roles, expectations, norms, relationships, and structures that constituted the DNA of the monarchies and affected, shaped, and then determined their emergence. The monarchies evolved and matured, still in the hydrocarbon-created soup, calcifying and reifying emerging tropes and approaches into day-to-day reality.

Therefore, it is no surprise that the history of the monarchies is cyclical, and the same problems and stresses reoccur. Wars (such as the one occurring now in Yemen), intra-Gulf blockades and competition, regional ideological challenges, foreign power interventions, domestic ructions, elite jockeying, the emergence of iconoclastic young leaders, migrant worker protests, economic crashes, and the twisting of the environment to sustain naturally unsustainable population numbers are not new. Similarly, the answers proposed by elites have an unmistakable similarity to them. Creating exclusivist national identities, expanding welfare-based ruling bargains, leveraging foreign powers as protectors, and relying on (often Western-authored) consultancies for answers are recurring policies.

This focus on the golden explanatory thread of continuity provided by the hydrocarbon paradigm is neither to ignore the agency of individuals and groups nor to suggest that nothing has changed. The role of migrant workers evolved from being politicized to increasingly docile, the state apparatus inexorably overcame and absorbed preexisting mechanisms of social organization; the monarchies shifted from an influence taker to an influence maker, proselytizing religious and ideological ideas; and, more recently, the UAE and Saudi Arabia used military force as a tool of foreign policy, marking a break from the past.

Nevertheless, with oil playing such a pivotal role as a factor of continuity in the Gulf's recent history—see figure 0.1 showing the state's proved oil reserves—it is essential to reflect on the impact as this paradigm evolves under increasing pressures.

On the demand side, burgeoning awareness and concern about the impact of climate change drive consumers, industry, and states to find

	Proved oil reserves (billion barrels)
Bahrain	0.19
Oman	5.37
Qatar	25.24
United Arab Emirates	97.8
Kuwait	101.5
Saudi Arabia	258.6
United States	47
World	1,662

FIGURE 0.1 Proved oil reserves. Figures: 2021 for the Gulf monarchies and 2020 for the U.S. and world totals.

Source: BP Statistical Review of World Energy (2021).

ways to ditch dirty fuels like oil for greener alternatives and to increase efficiencies to reduce their overall energy consumption. Meeting this demand on the supply side is a range of alternative fuels, ranging from ever-more cost-effective renewables to somewhat cleaner fuels like shale gas. Regardless, the hydrocarbon paradigm is based on dwindling finite resources.

The lesson is not that diminishing oil prices are simply a fiscal concern. Instead, *Security Politics in the Gulf Monarchies* reveals just how inextricably linked this political economy is to myriad facets that make up the fabric of the region's states across the political, societal, economic, military, and environmental spectra. The next iteration of evolution in the monarchies ever more away from its oil paradigm will be a change as never before—shorn of the one core facet of continuity that has underpinned the monarchies' stability in a turbulent century.

Ultimately, *Security Politics in the Gulf Monarchies* has four broad goals. The first is to examine the litany of challenges assailing the monarchies across the spectra of economics, politics, environment, defense, and society. Many challenges *look* like they are both novel and severe. However, this book's initial goal is to examine whether, under closer inspection, they are as profoundly new and challenging as they first appear. Indeed, it highlights deep levels of repetition in the region's trials and tribulations, rooted in the formative and still-enduring oil- and broader hydrocarbon-based regional economies. The rhetoric from regional leaders, the image emerging from the region's states, and the public relations blitz from the Gulf monarchies speak of states with modern, innovative economies that are either diversified or clearly in the process of diversification. But this book highlights that this is not really the case. Moreover, the monarchies need far more than mere economic diversification. Rather, if states are to diversify and shift their economies seriously away from reliance on oil and related hydrocarbon industries, it is far more accurate to see this shift as a far broader and more complex politicosocial and economic transition.

The second goal is to use contemporary history as a foil against which to contextualize today's surprisingly reminiscent trials and tribulations as an accessible way to add value to analysis of the Gulf monarchies. The opening epigraph from Schlesinger underpins the book's approach, offering an important reminder that too often it is easy to fall prey to the sin of presentism, succumbing to hyperbole when describing contemporary problems or developments that seem to be unprecedented in scale. This admonishment behooves scholars to address contemporary concerns in a longer-term perspective to avoid flitting from tweet to tweet, outrage to outrage, or decree to decree. The utility of this approach is not to observe, in a facile way, that just because the monarchies have survived low oil prices or hostile ideological challenges before, they can do so again. Instead, it is crucial to reflect on history to understand the tactics, tools, relationships, and skills deployed to confront similar issues in the past and to reflect on how the problems and solutions are changing in the present. This allows observers to take a more sanguine and informed perspective on today's changes.

Third, this book fills an important gap in the literature on the Gulf region. The recent tendency has been for books to focus on individual countries or specific themes like energy, security, societal issues, or migration.[6] Arguably, not since the heyday of the 1990s, with works by Rosemarie Said Zahlan and Gregory Gause, or Kristian Coates Ulrichsen's innovative 2011 monograph examining security in the region has there been a serious scholarly monograph that offers a comprehensive and comparative approach to looking at the six Gulf monarchies.[7] Given the significant expansion of the region's states as influencers in the wider Middle East, as well as myriad new developments internally, an up-to-date reflection on the region is overdue.

Moreover, too often, Gulf scholarship examines the region only through the lens of Western policies, histories, and archives. However, carefully and thoroughly rooted in the contemporary literature in Arabic and English and taking advantage of the recent digitalization of primary sources, this book pulls together diverse strands from various approaches, compiling them into one accessible, structured evaluation. More specifically, it folds into its analysis developments in the critical Gulf literature such as those focusing on the increasing agency and influence of migrant workers and early political action among Gulf nationals, successive generations of scholarship forensically examining the Gulf political economy, and contemporary Arabic language scholarship on the nature and sustainability of the rentier ruling bargain. Such insights are then harnessed and brought up to date, including reflections on the Gulf's reactions to the COVID crisis. In today's era of considerable flux amid the shifting of core elements of the ruling bargain, it is important to have a clear, unvarnished understanding of state-society interaction, not one merely rooted in Western perspectives.

Fourth, this book innovates by deploying the Copenhagen School's five-sector analysis of security as the key framing device for the first time in the Gulf context. Parts of the Copenhagen School's toolkit, such as the regional security complex, have been deployed in the Gulf context.[8] However, using the five-pronged typology examining the political, economic, societal, military, and environmental aspects of security allows a structured and systematic examination of the Gulf monarchies, rooted in one of the most significant developments in security studies in generations. It rightly acknowledges that to reflect on security concerns in a traditional way, with a majoritarian focus on military dynamics, would be too simplistic, especially in the Gulf monarchies. This would ignore subtleties highlighted by recent debates and developments in critical security studies that emphasize, for example, the importance of a more nuanced grasp of the meaning of security. Deploying this framing device, furthermore, provides a model for comparative political analysis and area studies alike.

LITERATURE AND APPROACH

Security Politics in the Gulf Monarchies fits into a lineage of literature that examines the stability of the Gulf monarchies. Indeed, the epitaphs of the monarchies were written on many occasions. In the 1920s and 1930s, such was the level of discord within the royal family and the litany of challenges facing the nascent state that experts predicted the sure failure of the Saudi state after Ibn Saud died.[9] The death knells for the smaller monarchies were similarly persistent in the early twentieth century, notably surrounding fears in London of their inability to fend off Saudi advances.[10] The stability and security of the young Saudi state continued to be questioned, particularly under the allegedly incompetent rule of Saud bin Abdelaziz Al Saud (r. 1953–1964) in the face of nationalistic forces on Saudi's northern, southern, and western borders.[11] The ability of the small monarchies to survive and prosper after the British withdrawal in 1971 was questioned, as was Bahrain and Qatar's decision not to band together with the Trucial

States—i.e., the seven Shaikhdoms that would become the United Arab Emirates in 1971—to form a nine-member UAE.[12] Oman suffered from a debilitating civil war that threatened the fundamental cohesion of the state and emerged from profound underdevelopment only in the mid-1970s.[13] Later, the Iran-Iraq war (1980–1988) spilled over with the targeting of the monarchies' oil tankers, about which they themselves could do virtually nothing. The 1990 Iraqi invasion of Kuwait proved just how vulnerable the monarchies were, with Saddam Hussein's forces waltzing across the border with minimal resistance, swiftly capturing the state.[14] Only foreign intervention saved the other monarchies from a potentially similar fate and subsequently freed Kuwait as well. Close relations with the United States shored up the monarchies in the aftermath, with the proliferation of U.S. military bases in the region.

Aside from these practical challenges to the monarchies, a thread in the broader academic literature has long assumed that monarchy is an anachronistic mode of governance. Many thought that it would be only a matter of time before the Gulf and remaining North African monarchies inevitably went the way of those Arab monarchies that fell in the 1930s and 1940s.[15] Samuel Huntington's conception of the king's dilemma—the idea that any reforms provided by the king would only lead to ever-greater demands for more reforms—was a core argument that bolstered the inevitable decline theory.[16] This approach fueled the wave thesis of democratization, which was popularized by Huntington's 1991 article and subsequent book *The Third Wave: Democratization in the Late Twentieth Century.* The first wave was in the early nineteenth century; the second came after World War II; and the third started with Portugal's Carnation Revolution in 1974 encompassing Latin American and Asian transitions in the 1980s and the post–Cold War democratization in former Soviet spaces.[17] The Middle East was conspicuous in its absence. However, from the weight of world history or as a result of specific mechanisms (such as the king's dilemma), it was too often assumed that Middle Eastern democratization was inevitable: Scholars were, as Sean Yom put it, "waiting to exhale."[18] Some saw monarchies as "an endangered species."[19] A quid pro quo emerged when the U.S.-led liberation of Kuwait saw its rulers loosely agree to redouble democratic endeavors, or at least stop terminating parliaments early, as had been the norm in the 1980s. Some saw this as another harbinger of democratization pressure in the Gulf.[20]

The Arab Spring uprisings beginning in late 2010 sparked another era of debate about the nature of governance in the Middle East.[21] For a time, it seemed that the fourth wave had arrived. However, this proved illusory, with democratic rollbacks, the resilience of autocracy, and a descent into civil war in almost all Arab Spring–affected states. The Gulf monarchies emerged from the Arab Spring in much better shape than many republics in the Arab world.[22] Certainly, Bahrain suffered from serious protests, but no government fell, as in Tunisia and Egypt (where it happened twice), and no Gulf monarchy descended into civil war, as Libya, Yemen, and Syria did.[23]

An argument can be made that much of this academic debate—the expectation of democratization and the search for reasons why Middle East states have not managed to transition—is imbued with problematic normative expectations.[24] From a Western-based standpoint, it may be "a rather sad indictment of Arab politics today that the word *democratization* has virtually disappeared from research-based literature on the Middle East."[25] However, if scholars were not expecting—if not hoping for—democratization, they might have realized earlier, had they examined the states themselves, that, as Emma Murphy continues, "authoritarian modes of rule are more deeply embedded than previously imagined."[26] More than being merely embedded, monarchies in the Arab world are thriving, particularly compared to many of their republican counterparts.[27]

Also, in the present, we cheat. We know where history's ark bent. Without realizing it, much of this literature unconsciously predicates its ideas, approach, and research on an unspoken assumption of an obvious end point for the trajectory for the monarchies: the assumption of inevitable decline or a certain transition from monarchical rule to a so-called modern system of governance. Two of the twentieth century's leading historians, Herbert Butterfield and E. P. Thompson, railed against the propensity of historians to unthinkingly start their analysis of the past with an end state in mind. Thompson criticized the "enormous condescension of posteriority," while Butterfield complained about historians who "produce a scheme of general history which is bound to converge beautifully upon the present."[28] In either case, whether a scholar knows who won the Battle of Agincourt or assumes that the monarchies will transition to democracy someday, analysis becomes skewed.

In assessing the salience of the challenges facing the monarchies, it is important to find a suitable way to structure the investigation. Concerns facing the region's states, as the body of the book explains, touch on myriad issues ranging from wars to population bulges to geopolitical shifts and migration. Without alighting on an organizing principle, framework, or theoretical model to direct analysis, a book-length project runs the risk of taking a directionless and scattershot approach. Worse, without a grounded approach, a book examining contemporary issues might be too influenced by presentism and the desire to follow what look (at the time at least) like important issues.

Given that *Security Politics in the Gulf Monarchies* is concerned with the contemporary security and stability of the six monarchies amid a panoply of challenges, the obvious theoretical roots are in international security studies (ISS).[29] A subset of the discipline of international relations, ISS emerged mainly in Europe and the United States after World War II, though its antecedents go back centuries. ISS means different things to different people. An earlier plurality of approaches narrowed after the brutality and scale of World War II and the self-evident need to focus on existential threats like wars, in which the military element was front and center.[30] Security discourse axiomatically focused on states as the critical protagonist (or referent, or actor) and military force as the key tool, with an explicit focus on warfare and the use of force as the prime concern.[31] Thus, given that to every hammer, a problem looks like a nail, to increasing numbers of those studying security studies, the answers to security problems were militarily shaped.[32] The pressures of Cold War bipolarity and the existential fears fostered by nuclear war reinforced the dominance of the military focus in most security scholarship.

Firmly rooted in this realist paradigm, particularly in North America, institutions created new programs. At the same time, newly founded think tanks, journals, and burgeoning scholarship shifted to meet the pressing need to understand the nuclear era (and secure the necessary funding).[33] Security studies evolved an entire subdiscipline—deterrence theory—which focused on managing this weapons-driven international order.[34] Realist-oriented understandings of security became ingrained in the DNA of American security and international relations scholarship. Even after the failure of the Vietnam War, there remained a resolutely hard-edged focus on the military tool in security studies and a focus on "war as an instrument of national policy."[35] Despite the preoccupation with military security and associated nuclear doctrines, the concept of security widened and deepened as the century progressed, particularly in Europe. A key innovation of ISS was to switch the focus from defense to security.[36] This slowly "opened up the study of a broader set of political issues" and shifted the locus of thought from military-based scholars and thinkers to the civilian realm.[37]

Led by scholars associated with Aberystwyth, Copenhagen, and Paris, the security agenda opened to consider referent actors other than the state; to question whether internal threats ought to be considered as valid as external ones; to examine if other facets of security (for example, human security) were equally as valid as military security; and to question whether a security issue was inextricably tied to conceptions of urgency and danger.[38] Many innovations were rejected (or just ignored) by U.S.-based academics,[39] who saw such widening as diluting the concept of security to such a degree that it lost coherence and utility. American scholars, journals, and PhD theses still tend to focus on variants of the realist school that reflect, albeit to differing degrees, the preponderant importance of a state-centric world and military-focused elements.[40]

Scholars in the Copenhagen School, led by Barry Buzan and Ole Wæver, sought a middle way "to move security studies beyond a narrow agenda which focuses on military relations between states while avoiding ending up with an all-embracing inflated concept dealing with all kinds of threats to the existence, well-being or development of individuals, social groups, nations and mankind."[41] One method was to diversify focus onto economic, political, societal, environmental, and military matters.[42] While this expansion of the topic remained too much for some, this five-pointed typology became widely used. The core book expounding this approach—*Security: A New Framework for Analysis*—garnered over 10,000 Google Scholar citations, and its ideas are applied across "the lexicon of international relations thought."[43]

This framework—or "organizational tool," as Huysmans describes it—provides the structure for chapters 1–5.[44] Using this sectoral approach offers a thoughtful tool for analysis. It makes sense in the Gulf to consider security in a broader context than merely the military apparatus and the use of force. It would be a mistake to ignore or marginalize the role of leaders and their influence on state policy in the Gulf context, which realist-oriented theory tends to do to varying degrees.[45] While the role of individuals must not be overemphasized, Gulf history is replete with examples of leaders profoundly shaping state policy, expedited by relatively few domestic obstacles, such as formal parliamentary scrutiny, and facilitated by often significant hydrocarbon revenues.[46]

Nevertheless, it would be foolhardy to entirely reject a realist approach when examining international politics in the Gulf. This is a region with archetypal examples of stronger states doing "what they can" while weaker states "suffer what they must," as Thucydides put it in his Melian Dialogue, one of the classic realist texts. The 1990 invasion of Kuwait by Iraq is the ultimate example of this kind of depredatory action that realist logic expects. Little wonder that Raymond Hinnebusch describes Middle Eastern leaders as "quintessential realists, preoccupied with the threats that are so pervasive in the MENA region."[47] Consequently, seeking to draw insights from realism but reject its overly onerous and unrealistic bounding, scholars like Hinnebusch and Gerd Nonneman use a complex form of realism. They take the core insights from realism but nuance them in the Middle East context.[48]

Security Politics in the Gulf Monarchies follows this kind of approach, emphasizing within the five-point Buzan framework the importance of regional threats, the struggles for power, the prevalence of security concerns at multiple levels, and the primacy of regime survival for leaders.[49] This understanding of realism argues that states are the critical actor to examine when considering questions of regional security and stability. Indeed, as Edward Kolodziej persuasively argues, this is for very good reason:

[the state is] the principal unit of political organization of the world's populations. . . . It has defeated all other competitor systems of political organization. . . . While other associations, like the Catholic Church or Muslim religion, also command the loyalty of their adherents, none possesses either the depth of commitment of national populations to their states or the state's material power.

The second and equally important reason for pivoting much of the discussion on the state is that the modern state . . . is the repository of a monopoly of legitimate violence. . . . These capabilities consist of police, military forces, and a judicial and administrative system. . . . Since security studies is concerned with the use by actors of force and violence, it seems reasonable that we know more about the greatest wielder of violence first—the state.[50]

This does not detract from the reality that one can recognize the influential nature of the state but still focus the examination on other actors as important "referent objects," as the theoretical literature puts it. There is a range of other groups whose security is imperiled or frequently ignored in the Gulf context, including Shia minorities in the Sunni-majority states, women, or migrants who make up one-third of the Gulf monarchy population.

However, *Security Politics in the Gulf Monarchies* focuses on the state as the key actor as well as its security and stability. This approach follows that taken by Arnold Wolfers. In his seminal 1952 article examining the meaning of security, he argued that the first step, inherent to the research question, was deciding whose security was going to be the focus of the inquiry.[51] No decision is inherently correct or incorrect; rather, it merely reflects the focus of analysis. In this case, the focus of the research question and subsequent investigation, analysis, and evaluation is the state. Moreover, given that this book strives to provide scholarly and accessible analysis for a range of policy, academic, and research communities, as well as those casually interested in Middle East issues, it makes sense to speak in a pragmatic language reflecting the reality that states clearly remain, despite challenges, the preeminent actors in regional and international politics.

Chapters 1–5 thus focus on political, societal, economic, military, and environmental sectors as they affect the Gulf monarchies. Taking the Gulf monarchies together as a unit of analysis is not unusual. Analyzing states that share the same security concerns is well grounded in the theoretical literature. Indeed, another innovation of the Copenhagen School was the regional security complex (RSC) concept. The antecedents of this concept go back to the early 1980s and Buzan's *People, States, and Fear*, as well as its subsequent editions, but it came to the fore as the 1990s progressed. In particular, with the collapse of the Soviet Union and the bipolar world order, the importance of regions is widely thought to have increased.[52] In their 2008 book, Buzan, Wæver, and de Wilde define a RSC thus: "A security complex is defined as *a set of units whose major processes of securitization, desecuritization, or both are so interlinked that their security problems cannot reasonably be analyzed or resolved apart from one another.*"[53] They suggest that the Middle East may be classed as one RSC, while the Persian Gulf ought to be considered a subcomplex.[54] This approach fits with the Gulf monarchies, where the study of politics, security, and international relations is often tied up with threats and opportunities that emerge from its wider subregion and states like Yemen, Iraq, and Iran. Moreover, this kind of approach—the marrying of an RSC-based analytical approach with the Gulf region—has been undertaken by leading regional scholars. Gregory Gause has followed this approach twice in analyzing the security and international relations of the Gulf, while Kristian Coates Ulrichsen and Henner Fürtig also explicitly consider security a regional and a relational matter.[55]

This book examines the monarchies together, as states with important differences but ultimately with more similarities and elements of continuity. Indeed, the core theme underpinning the book's analysis, approach, and conclusions concerns the role of oil and the wider hydrocarbon industry acting as a uniquely shaping element across the monarchies. These industries created and deeply embedded path dependencies that directly forged the type of states that emerged, bringing tremendous wealth to a region that otherwise would have developed at a fraction of the pace. But there is no such thing as a free lunch. Oil brought myriad benefits, but costly externalities came with these many boons. Although Gulf governments sporadically struggled to secure and stabilize their states, oil wealth—and the structures, advantages, and relations that it gave elites—facilitated the states to overcome their many and varied challenges.

However, the oil and wider hydrocarbon economy is ever more challenged in a world of growing renewable and other energy alternatives and the mainstreaming of climate change awareness. As the International Monetary Fund (IMF) and other bodies have long noted,[56] these changing realities pose existential challenges to the economic status quo of the Gulf monarchies within foreseeable time frames. Many note that the monarchies have been seeking to diversify their economies for decades now. This may be so, but startlingly little progress has been made. Moreover, this sentiment of economic diversification singularly fails to capture the change required. As this book highlights, deep-rooted change is required across the political, economic, societal, military, and environmental spectra if the states are to transition from ones rooted in the hydrocarbon paradigm.

1

POLITICAL SECURITY

The proclamation that the Gulf States' demise is imminent reminds this reviewer of an article published in 1975 by a prominent Gulf analyst. The author assigned percentages to his predictions of how many short years it would be before each of the Gulf States reached their downfall. His conclusion was that the Arab monarchies would be the first to disappear while Pahlavi Iran would outlast all the others. Myriad pronouncements of the death of the Al Saud state have circulated regularly since the latter days of King Abd al-Aziz in the early 1950s, and the other states have received similar estimates. Predicting is a notoriously dangerous proposition.

PETERSON (2014)

Of the 193 states in the United Nations (UN), in only ten are monarchs the decisive actors: Morocco, Jordan, Brunei, Eswatini, Saudi Arabia, Kuwait, Bahrain, Oman, Qatar, and the United Arab Emirates (UAE).[1] This form of governance of 5 percent of the world's states is entrenched in the Gulf. Saudi Arabia's ruling family, the Al Saud, stamped their family name on the state. Meanwhile, the Al Sabah in Kuwait, the Al Khalifah in Bahrain, the Al Thani in Qatar, the Al Said in Oman, and the Al Nahyan and Al Maktoum families in the UAE are preeminent in terms of their local importance.

However, as Lisa Anderson notes, most monarchs in the Middle East and North Africa (MENA) have scarcely been in power for more than a century.[2] There is still (just barely) a generation of people alive who pre-date the formal creation of Saudi Arabia in 1932 or who lived in an Oman divided in two, without the overarching control of the Al Said dynasty. Moreover, it is not difficult to conceive of an alternative history where, had a battle gone one way and not another, we could be dealing with the Kingdom of Rashidi Arabia, the Al Musallam of Qatar, the Al Qasimi in the UAE, and so on. John Peterson makes a similar point:

> In 1935, the British Foreign Office produced a memorandum called "The Seven Independent Arabian States." . . . But of those described a half-century ago (Yemen, 'Asir, al-Hijaz, Najd, Kuwait, Jabal Shammar, and Jawf), only two still exist in similar form [i.e., Kuwait and Yemen]. . . . This immense change provides an illustration of the fragile and transitory nature of traditional Arabian states, given their foundations on shifting tribal allegiances, their absolute dependence on strong and capable leadership, and their lack of firm territorial grounding.[3]

Today's monarchies overcame myriad problems, threats, and challenges. Delineating the specific kind of political challenges they faced is tricky. Buzan et al. see such political matters as the "widest" area as "all threats and defenses are constituted and defined politically."[4] It is, therefore, essential to sharpen the focus of what is and is not considered under the rubric of the political security agenda. At its core, political security "is about the organizational stability of social order(s). The heart of the political sector is made up of threats to state sovereignty."[5] A central struggle is ideational and political security revolves around giving or denying recognition, support, or legitimacy to potential competitors.[6] Accordingly, although there can be myriad specific threats, Buzan et al. argue that they are best categorized as emanating from three locations: substate groups (tribes, social groups like unions, the royal family, or other elite challengers), pan-regional ideational challenges (e.g., pan-Islamism, pan-Arabism), and suprastate concerns (e.g., the Arab League).[7] There is often nothing separate about these challenges. Instead, an analysis of the contemporary history of the monarchies repeatedly demonstrates that international forces and regional ideologies persistently agitate substate groups.

This chapter opens by focusing on the founding and development of the Gulf monarchies in the twentieth century, often under empires or influential international actors and facilitated by ever-larger oil incomes. The Ottoman and particularly the British empires oversaw the emergence of several Gulf monarchies. But even for Saudi Arabia, a state that did not emerge from British or Ottoman suzerainty, foreign states—mainly the United States—provided pervasive logistical and technical support as the Saudis emerged to found inter alia their hydrocarbon industry. Part and parcel of the advent of these extractive industries, and accompanying the founding of the rudiments of the modern state machinery, was a vast influx of foreign workers bringing them foreign ideas. These factors were to shape, from the ground up, the nature of the Gulf monarchies. These workers built, designed, and staffed nascent ministries, while their at times revolutionary ideas percolated around Gulf societies. This elicited a security-minded reaction from authorities. Foreign workers were increasingly controlled and cowed by the emergence of strict nationality laws and stricter policing measures. In reaction, Gulf citizenship became more exclusive and often explicitly set against the foreign "others" who numerically dominated the state population.

With the expansion of the oil and hydrocarbon industries came the vast expansion and transformation of states to today's highly developed entities. Leaders further deployed these growing (and then booming) revenues to lock themselves into power, countering domestic and regional threats. Indeed, leaders preferred to deploy fiscal resources to counter these issues, displaying what might be termed a "rentier mentality." Against local threats, citizens were often induced into political quietism with the employment by some of the world's most generous welfare states of a smorgasbord of subsidies, jobs for life, opportunities for connected families to earn considerable sums, and a low-tax environment. This dampened citizen expectations of political participation and successfully undercut meaningful opposition movements.

Regional pressures swirled around the developing Gulf states. On the Arabian Peninsula, from the 1950s, Yemen and Oman were beset by civil wars, often driven by a concerning mix of communist and pan-Arab ideologies. When Egypt's president, Gamal Abdel Nasser, landed thousands of Egyptian troops in Yemen in the early 1960s to support the overthrow of the old Yemeni monarchy in favor of local revolutionaries, the Gulf monarchies looked on with unabated concern. U.S. fast jets protected Saudi Arabia as Yemen descended into a proxy conflict, while British and Iranian help was needed to crush the Dhofar rebellion in Oman. In other words, foreign relations, predicated to a substantial degree on the importance of the region's oil supplies, were critical to defending the monarchies from clear and present dangers. To secure these relations, expensive Western military equipment was often acquired at least partly—and at times explicitly—to induce relations with significant Western powers to protect the status quo. This process only became starker with the establishment of numerous foreign military bases on the Peninsula from the 1990s onward. States also sporadically sought to engage in dinar diplomacy to rent regional alliances and otherwise push their agendas.

There are various plausible alternatives to these approaches. Engaging in greater regional diplomacy, striving to build as opposed to buying regional kudos or influence, and attempting to meaningfully forge national armed forces could have gone some way toward securing states on the regional or international level. Domestically, openings for meaningful political participation could have been pursued as a method to engage with bubbling local issues. But these ships have sailed. Path dependencies have long been instituted whereby expectations, structures, relations, and norms have been set in particular ways. The very strategies employed to develop the state and secure power for elites were often double-edged. So development was required, paid for with oil receipts and demanding an immense influx of foreign workers. In turn, this tended to irritate domestic constituencies, forging an ever-more-exclusivist national identity. It presented authorities with real challenges to security and stability as migrant workers became both a transmission method of these potentially seditious ideas and a large constituency that could be influenced to the point where they posed a threat. Consequently, a consistent reaction from Gulf elites was to externalize security concerns by inducing international powers into positions where they could support the status quo.

Today's politics in the Gulf monarchies is as vibrant and stagnated as ever. Tremendous change is occurring at breakneck speed as the Overton window denoting the limits of possible action is consistently challenged, stretched, and reforged. This is particularly noticeable in Saudi Arabia. Under the de facto leader Mohammed bin Salman Al Saud, the role of women has been transformed. Women are emerging in large numbers as economically active citizens as social, religious, and legal strictures and structures are speedily reformed and the young leader simply blows through taboos that most assumed were entrenched. The story is similar regarding the balance in Saudi politics between political and religious groups and the hitherto-presumed necessity of retaining some balance at the uppermost levels of the Al Saud family. However, such shibboleths wilted under the reforms that Mohammed bin Salman bulldozed through. Ultimately, he has consolidated power like almost no leader before him, intimating that a significant change from the past is taking place. However, in a longer-term view, Gulf history is replete with young leaders coming to power—Sultan Qaboos bin Said Al Said in Oman and Hamad bin Khalifah Al Thani in Qatar, among others—who rip through norms with deeply iconoclastic policies, shattering the status quo in the process.

As dangerous as it may be to instigate such profound, sometimes wrenching changes in a seemingly unfeasible short period of time, it is tempting to conclude that it is only through shock therapy that enough change is likely to transpire in the monarchies. The oil- and hydrocarbon-rooted political bargain that pervades contemporary society provides powerful incentives to maintain a business-as-usual approach as much as possible. The paradigm shift that the monarchies will need to endure in shifting away from an oil-rooted existence ultimately mandates little less than the reformulation of state-society relations.

∽∾∾∿

The first section of this chapter, "Founding and Developing," focuses on the founding and initial development of the monarchies. It examines the critical role that early waves of foreign labor played in both the pragmatic construction and design of state institutions, but also in bringing swathes of new and challenging international currents of ideas to the nascent monarchies. This prompted the internationalization of the monarchies, swiftly presenting early leaders with a litany of changes to the political security of their growing states, exacerbating febrile local political issues. The second section, "Consolidating and Modernizing," examines how monarchs dealt with age-old problems, such as competition from tribes or religious pressure, in the consolidation of new, modern, independent states. The third section, "Reforming and Defending," analyzes the varied pressures for democratization and the state responses. The discussion moves forward to examine how the monarchies dealt with the varied pressures and challenges that emerged from the 2010 Arab Spring. The final section, "Leadership and Change," examines contemporary elite dynamics through a historically comparative lens across the monarchies.

FOUNDING AND DEVELOPING

FOREIGN WORKERS AND FOREIGN IDEAS

Today, the Gulf monarchies are known for supporting some of the oddest population dynamics in the world.[8] Not only are Gulf nationals a minority in their own lands—sometimes outnumbered around 9:1—but local populations are overwhelmingly male, with approximately 3.7 men for every woman.[9] With these disparities come concerns, none of which are new. Even before the advent of oil, migrant workers posed a challenge to Gulf leaders. One of the first collective protests occurred in 1923 in Bahrain's diving industry due to newly imposed regulations.[10] This soon escalated, and 1,500 divers attacked a police station to free strike leaders and the local Indian police shot two people.[11] The strikes concerned both British and local leaders, as they threatened to undermine the stability of the social order. A British representative noted that

> these divers number some thousands of ruffians and semi-savages from a dozen different countries without any families present to restrain them; the danger of leniency is at once apparent, particularly when the small number of the armed forces of the State are considered and also the appalling suddenness with which these outbreaks can occur. Sticks and clubs are always at hand and a small crowd may swell into thousands in a few minutes.[12]

Not only did their sheer numbers raise salient questions about the continued ability of the proto-governments to keep order, but striking workers cut deeply into rulers' revenues. Elsewhere, in 1931 drivers for Abdulaziz Al Saud (Ibn Saud) protested and were "repressed . . . beaten and deported."[13] Foreshadowing the interplay between international ideas and agitated workers, exiles who returned to South Yemen in the 1920s fell under the influence of Indonesian nationalism and British socialism, such that they launched a petition in 1927 to unify the two Yemeni states, albeit to no avail.[14]

Education has long been a locus for agitation. In 1929, Syrian head-masters organized a strike—in "an Egyptian manner"—at several schools in Bahrain, seeking a range of better working conditions and less British interference.[15] After rejecting the petition, the British saw that the ring-leaders were "dismissed and sent off by boat on the same day," which prompted "a hysterical demonstration."[16] Such protests highlight the min-gling of regional ideas brought by individuals and groups to the Peninsula with local causes.

In Bahrain, Persian and then Indian workers became the mainstay of the Bahrain Petroleum Company (BAPCO). However, the former con-cerned the British as potential fifth columnists, and the latter concerned the Bahrainis for their propensity to strike, demanding better conditions.[17] The 1938 BAPCO strike is, somewhat incorrectly, regarded as one of the first serious examples of worker collective action (as will be explored in greater detail later in this chapter). It came amid the 1936–1939 Arab revolt in Palestine; not only was that the "most sustained anticolonial uprising against the British in the twentieth century," but a vital target of the insurgency campaign was the oil pipeline from Iraq.[18] Such ideas—using collective action targeting the energy infrastructure to make social and political demands—flowed via imported migrant workers to Bahrain and the rest of the Gulf.

Khaldoun Hasan al-Naqeeb terms these protests among expatriates and nationals as being concerned with reform, and later protests from the late 1950s as being inspired by independence and nationalization demands.[19] In the Gulf, 1938 is sometimes termed the "year of the majlis [parliament]." In that year, Kuwaiti merchants protested and instigated the creation of a majlis that had "legislative, executive as well as . . . some degree of judicial power."[20] Dubai followed this lead, and disenfranchised royals joined local merchants to establish a reform movement that instituted changes inter alia to local education.[21] Fueled by regional participatory sentiment, such moves concerned leaders and British authorities because they were rooted in local society, lending them a legitimacy that threatened the status quo.

This was a high watermark of political participation, limited as it was. A combination of sheiks enriched from their oil concessions and support from the British (or American) government undercut such moves. Although small compared to the vast sums that Gulf oil fields would later produce, initial payments and royalties from international oil companies strengthened local rulers.[22] In Kuwait, the majlis experiment ended when merchants tried to expand their powers over the distribution of oil revenues and the elites in the Al Sabah, with the support of the British, stymied the majlis then dissolved it in March 1939.[23] Similarly, in Dubai, within a year, the ruler mustered sufficient support from loyal soldiers paid for by oil royalties and British support. Political stability for the elites increased for a time.

However, the monarchs were in a bind. Income from oil looked transformative, but it was risky to exploit. It meant entering into agreements with U.S. and UK corporations, which left rulers vulnerable to accusations of being stooges of so-called imperial states. It also required a vast expansion of migrant workers in the population to build state infrastructure. This posed various issues, from facilitating the transfer of controversial ideas to irritating Gulf nationals who were becoming minorities in their own country. Much of the contemporary history of the monarchies was an exercise in balancing these contradictory positions.

For the elites, external support was often the answer. After defeating Ibn Saud's invading forces at the Battle of Jahra in 1920, Kuwait's leader, Salim Al Mubarak Al Sabah (r. 1917–1921), turned to the British for protection against a Saudi counterattack. Although this ploy worked, Ibn Saud still believed that Kuwait belonged to him, as its people originated from Saudi heartlands, and that he ought to be able to tax Kuwaiti profits. Despite trying to appease Ibn Saud financially, with no success, Shaikh Ahmed Al Jabir Al Sabah (r. 1921–1950) ultimately refused the demands, and Ibn Saud launched a punitive, two-decade-long blockade of Kuwait.[24]

As the size of Saudi oil fields became evident in the 1940s, it became clear that the state required a fundamental transformation to realize their potential. The Dammam–Riyadh railway project alone required 15,000 migrant workers, while Saudi Aramco employed over 20,000 in the early 1950s.[25] Oil industry protests were sporadic, starting as early as 1945.

Important stoppages occurred in the early 1950s, when a series of inter-linked and mutually supporting strikes were launched.[26] Demands ranged from better pay and working conditions to removing a U.S. military base from the kingdom; little wonder that the U.S. Department of State mused that the strikers were "followers of the Communist line."[27] Bahraini authorities also struggled with strikes. Concessions to agitators were offered initially in 1956 in the face of workers' organization into a union. However, leaders were soon arrested for sedition, sentenced, and exiled to St. Helena.[28]

This occurred when the United States and the United Kingdom, expe-riencing strikes around the Gulf region, used their foreign intelligence services to launch a coup against the popularly elected Iranian prime minister Mohammed Mossadegh in 1953 for threatening to nationalize Iranian oil assets.[29] Such naked colonial aggression added to growing pan-Arabist sentiment emanating from Nasser's Egypt. Gulf leaders were torn between supporting the nationalist ideals of Nasser, which were pop-ular domestically, and the realities that they both needed ongoing UK and U.S. security and technical support, something inimical to the thrust of Nasserist policies. There was also the underlying awkwardness of con-servative monarchies genuflecting to an Egyptian republican government that had just overthrown its monarchy.

REGIONAL CHALLENGE AND CONTESTATION

Gulf monarchs tried to have their cake and eat it too. The Bahraini lead-ership met with Nasser in 1956 as he transited the region, while an influ-ential Bahraini exile, Abdul Rahman Al Bakir, used Egypt's propaganda (or soft-power) tool *Sawt Al Arab* (*Voice of the Arabs*) to pontificate against the Bahraini regime.[30] Elites in Qatar jockeying for power sought to boost their domestic legitimacy by echoing Nasserist rhetoric.[31] In Kuwait, Iraqis and Egyptians carried the Nasserist message. The Kuwait Democratic League emerged in 1954, criticizing the egregious spending and waste of the leading sheikhs. When Nasser called for a strike in 1956, 4,000 demonstrators protested in Kuwait.[32] Lest such sentiments infect Kuwaitis too much, the ruler responded with "social policies and nationality laws to create as much of a rift as possible between expatriate

Arabs and Kuwaitis."[33] Such policies succeeded, and the dislocation of Kuwaitis and expatriates became endemic.[34] Strikes beset Qatar during the 1950s, with divers, enslaved people, oil workers, and Al Thanis agitating at different times.[35] In Bahrain in the mid-1950s, a "cross sectarian nationalist political movement"[36] emerged, recruiting up to 14,000 workers, driving protests, and unnerving the government.[37] Under advice from the British government, these groups were repressed, with their leaders arrested and deported.[38]

Nasserist politics affected Saudi politics. Before Faisal bin Abdulaziz Al Saud became king (r. 1964–1975), he jockeyed for power with his brother, Saud bin Abdulaziz Al Saud (r. 1953–1964). The latter was the first to succeed his father and founder of the current Saudi state, Ibn Saud. Faisal and Saud considered joining the growing United Arab Republic (UAR), then consisting of Egypt and Syria, in the charged regional atmosphere. They were also pressured to denounce U.S. relations, which were critical to the state's defensive stability and its economic income (via Saudi Aramco, the joint U.S.-Saudi oil company). By 1958, Faisal—as regent (acting king) for a time—steered the Saudis toward a "neutrality and Arab nationalism" policy.[39] Seesawing Saudi politics saw Saud regain power in the late 1950s, and he swung toward the pan-Arab regional mood, promising not to renew the U.S. lease on Dhahran Air Base when it expired in May 1961.[40] However, regional politics again shifted domestic priorities. September 1962 saw the military overthrow the Yemeni leader, Imam Mohammad Al Badr, and proclaim an Arab republic. The Egyptian army, navy, and air force landed quickly in support, indicating that Nasser had known what would happen.

In this burgeoning Arab Cold War, the Gulf states built alliances against Nasser's Egypt. With a state to build, and without a prominent ideology to deploy against Nasser, exiled Muslim Brotherhood members from countries like Egypt, Iraq, and Syria helped in both regards. Their clerical expertise made them ideal workers to establish and staff the emerging Gulf ministries. At the same time, their experience, links, and religious legitimacy were adopted and used by the monarchies, such that in Saudi Arabia, "the Muslim Brotherhood were put in charge of the whole Saudi counter-propaganda apparatus, especially the Saudi media sector."[41] The Brotherhood was used to defend the state from pan-Arabist and left-wing threats that fostered a coup attempt in the Royal Saudi Air Force in 1969.[42]

Nor would this be the last time that the Saudi state deployed such means to counter ideational threats.[43] Otherwise, the Brotherhood dominated the development of Qatar, Kuwait, and the UAE to varying degrees, often using the states as vehicles to organize and promote their message.[44]

No Gulf monarchy struggled with its stability more than Oman. Deep cultural and religious divisions at the substate level split it into pieces. At the turn of the twentieth century, the Al Busa'idi dynasty broadly controlled Oman's north coast and the seaside town of Salallah in the far south. However, imams from the Ibadi sect of Islam held sway in the interior. Battles broke out repeatedly from 1913 to 1915. The British intervened to restore stability because they did not want to provide Sultan Taimur bin Faisal (r. 1913–1932) with troops to defend his position in perpetuity. The two Omani sides were engendered to an agreement at Seeb in 1920, de facto giving Ibadi imams power in the interior, but with enough wiggle room for the sultan to retain a theoretical sense of sovereignty throughout Oman.[45] However, oil found in the interior near the Buraimi Oasis—a long-disputed area between Oman, the Trucial States (the seven Shaikhdoms that would become the UAE in 1971/2), and Saudi Arabia—changed calculations. With the imamate changing positions to support the Saudi claim in 1954, the British reacted. For the rest of the 1950s, British military forces attacked the imamate, eventually routing it and asserting the authority of Taimur's successor, Said bin Taimur (r. 1932–1970) to a greater degree.[46]

In the 1960s, the monarchies continued to pivot, bend, and shimmy under the pressures of international ideological winds. First, crises in Yemen provided the Gulf monarchies with a troubling vision of their potential future. The first republic of modern times was established on the Peninsula when in September 1962, Egyptian-trained officers trundled their tanks into the capital of Sana'a, overthrowing the monarchy in North Yemen. Witnessing the demise of a centuries-old, deeply rooted monarchy at the hands of Nasser-inspired populism can only have been foreboding for other monarchs. The monarchies tried for eight years to support and reinstall royalist forces, while Nasser supported republican forces in the north with troops. This meant that the Arab world's most popular leader, leading the Arab world's most populated country, who propagated a deeply antimonarchy line to significant effect, landed thousands of troops on the Peninsula in a country with a vast, near completely unguarded 1,600-kilometer (994-mile) border with the Gulf monarchies.[47] The new Yemeni Arab Republic (YAR) also received an influx of political exiles eager to engage in ideological hostilities.[48]

Second, with increasing agitation from North Yemen starting in the mid-1960s, South Yemen descended into civil war. Even though the port city of Aden was the UK's most important military installation between Portsmouth and Singapore, and the United Kingdom had long offered support guarantees to local tribes and loyal forces, it abandoned its position to rebels. The last British troops had withdrawn by 1967. Not only was a Marxist state, the People's Democratic Republic of Yemen (PDRY), installed, but from the perspective of the rulers of the Gulf monarchies, the British had proved to be fickle and untrustworthy precisely when they were needed most.

Third, as the PDRY emerged, leftist sentiment spread, and another battleground developed on the Omani-Yemeni border in the province of Dhofar from the mid-1960s onward. Rebels challenged the monarchy for a decade and became a cause célèbre in much the same way that the Spanish Civil War was to the generation of George Orwell leftists. The Marxist South Yemen state—the Cuba of the Middle East, replete with Mao and Lenin badges[49]—and the ongoing conflict in Dhofar corralled a motley group of international supporters from Palestine to East Germany to China.[50]

Fourth, this activity spilled over into the Gulf monarchies. Bahrain's repressive policies of the 1950s backfired. Enflamed by pan-Arabist sentiment, indignant at continuing British colonial rule, and ignited by the firing of hundreds of workers from BAPCO, the intifada Maaris (the March uprising) emerged in 1972 as the first national strike. The government reaction was swift and harsh, putting down the movement, arresting and deporting its leaders, and imposing emergency laws.[51] This prompted the creation of new underground movements like the Bahrain National Liberation Front.[52]

Fifth, stung by the Aden debacle and facing the twin pressures of financial difficulties and a decolonization policy, the British government announced in 1968 that it was pulling forces back from East of Suez. This gave the monarchies of Qatar, Bahrain, and the Trucial States three years to figure out what to do: strike out as independent states or join together. Despite sporadic anti-British protests, there was minimal evidence of a large-scale desire to end British rule—little wonder considering the apparent regional dangers. Indeed, 1968 looked for a while like a turning point, whereby "the whole region might be taken over by broadly left-leaning popular movements, guerrillas, and army officers."[53]

LEADERSHIP TRIALS AND TRIBULATIONS

In the founding and development of the Gulf monarchies, varied interlinkages between substate threats and regional concerns provided a smorgasbord of issues for leaders to deal with and their challengers to take advantage of. Indeed, the ruler's son, brother, or other male relative proved to be a continual source of threat. Ibn Saud survived multiple assassination attempts in the 1930s and 1940s as he struggled to consolidate rule over fractious tribal lands.[54] Britain's leading Arabian experts, including T. E. Lawrence, David Hogarth, most of the Arabian Affairs department in the Foreign Office, as well as the U.S. vice-consul in Aden expected the nascent state to implode without Ibn Saud.[55] His approach to knitting together a divided tribal and familial landscape was to marry approximately fifty times, bringing prominent families into his political orbit. One problem with this approach was that he sired over one hundred children, and each male had at least a basic claim to the throne. In 2000, Mai Yamani opined that there might be up to 100,000 Al Sauds or those from the Al Sheikh lineage (i.e., those from the religious half of the Saudi ruling bargain) who could technically be described as in the Saudi elite, with a ruling class of 20,000.[56]

The Sudairi seven, the sons of a crucial marriage between Ibn Saud and Hessa bint Ahmad Al Sudairi, became an influential group that dominated Saudi politics. They included the kings Fahd (r. 1982–2005) and Salman (r. 2015–) and some of the most influential and powerful ministers of defense (Sultan: 1962–2011) and the interior (Nayef: 1975–2012), both of whom were also crown princes for seven years in total. This consolidation of power, whereby these brothers seemed to support each other for decades, allowed a certain stability or predictability at elite levels in Saudi Arabia. However, it is important not to reify the importance of this group. It was not preordained that it would dominate, nor that its dominance would last, nor that this kind of modus operandi—of a faction of a family taking over—is a natural part of Saudi elite culture.[57]

Throughout the 1960s, the state's leading Islamic scholar, the Grand Mufti Mohammed Ibrahim Al Shayky, founded a range of educational and judicial institutions. This forged a cadre of religious civil servants with a vested interest in the continuance of such a system.[58] Such moves constituted the modern institutionalization of religious power as a challenge to Al Saud political authority. Countering, Faisal continued modernization plans establishing a nonreligious court system, among other progressive policies like opening public schools for women in 1960.[59] With Al Shaykhs's death in 1969, Faisal regained the upper hand. The office of mufti was dissolved, and although the Committee of Senior Scholars replaced it, its successor institution was weaker. Undeterred, the religious institutes trundled along, taking advantage of the oil boom to mushroom using the organizational experience of their Muslim Brotherhood members to expand.[60]

Although other Gulf royal families are much smaller in absolute numbers, they contain the same dramas, threats, and challenges from which a central ruler emerged to found and shape the state. Ibn Saud is the Saudi founding father, while this role is claimed by Mubarak the Great (r. 1896–1915) in Kuwait, Zayed bin Sultan Al Nahyan (r. 1966–2004) in the UAE, Jassim bin Mohammed Al Thani (r. 1878–1913) and Hamad bin Khalifah Al Thani (r. 1995–2013) in Qatar, Isa bin Salman Al Khalifah (r. 1961–1999) in Bahrain, and Sultan Qaboos bin Said Al Said (r. 1970–2020) in Oman. Each found different ways to develop his role and legacy, shoring up legitimacy and safeguarding the stability of the state with himself and his nearest and dearest at the apex (with the partial exception of the sultan on this last point, who had no children to finagle into positions of power). Despite the same broad dynamics at play, no two Gulf monarchies developed the same mechanism to stabilize their political milieu.

The nature of Kuwait's emergence as a port city meant that local merchants were independently wealthy compared to the ruling family, the Al Sabah, and a more balanced picture emerged.[61] Only the advent of oil would truly tilt this balance. Still, the political culture was set by then: Kuwaiti people expected some form of political participation not found elsewhere on the Peninsula.[62] This was consecrated in the Kuwait Parliament, which checked Al Sabah rulers to varying degrees. Similar dynamics are found in Bahrain, where there is a long-established royal family—the Sunni Al Khalifa—whose roots reach back to the late eighteenth century. That Bahrain was a well-resourced archipelago with water, dates, and pearls gave it a regional head start. A thriving economy emerged, which fostered the creation of a monied merchant class. With a state that developed educational systems and ministries before Qatar, the UAE, or Saudi Arabia, a literate population emerged receptive to regional sentiments.

As noted earlier, these factors coalesced into tumultuous decades from the 1920s to the 1960s.[63] The associated rioting and strikes, Omar AlShehabi argues, were seen and dealt with by authorities through a sectarian lens.[64] Policy reactions became focused on Shia communities as the problem, rather than socioeconomic issues. That the Sunni Al Khalifah wrestled to stamp out the striking and agitation of the 1950s and 1960s among the majority population (i.e., the Shia) meant that the space for disagreement among Al Khalifah elites narrowed.

In contrast, Qatari politics was more dominated by the royal family, where elite struggles were acute, and the Al Thani family developed a reputation for being rapacious.[65] This led to exasperated abdications and mini-coups in the nineteenth and early twentieth centuries. The advent of Khalifah bin Hamad Al Thani (r. 1972–1995) changed this pattern. By assiduously developing the state rather than just enriching the family as his predecessors did, he embedded himself and his immediate descendants in power by successfully seeking a broader source of legitimacy than the Al Thani family in itself.[66] In Oman, Sultan Qaboos founded the whole corpus of the contemporary state and dominated it for five decades.[67] No nation on earth was as closely associated with one leader as Oman was with Sultan Qaboos, which leaves a problematic legacy for his successor, Haitham bin Tariq Al Said (r. 2020–).

Zayed bin Sultan Al Nahyan (r. 1966–2004) is nearly universally credited with founding the modern UAE, while enormous hydrocarbon deposits in Abu Dhabi territory helped him consolidate a preeminent position amid the seven emirates.[68] Initially, a united group of Arab emirates was expected to include the Trucial States, Bahrain, and Qatar, a sensible project given the myriad nearby dangers posed by far larger states like Iran, Iraq, and Saudi Arabia.[69] However, long-term divisiveness between Qatar and Bahrain killed this plan. Even without these two extra statelets, UAE politics was far from straightforward. Ras al Khaimah (RAK) only joined the UAE in 1972, nearly seven months after Abu Dhabi, Dubai, Sharjah, Ajman, Umm Al Quwain, and Fujairah transitioned from the Trucial States to the UAE. RAK and Dubai kept their own military forces into the 1990s, and Abu Dhabi was only officially made the capital in 1996, hinting at lingering intra-Emirati wrangling stemming from centuries of rivalry.

CONSOLIDATING AND MODERNIZING

The Gulf monarchies achieved independence at different times. Saudi Arabia was never under colonial rule, and Ibn Saud founded the contemporary state in 1932. The other monarchies became independent from British control over the next half-century: Oman in 1951, Kuwait in 1961, and Qatar, Bahrain, and the UAE in 1971. For most monarchies, the rise to independence coincided with a significant influx of hydrocarbon wealth. This gave leading sheikhs a considerable advantage, further rooting their families at the apex of society and enriching them to profound degrees, but challenges still came thick and fast. AlShehabi argues that traditional ruling structures, changed mostly under colonial pressure, resulted in a new form of rule. When combined with the usually vast oil revenues, the new type of rule in the Gulf is best described as "petro-modernized Absolutism."[70] Despite the structure of power favoring the rulers strongly, the newly independent monarchs needed to consolidate and modernize their rule, and they tended to go for cooptation and consolidation as opposed to outright repression.

While some aspects of traditional polities remained encased in aspic, notably the role of the ruler and the family from which he came, everything else around him and his core elite was changing, from the size and complexities of society to the nature of the administration system and a proliferation of international relations.[71] Different monarchies progressed at different rates. Sultan Said bin Taimur of Oman actively avoided developing the Omani state, believing that modernization would bring more problems than it solved, as Huntington's King's Dilemma (the argument that modernization is often inherently difficult for monarchs to undertake as it inexorably leads to greater demands for ever more reforms) predicted.[72] In contrast, in the mid-twentieth century, Kuwait and Bahrain were the Dubai of their day: the most developed city-states in the region, basking in international limelight. Their relatively advanced development stemmed from their histories as regional trading hubs and the cosmopolitan hue that this bequeathed.[73] For example, Bahrain's relative commercial and international importance was shown by the fact that the first British Airways scheduled flight of the Concorde supersonic airplane was to Manama, on January 22, 1976.[74]

The oil-fueled expansion of Gulf bureaucracies and state institutions was added atop age-old mechanisms of leaders dishing out favor and finance. Sometimes, leaders and their diwans (royal courts) directly dispensed rent revenues, land, institutional control, or opportunities to run a business.[75] Opportunities for nationals to turn up to see the leader at his regular open majlis or diwaniya and plead their case for the leader's intervention or financial support are rooted in the realities of Gulf politics.[76] Although micromanaging persisted—some monarchs still insisted into the 1980s that they (debilitatingly) sign all state checks above $50,000[77]— such ad hoc approaches were phased out as states modernized and industrialized and their income skyrocketed.[78]

When facing substate groups that enjoyed significant reserves of legitimacy, governments tended to coopt and outmaneuver them. Indeed, development is not a neutral tool. Building infrastructure, schools, housing, industry, and seemingly mundane investments in agriculture (usually via subsidies) are mechanisms to forge and fix the state's preeminent role in society, boost its legitimacy, and (strive to) ensure stability. In Saudi Arabia, for example, subsidy regimes and development projects embodied "Saudi authority in tangible, visible, and material forms . . . which further reinforced centralized power and strengthened the state's grip on their lives."[79] Although religion would remain the core glue of the Saudi state, the mantras of modernization and development became new national dogmas and a new national narrative, with the centralized, king-led state driving it along.[80] A cult of personality emerged around Faisal and his various development plans, backed by billions of dollars of investment.[81] Saudi leaders "believed that mastery over the environment would translate into credibility, both at home and abroad, legitimizing the government to its subjects and its neighbors. . . . Environmental services, including irrigation projects, loan programs, dam building, and training, formed an important part of the kingdom's image-building program."[82] The same processes can readily be seen elsewhere in the Gulf, as in the UAE with Shaikh Zayed's environmentalism and Sultan Qaboos's reputation as a state builder.[83]

Bedouin tribes, once the critical political constituency that controlled the majority of the wealth on the Peninsula, were clientalized and inducted into the state.[84] Many bedouin tribesmen joined the Saudi Arabia National Guard (SANG), as this offered a stable income in an era when the military duties of tribes were revoked.[85] This and broader centralization projects of states undercut the traditional levers of power available to tribes. For example, instead of going to a tribal chief to arbitrate a commercial or social dispute, as previous generations did, official court systems replaced this function, denuding tribal leaders of another aspect of their legitimacy and power and transferring it to the state. Ultimately, such oil-fueled approaches atomized Saudi society, "emasculated"[86] traditional Bedouin tribes, and installed the state as supreme.[87]

This logic was exemplified throughout the Gulf region, albeit in different ways. Wealthier city-states like Qatar and Abu Dhabi could offer the world's most generous cradle-to-grave welfare state, but without significant taxation burdens on citizens, which engendered political apathy.[88] Even in Bahrain and Oman, countries with comparatively much smaller oil reserves, their outputs still afforded leaders sufficient revenue to forge similar—though less generous—welfare systems with the same "no taxation for no representation" mantra.[89] Having said that, as contemporary historiographies show, Gulf states also used the stick as well as the carrot to retain control, as explored later in this chapter.[90]

In the Saudi case, the religious class—the ulama—enjoyed a privileged spot in the state structure because of the religio-political origins of the Saudi state. They were thus a seemingly immovable but influential object. King Faisal's answer in the 1960s was to bureaucratize them, using the state to envelop them. Thus, although given room to influence spheres such as education and the judiciary, this approach imposed structures that impeded them from exerting authority elsewhere.[91] Similarly, influential members of ruling families and leading merchant families were brought into the state and given access to a fiefdom. Examples abound in the Gulf. In Saudi Arabia, Prince Sultan bin Abdulaziz Al Saud in the 1980s and 1990s became synonymous with the Saudi Ministry of Defense when he stood accused of skimming billions of dollars from various arms deals.[92] Such approaches were effective at coopting rivals and fostering broad elite stability.[93]

Naturally, most cooptation did not involve multibillion-dollar weapons deals. A common mechanism across the Gulf saw an individual or family appointed as (often the sole) sponsor to foreign companies entering local markets.[94] This gave such sponsors the ability to earn phenomenal sums of money as the intermediaries for Nissan, Pepsi, and every other international company needing to operate in the state. The explicitly implicit quid pro quo was that sponsors were brought into existing systems, enriched, and consequently indebted to the status quo.[95]

Such approaches did not stop all forms of competition. Competing claims for legitimacy were strong in Oman as Sultan Qaboos's reign started. Since ascending to power in 1970, Sultan Qaboos inherited "a territory without a state"—such was Oman's chronically underdeveloped nature.[96] He had to both construct a state and cement his place as the preeminent leader against other claims, such as those from tribal or Ibadi sources.[97] His core strategy was to use oil revenue–fueled development to coopt people and groups. He offered amnesty for political opponents, and lucrative sinecures and monopolies for prominent oppositional leaders. This gave them access to economic opportunities in state-run businesses and bureaucracies.[98] Many new positions were in the capital of Muscat, meaning that would-be leaders "were cut off from their traditional power basis, which greatly weakened their political and social influence."[99] Accordingly, former rivals were not humiliated but rather enriched, and both brought and bought into the new system.

Neither tribes nor their influence disappeared, nor were they entirely marginalized. In Qatar, tribes settled in clusters in and around Doha, the capital, reinforcing their identities as the state evolved.[100] However, the government diminished the power of tribes by carefully apportioning official roles to different tribes and creating broader welfare policies that forged dependencies on the state.[101] In Kuwait, the central government disrupted tribal and other groups with such devices as planning laws, atomizing them to dilute their coherence and their wider organizing power as a rival group.[102]

The tribal picture in the UAE is different, as it is a federal state with seven component statelets, each ruled by its own tribe: Abu Dhabi and the Al Nahyan, Ajman and the Al Nuaimi, Dubai and the Al Maktoum, Fujairah and the Al Sharqi, Ras Al Khaimah and the Al Qasimi, Sharjah and the Al Qasimi, and Umm Al Quwain and the Al Mu'alla. The state gradually professionalized and centralized its affairs, undercutting any substantial role for tribes. The federal judicial system overtook tribal leaders as arbiters. The ruler focused less on strategizing how to control different societal elements and transitioned to a fatherly figure administering the state. Services were given regardless of tribal hierarchies, and succession was managed via the crown prince, a new invention.[103] Andrea Rugh opines that today, it is practically impossible to usurp a sitting Emirati leader—a profound change from the assassinations and coups of yesteryear—such are the layers of security, but also institutional encumbrance.[104] Accordingly, rulers do not need to marry many times—as they did in the nineteenth and early twentieth centuries—to unite a coalition.[105]

Independence came at a tricky time for Bahrain, which was recovering from the general strikes in the late 1950s and mid-1960s. The state did not join the putative united group of Arab emirates, partly because, aside from its long-term aggravation with Qatar, the government attempted to listen to domestic sentiment that favored independence.[106] Once independent, the government established its own unicameral parliament elected by universal male suffrage in 1973. However, regional political winds and a legacy of Bahrain's contentious politics retained influence. The Ba'thist-dominated parliament was obstructionist to government plans to pass what it saw to be important security legislation. Fearing this challenge to his legitimacy and rule, Shaikh Isa bin Salman (r. 1961–1999) suspended the constitution and parliament in 1975, and it was not restored until 2001. This once again forced groups to go underground and organize. One such group was Al Jabhat al Islamiyya lil Tahrir al Bahrayn (the Islamic Front for the Liberation of Bahrain, IFLB), which, from 1976, sought inter alia to topple the government and install a Shia Islamic regime.

Given that Bahrain is widely considered to be a Shia-majority state ruled by a Sunni monarchy, such a threat carried particular salience. The IFLB and other groups were encouraged morally and physically by the Iranian Revolution in 1979. The leader of the IFLB was Mohammed Taqi Al Modarresi, a prominent Shia theologian. As well as proselytizing for a Shia theocracy via lectures, books, and appearances in Bahrain, the UAE, and Iran, he was accused of planning an attempted coup in 1981, which he neither denied nor admitted.[107] While there is no smoking gun, the circumstantial evidence is overwhelming as to the involvement of Iran with the IFLB and this plot.[108] This attempted coup increased tensions between the government and substate actors. The Bahraini government came to see these security threats as a clear and present danger to its legitimacy and stability.[109] The government reacted accordingly, engendering Sunni groups in opposition to affect a balance, while police-led actions (e.g., surveillance, arrests, expulsions) became the norm as the 1980s progressed.[110]

It was a similar, if less fraught, situation in Kuwait. Reacting to lingering pan-Arab sentiment, domestic angst at the rising numbers of foreigners, and imminent independence, a stream of legislation was passed in 1959 and 1960 to classify the exclusive privileges of Kuwait citizens.[111] By so clearly privileging Kuwaitis with unique opportunities to establish businesses or with other benefits (such as subsidies and healthcare), the British ambassador in 1960 opined, "Now the born Kuwaitis have seen that the maintenance of their own privileges probably depends on the survival of the Sabah."[112] When Kuwait obtained independence from the United Kingdom in June 1961, Iraq's prime minister, Abd Al Karim Qasim, announced that Kuwait was "an integral part of Iraq."[113] This was an imminent threat to the social order in Kuwait, let alone the legitimacy of the ruling family. In reaction, British forces returned to Kuwait, others were put on alert in Bahrain, and equipment was returned to the region to prepare to resist an invasion. Although there were no formal alliances in place, the United Kingdom assumed the mantle of planning for the defense of Kuwait to the point where code words were established: "Oban" meant "Iraqi invasion appears imminent," "Ripley" meant "Amir has requested intervention by British forces in view of increased threat of Iraqi aggression," "Ulster" asked for British intervention in view of prospective invasion, and "Wharton" meant "invasion confirmed."[114]

This deterrence worked. After the peak of the crisis, driven by a desire to boost his regime's popular, quasi-democratic legitimacy against any putative Iraqi threats, the ruler swiftly promulgated a constitution in 1962.[115] The next year, all literate Kuwaiti males were allowed to stand for election.[116] The new constitution established a system that affirmed the

Al-Sabah as the hereditary and inviolable rulers of Kuwait, with succession limited to male descendants of Mubarak the Great. The parliament was to set the emir's salary and vote on his choice of crown prince, who was also to serve as the parliament's prime minister. The selected prime minister was then to appoint sixteen cabinet members, only one of whom needed to have been elected to the parliament. This system allowed the emir to install family members in key posts. Significantly, political parties were not allowed, and the emir retained the power to dissolve parliament at any time, on the proviso that he would call for elections soon afterward. It was decided that the emir could pass urgent laws whenever the parliament was not in session. Instead of members of parliament voting directly on the cabinet's proposals, they could call for votes of confidence if they gathered at least ten votes.[117] The British ambassador at the time haughtily argued that the parliament's

> overpowering silliness . . . frustrates such few sensible schemes as the government does put to it . . . [the parliament will find] selfish, trivial or backward-looking issues over which to bicker; but so long as it provides a vent for its particular brand of folly it can, perhaps, be argued that it is a kind of safety-valve against a political upheaval that would produce something worse.[118]

This sentiment reinforces the notion that the parliament had more to do with ensuring the stability of society in its current manifestation, as opposed to advancing a democratic cause for normative reasons.

Indeed, whenever the Kuwaiti elite could, it canceled parliament, and when it needed the body back, it was reinstated. Facing intransigence from the parliament, the ruler unconstitutionally dissolved it in 1976. Although the emir does have the right to dissolve parliament, in this case he ignored strictures demanding fresh elections within a set time frame. In 1981, the parliament was reestablished, as the Al Sabah sought to harness popular legitimacy in the face of the twin threats of the 1979 Iranian Revolution and the 1980–1988 Iran-Iraq war. At the same time, the number of voting districts went from ten to twenty-five in order to dilute the votes of the more intransigent politicians and enfranchise more pliant groups.[119] The budgets proposed were "highly expansionary," including extra subsidies for fuel as the Al Sabah inculcated and ensured the loyalty of typically more marginalized social groups in the parliament.[120]

Although this worked in the short term, the consistent expansion of the franchise by the government for the purpose of getting new groups to vote for them stoked resentment among traditional classes. These groups saw the ethos of the parliament as a check on the government being diluted and their state's wealth being spread around ever further, at their expense. Meanwhile, those more recently enfranchised groups saw these machinations as an opportunity to get hold of some of the state wealth that they had been deprived of and the traditional political classes had hoarded for so long. This is the kernel of the acrimonious tone in Kuwaiti politics that remains to this day. Given that obstreperous parliamentarians have enough power to block government legislation, it has proved to be an enduring recipe for enduring parliamentary intransigence.

REFORMING AND DEFENDING

PARTICIPATION AND PARTIAL REFORM

The transition to a post–Cold War world precipitated another wave of democratization, this time in the post-Soviet sphere.[121] Amid the wider "waves" thesis of the progress of democracy—the notion that democratization in one country engenderers a domino effect nearby—many assumed that the Middle East was ripe for change.[122] Such sentiments were galvanized by the invasion of Kuwait in 1990 by Iraq. Operations Desert Shield and Storm, led by the United States, protected Saudi Arabia and repulsed the Iraqis from Kuwait the next year.[123] Aside from the financial cost required to rebuild the Kuwaiti state (approximately $65 billion), the invasion prompted a multifaceted shift in regional politics.[124]

Democratic pressures were acute in Kuwait, which had the region's most democratic (but stymied) political culture, with more than half of its parliaments dissolved since the 1960s.[125] As Kristin Smith Diwan notes, the rulers of Kuwait rested their legitimacy on a number of factors, including protecting the state through controlling its international relations and the management and sale of oil for the state's benefit.[126] On both counts, the invasion and decimation of the state counted as severe blows to these pillars of Al Sabah legitimacy, with charges leveled at senior royals that they not only failed the country but fled and abused Kuwait's Future Generations Fund (FGF).[127] They were duly punished in the reinstated elections in 1992, when a range of tribal groups, Islamists, and liberals sought greater accountability, representation, and even power sharing.[128] This opposition-led parliament led so-called fact-finding missions whose reports scathingly attacked Kuwait's leadership, while immunity was rescinded for royals who were prosecuted for embezzling funds.

Toward the end of the 1992 parliament, opposition unity dissipated as latent differences between liberals and Islamists emerged over segregating Kuwait University. This provided the Al Sabah with an opportunity to reassert dominance and counter threats to their legitimacy, stability, and control. They emphasized Kuwait's history of consensus (with the Al Sabah munificently atop it) and criticized the opposition for dividing the country. Higher oil prices allowed the rulers to continue the practices of the 1980s, gerrymandering constituencies to bring in new groups, especially disenfranchised tribal ones, enriching them and tying them to the Al Sabah and the ruling coalitions.[129] In the 1996 elections, although Islamists dominated, the government won a working majority.

Nevertheless, politics in the 1990s remained conflictual, with bitter so-called grillings coming to the fore. This language is interesting. In Arabic, the term *istijwab* means "interrogation," "questioning," "hearing," "interview," or "interpellation" in a parliamentary context. But the standard translation for it in English is a "grilling," a term nicely conveying the hostile and conflictual nature of the process.

Operation Desert Shield in 1990 necessitated the deployment of hundreds of thousands of (mostly) Western soldiers to defend Saudi Arabia. It was an embarrassment for the Saudi elite that its armed forces were not up to the job and had to rely on non-Muslim men and women to defend their lands. Consequently, elites relied on a fatwa from the Council of the Committee of Senior [Religious] Scholars to sanctify calls for foreign forces.[130] The scholars acquiesced, but their price was increased religious control of social spheres like education, a descent into "bottomless Islamization," as Gilles Kepel put it.[131] Combined with rising protests, notably from women drivers taking advantage of the world press focus on the kingdom, this posed a concern for the elite.

King Fahd in Saudi Arabia received a petition in 1992 asking for reforms. While the organizational stability of the Al Saud was not threatened, the elite needed to react. Fahd promulgated a quasi-constitution called the Basic Law, discussing a new consultative council and regional systems of provincial government. The council was an appointed, advisory-only body but grew from 60 members in 1996 to 90 in 1997, 120 in 2001, and 150 in 2005.[132] More petitions were delivered to Fahd in 2003—the "year of reform"[133]—calling for the council to be given inter alia legislative powers, with elected members and an independent judiciary. Petitions also saw the coming together of several kinds of groups who, in increasing numbers, protested and made demands of the king.[134] In the following National Dialogue, a poll found that 85 percent of respondents wanted political reforms, and 90 percent wanted more rights for women. The government ultimately responded in 2003 and 2005, allowing elections for half of the Shura council and giving the body limited legislative powers, access to more government data, televised debates, and other opportunities to question ministers.[135] In the first elections in 2005, Islamists won comprehensively, thanks, Stephane Lacroix argues, to their links to Saudi Muslim Brotherhood groups with organizational experience brought from places like Egypt.[136] In dealing with widespread protests and petitions, Saudi under King Fahd and regent Abdullah reacted mostly with conciliatory gestures and political reforms.

Democratic impulses, catalyzed by the 1990 Gulf War, were felt across the monarchies. Bahrain struggled with protests in the 1990s—its own intifada—as Shia villages protested and were repressed by the government.[137] Aside from such a direct response, Toby Matthiesen argues that the Bahraini government altered the state's demographic makeup, encouraging the settlement of Sunnis from abroad to boost their numbers against the majority Shia.[138] In addition to these sticklike measures, as a carrot, the government reinstated parliamentary elections in 2002 after a thirty-seven-year hiatus, which instigated the typical back-and-forth between the elected officials striving to influence government policy and the intransigent ministers and royals.[139]

Similarly, Oman's quietism was interrupted when in 1994, over 400 "Islamic militants" were arrested for plotting to overthrow the government. Although only around 150 were eventually tried and sentenced, their number included influential tribal actors, government undersecretaries, and the newly appointed Omani ambassador to the United States.[140] The sultan soon commuted all sentences in a quintessentially diplomatic and assuasive Omani way, but this constituted "the first public (and officially recognized) mark of dissatisfaction towards authorities since the Dhofar war."[141] The mid-1990s saw a significant economic shift, attempting to refit the Omani economy to deal with dwindling oil supplies, a youthful, demanding population, and the promulgation of the Basic Law of the State. This was a document that officially laid down inter alia Oman's form of government and succession structure. It was greeted as a positive move toward political liberalization, even though the sultan's power remained paramount.[142]

Qatar had a little burst of ersatz democratic experimentation. When Crown Prince Hamad took power from his father in 1995, he decoupled the role of prime minister from that of the emir, separated his finances from the state, and oversaw the enfranchisement of women—a regional first—by giving them the ability to stand for a newly appointed advisory body, the Central Municipal Council (CMC).[143] These elections took place every four years from 1999, although the body is broadly seen as toothless, with no legislative or executive power.[144] Ever-smaller percentages of Qataris vote in the CMC election. Survey data suggests that the token nature of the CMC elections, not a lack of desire to vote per se, is to blame for the dwindling turnout.[145] During the Arab Spring, Qatar was the only Arab nation to see no protests.[146] A manifesto did emerge there from a local academic and thinker, Ali Khalifah Al Kuwari, *al Shaab Yurid al Islah fiy Qatar Aydan* (*The People Want Reform in Qatar Too*).[147] This rumination on reform and democratization was far from radical; instead, he sought a slow transition amid broadly similar political structures.[148] It was, nevertheless, ignored.

FRICTION AND REVOLUTION

During the Arab Spring, the stable order of some of the region's most established autocrats crumbled as their legitimacy was fatally undercut by substate movements that were fanned and exacerbated by regional currents of thought and support. Some incumbent elites were evicted from power (Tunisia, Egypt). Others clung on with varying degrees of success as their states descended into civil war (Syria, Libya, Yemen), and still others were shaken by large-scale uprisings (Bahrain) or suffered relatively minor but still-concerning protests (Saudi Arabia, Oman, Jordan).

The UAE saw the rise of Islamists as the sum of all fears, prompting an era of interventionism never seen before. Worse still from the perspective of the monarchies, when protests erupted in Bahrain and Egypt, the United States—a state perceived as a close friend and de facto stability guarantor for decades on end—offered no protection. President Barack Obama offered a conciliatory line, encouraging states to engage with protestors— far from the staunch support of the status quo that the elites expected.[149] Stripped of confidence in U.S. relations that had been assiduously courted for many decades with up to $500 billion in defense spending, the UAE and Saudi Arabia launched a series of counterrevolutions.[150]

Indeed, the Arab Spring exacerbated a split in the monarchies that had been growing for some years. On one side is Qatar. Its elite have no ideological aversion to working with Islamists when they need to. They often supported groups on the Islamist spectrum with financing, weapons, diplomatic support, and publicity.[151] However, at the same time, there is little evidence of a specific *preference* to support Islamist groups actively. There is no ulama or other institutional religious body with any detectable influence on Qatar's elite, pushing them to support Islamists.[152] The character of the contemporary Qatari state, most notably in its domestic policy choices, is hardly one that emerges from Islamist-influenced politics. In the late 1990s and 2000s, the Qatari state underwrote myriad liberal projects of Sheikha Moza bint Nasser al Misnad, the consort of Hamad bin Khalifa al Thani and the mother of Emir Tamim bin Hamad Al Thani. Indeed, Moza was one of the most powerful and influential women in the entire history of the Arab world.

It is arguably best to see the Qatari elite as simply pragmatic rather than religiously dogmatic. They view Islam as having an abiding, irrefutable, and irreconcilable place in the Arab world, so it would be folly to try to somehow prevent it from exerting influence on governance.[153] As a small state of around 300,000 citizens, Qatar naturally lacked depth or range in its diplomatic corps. So, in the execution of Qatar's foreign policy during the Arab Spring, the state leveraged long-existing contacts with the Muslim Brotherhood—a group with a century's organizing history and tens of thousands of active members across the region.[154]

Qatar pursued these policies thanks to the considerable freedom of movement that its elite possessed at home. The Al Udeid Qatari Air Force base, the regional headquarters of the U.S. Central Command (CENTCOM), oversees and runs U.S. military operations for an entire segment of the world—from the coast of the Horn of Africa to Afghanistan.[155] With a homogenous population and the world's third-largest gas supplies and large oil supplies relative to its size, Qatar is by far the wealthiest country on Earth per capita. This has a calming effect on Qatari society, whose residents consistently show minimal interest in democracy.[156] The point is that these Arab Spring policies are luxuries. Indeed, uniquely, Qatar's elite can engage with any group it wants—Israel, Iran, the United States, Hezbollah, Hamas, the Muslim Brotherhood, a smorgasbord of Islamist militias in Libya, or Al Qaeda affiliates in Syria[157]—with no concern about significant domestic fallout or any obvious financial opportunity cost.

However, the very fact that Qatar's Arab Spring policies were so willful is just one of the many issues that rankle the UAE, the state very much on the other side of this debate. The UAE sees Islamists as inherently untrustworthy: if you give them an inch, they will take a mile and pose a threat to societal and political stability. From the perspective of UAE leaders in Abu Dhabi, the history of local Islamism bears this out, as do the realities of the Arab Spring.[158] Their logic flows that for decades, Islamists argued that all they wanted was a social space and the opportunity to educate society, and they had no yearnings for political leadership.[159] However, when opportunity presented itself, as during the Arab Spring, they struck.[160] Across the region, the UAE sees Islamists emerging and clamoring for power—and sometimes taking it. Within the UAE, the elite received petitions (albeit polite, respectful ones) from Islamist voices asking for further enfranchisement and a broader role in society. Abu Dhabi leaders saw these demands as being incremental and giving the lie to decades of protests from such groups that they had no such agenda.[161]

Consequently, today, it is an article of faith with the leadership of Abu Dhabi that the growth of Islamist forces is a near-immediate and obvious threat to the stability of their state and that of other countries around the Arab world.[162] They see such groups ranging from the extreme end, like Al Qaeda and the Islamic State (IS), to the more moderate end, encompassing the Muslim Brotherhood as part of the same problem. Indeed, as Abu Dhabi leaders point out, the Muslim Brotherhood is actively seeking to implement Sharia law as their ultimate, stated goal.[163] Accordingly, the UAE sees the kind of politics that Qatar has long promoted as an active danger to regional political stability. Wherever religious principles outmatch and overtake political considerations in the Arab world, with groups like the Taliban, in the Islamist-soaked politics in Palestine, or wherever Islamist dogma enjoys such influence for so long, the result has reliably been the immiseration of the body politic. From the UAE's perspective, Islamist politics has already upended the suboptimal but broad stability in Egypt, Syria, Libya, and Yemen. Thus, the Abu Dhabi elite are convinced that they know the core problem in the Arab world: the mixing of religion and politics. Therefore, the solution is obvious: fervently support a Jeffersonian approach, advocating the separation of church (or, rather, mosque) and state.[164] Equipped with wealth, experience, and a highly professionalized state, the UAE felt compelled to act and promote its ideals in an era of tumult.

First, the UAE was the critical force behind the attempted cowing of Qatar. Within six months of Emir Tamim coming to the throne in 2013, the UAE, Saudi Arabia, and Bahrain withdrew their ambassadors from Doha, with implicit threats that Qatar's only land border (which is with Saudi Arabia) could be closed. There were multiple reasons for this move. Building anger over many years of Hamad bin Khalifah's status quo–challenging policies—supporting Islamist groups around the region, defying regional containment policies toward Iran, bankrolling Al Jazeera's taboo-breaking news coverage, engaging with Israel—meant that the troika wanted to force the young emir to radically change the state's policies.[165] At the time, this was shocking and unprecedented. Within months of the withdrawal, Saudi Arabia under King Abdullah was playing a mediating role between Qatar and the UAE. By the end of the year, an agreement was fashioned so that Qatar could host the annual meeting of the Gulf Cooperation Council (GCC) in December. Qatar signed agreements promising to curtail some of its more pointed foreign policies, and the issue was settled, albeit to no one's satisfaction.[166]

Second, in June 2017, the UAE, Saudi Arabia, Bahrain, and Egypt led an unprecedented blockade of Qatar. The severity and range of the blockade—from closing Qatar's border with Saudi Arabia and cutting off Qatar from regional airspace to forcing the repatriation of Qatari nationals and refusals to allow reshipment to Qatar from the region's main port in Dubai—shocked observers in the region and farther abroad.[167] Qatar was charged with a wide array of crimes. Still, the core issue remained the same: Qatar, as a homogenous, stable, exquisitely rich state, with no hint of internal discord, was exacerbating, often severely and without heed for regional sentiment, the stability and security of other monarchies and Arab states farther afield. Thus, the same issue that had plagued Gulf leaders for a century—concern about challenges emanating from regional arenas affecting domestic dynamics—was still center stage. However, this time it was not immigrant workers or disgruntled local cliques who were agitating; instead it was Qatar, one of their allies.

Qatar's role as an Islamist-supporting state during the Arab Spring was the final critical element to the decision to blockade the country. This also explains why Egypt was such a vociferous supporter of the blockade, given the loathing of President Abdel Fattah el-Sisi of his predecessor, Mohammed Morsi, the politician from the Muslim Brotherhood who had held power for a year and whose government received tens of billions of dollars' worth of support from Qatar. Bahrain also charged Qatar with nationalizing Bahraini Sunni citizens and contributing to the demographic destabilization in the state. Details of this charge remain unclear, but even a small nationalizing of Sunni Bahraini citizens, even if they are just joining family members in Qatar, is likely to concern Bahraini leaders who are deeply sensitive to the state's demographic and sectarian makeup. Bahraini leaders were similarly furious at Qatari think tanks teaching (or evangelizing, as those in Manama would see it) non-violent protest tactics.[168] Such examples again speak to the core concern and charge: Qatar's apparent disregard for the security and stability of its fellow monarchies. Qatar is no innocent state, and its foreign policies have contributed to regional instability. However, Qatar is far from alone here: consider the record of Saudi Arabia's proselytization of its Salafi religious doctrines from the 1960s to the 2000s, or the role of Kuwait, which according to the Obama administration, is the Gulf state most culpable for allowing terrorist financing in recent years.[169]

Qataris are sure that the blockade nearly included military action against the state, threatening its sovereignty most egregiously, and only the concerted mediation of U.S. secretary of state Rex Tillerson stopped this from occurring.[170] Though a heartfelt sentiment in Qatar, there is no concrete evidence of this threat. The punitive blockade plus the latent threat of invasion had a transformative effect on the Qatari polity. It demanded that Qataris return home from Bahrain, Saudi Arabia, and Egypt—and often vice versa—whether they were studying, living, or working there. Given the high level of regional intermarriage and the normality of the dispersal of families and tribes between the monarchies, this directly affected citizens. The establishment of a hotline and a mechanism for citizens to visit family was widely deemed insufficient and impractical.[171]

The idea behind the blockade was inter alia to cut off Qatar's most important sources of imports to pressure the government. Initial reports of supermarket shelves emptying likely pleased the blockade's planners: they actively sought to engender local anger, confusion, and panic to induce the Qatari government to capitulate. As such, the action sought to directly undermine the social order in Qatar. However, in reality, the opposite happened—Qatar ultimately boosted its domestic resilience (discussed in more detail later in this chapter).

A third, interrelated part of the quartet's attempts to—from their perspective—restore regional stability is the support of anti-Islamist nationalists around the wider MENA region. Thus, the UAE supports, sometimes with alleged backing from Saudi Arabia and Egypt, the forces of General Khalifa Belqasim Haftar in Libya against Islamist forces, some of whom had been backed by Qatar.[172] Similar allegations are made about the quartet seeking to support a counterrevolution in Sudan.[173]

LEADERSHIP AND CHANGE

Sometimes the centrality of leaders can be overplayed. Institutions are important. Even young ones established within living memory have a honed ability to preserve and expand their influence and absorb shocks and changes in myriad layers of bureaucratic and institutional rules and regulations.[174] Nevertheless, it is not unreasonable to focus, quite extensively, on the influence of leaders in the Gulf context.[175] They have the power and purview to profoundly shape the state, and except in Kuwait, they are not impeded by one of the stickiest forms of institutional impediment—namely, democratically elected parliamentary bodies.[176] As such, scholars focus on succession issues as critical to the maintenance and stability of the existing social order.[177] Such problems are typically opaque to almost everyone, while rules and laws governing these processes are invented and then ignored and bypassed with alacrity.

Consequently, there is a tendency for discussion in the scholarly community to be circular, with presumed rules, whether formal or informal, emerging to mutual agreement and reification. So when it comes to ascertaining who might succeed to power in Saudi Arabia, experts pontificate that esoteric and vaguely Orientalist motifs such as "success in battle, generosity in victory, and wisdom in mediation" are important variables.[178] This, as well as a litany of other apparent rules—from this and not that side of the family, whose mother must or must not come from a particular segment of the family—get undue deference until they get ripped asunder by the realities of Gulf politics.[179] Thus, this subject needs to be addressed cautiously. The best an analyst can do is outline the status quo and offer a historically informed view of contemporary issues. The reasoning here is that, while history does not automatically repeat itself, it likely provides a culturally and sociopolitically attuned understanding of the art of the possible.

ALL CHANGE? SAUDI ARABIA

Scholarly discussion has long been most fevered about transitions and elite changes in Saudi Arabia. The rise to power of Mohammed bin Salman Al Saud curtailed long-emergent concerns about how Saudi politics would deal with leadership skipping a generation and passing from the sons of Ibn Saud to his grandsons. Viable and compos mentis candidates from the second generation were in short supply. The first age-related issue occurred with King Fahd (r. 1982–2005). He suffered a severe stroke in 1996 in his seventies, meaning that he was removed from de facto power for the last decade of his reign, and Abdullah, his crown prince, was regent. In turn, Abdullah (r. 2005–2015) ruled into his ninetieth year, which led to speculation about his health and ability to do the job. A further sign of the aging pool of pretenders to the throne saw King Abdullah outlive two of his crown princes. Prince Sultan was heir apparent from 2005 to 2011 and died at the age of eighty-five, and Prince Nayef, his successor, lasted under eight months in the role, passing away in 2012 at the age of seventy-eight. Such deaths intensified discussions of the generation jump, given the dwindling "windows of lucidity" of ever more geriatric leaders.[180] Nevertheless, this jockeying for position was peaceful compared to similar events in the twentieth century that led to bitter wrangling at the top. Such instances threatened to split the Al Saud family, which deeply concerned Ibn Saud, who saw elite issues as the reason for the dismemberment of the second Saudi state.

To address the succession issues, formal and informal rules have changed and evolved. In 1992, King Fahd introduced the Basic Law, formalizing the king's right to name and change his successor, and in 2007, an amendment formed the Hayat Al Bayah (the Allegiance Council). Theoretically, this body would consult with the king on picking a successor and ratify his choice. However, the practice of this procedure failed at the first hurdle. In 2014, King Abdullah tried to line up Muqrin bin Abdulaziz Al Saud to succeed Crown Prince Salman, even decreeing that this decision could not be changed. But it was. King Salman (r. 2015–) swiftly evicted Muqrin from his position in line to the throne, appointing Mohammed bin Nayef.[181] This meant that for the first time, a grandson of Ibn Saud was in line to the throne. The choice meshed well with scholarly expectations. Mohammed bin Nayef had long cultivated a reputation as a hardworking, effective, and internationally well regarded leader in the Ministry of the Interior, particularly with counterterrorism portfolios.[182]

However, Mohammed bin Nayef was soon displaced by an individual who emerged from near obscurity, at least as far as outside observers were concerned. Mohammed bin Salman (b. 1985) swiftly rose through the ranks to consolidate his place as king-in-waiting, with more power than any individual since Ibn Saud (Figure 1.1).

Adviser to Council of Ministers	April 10, 2007
Special adviser to his father (then governor of Riyadh)	December 28, 2009
Minister, chief of Crown Prince (Salman's) court	March 3, 2013
General supervisor, Minister of Defense's Office	July 13, 2013
Defense minister, chief of Royal court	January 23, 2015
Chairman of Council of Economic and Development Affairs	January 29, 2015
Chairman of Board for the Public Investment Fund (PIF)	March 23, 2015
Led the war against the Houthis in Yemen	March 26, 2015
Deputy crown prince	April 29, 2015
Chairman of Higher Council for Saudi Aramco	May 1, 2015
Crown prince	June 21, 2017

FIGURE 1.1 The evolution of Mohammed bin Salman (b. 1985).

Mohammed bin Salman profoundly changed elite structures and decision-making modalities, if not the very nature of sociopolitical relations in Saudi Arabia; as Nathan Brown notes, his decisions "seem to be products of a different country."[183] As deputy crown prince, he showcased the extent of his power, launching the war in Yemen as the newly ensconced defense minister in 2015. Such a dangerous, large-scale mobilization, seeking to attain maximalist political ends by vanquishing a hardened, experienced asymmetric foe like the Houthis (discussed in more detail in Chapter 4), is a first in the contemporary history of the Gulf monarchies. The international coalition assembled for "Operation Decisive Storm"—playing on the Western-led operations Desert Shield and Desert Storm in 1990 and 1991—was the largest in Arab history. This gambit was interpreted as Mohammed bin Salman's way to galvanize and mobilize Saudi public opinion behind him as a new, vigorous leader amid a propaganda blitz.[184]

Domestically, Mohammed bin Salman was transformative. A flagship policy was the announcement in September 2017 that it would become legal for women to drive cars in the kingdom.[185] The fact that it was illegal for women to drive in Saudi Arabia had long been one of the touchstones of critique of Saudi Arabia. Its symbolic importance outstripped the realities of the issue's salience. This is to say that arguably more important and impactful concerns about women's rights—such as their ability to travel, open a bank account, or engage in work without the agreement of a male family member—are more pressing issues by most assessments. However, the symbolism of women driving is tough to beat. Consequently, this issue became the third rail of Saudi politics. King Abdullah was relatively progressive. He established a university where men and women studied together, called King Abdullah University of Science and Technology (KAUST). He appeared in photographs with women without their faces covered, something that was unthinkable until it happened. In 2012, he decreed that women could stand for election to the Consultative Council, and he appointed the state's first woman to the office of deputy minister.[186] Nevertheless, the driving issue remained too divisive. Although he was powerful as king, he received pushback from clerics as he made some of his more progressive ventures.[187]

In this context, Mohammed bin Salman's grasping of this issue—when he was but a newly ensconced crown prince in his early thirties—was symbolically important for both women's issues, in demonstrating the reach of his power, and his desire to shake staid taboos. Notably, the decree was announced live on Saudi state television "and in a simultaneous media event in Washington."[188] There are a couple of conclusions to draw from this issue and its announcement. First, it is essential to note that Mohammed bin Salman effortlessly blew through what was perceived to be one of the core taboos at play in the Saudi state, ignoring the institutional power of the clergy and the blocking role that they were believed to play with such issues. Second, choosing this issue so early on and announcing it in Washington, D.C., signaled a desire to rebrand the Saudi state with himself at the helm as a quasi-revolutionary leader.

Similar policies successfully enacted by Mohammed bin Salman included the abolition of the need for women to obtain permission from their male guardians (a husband, or even a son) to undertake myriad actions like opening a bank account or leaving the country.[189] Other policies in this vein included facilitating the return of cinemas to the kingdom and hosting international events (car races, concerts, and—nearly beyond belief—large-scale raves) as part of a broader attempt to build an "entertainment industry from scratch."[190]

Mohammed bin Salman was similarly iconoclastic in the economic sphere, a subject discussed in more detail in chapter 3 of this book. Under his father's auspices, Mohammed led a bonfire of the quangos (quasi-autonomous nongovernmental organizations) and their replacement with new, streamlined councils.[191] Notably, two influential committees emerged—the Council for Economic and Development Affairs (CEDA) and the Council for Political and Security Affairs (CPSA)—replacing at least a dozen preexisting institutions. Mohammed bin Salman headed CEDA and was a member of CPSA initially, the only individual to be involved with both organizations in any capacity. When Mohammed bin Nayef was ousted as crown prince in June 2017, Mohammed bin Salman replaced him as head of CPSA, thus taking control of the state's two most critical governing institutions.

The most important impact of the creation of the CEDA was that it allowed the restructuring of Saudi Aramco, the state oil company that provided 68 percent of state revenue in 2019.[192] The company was entirely separated from the Ministry of Petroleum and Mineral Resources, "giving it greater operational independence," akin to similar moves in recent years by Qatar Petroleum (now Qatar Energy) and BAPCO.[193] The old board structure was dissolved, and a new one was created with Mohammed bin Salman as the chairman. This was a profoundly unusual move, as hitherto Al Sauds had avoided taking such a direct role in Saudi Aramco, wanting to leave the company—the state's golden goose—above the fray of internecine politics.

Nevertheless, with the pieces in place, Mohammed bin Salman announced yet another taboo-breaking plan: to privatize Saudi Aramco, move control of the firm to the Saudi Public Investment Fund (PIF), and float 5 percent of the oil company on a stock exchange to raise up to $2 trillion (or so he hoped). The theory behind this was to give the PIF the financial strength to act as a transformative institution in Saudi Arabia, to symbolize an era of change in the country, to introduce more transparency into Saudi Aramco via the listing, and, overall, to catalyze the transition of the state's economy to a post-oil era. The blueprint for this transition is Mohammed bin Salman's Vision 2030 document. This far-reaching plan includes inter alia the creation of a new, $500-billion city, NEOM, slated to be thirty-three times the size of New York City.[194]

Seeing foreign direct investment (FDI) as a central plinth of his plans to transform the state, in October 2017, Mohammed bin Salman hosted a jamboree of an investment conference at the Ritz-Carlton Hotel, on the edge of Riyadh's diplomatic district. Attended by some of the world's most prominent businesspeople and hedge fund managers, this event, dubbed "Davos in the Desert," caught the world's attention and was further grist to the Mohammed bin Salman zeitgeist. Breathless commentary followed, gushing about the reforms and potential that existed in Saudi Arabia.[195] In November 2017, Thomas Friedman, a *New York Times* op-ed columnist, wrote that "the most significant reform process underway anywhere in the Middle East" was happening in Saudi Arabia, masterminded by the young and dynamic crown prince, Mohammed bin Salman.[196] But history should have given such observers pause. August institutions like the *New York Times* have long described Saudi kings as enlightening reformers. From King Saud being seen as "more progressive and international-minded than his autocratic father," similar sentiments were penned in 1960, 1962, November 1963, December 1963, twice in November 1964, 1965, April 1975, June 1975, 1979, 1982, August 1991, November 1991, 1992, 1996, 2000, 2002, and 2005.[197]

Barely a week after the Saudi Davos ended, the Ritz-Carlton again played host to some of Saudi Arabia's most important, influential, and well-known individuals—but this time they were under arrest, by order of the crown prince, on charges of corruption. The crackdown was unprecedented in its scale and reach, including prominent royals. Waleed bin Talal Al Saud was a billionaire and the state's wealthiest and most prominent investor, with stakes in blue-chip Western companies like Twitter and Citigroup. Miteb bin Abdulla Al Saud was the most influential son of King Abdullah and the former head of the SANG, an institution long understood as one of the critical nodes of power among the factions of the Al Saud family. Other Al Sauds, including former senior ministers and Ethiopian billionaire Mohammed Al Amoudi, were scooped up as well. Details of the arrests and the outcomes remain opaque to this day. The *New York Times* reported that 381 people were summoned in one way or another, and over $100 billion was recouped.[198]

These two events at the Ritz stand in glaring contrast, with one deeply undercutting the other. Investors prioritize certainty and the rule of law. Saudi authorities argue that the legal foundation of the arrests and the expropriation of their assets in compensation for their crimes were firmly under Saudi judicial auspices. However, few international investors will be comforted by such an assertion, given how ad hoc and opaque the whole episode looked to those abroad. As one investor put it to the *Financial Times*, "Half my Rolodex is in the Ritz right now. And they want me to invest there now?"[199] While Saudi Arabia remains a target for investment, the price demanded by investors can only have increased, probably significantly. But Mohammed bin Salman reasoned that this was a price worth paying for displaying his uncompromising attitude toward corruption. This message, several Saudi interlocutors insisted, reached every corner of Saudi society and received substantial popular support.[200]

But then the de facto rule of Mohammed bin Salman oversaw one of the darkest periods in Saudi history. Jamal Khashoggi was a Saudi exiled in the United States and a journalist for the *Washington Post*. An elite insider in Saudi society for decades, a veteran journalist and editor, and a regular on the international conference circuit discussing Saudi matters, he was a progressive individual who mildly critiqued Saudi policies. In 2018, he was lured to the Saudi consulate in Istanbul, where he was accosted, killed, and dismembered (his body has yet to be found) in what remains a singularly gruesome episode. Leaks from the U.S. Central Intelligence Agency (CIA) suggest that the spy agency finds Mohammed bin Salman culpable for the incident, and the U.S. Senate "passed a resolution holding him personally responsible for the crime."[201]

This rendition gone wrong (or perhaps, simply, this assassination) of Khashoggi is part of a more extensive set of policies that seek to control the Saudi narrative and shut down criticism. While there have been some unambiguously positive moves in the realm of women's rights in Saudi Arabia, several of the most prominent activists who have been fighting peacefully for their rights for decades have been arrested on a range of charges.[202] There has also been a clampdown on figures on the conservative and liberal ends of the religious spectrum.[203] Further, there has also been a rash of policies undertaken that are similarly surprising and similarly pugnacious. In 2017, the Lebanese prime minister Saad Hariri was summoned to meet with Mohammed bin Salman, whereupon he was detained and forced to read a resignation letter live on television, with a Saudi minder visible in the shot.[204] In 2018, in reaction to a run-of-the-mill tweet by the Canadian foreign minister Chrystia Freeland calling for the release of Saudi activists, Saudi Arabia officially cut off ties with Canada, suspended trade and investment, canceled direct flights, and announced the withdrawal of Saudi students studying in the country.

These policies indicated the emergence of a new era in Saudi Arabia where no taboo is sacred. Controlling critical economic and security councils as crown prince, and swatting aside individuals heretofore considered influential, Mohammed bin Salman has consolidated power more thoroughly than any predecessor since Ibn Saud. The bulwark of the SANG, for over fifty years under the leadership of the Abdullah side of the family, proved to be of no use in defending his descendants. Similarly, the religious establishment was understood since time immemorial in Saudi Arabia to have power over crucial sections of state-society relations. From this position, they were assumed to be an impediment to progressive reforms by virtue of their influence over (it was presumed) millions of Saudis. Nor was this religious influence thought to be limited to the establishment. Salman Al Odah was one of the state's most prominent clerics, with a Twitter following of over

13 million, and as such he was the embodiment of the kind of individual assumed to have real power in Saudi Arabia. But he was simply arrested in September 2017, with barely a detectable murmur, like many others before and since.

Mohammed bin Salman wants to control the narrative of the state and the pace of change. Therefore, he has lashed out at liberal and conservative clerics, women's rights pioneers, and critical journalists, and he has narrowed the scope of Al Saud power, centralizing control. However, no autocrat can rule by fear alone: every leader needs key constituencies of support. What Mohammed bin Salman has done is shift the poles of support from Al Saud nodes and clerical institutional support to, in essence, a more populist mandate, striking "a new balance."[205] Far more than merely doling out more subsidies, more jobs, and financial benefits—although King Salman did do this, offering up to $32 billion worth of such bonuses upon ascending to the throne[206]—Mohammed bin Salman has ignited a new phase of Saudi nationalism.[207] His Vision 2030 explicitly strives to create opportunities for Saudi Arabia's vast young population, indicating Mohammed bin Salman's careful focus. The uncompromising crackdown on elite corruption, the war in Yemen, and pointedly trying to secure Saudi strategic goals are all elements stoking this new wave of assertive nationalism in the kingdom.[208]

The question of succession in Saudi Arabia has been set aside by most analysts. Given Mohammed bin Salman's youth, his purging of obvious rivals, and his viselike grip on the levers of power, he is universally expected to take control when his father, King Salman, already in his eighties and increasingly frail, dies. Only a black swan event like an assassination (as befell Faisal in 1975) is thought likely to impede his rise to the throne. If precedent is any guide, it seems likely that Mohammed bin Salman could oversee Saudi Arabia for decades.[209]

SOME CHANGE? KUWAIT AND OMAN

Succession issues in Kuwait are fraught. Historically, Mubarak the Great infamously took power in 1896 by killing two of his brothers, one of whom was the ruler. However, he made up for this inauspicious start by forging Kuwait as an independent state with British help. A loose succession

Mubarak the Great (r. 1896–1915)	
Al Jaber	**Al Salem**
Jaber bin Mubarak (r. 1915–1917)	
	Salem bin Mubarak (r. 1917–1921)
Ahmed (r. 1921–1950)	
	Abdullah (r. 1950–1965)
	Sabah (r. 1965–1977)
Jaber Al Ahmed (r. 1977–2006)	
	Saad Al Abdullah (r. 2006–2006)
Sabah Al Ahmed Al Jaber (r. 2006–2020)	
Nawaf Al Ahmed Al Jaber (r. 2020–)	
Crown Prince Meshaal Al Ahmad Al Sabah	

FIGURE 1.2 Succession to the throne in Kuwait.

mechanism emerged, whereby rule would alternate between the decedents of Mubarak's sons, Salem and Jaber (Figure 1.2).

But this has not always worked. Power skipped directly from one Al Salem to another in 1965, giving that side of the family twenty-seven years of rule. Similarly, in 2006, a constitutional crisis erupted. On the death of Jaber Al Ahmed, power moved to the other side of the family, but Crown Prince Saad Al Abdullah was so ill that it was not even clear he could take the oath of office. Amid newspaper editorials encouraging Saad to step aside and the head of the National Guard lobbying for him to stay, the matter ultimately was decided by the parliament. As per the constitution, members of Parliament (MPs) removed the would-be emir on health grounds and chose Sabah Al Ahmed Al Jaber as the head of state. As the *Gulf States Newsletter* noted,

Elected representatives of the people have, for the first time, decided the legitimacy of a ruler in Arabia. . . . Citizens of the Gulf Co-operation Council countries have been treated to the spectacle of a full-scale constitutional crisis that has been resolved by open political negotiation, public pressure and, crucially, the intervention of an elected parliament rather than secret family deals or a palace putsch. . . . In the West, the

events of the past two weeks have been portrayed as a picturesque orien-
tal soap opera. But this complacent depiction misses the real significance
of a Gulf society and ruling family grappling to reconcile tradition with
the demands of modern power and accountability.[210]

Emir Sabah chose his brother Nawaf to be crown prince. At the time,
analysts speculated that the Jaber/Salem "alternating succession has
apparently been consigned to history."[211] With the 2020 transition upon
the death of the ninety-one-year-old Sabah, this alternation was again
ignored with the appointment of Nawaf Al Ahmad Al Sabah as emir and
Mishal Al Ahmed Al Jaber Al Sabah as the crown prince. This transition bucked the regional trend for young leadership, as in Saudi Arabia
and Qatar, or dynamic leadership, as in the UAE. With Nawaf being born
in 1937 and facing a series of serious health conditions, within fourteen
months, he had handed considerable powers to his (also nonagenarian)
crown prince, Mishal.

Whenever Kuwait passes the torch to the next generation, the new,
younger leader will still be confronted by the immovable structure that is
Kuwaiti parliamentary gridlock. Although elites sought to curb its powers
by gerrymandering districts and unconstitutionally canceling the parliament, these measures have only stoked resentment. Despite these challenges, the parliament's oversight powers remain deeply rooted.[212] Kuwaiti
politics suffered from the jockeying for position between would-be rulers
in the late 2010s, and resurrecting such an era would be damaging.[213]
However, speaking to the broader stability of social order, the Kuwaiti
system showed in 2006 its ability to deal with contests for power. In that
instance, the legitimacy derived from parliament proved crucial in facilitating the unseating of one soon-to-be emir and his replacement. In this
sense, it is tempting to tentatively assume that the nature of Kuwait's transition is broadly secured by state rules, norms, and institutions that have
been tested and proven.

Ever the regional outlier, Omani politics bucks various trends. While
close family members elsewhere play decisive roles as ministers or
advisers, Sultan Qaboos was more isolated in Oman. As he was developing his rule, key advisers earned their positions as a quid pro quo for
supporting the sultan as he came to power.[214] Indeed, the story of elite
politics in Oman is suffused with the centrality of the sultan himself. He

knitted the state together after putting down a rebellion in the 1960s and 1970s in the Dhofar region. He dominated the Omani state as sultan, supreme commander of the armed forces, and nominal ministers of defense, foreign affairs, and finance. Although the sultan had the title of foreign minister, in practice Yusuf bin Alawi bin Abdullah was the sultan's minister responsible for foreign affairs (1997–2020). Nevertheless, for strategic direction, the sultan remained vital.

After half a century in power, Sultan Qaboos was the Arab world's longest-serving ruler when he died on January 10, 2020. Succession in Oman was long one of the region's more curious processes. No official successor was appointed, there was no leading candidate, and there was no transparent process. The Basic Law of the State (the so-called White Book), promulgated in November 1996, stipulates that a clique of around forty senior Omanis must agree on a successor within three days of the sultan's death. If that does not work, as per a 2011 amendment, designated individuals will consult the famous letters in which Sultan Qaboos wrote his nomination.[215] Speaking to how this process became overly mythologized, one well-known French journalist noted that one copy was found in a "multi-coloured Japanese pagoda-shaped" safe in Muscat, and another copy was 1,000 kilometers to the south, in Salalah.[216] Although Qaboos was an autocrat who held onto all the key portfolios of power, the *Financial Times* described him as "widely loved" in its obituary.[217] Although this sounds quaint and anachronistic, Gulf scholars will surely testify that they routinely receive a similar answer whenever they ask a similar question. The sultan is a tough act to follow.

In the end, rather than engaging in (potentially) three days of discussion as expected, Oman's defense council met within hours of the sultan's death, opened one of the famous letters on live television, and anointed Haitham bin Tariq as sultan. Doing it so quickly left no room for squabbling, made the process transparent, imprinted Sultan Qaboos's imprimatur upon Haitham, and gave the impression of smooth continuity.[218] In a country whose top leadership remembers a time when their state was deeply riven into factions, such a clean, quick transition to a new leader was of paramount importance.

Although this hurdle was smoothly cleared, Sultan Haitham faces an array of profound challenges, many of which threaten to undercut Oman's hard-fought stability. The problems for Haitham are primarily economic.

Oman has seen protests in recent years as its citizens, as elsewhere in the region, voice displeasure over a smorgasbord of grudges ranging from a lack of economic opportunities to corruption. There are compelling concerns that Oman's financial predicament is perilous (as discussed in more detail in chapter 3). Without the mystique of Sultan Qaboos, the nation's founder and father keeping tensions in check, concerns may transition to threats to Oman's stability. It seems likely that, whatever the policies of Haitham, he will need to seek financial assistance if the mismatch remains too great between people's expectations and what the state can deliver.

The obvious places from which to seek assistance are China, other Gulf monarchies, and international institutions like the International Monetary Fund (IMF). Financial support from each comes with different prices. China demands something akin to (often huge) stakes in Omani companies or infrastructure projects. The IMF demands structural changes along neoliberal lines, such as trimming the public wage bill, which would be unpopular domestically. And different monarchies come with their own varying issues. Saudi Arabia is facing its own economic crisis in the coming years, as is Bahrain. Kuwait is a likely source of support if its intransigent parliament does not interfere. Qatar too is expected to offer support, although accepting significant help from Doha is liable to place Oman in a more problematic position with the UAE. Given that the UAE is potentially a good source of assistance, this is a concern, but their bilateral relations remain frosty. Historical bitterness in their relations goes back generations, with irredentist issues and ongoing wariness about contemporary borders. This includes the Omani enclave of the Musandam Peninsula and the Emirati counterenclave of Nahwa (i.e., Emirati land within Omani land, which is within Emirati territory).[219] Recent issues with Emirati spy rings having been caught and sentenced in Oman further complicate relations.[220]

However, Oman is far from friendless, and it is informative to reflect on which leaders paid their respects in person upon the sultan's death. The leaders and de facto leaders of Saudi Arabia, Kuwait, Bahrain, Qatar, Jordan, and the UAE all traveled to Oman, while the Iranian foreign minister represented his country. They were joined by Japanese prime minister Shinzo Abe, seniormost royals from Belgium and the Netherlands, and the German president, Frank-Walter Steinmeier. In contrast, China only sent its science and technology minister, there was no conspicuous Russian delegation, and the U.S. delegation was late, arriving the day after official mourning ended, and surprisingly low-level being led by newly confirmed Energy Secretary Dan Brouillette. Britain, meanwhile, sent as many senior leaders as realistically possible, including Prince Charles, Prime Minister Boris Johnson, Secretary of State for Defence Ben Wallace, and Chief of the Defence Staff Nick Carter.[221] Thus, although Haitham has a delicate socioeconomic hand to deal with, along with some nearby frosty relations, he will have a healthy amount of domestic goodwill and an array of international allies to rely upon in the short and medium term.

MINIMAL CHANGE? QATAR, BAHRAIN, AND THE UAE

It is widely assumed that Abu Dhabi is the dominant emirate in the UAE. This is mostly true, but as always, the devil is in the details. Abu Dhabi is the largest emirate, over six times bigger than all the other emirates combined. It is also the wealthiest, with over sixteen times the amount of oil, resulting in, for example, Abu Dhabi's per capita income being approximately six times that of Ajman.[222] Nevertheless, Abu Dhabi was recognized as the formal capital only in 1996, after tentative plans to build a new city and capital called Karama on the Abu Dhabi–Dubai border were shelved. Since the millennium, Abu Dhabi has emerged to increased prominence, notably in its foreign policy.[223] A well-equipped and strong military were tools that the state used to achieve its policy ends.[224] Although this might sound normal, the active deployment of Gulf militaries in harm's way in wars of choice is new. Emirati military capability is understood as the brainchild and under the control of Mohammed bin Zayed.[225]

Another facet of Abu Dhabi's rise to power is the relative decline of Dubai, not least because of the latter's multibillion-dollar financial bailout of the latter in the wake of the 2008 financial crash, which signaled a decisive shift in the UAE's center of gravity toward Abu Dhabi.[226] Indeed, the world's tallest building—the crown jewel of Dubai—had its name changed barely minutes before its official opening from the Burj Dubai (the Tower of Dubai) to the Burj Khalifa (Khalifa's Tower), after Khalifa bin Zayed Al Nahyan, the president of the UAE and emir of

Abu Dhabi. The change of name was so spontaneous that no one in government even registered the Internet domain name burjkhalifah.com.[227] Few would argue that Dubai (or any of the other emirates) has a distinct foreign policy. Instead, Abu Dhabi sets the tone and directs UAE foreign policy.[228]

However, Abu Dhabi's dominance can be overplayed. The leadership in the UAE's capital takes a hawkish approach toward Iran. Going back to Wikileaks discussions in the 1990s and 2000s, it is clear that Mohammed bin Zayed has long displayed a particular concern about the kinds of threats Iran poses. Indeed, if anything, Mohammed bin Zayed (and consequently UAE policy) became increasingly contra-Iran. Gone were the days when three emirates supported Iran during the Iran-Iraq war in the 1980s (Dubai, Sharjah, and Ras Al Khaimah), while the others supported Iraq.[229] Rather, the UAE state, under Abu Dhabi's auspices, launched a war in Yemen motivated mostly to counter what it saw to be Iranian proxy forces.[230] Despite Abu Dhabi's aversion to Iran and its desire to see the United States exert "maximum pressure" on the state, Dubai remains by far the region's largest trader with Iran, at $19 billion per year.[231] Indeed, Dubai is a critical offshore trading center for Iran, accounting for up to $300 billion of investment at one point, according to the U.S. Congressional Research Service. Relatedly, there are up to 600,000 Iranians living in Dubai.[232] As much animosity as there is in Abu Dhabi to Iran and its varied regionally destabilizing policies, in the absence of any credible alternative and with the considerable structural weight of Dubai's Iranian relations, its more accommodationist approach to Iran in 2022 is not ultimately that surprising.

Like Saudi Arabia, the UAE is going through an era where building nationalism, often with a martial tinge, is an increasingly active focus.[233] The UAE started this push in 2006 by introducing a law on reserve service in the military. In 2008, a revamped school curriculum on citizenship was introduced; in 2009, laws were passed referring to emergency mobilization; in 2014, the state introduced basic universal conscription; in 2015, military camps for high school children were introduced; in 2016, a national volunteer service was announced, and basic training was extended from three to four months.[234] The goal is to create a new type of educated citizen who would forge a new relationship with the state.[235] Much of this revolves around creating new, intense forms of patriotism, many of which have military links. Hence, the ever-larger military components to national holiday parades, the establishment of a Martyr's Affairs Office in the Office of the Crown Prince of Abu Dhabi, the memorialization of the war in Yemen in the UAE, the commemoration of losses with a new national holiday called Martyr's Day, and the Union Fortress military demonstration, which became "a national identity moment incorporating military drills, patriotic music, and pictures of each emirate's leaders together."[236] One of the key goals of these approaches is to forge a closer-knit sense of UAE identity so that, theoretically at least, it makes the state more resilient to alternative conceptions of belonging. In this sense, the modern UAE is continuing plans and projects undertaken by earlier leaders to shore up stability against the legitimacy of other substate competitors. Indeed, the broad direction of the UAE state remains set. President of the UAE Khalifah bin Zayed suffered from a long-term illness meaning that Mohammed bin Zayed, the Abu Dhabi Crown Prince, was regent and de facto ruler of the UAE. Thus, with Khalifah's passing in mid-2022, power transitioned smoothly to Mohammed bin Zayed.

As noted previously, mostly thanks to his Emirati frenemies, Tamim bin Hamad Al Thani endured a baptism of fire as emir of Qatar. While in hindsight, the Qatar blockade ended and the states suffered no lasting damage, at the time Qatar's leaders were convinced that it nearly included military action against the state, threatening its sovereignty most egregiously, and only the intervention of senior foreign statespeople like Rex Tillerson stopped this from occurring.[237] The punitive blockade plus the latent threat of invasion changed the Qatari polity. Qatar lodged a number of grievances against the blockading states in international bodies. Qataris felt the blockade was wildly unjust, and an organic outpouring of nationalism in Qatar ensued.[238] A wide range of Qataris, from local artists to poets to singers, found ways to voice their support for the state. At the same time, tens (if not hundreds) of thousands of residents signed petitions, put up posters of Emir Tamim, and adorned cars and buildings with Qatari bunting and flags.[239] A portrait of Tamim incorporating the phrase *Tamim Al Majd* (Tamim the Great) became ubiquitous in Qatar. The quartet used tribal levers of power, allowing or encouraging large gatherings of the Al Murrah tribe on Qatar's borders to destabilize further.[240] Qatar reacted swiftly and removed the citizenship of dozens of members of the Al Ghufran segment of the Al Murrah tribe, to some international condemnation, but it evoked only a minimal noticeable ripple in Qatar itself.[241] There were also tribal protestations in Bahrain, including 190 tribes and families issuing statements stressing their allegiance to the Bahraini monarch and condemning Qatar and its "seditious" news network, Al Jazeera.[242] A range of potential alternative Al Thani leaders emerged. But each one of these ventures was ultimately little more than an embarrassment, posing no threat to the legitimacy of Qatar's ruling clique. If anything, Qatar's Tamim-led government was boosted by these hamhanded attempts at subversion, with Qataris indignant that foreign states could put up a patsy so transparently and think they would fall for it.

Internationally, Qatar reforged vital relations. Instead of buying one or possibly two types of advanced fast jets from the United States, France, or the United Kingdom exclusively, Qatar replaced its fleet with all three platforms. In December 2017, Qatar bought thirty-six U.S. F-15s and twenty-four British Typhoons, and in March 2018, they added another twelve French Rafales to an initial order of twenty-four.[243] Thus, the Qatari fleet increased from twelve fast jets to at least ninety-six. This means that, based on these deals alone, Qatar is spending upward of $15 billion in each of the military-industrial complexes of three of its closest international allies, all of whom operate military bases in the Gulf region. While these decisions will theoretically give Qatar formidable air capabilities at least in the medium term, it is far more persuasive to see these acquisitions as primarily political.[244]

First, with a population of around 300,000, it is impossible for Qatar to train a sufficient number of pilots, logisticians, and technicians to meaningfully staff these planes. Of course, Qatar can and will import workers for these roles, but their level of expertise will make this option exceedingly expensive. Furthermore, the question will always remain: Will a contracted foreigner go to war for their paymaster? Second, no Air Force commander would want to operate different fast jet platforms in this way, as the logistics, training, procurement, maintenance, operation, and integration of three new, complex, and temperamental platforms is unnecessarily complex. Either way, the upshot is that these three influential nations with permanent seats on the UN Security Council are invested in Qatar's stability and status quo. The nature of these deals means that

Qatar worked with the United Kingdom to stand up a new Royal Air Force (RAF) squadron, integrating Qatar into critical UK defense decisions. This is the first time since World War II that the United Kingdom has jointly formed a squadron with any other nation.[245]

The blockade also meant that Qatar swiftly transitioned a Turkish training mission in the Doha into a "base." Extra Turkish troops arrived in Doha within hours of the blockade being launched and increased in number over time to the low thousands, meaning that almost exactly a century after the Ottoman military base closed in Doha, Turkish troops returned. From Qatar's perspective, this further enhanced the fundamentals of the state's security, helping to keep in abeyance the threat posed by the quartet to state sovereignty.[246] The orders of the Turkish troops in Qatar—whether to strive to fend off an incoming invasion—remain unclear. Nevertheless, their presence would have deeply complicated the calculations of any aggressor, adding an essential layer of deterrence. Moreover, with Turkey being a member of the North Atlantic Treaty Organization (NATO), this meant that Qatar induced the stationing of yet more foreign forces on its land that come with Article 5 provisions (i.e., an attack on one NATO nation is considered an attack on all).

Under the pressure of the blockade, despite near-universal local support,[247] the government felt the need to exert control over social and media spheres in Doha. Such regressive moves are not symptomatic of the draconian evolution in Qatar. However, they mirror a narrowing of public space throughout Gulf politics. Like many monarchies, Qatar has instituted new media laws that evoke concern.[248] The censoring of books and other independent initiatives by the Ministry of Culture adds to a sense of backward movement in the nation.[249] Authorities seem notably animated by discussion about the historic plurality of Qatari nationalism, in contrast to state-led narratives to homogenize and project a single, united vision of one "Qatari tribe."[250]

Qatar proved nimble in the realm of commerce and trade, swiftly finding ways to replace blocked import routes. Normality was restored to its domestic markets, and long-term new routes, mostly via Iran and Turkey, were implemented. After the initial crisis abated, Qatar pursued tactics to ensure that it will never again be as reliant upon the UAE and Saudi Arabia. Using its new Hamad Port, which became partially operational in December 2016, the state signed up a range of multidecade deals with some of the world's leading shipping companies to supply it. Similarly, to cite one small example, Qatar increased the capacity of a local dairy company to make up for the shortfall that arose when Saudi imports were cut off. Because of the expansion of Baladna (whose name means "Our Country"), Qatar became self-sufficient in milk by spring 2019. Overall, Qatar survived the blockade by finding new import sources, redoubling international alliances, and strenuously engaging in the media to make their case. Its stock market rebounded, international credit agencies reraised its scores, society was galvanized, and Emir Tamim became lionized. Qataris feel that they won. Relations were restored with the blockading states in a meeting in Al Ula, Saudi Arabia in January 2021, with Qatar offering no obvious concessions. Emir Tamim is seen as the architect of Qatar's successful response to the blockade, and his position is stronger than ever.

No Gulf monarchy was hit harder by the Arab Spring than Bahrain. Prolonged large-scale protests took place from February 2011 onward. The demands of key protesting groups were maximalist, including the disbarment of royals from senior government positions and the installation of a constitutional monarchy with an elected prime minister and parliament.[251] Popular agitation in Bahrain was not new; as discussed earlier in this chapter, Bahrain has one of the most consistent histories of strikes and political unrest in the region.[252] However, this time it was different. A combination of the demands themselves, the scale of the protests, the regional atmosphere of revolution, sporadic, small-scale violence, and an abiding concern that Iran would influence the Shia Bahraini population to ferment discord and exert control over Bahrain coalesced, such that the Bahraini elite considered the protests as an imminent threat to the social order and an ideologically rooted competitor to the state's legitimacy. They reacted strongly, and the police and military forces disbursed protestors and put down the protests harshly. The Bahrain Independent Commission of Inquiry (BICI), set up by the king to investigate the conduct of Bahraini authorities, ultimately provided a "devastating and embarrassing indictment of his security forces."[253] As well as attributing the deaths of three police officers to the protestors, it found that "the security services used 'excessive force'; that security forces killed at least 19 protesters during February and March 2011 and another five died under torture in custody;

and that there was a 'systematic' policy of torture and abuse, designed both to elicit confessions and to punish people. The BICI also found no evidence of Iranian involvement in the protests."[254] The recommendations made by the royally decreed report were slow to be implemented, and many remain undone.[255]

Elections to the state's National Assembly in November 2018 elicited high voter turnout (67 percent, according to the government). Nevertheless, Ronald Neumann, a former U.S. ambassador to Bahrain, in a generally sympathetic article, simply stated that in reality, politics in the state was "dead."[256] The assembly's powers have been reduced, the main Shia opposition party is banned, and electoral districts have been gerrymandered to prevent a Shia bloc from emerging.[257] Despite ongoing socially liberal policies in the state—such as attitudes toward female leadership and notional religious pluralism—Neumann argues that the suspension of meaningful politics is a price worth paying for a return to a broadly stable and peaceful state after the tumult of Bahrain's Arab Spring experiences, and given the outright hostility of Iran to boot.[258] As elsewhere in the Gulf, wide-ranging media laws are used to circumscribe online activities with the threat (and reality) of arrest and prosecution.[259]

A triumvirate has long dominated Bahrain. The king, Hamad bin Isa Al Khalifah, came to power in 1999. His uncle, Shaikh Khalifah bin Salman Al Khalifah, was the longest-serving prime minister in the world, having taken the role in 1971, and he was one of the state's most influential individuals until his death at eighty-four in 2020. King Hamad's son, Crown Prince and Prime Minister Salman bin Hamad Al Khalifah, is in his fifties and clearly in line to the throne. He was appointed prime minister upon Khalifah's death. The broad sentiment runs that this is now an opportunity for a far more open-minded individual—the crown prince—to institute progressive-oriented changes without the powerful conservative de facto veto of Khalifah to intervene.[260]

⸻ ❧ ⸻

Security in the political realm is inherently concerned with the stability of the existing social order. Any number of threats can be ranged against such a broad target, including those emerging from ideational, economic,

military, and environmental vectors. Such threats emanate from a combination of substate, regional, and suprastate locations. All of this makes
political security a particularly wide-ranging issue.

Today's core substate concerns are not so dissimilar to those plagu-
ing the rulers' ancestors. Carefully balanced tribal dynamics continue to
influence state actions. The quartet's attempts to leverage the Al Murrah
tribe as a wedge to pry open Qatari society during the 2017–2021
blockade or to gin up and promote some alternative Al Thani leader
were precisely the same tactics deployed over past decades, and indeed
centuries. The fact that these tactics did not work is interesting and sug-
gestive, meshing with broader evidence and intimating that tribal levers
of influence are waning when faced with the might of the state-driven
national identity.

The Gulf monarchies have evolved considerably since the quip that
they, and the rest of the Arab world bar Egypt, were mere "tribes with
flags." This is hardly surprising. Gulf governments have spent intense
amounts of money building their states and consciously forging national
identities, delineating this and not that tribal song or dance as the correct
and accurate version. The eternal question remains of how far national
identities and understandings of what it means to be a citizen of a Gulf
country can be delinked from the overprivileged lifestyles that generations of oil wealth have baked into society. Layers of the Gulf state-cit-
izen bargain have been removed across many monarchies, and they
have not been replaced by meaningfully more democratic elements. For
example, considerable indirect taxes in Saudi Arabia, Oman, Bahrain,
and the UAE are a reality today, as are signs of the UAE government
moving to introduce competition for long-held family monopolies.[261]
Instead, states seem to be ramping up a newly energized form of nationalism, tightly focused on the status quo leadership, as the state's new
organizing principle.

Inevitably, in an autocratic region going through a conspicuously
controlled and securitized moment where dissent is, overall, as verboten
as it has been in decades, these changes look like they have taken hold.
The artifacts of support—epic flag-waving at national holidays, syco-
phantic social media fawning over leaders, docile and supportive local
press, nationalistic soap operas—are as obviously in abundance as they
are skin deep.

Such attempts to reforge national identities, rallying around the flag under the benevolent guidance of leaders, were catalyzed by the Arab Spring, when several monarchies felt regional winds of ideological challenge tickle and agitate their societies once again. The transmission source this time was not foreign workers, but international media. In addition to a mixture of economic soothing and security crackdowns, the vigorous attempts to reforge national identities seek to set up monarchies for a new, tighter fiscal age.

Today's leaders no longer feel the need to genuflect to regional or international ideologies. Instead, as a consequence both of being ever more sure-footed in their role as regionally influential states and declining U.S. primacy, they have evolved such that leaders take a pick-and-mix approach to devise unique organizing principles for their states. Certainly, the Gulf monarchies no longer feel the compulsion they once did toward democratization. If the United States ever did pursue a meaningful democratization agenda in the Middle East and elsewhere, that agenda today is over amid the rubble, failure, and humiliation of Iraq and Afghanistan. The European Union (EU) gamely plugs away at a human rights–led foreign policy, to little avail, while individual member-states—and the United Kingdom now out on its own—undercut any such approach with alacrity. The core competitor here is China, which is correctly seen as marrying dizzying economic growth and globe-spanning competitiveness with highly centralized, highly autocratic, but broadly stable state control. Such a concept amounts to manna from heaven for the monarchies. Most take China's core promise of development with control and tweak it to their own specific circumstances.

These new state-society relations and adopted models will come under greater scrutiny in the medium and long term. Substate challenges are dwindling in importance so far, but past performance is not necessarily to be taken as a guarantee of future results. Indeed, as the Peninsula's states struggle with the transition away from hydrocarbon-based economies in the ensuing decades, increasing agitation among citizenry is likely as they adjust to new expectations and the loss of privileges. The turn against foreign workers, already evident in examples across the region but particularly noticeable in Saudi Arabia and Kuwait, will become even more strident as citizens lash out against the myths of foreigners as net drags on economies.

The trend (or at least the attempted trend) to tighten space for social interactions about political matters comes with a range of concerns. With decision-making often being uberconcentrated at the absolute apex of societies, there is the perennial concern that such small groups have become captured by bad ideas. This concern was first identified in the U.S. context by Irving Janis's *Groupthink* and Graham Allison's *Essence of Decision* and their studies of the small-group dynamics around President John F. Kennedy during the Cuban missile crisis.[262] These studies are conspicuously relevant to the Gulf monarchies. Indeed, the Gulf blockade is undoubtedly the quintessential example of this phenomenon. The idea percolated among elites, but because of the rise of an increasingly controlled and authoritarian moment, too few people questioned the fundamental logic of the charges. Essentially, all commentators not from Saudi Arabia, the UAE, Bahrain, or Egypt thought that the blockade charges against Qatar were ludicrously overhyped. No examples leap to mind of anyone from these four states openly questioning the gratuitously trumped-up policies, hardly surprising when showing sympathy for Qatar became a criminal offense. While the Gulf monarchies have now reconciled and this peculiar blockade fever has broken, it remains concerning that such a break premised on alternative facts could transpire.

In the supraregional sphere, the U.S. moment in the Gulf is winding down, even if this is likely to be measured in decades rather than years. The attacks of September 2019 on the world's most important oil processing facility at Abqaiq (and also on Khurais) in Saudi Arabia was a moment that will come to define the next half-century in the Gulf. This attack revealed in an unimaginable way for the monarchies the sheer pointlessness of their ploy of courting relations with the United States over multiple decades, with hundreds of billions of dollars' worth of purchases. U.S. political deterrence and defensive technologies failed at their primary duty to prevent an attack on inter alia oil-related critical national infrastructure. Subsequently, with the U.S. emperor bracingly shorn of its clothes, and with no meaningful reaction emerging from the Donald Trump administration, the monarchies recalibrated.

Within eighteen months, Saudi Arabia restarted direct negotiations with Iran. By late 2021, the UAE signaled its intention to pull out of a $23 billion acquisition of F-35 U.S. fast jets. At the same time, the UAE national security adviser, Tahnoon bin Zayed Al Nahyan, went on a reconciliatory tour in the Gulf, Turkey, and Iran. The latter part of the tour led to the restoration of UAE-Iranian diplomatic relations in summer 2022 and the notion of a visit by Ebrahim Raisi, the Iranian president, to the UAE, a hitherto thinkable policy in the contemporary Gulf, indicating just how much the hawkish Abu Dhabi leadership has profoundly recalibrated its approach. Moreover, the UAE also abstained from voting on the February 2022 U.S.- and Albanian-drafted Security Council resolution condemning Russia's invasion of Ukraine. By doing so, the UAE signaled its independence from U.S. pressure and, by joining India and China in abstaining, a desire to more carefully take heed of the position of Asian states as it forges its own pragmatic approach to the world.

2

SOCIETAL SECURITY

If there is anything special about the international politics of the Middle East, it is the power of identity.

HINNEBUSCH (2016)

The societal sphere is concerned with identity, how individuals see themselves, and where they place themselves in the state. As Barry Buzan, Ole Wæver, and Jaap de Wilde note, rarely do state and societal boundaries match perfectly.[1] Sometimes phrased as a mismatch between state and nation, this disjuncture is a redolent issue in the Middle East and North Africa (MENA) region. Societal security inherently focuses on whichever "we" is relevant to the given context and reflects how and to what degree that identity is challenged. This "we" can refer to clans, tribes, villages, city-states, extended families, ideologically linked groups, religiously affiliated people, ethnic units, civilizations, or minorities united by other characteristics.[2] The relative importance of various societal groupings and the salience of the challenges they face (or pose) depends on the context. It might not make much sense to focus on clans in contemporary Scotland as identity markers affecting broader societal stability. However, it might make sense to focus on tribes on the Arabian Peninsula.

In a postcolonial setting like the Middle East, where borders have often been drawn by external powers often heedless of local societal and cultural histories and realities, states can be shot through with irredentism and conflicting state-societal conceptions of their identity.[3] As the young states on the Peninsula form their narratives—or, as Eric Hobsbawm put it, "invent" their traditions—there is competition to state narratives from other forms of belonging far older than the state itself. Certainly, there is plenty of redolent belonging material for state authorities to work with.[4] Nevertheless, this issue is complicated in the Gulf by the nature of the region's oil-rooted rentier economy, which often confers significant benefits on citizens. This creates a strong incentive to become a citizen wherever possible, which energizes strong in-group and out-group dynamics. This is seen in Kuwait with its bidoon issue (meaning those "without"—in this context, a passport and thus lacking Kuwaiti citizenship). This group of typically long-term residents is seen as not being originally Kuwaiti, but incomers who seek a share of the state's wealth, which generates keenly felt protectionism over obtaining citizenship.

Buzan, Wæver, and de Wilde note that the societal security agenda tends to be set by three kinds of threats: migration, horizontal competition (from neighboring cultural and linguistic influences), and vertical competition (from regionalist projects and ideas). However, because the sources of societal insecurity and the "we" in question emanate from (sometimes unique) local circumstances, the specific character of each challenge needs to be heavily contextualized to decipher whether there are any specific sources of societal security and insecurity to be addressed.

The Gulf monarchies acutely feel the challenge to societal security posed by migration, as foreigners often vastly outnumber locals. This dynamic puts pressure on the stability of existing societal and cultural norms due to threats of dilution and change. This is not a new problem. Instead, the monarchies have over a century of experience dealing with large numbers of migrant workers, and they have developed routines, laws, and policies to deal with the issue.

A range of reoccurring horizontal challenges emanates from within the Gulf. Tribal links often span states regardless of modern borders and provide an "us" for people to identify with containing strong familial and historical resonance. State building projects crafting national narratives, fueled by hydrocarbon wealth to varying degrees, compete with such identities. Similarly, pan-state religious linkages have long presented alternative sources of belonging, consistently offering unfolding iterations of challenges to the monarchies. Great debate—and concern—emerge, for example, from discussions of where Bahrain's and Saudi Arabia's Shia populations derive their theological direction (or *marjaa*), or whether they religiously (and thus politically) orient themselves toward religious influence in Qom, Iran, or Najaf, Iraq. From the government's perspective, this issue boils down to the thorny question of where loyalty lies. Governmental securitizing of these concerns can perversely reinforce alternative identities fostering an "us against them" dynamic (i.e., the religious group against the state authorities). These pressures have long been apparent and have become ever more securitized in recent decades.

Societal challenges along vertical lines emerged notably in the 1950s and 1960s, with acute challenges from pan-Arab ideologies emanating initially from Egypt. Only with Israel's humiliation of Egypt, Syria, and Jordan in 1967 did this challenge cease, even if the sentiment lingered. Arguably the obvious change in regional relations emerged in much more recent times, with traditional region-leading states like Egypt, Syria, and Iraq being ever more economically sclerotic or mired in civil war. Into this gap, hydrocarbon-fueled Gulf monarchies led by Qatar and the United Arab Emirates (UAE) emerged to new levels of regional influence.

It is also interesting to examine the evolution of a *khaleeji* identity (*khaleej* means "gulf" in Arabic, and *khaleeji* means "gulfy," as a way to describe an individual from the Gulf) and the founding of the Gulf Cooperation Council (GCC) as a collective regional organization in 1981. At the local level, *khaleeji* identity retains a natural relevance. Many families have relatives in multiple Gulf states, and work, travel, and study throughout the monarchies have long been normalized. However, collectively as a political project, the GCC provides a perennial puzzle. It is a group of states united by myriad cultural, historical, religious, and political elements facing off against a deeply concerning, large, and menacing "other" in the form of Iran. Nevertheless, individual grievances among states and persistent squabbling, typified by the risible blockade of Qatar, stymie meaningful progress toward forging a united political bloc.

Indeed, further challenging any form of collective *khaleeji* identity is the rise of individual nationalisms in the contemporary era, manifested not least in the ever-increasing scale of national day festivities. This is not to say that this search for and crafting of an identity is new: elites have been using archaeological digs and museums to shape national histories for generations. Instead, today's efforts are exponentially better funded and professionalized. Otherwise, Gulf nationalism has been conspicuously energized in recent decades by events. Kuwaiti society was galvanized in the aftermath of the invasion of Iraq, just as Qatari society organically rallied around the flag and Emir Tamim in the face of the 2017–2021 blockade, which was universally felt to be an outrageous threat and imposition. As the 2010s wore on, Emirati nationalism took on an ever-more-martial tone, driven by the state's involvement in the war in Yemen. Under Mohammed bin Salman's de facto rule, Saudi Arabia also saw a reinvigorated sense of nationhood as he pushed through a range of dynamic, modernizing policies.

The first section of this chapter, "Migration and Influence," examines the impact and influence of migration on Gulf society. The overall effect was overwhelming. The scale of the influx and the accompanying dizzying speed of change profoundly shaped the budding monarchies. Over time, locals developed an ever-harsher attitude toward foreigners as in-group and out-group differences became ever sharper and deeply ingrained. The second section, "Islam and Tribalism," focuses on how some of the archetypal societal features of life on the Arabian Peninsula, such as the bedu (or bedouin) and hadar dynamics, evolved as states grew stronger. Similarly, following the evolution of the regional role of Islam reveals it as both a challenge to the state and a tool wielded by the state. The final section, "Globalization and Identity," reflects on how these aforementioned concerns have come together, along with wider homogenizing pressures, to forge the Gulf society as it is today. Today's Gulf states are ever more robust and all-encompassing. Neither tribes nor religious actors are irrelevant; however, they are increasingly relegated to state-controlled or sanctioned forms of mediated pageantry.

MIGRATION AND INFLUENCE

Migration is not new to the Peninsula. Trade and pilgrimage have endowed the region with a globalized and heterogeneous composition to its socioeconomic life for centuries. Oman once held colonies in modern-day

Tanzania and Pakistan, for centuries Dubai has been an outward-facing entrepôt port city, and Kuwait City was once such an international melting pot that it was referred to as the Marseilles and the Paris of the Gulf.[5] Slavery was also a significant source of influence, with around 100,000 men employed or enslaved across the Peninsula in pre-oil days, albeit an influence that remains under-researched given the subject's sensitive nature.[6]

As the 1920s advanced, more diverse sources of labor were sought as the proto-states transitioned from their "natural state" to establish rudimentary facets of a modern state ranging from roads to schools to civil administrations.[7] These tens of thousands, hundreds of thousands, and then millions of foreigners were—and remain—critical to state development, even if their role is often elided by a depoliticized history that tends to focus on the raw facts of swift, oil-fueled progress.[8] Until recently, absent from much Gulf history as active, participating, and influential actors, foreign workers exerted tremendous influence as foils, as an "Other" against whom local identities were forged in a time of significant change.[9]

From the turn of the twentieth century, the influx of labor from Yemen, India, Persia, and later Egypt, Iraq, and Syria catalyzed agitation and protest.[10] In an era without social media or 24/7 international news, the workers themselves became the transmission source of new ideas and new ideologies. They brought to the Gulf their formative experiences and shaped the monarchies from an embryonic stage:

> These migrants came from cities and regions shaken by the collapse of the Ottoman Empire and the advent of direct colonial rule and Zionist settlement and marked by the rise of nationalism and popular movements. The Arab revolt of 1916–1918, the Egyptian uprising of 1919, the Iraqi uprising in 1920, the Syrian revolts from 1920 onward, the example of Turkey, and the increasingly intense Palestinian struggle against dispossession were intensely discussed, along with a labor upsurge in Egypt, the growth of worker protest in the Mashriq and Palestine, and the appearance of a class-inflected peasant-guerrilla movement in Palestine during 1936–1939.[11]

As detailed in chapter 1, the wave of protests that struck in the 1950s and 1960s were often led and populated by migrant Arab laborers. Their effect on indigenous Gulf society was diverse. Immigration and idea transmission from migrants exacerbated cleavages in Saudi society. Nationals from more liberal regions like the Hijaz supported Palestinians and Egyptians in solidarity, while those from the more conservative interior Nejd regions did not.[12] Demonstrators in Bahrain chanted, "The fellow Arab is not the foreigner," echoing the sentiment of the age but threatening the exclusivity of being a Bahraini national, with the benefits this accrued.[13] In Kuwait, pressure from the indigenous, dominant merchant class initially drove a laissez-faire immigration policy to staff, build, and run their business interests.[14] Similarly, in the late 1950s and early 1960s, 95 percent of teachers and over 98 percent of doctors and nurses were non-Kuwaitis.[15] Kuwaiti leftists supported relaxed immigration policies and were agitated by the poor treatment of so-called deserving Arabs compared to the naturalization of the illiterate bedu. They sought a stronger governmental stance on international Arab issues.[16]

But as increasing numbers of Arab expatriates organized and pursued pan-Arab positions like the free movement of Arab labor, countervailing communities emerged. Some Kuwaitis tried to block any straightforward naturalization processes for Palestinians.[17] At the same time, the royal family and their traditional bedu supporters saw emerging foreign groups as "competitors in the labor market and . . . a drain on financial resources."[18] Consequently, laws were driven through parliament, such as the Aliens' Residence Law and the Nationality Law of 1959, that circumscribed the rights of foreigners. Sharon Stanton Russell argues that these (and other similar) laws had four aims: to regulate labor for local requirements; to control immigration via checks, controls, and permits; to promote immigration from politically close states via wavers; and to embed within Kuwaiti society a core difference between nationals and foreigners that privileged the role of the former.[19] The swiftly growing numbers of foreigners in Kuwait prompted the government both to slow the rate of immigration and to naturalize more bedu as a local alternative, which, because of their low levels of education, only increased the burden on the state.[20]

Across the Gulf, the need for immigration spiked in the 1970s for two different reasons, which required different policy responses. First, with the emergence of independence for Qatar, Bahrain, and the UAE in 1971, these states' unfeasibly small population base needed to be addressed.

In 1971, Abu Dhabi's population was around 20,000, which prompted its leadership to grant citizenship widely, but not exclusively, to tribes linked to the Bani Yas, the primary tribal grouping of the Al Nahyan ruling family.[21] Recruitment from Yemen took place, such as with the Manahil from Hadramawt or the Yafi and the 'Awlaqi, none of whom enjoyed any particular closeness to the Bani Yas. Similarly, the Za'abis switched from Ras Al Khaimah to Abu Dhabi just before independence.[22] Many of the Yemeni-originated Abu Dhabi citizens served in the police and the armed forces. Such policies had the effect of embedding yet further the tribally based nature of Abu Dhabi politics, making the central government—as everywhere in the Gulf—the font of munificence, subsidies, and livelihood, and loyalty was expected in return.

Second, as Gulf revenues soared when they cut oil supplies to key Western nations in 1973 spiking the price of oil, the monarchies' demand for foreign workers rose steeply, given their critical role in the physical construction, development, maintenance, and running of the various new infrastructure and industrial projects. To avoid the politicization that came with Arab expatriates and secure a more quiescent (and often cheaper) source of labor, Asian migrants were preferred in increasing numbers.[23] These new migrants, as well as a range of more oppressive checks on existing Arab workers, "unstitched" immigrants from oppositional local debates such that "by the 1990s, migrants had become an adjunct rather than a challenge to monarchy."[24] New nationality laws consistently ratcheted up the exclusiveness of what it meant to be a Gulf national. Law Number 21, promulgated in Qatar in 1989, banned certain Qataris—ministers, deputy ministers, those in the foreign services, and in the security or armed services—from marrying non-Qataris, while a similar law was passed in Oman and the UAE soon after.[25] Rooted in a reaction against foreigners, states were shaping legal concepts of what it was to be a national.

Iraq's invasion of Kuwait in 1990 further redefined societal relations. Palestinian support for Saddam Hussein's attack and Yemen's attempt to be neutral both backfired. These positions were viewed as gratuitously ungrateful, plugging into lingering resentment about the generosity of the Gulf monarchies toward Arabs.[26] Kuwait expelled 350,000 Palestinians in 1991–1992, and Saudi Arabia expelled up to 1 million Yemenis. The numbers of Arabs as a proportion of the overall population in Saudi

Arabia fell from 91 percent to 75 percent from 1975 to 2004, and from 80 percent to just 30 percent in Kuwait from 1975 to 2003.[27] Policies to diversify the Arab population of the Gulf states became law. Societally, foreign workers thus became even less a part of the fabric of these societies. Instead of engaging with local or international politics or developing any sense of a participatory role in the state, workers became, as a rule, isolated in camps that often were far from population centers in industrial zones. The nature of contracts also changed as open-ended roles changed for project or time-limited residence permits so that when the job ended, the workers returned home.[28]

Plenty of strikes have taken place in recent decades. However, they have been on a much smaller scale overall than those of the 1950s and 1960s. Also, they have revolved around "only economic-corporate demands" and lack an overtly political dimension.[29] In other words, those who constitute the majority of the region's society, the usually lower-paid foreigners, have evolved to the point where they are coopted into the political economy of the monarchies. They are *homo economicus*, denuded of a political role.

Social attitudes reflecting these economic realities calcified, and Gulf societies became rigidly stratified. The days when the British defended the economic prerogatives and institutionalized advantages of Indian merchants over locals in the Trucial States have long gone. Gulf citizens are privileged in myriad ways by their governments, from access to some of the most generous welfare states in the world to employment laws and programs (e.g., Qatarization, Saudization, etc.) mandating that specific percentages of locals be employed in a given endeavor. Within this thin top stratum there are, as ever and everywhere, degrees of privilege.[30] Occasionally, nonroyal families, such as the Al Attiyah in Qatar, were given governmental stipends, though such privileges are usually reserved for royal family members, and even then the amount depends on their closeness to the specific lineage in charge.[31]

A Wikileaks cable detailed how this used to work in Saudi Arabia. The Office of Decisions and Rules in the Ministry of Finance oversaw the disbursement of $800–$270,000 per month to thousands of Al Sauds.[32] While these figures are from the 1990s, and Mohammed bin Salman has narrowed the pinnacle of society, an approximation of this system remains. Steffen Hertog even argues that under King Salman, the material wealth available to the Al Sauds has increased.[33] Such stipends pale in comparison to wider opportunities afforded to selected, close, loyal individuals—royal or otherwise—who are given control of fiefdoms from which they can extract profits.[34] Such policies are a core part of the government's cooptation strategy.

There is a widely perceived pecking order, in which Caucasian Westerners sit below nationals.[35] The salary packages of such foreigners are usually less generous than those of citizens, although there are exceptions for elite advisers.[36] Some of their perks, such as airfare and home or private education for their children, are resented by the local population.[37] Nevertheless, all foreigners live in the Gulf under the permanent reality that contracts may be canceled at any point, revoking their right to live in the state with no realistic legal recourse.

An intermediate layer comprises educated Arabs, often from Egypt, Lebanon, Syria, and Jordan, or those from India or Southeast Asia more generally who often do similar jobs as Westerners.[38] However, according to one multidecade business salary survey, someone from Asia receives 26 percent less on average than a Westerner for doing the same job, while an Arab receives 15.7 percent less.[39] Lowest on the totem pole are manual laborers, often from the Indian subcontinent or sub-Saharan Africa, and domestic workers (e.g., nannies, drivers, and cleaners) often from elsewhere in Southeast Asia (e.g., the Philippines and Indonesia). These individuals and the culture they bring—or "foreign matter," as Paul Dresch accurately puts it, capturing perfectly the anodized way that such people can be viewed—means that nationalities are associated with a specific job (e.g., the Philippines with maids, or Nepal with construction).[40]

Despite the reality that the monarchies would grind to a halt were these workers to leave, there is often a palpable dislike of such "foreign matter" by local populations. Authorities do what they can to minimize the impact of these hundreds of thousands of residents. Many are crammed into accommodation camps far from downtown areas, and authorities try to segregate these individuals in their leisure time, banning single men from malls or creating their own spaces in industrial areas.[41] However, editorial pages of local newspapers and local radio stations often focus on the malign influence of foreigners on local customs and traditional aspects of life.

This overt presence of "foreign matter" has the effect of further rarefy-
ing Gulf citizenship and national identity among Gulf nationals, forging
in-group dynamics against a definite out-group driven by the feeling of
being outnumbered.[42] It has also resulted in pressure from society to make
ever more stringent the legal basis for Gulf nationality and ever-greater
draconian controls of foreigner employment, as in the kafala system.[43]
This system of sponsorship, found across the Gulf, holds to greater and
lesser degrees that employees remain dependent on their employer for
their immigration and contract. The power in this relationship is disproportionately in favor of the employer, a factor that has long been central in
allowing systematic abuse by companies. International pressure focused
on those monarchies looking for attention—notably the UAE and Qatar—
has seen some changes for the better.

However, governments can only do so much, given that the root of
this issue stems from strongly felt desires among the citizenry to use the
kafala system as a method of control and profit-making.[44] Partly, this is
a small-scale concern. Sentiments and complaints pervade Gulf society
about the expense and difficulties that nationals endure in order to bring
workers to the monarchies (fees for recruiting agencies, visas, flights,
etc.). Also, with (often multiple) domestic workers like drivers and maids
being the norm, especially in the smaller and richer monarchies, nationals are loathe to then allow workers to change jobs quickly and easily,
considering the potential expense and upset that might ensue. Similar
logics work on a larger scale too. Powerful business interests want the
kafala system to remain as a rule, as it allows for the control of systematic
cheap labor, which is an advantage that is built into the profit margin of
industries.[45]

Despite social tension in the monarchies rooted in the often-
overwhelming number of foreigners, governments perversely still build
foreigners into their political economy. From the millennium onward,
new laws emerged in Bahrain (2001), Oman (2004), Qatar (2006), and
Saudi Arabia (2010) allowing foreigners to own property in designated
areas, tied to long-term residency permits.[46] In 2021, the UAE announced
that it would offer citizenship to especially so-called talented foreigners.
This marks a "qualitative and fundamental shift" in Gulf approaches to
foreigners as leaders actively court migrants for the long term.[47] To do
this, they change legal structures and build into local economies vast real

estate ventures predicated upon the indefinite residence of several million of these no-longer-temporary workers.[48] There are a variety of long-term implications of such moves. They inhibit Gulf nationals' entrance into labor markets, irritate locals due to a lack of consultation, contribute to antiforeigner sentiment among citizens, and spike concerns about foreigners being used to alter state demographies, as is alleged in Bahrain's security and defense forces.[49]

ISLAM AND TRIBALISM

The history of the people, rulers, and states on the Peninsula, with some notable exceptions, is one of a primarily shared sociopolitical experience: they are united more than they are divided. The traditional approach to politics on the Peninsula suggests that it is fundamentally rooted in the "immutable characteristics of Islam and tribalism."[50] By mastering these facets of life, the argument goes, ruling families emerged to prominence. Gregory Gause, arguably the most respected scholar of the region, cautioned back in the 1990s that this kind of view "is not so much wrong as it is outdated."[51]

Two quintessential images dominate in terms of tribalism as a core societal organizing principle on the Peninsula. First, there are the bedouin or bedu tribes roaming and raiding in the deserts, with their own socio-economic, political, and cultural mores.[52] Then there are the more settled hadar, many of whom were the seafaring Arabs of port settlements, buzzing around the coasts fishing, trading, and—from the British if not the local perspective[53]—engaging in piracy.[54] The bedu motif is an omnipresent historical trope, but C. D. Matthews argues that they have probably been outnumbered by settled counterparts "throughout the recorded history of Arabia."[55] It is also important not to oversimplify pre-oil governance on the Arabian Peninsula into just a hadar-bedu dynamic.[56] Nevertheless, for the bedu in particular, with their unique poetic traditions and political economy, this existence can be characterized as a distinct organizing principle and a challenge to any other authority.[57]

Slowly, as the eighteenth and nineteenth centuries progressed, the tribal bedu's modus operandi was assailed by other horizontal organizing principles for kinship and legitimacy. Wahhabi powers in proto-Saudi Arabia offered a robust competing ideological organizing system, with its own religiously based, centralized, and institutionalized approaches.[58] In the case of Saudi Arabia, Abdulaziz Al Fahad notes that

> the last and decisive encounter between the two conceptions of political organization, that of hadar central authority and Bedouin tribal independence, took place on the plains of Sbila in central Arabia on March 30, 1929. Subsequently . . . the Bedouin's military, fiscal, judicial, and territorial autonomy was decisively ended. In its place, the idea of one supreme leader (later to be named the king), Shari'a law, payment and collection of taxes . . . and monopoly of the legitimate use of force by the central authority were firmly established.[59]

The introduction of firearms, and critically, the rise of the modern, oil-fueled Saudi state "rendered traditional Bedouin life simply impossible."[60] Khaldoun Hasan Al-Nakeeb pointedly notes that traditional forces like tribes and religious sects were "transformed into something resembling a decrepit lumpen proletariat in air-conditioned ghettos on the fringes of the metropolitan petroleum cities."[61] Indeed, the bedu were seen as backward, and Arab governments, the Arab League, and even the United Nations (UN) called for their sedentarization.[62] In Kuwait, the very architecture of town planning and the design of houses were in part driven by the desire to break up traditional modes of societal life.[63] Across the region, bedu tribes took advantage of state-led work opportunities and engaged in emerging health and education programs. In Saudi Arabia, many joined what would become the Saudi Arabia National Guard (SANG) as the government used expanding revenues to coopt tribes by encouraging their dependency on governmental assistance. This allowed tribal leaders to form their own brigades, retaining symbolic linkages to their traditional martial, directive role if ultimately they were just a denuded cog in a modern institution.[64]

Bedu tribal dynamics were neither forgotten nor ignored, but their role changed from the higher-most organizing principle of the group to a mediated pageantry. Fabietti argues that this led to "detribalization" among the bedu. Donald P. Cole agrees to a point, noting that the bedu were "economically, politically, and legally" detribalized, but socially they continued and even prospered.[65] Markers of tribal identities expanded, with the increased use of tribal surnames harking back to bedu lineage and a shared sense of "Bedouin-ness" focusing on common histories.[66] The bedu identity became a signifier of a generic heritage that many, in a time of swift, oil-fueled change, were eager to latch onto, whether from bedu lineages or not.[67] Consequently, states began to actively develop bedu narratives, mirroring the "invention of tradition" that Hobsbawm argues had taken place in Europe centuries before.[68] In Kuwait, in the 1960s, "Bedouin Hour" was a popular radio show.[69] Those who can "remember" their tribal background are "diminishing day by day," such that by the end of the 1970s in the UAE, only 15 percent of citizens could meaningfully make such a claim.[70] In the UAE, horse and camel races were initiated, further tying into a quasi-bedu heritage. Across the Gulf, bedu history is being revived or purely invented, focusing on falconry, camel racing, and pearl-diving.[71] Local tourist and heritage industries actively adopt Orientalist images of bedu heritage both to attract tourists and to reinforce foundational state myths.[72]

States politicized and deployed aspects of bedu history where it suited their purpose. Saudi leaders took advantage of tribes, claiming that wherever they roamed was ipso facto Saudi territory.[73] Accordingly, Ibn Saud claimed much of the Qatari hinterland into the 1950s via the peregrinations of the Al Murrah tribe that spanned the border.[74] In the 1960s and 1970s, Kuwaiti bedu became useful ballast for the government. By enfranchising bedu from the Kuwait-Saudi border and giving them passports, the Kuwaiti government coopted tens of thousands of new voters to support the government in the feisty parliament.[75] More recently, Kuwaiti politicians used the specter of the hadar versus bedu dynamic to try to divide and rule, something that is all the more bizarre in the Kuwaiti case, given the state is 99 percent urbanized, and there are no longer any bedu.[76] Nevertheless, these political dog-whistles are marshaled to delineate, in the Kuwaiti case, who is and who is not an original Kuwaiti national, with the rights and access to welfare this grants.[77]

Bedu tribes have been useful pawns for different states. In 1996, there was a coup attempt against the new Qatari emir, Hamad bin Khalifah Al Thani (r. 1995–2013). Saudi Arabia was implicated following the arrest of members of the Al Ghufran subsection of the Al Murrah tribe. Many were sentenced to jail, and as part of the punishment, 4,000–10,000 members of the Al Murrah had their Qatari citizenship temporarily revoked.[78] In 2010, Saudi's King Abdullah requested that those Al Murrah remaining in jail be released. Hamad bin Khalifah complied, and they were flown to Jeddah.[79] The divisive Al Murrah issues came to the fore again during the 2017 Gulf blockade of Qatar. Saudi authorities tried to play the tribal card, encouraging thousands of bedu to assemble on the Saudi side of the Qatari border. Qatar again withdrew passports from around fifty individuals in response, including the head of the Al Murrah, Shaikh Taleb bin Lahom bin Shuraim.[80] Qataris saw several appearances by bin Shuraim on Saudi television in 2017 as provocative, as if he were trying to ferment discord among the Al Murrah in Qatar.[81] Apparent attempts by Saudi Arabia and the UAE to support alternative rulers in Qatar failed resoundingly.

The withdrawal of passports from troublesome tribal elements has long been a tool used to stifle dissent to weaken alternative horizontal modes of belonging. In 1954, authorities stripped Sunni leaders Abdul Rahman Al Baker, Abdelaziz Al Shamlan, and Abdul Ali Al Alaywat of their Bahraini citizenship because they agitated against British rule. They were deported 7,665 kilometers away, to St. Helena.[82] More recently, the power of passport withdrawal became increasingly potent because states have successfully inculcated a dependence on them among the tribes through the provision of welfare (including schooling, health care, unemployment benefits, and job opportunities). The rationales used by each state reflect its political concerns. Kuwait's government focuses on troublesome political activists as shown in 2014 when eighteen nationals lost their passports.[83] Bahrain revokes the citizenship of Shia citizens convicted or suspected of working against the government.[84] The UAE used this tool to counter domestic critics of the lack of reform in the Arab Spring era.[85] Kuwait and the UAE also sought to give their passport-less minorities and troublesome individuals other nationalities, such as by forging agreements with the Comoros Islands.[86]

In addition to tribalism, religiosity in one form or another is a feature of sociopolitical life on the Peninsula. Moreover, tribal and particularly religious challenges arguably play an outsized role in the Gulf monarchies, as Hootan Shambayati argues:

> When the government is financially autonomous from its citizens, conditions are ripe for challenging the state on noneconomic grounds.

In rentier states only moral and ideological commitment obliges the government to increase the national wealth, to provide services, and to consult the population. In other words, the relation between the ruled and the rulers is defined in moral and ideological, not economic terms. Consequently, organized challenges to the state are based on moral and cultural issues, where rentier states are most vulnerable.[87]

Except in Ibadi Oman, Sunni Islam remains the dominant religion among Gulf nationals, and all state constitutions are rooted in Sharia law.[88] John Duke Anthony describes such religious factors as "serving as a unifying force within and among the officialdom of these states."[89] Overtly acknowledging such "ties of special relations, common characteristics, and similar systems founded on the creed of Islam which binds them," the six monarchies on the Peninsula joined together in a collaborative regional organization, the GCC, on May 25, 1981.[90]

While true in the abstract, the devil is in the details, and one is reminded of Gause's refrain about tribes—that such sentiments are not wrong, but dated. Regional religious similarities belie a cornucopia of differences, large and small, in and among the monarchies. For example, Saudi Arabia and Qatar are the only states officially adhering to the Wahhabi school of Salafi Islam. Yet state policies have been starkly different in recent decades.

Particularly in the 1970s and 1980s, Saudi Arabia sought to proselytize a Wahhabi message. It established an infrastructure to do so, from universities to charities to specific sections of the Foreign Ministry.[91] In Qatar, the state's Islamic outreach center Al Fanar espouses a moderate Salafi line. The Qatari state mosque, finished in 2013, was named the Imam Muhammed bin Abdulwahhab mosque. However, it is not clear how the fact that Qatar is technically a Wahhabi state makes a pragmatic impact. Their Wahhabi nature has not prevented Saudi Arabia and Qatar from pursuing diametrically opposed policies: for a long time banning women from driving versus having a woman as one of the most influential leaders in the region, and so on. The point is that the state's religious makeup is not deterministic of policy outcomes; hence states with nominally similar religious foundations pursue very different policies. Indeed, it is the nature of the country, of the government, and of the leadership that drives policymaking.[92]

Scholars argue that mixing Saudi Wahhabi ideas in the twentieth century with ideas brought by immigrating exiles formed a new strain of political Islam. When tens of thousands of persecuted Islamists fled the autocracies in Egypt, Syria, and Iraq in the 1950s and 1960s, they were welcomed into the nascent Gulf monarchies for intertwined reasons. In the Arab Cold War between the Gamal Abdel Nasser–led nationalist bloc against the Saudi-led conservative Gulf bloc, such individuals provided the ideological thought, experience, and education that the monarchies required to defend themselves. Notably, in Saudi Arabia, such individuals "were put in charge of the whole Saudi counter-propaganda apparatus," particularly the educational establishments and the media.[93] As well as serving ideologically rooted goals, they played a crucial role in designing and running many of the nascent ministries across the Gulf, their university education from Egyptian and Iraqi establishments standing them in good stead. As one of Stephane Lacroix's interviewees put it, "the Muslim Brotherhood literally built the Saudi state and most Saudi institutions."[94] Even accepting some degree of hyperbole, the same is true across the monarchies, with Egyptian, Syrian, and Iraqi exiles playing formative roles in "starting the state" in Qatar, as well as in the UAE.[95] In Kuwait, for example, Muslim Brotherhood members and those influenced by them wrote and implemented educational curricula. Moreover, these ideas became the foundation of education planning—setting up, running schools, and providing textbooks—throughout the smaller Gulf states thanks to Kuwaiti largess.[96] Indeed, it was only in the 1990s that the UAE began to author its own school textbooks.[97]

There is nothing new about actors in the Gulf monarchies instilling a conservative religious agenda in state education and practice. The religious half of the Saudi political bargain has long sought to control state mores, instilling their understanding of a staunch religious orthodoxy around the Peninsula, which they did from a position of considerable power. Joseph Kraft notes that at one stage, "Members from the Al Shaykh dynasty held ministerial positions in Justice, Pilgrimage Affairs and Religious Endowments, Higher education, head of the . . . security force in the Interior Ministry, and director of military intelligence in the Defence Ministry."[98]

Still, the influence of the exiles from Egypt, Syria, and Iraq was sizable. As Lacroix detailed, a particular mixing of ideas occurred between this foreign influx and local counterparts that came to shape the core forces that influenced the nature of Saudi society from the 1960s onward.[99] The sahwa—short for *al sahwa al islamiyya* (the Islamic Awakening)—is the name of the indigenous Saudi Islamist movement that emerged from the 1960s, which comprised a mix of foreign Muslim Brotherhood Islamists and Wahhabi thought, Saudi scholars, and Saudi institutions. This hybrid Saudi-Muslim Brotherhood discourse and approach borrowed from both sides. It internalized the "extreme social conservatism" prevalent in Saudi Wahhabism, as with their intolerance of non-Wahhabi Islamic groups and innate misogyny, and borrowed Muslim Brotherhood approaches to forging an Islamic state and their hostility to Western influence.[100]

These foreign influences played directly into preexisting societal cleavages. The government wielded the sahwa in the 1960s and 1970s to combat the rising tide of leftist populism in the kingdom, whose ideas underpinned several coup attempts. After the attack on the Great Mosque in Mecca in 1979—in which the most important site in Islam was seized by terrorists, held for two weeks, and was freed only with the help of foreign special forces[101]—the sahwa was given more leeway and opportunity to spread its influence on behalf of the state.[102] Safeguarding pilgrims and the site itself is enshrined in Saudi Arabia's Basic Law of Governance. Saudi leaders have long placed custody of Islam's two holiest shrines as the basis for their legitimacy.[103] Making this all the worse was the fact that earlier in the year, the Iranian revolution evicted an American stooge of a leader, the shah, installing a hostile, youthful, revolutionary Shia theocracy. On Christmas Day, the coup de grâce of 1979 was the godless Soviet invasion of Afghanistan, a Muslim nation. Saudi authorities—and to a lesser, though still significant degree, the other monarchies—saw supporting jihad in Afghanistan as a practical and powerful way to signal their piety and to rekindle and rebolster their religious legitimacy.[104]

The leeway for religious authorities in the kingdom to expand their influence increased, while Islam nominally became a central rational and organizing principle for Saudi foreign policy. Cinemas were banned as part of the backlash after the Mecca seizure, in order to prove the state's piety. In 1986, King Fahd changed his official title to "Custodian of the Two Holy Mosques," signaling the importance of the religious role to him and the Saudi state. This was in addition to myriad expansions of foreign policies using religious tools.[105] In the words of Buzan, Wæver, and de Wilde, this is how "ideas and practices" surrounding armed jihad came to be an important way that individuals in the monarchies identified themselves.[106]

By the end of the 1980s, the Soviets were defeated in Afghanistan, the Iranian threat was diminishing in an era of Arab-Iranian détente, and the monarchies felt secure. The emergency measures undertaken earlier in the decade to whip up religiosity calmed. Still, a generation of mostly young men had been radicalized and battle-tested, and they were to provide the core of the burgeoning Islamist terrorist threat over the next four decades.[107] It has long been reported that Osama Bin Laden offered the services of his mujahedeen to defend Saudi Arabia against Iraqi aggression in 1990.[108] This offer speaks to the quasi-sanctioned and state-supported actions (by Gulf monarchies, also with U.S. funding) of the mujahedeen until that point. But this offer was rejected, with the Saudi elite preferring to call on infidels to defend the land of the two holy places. From this point onward, Al Qaeda became an implacable foe of the governments in the Gulf.

In August 1990, Iraq invaded Kuwait. Operations Desert Shield and Desert Storm, spearheaded by the United States, precipitated the presence of vast numbers of foreign troops throughout the Gulf. No regional leader wanted such an overt presence. It was embarrassing to admit that, even after significant spending, leaders could not defend their own countries. This was compounded by the need to reach out to Western powers after decades of independence. Leaders were notably concerned about appearing too close to the United States, whose unstinting support of Israel against the Palestinians was deeply unpopular.[109]

Across the monarchies, the 1990s witnessed contestation as various groups emerged with notions of reform. Governments responded to public pressure in varied ways. Kuwait restored its parliament, while Saudi Arabia and Oman each promulgated a Basic Law in 1992 and 1996, respectively, which increased participatory government infrastructure.[110] Notable Islamist clerics in Saudi Arabia led campaigns against the Western presence. In Saudi Arabia, Salman Al Odah, amid an array of demanded reforms (such as the formation of a specific army to wage war against Israel), called for the replacement of the state's highest religious authority, Grand Mufti Abdelaziz bin Baz, for legitimating the U.S. deal. Supported by 450 Islamists, a petition was addressed to King Fahd in 1991.[111]

For a state like Saudi Arabia, whose foundational forms of legitimacy rest atop religion, such challengers posed a horizontal threat to the state. Ultimately, the state responded in 1994 by jailing Al Odah, leading members of the Sahwa, and hundreds of his followers.[112] In 1999, Sahwa members like Al Odah emerged from jail as reformed moderates who stuck to the state line, although in the 2000s, he began to push for reforms once more.[113] With the Arab Spring, Al Odah and his fellow travelers felt able to voice more trenchant criticism, again linking regional winds of change to local issues on the Peninsula. He admonished Gulf governments that they are "fighting Arab democracy, because they fear it will come here," and published works that were swiftly banned, arguing from an Islamic perspective that democracy was the only "legitimate form of government."[114] Such outspokenness earned him ever-greater censure from the government and increased fame.[115]

However, by the imprimatur of Mohammed bin Salman, no influential alternative source of agenda-setting was tolerated. Saudi Arabia has one of the highest Internet penetration rates globally. One study even claimed that 41 percent of Saudi's online population used Twitter—the highest proportion in the world.[116] In conjunction with a more closed culture and a lack of public places to openly discuss politics, Twitter is far from a frivolous social media tool; rather, it acts as more of a "town square," while Iyad El Baghdadi called it "the Parliament of the Arabs."[117] Consequently, just as Mohammed bin Salman wants to preserve his freedom to act without formal parliamentary oversight, he wants to retain control from informal horizontal challenges to his power, whether from religious clerics, women's rights protestors, or agitating princes. Likely under the direction or suggestion of the de facto leader Mohammed bin Salman, in 2022 King Salman added a new holiday called "Founding Day" to the national calendar. This shifted focus of the state's foundation from the previous focus on 1744, when the Al Saud (political) and Al Sheikh (religious) sides founded their entente, to 1727, when the first Saudi state was founded.[118] This follows the pattern of seeking to downplay other forms of traditional legitimacy. The use of a new national holiday to do this mirrors other national day shifts, such as in Qatar.

Elsewhere in the Gulf, the UAE and Qatar increasingly became locales of significant Islamic influence, both near and far. Like many fellow students, Yusuf Al-Qaradawi arrived in Qatar in 1961 as a part of the outreach proselytization program of Egypt's great center of Islamic learning, the Al Azhar. Although these agents of the Al Azhar and similar organizations played a key role in building myriad institutions, as noted in the Saudi example, few developed the level of influence that Al-Qaradawi had. Indeed, he carved for himself a preeminent place in Doha, replacing preexisting Wahhabi doctrine, institutions, and practice with what might loosely be seen as Muslim Brotherhood–oriented alternatives.[119] Moreover, actively supported by the Qatari state, Al-Qaradawi's approach was popularized first locally, via inter alia a local television program called *Hady Al Islam* (*Islamic Guidance*), and then internationally via the Al Jazeera television channel, where his program *Sharia wa Haya* (*Sharia and Life*) became one of the most-watched shows in Arab television history.[120] Al-Qaradawi was, in many ways, a master marketer of his ideas. He became the first "Global Mufti" (or Islamic jurist), whose popularity was rooted in both the position and opportunities afforded him by Qatar, which inter alia he consecrated into forming the International Union of Muslim Scholars (IUMS), and his popular *wasatiyya* ("middle way," or moderate) jurisprudential doctrine approach.[121]

However, his moderate approach was not moderate enough for many. His former deputy in the IUMS, Mauritanian scholar Abdullah Bin Bayyah, quit the organization to found the Forum for Promoting Peace in Muslim Societies (FPPMS), based in Abu Dhabi. In this endeavor, Bin Bayyah formulated his doctrine, the jurisprudence of peace, to contrast directly with Al-Qaradawi's jurisprudence of revolution, which he developed during the Arab Spring.[122] Furthermore, the UAE sought to counter the IUMS with its own equivalent, the Muslim Council of Elders, which was established in Abu Dhabi as a transnational body of scholars in 2014 that took a more ecumenical approach.[123] Otherwise in the UAE ecosystem, Sufi traditions and voices, which are typically seen as positing a quietist dogma, have come to the fore, such as with the UAE-based Tabah Foundation. These efforts, in conjunction with other initiatives such as the creation of a Ministry of Tolerance and the visit of Pope Francis to the UAE in February 2019, revolve around the UAE striving to control and change dominant Islamist discourses in the Arab world and beyond.

In 2016, these ideas emerged notably in a conference in Grozny organized, at least in part, by the Tabah Foundation. This event sought to reflect on the question "Who is a Sunni?" and is interpreted as a part of the UAE's mission to deradicalize regional Islamist doctrines, corralling rejection of extremism. Interestingly, though, the conference included no Saudi, Salafi, or Muslim Brotherhood scholars, fueling speculation that the UAE was seeking to usurp traditional Saudi roles in this sphere.[124] This kind of approach seeking to depoliticize Islam fits into broader Emirati Jeffersonian approaches to foreign policy.[125] Also, with such a centralized and institutionalized locus of Islamic authority (the UAE also introduced a national Fatwa Council in 2018), this represents a mechanism for Emirati leaders to exert greater control over Islamic messaging and influence. Aside from such state-driven ideational shaping and competition, societally rooted Islamists remain a force in politics to varying degrees in the smaller monarchies, typically in three arenas: "electoral campaigns (in Bahrain and Kuwait); charities and [nongovernmental organizations] for social influence; and positions in government ministries for direct access to policymaking, as well as for means of enhancing recruitment."[126]

The UAE and Saudi Arabia decreed the Muslim Brotherhood a terrorist organization in 2014, formally shutting down Islamist-based politics in these states (although it had been on life support for some time).[127] Indeed, in Saudi Arabia, under Mohammed bin Salman, alternative sources of quasi-political organization are circumscribed, whether they emerge from a religious or a feminist angle. In contrast, members of local Brotherhood groups have long been part of the parliamentary furniture in Bahrain. However, they failed to win a seat for the first time in 2018 (although Salafis retained seats) as the parliament became ever more anodyne.[128] In Kuwait, Brotherhood and Salafi actors continue to exert influence in parliament.[129] Well institutionalized, Islamists are one of many groups in the state that exert influence socially via groups, gatherings, and societies.[130] After exerting quiet influence in Qatar over the decades, the local Muslim Brotherhood group disbanded in 1999, arguing that the state was providing sufficiently for its people. Unsurprisingly, in Qatar, there is negligible formalized religious influence through elected bodies, although "informal influence persists," if in a marginal way, from local Qatari Salafi quasi-organizations.[131]

Oman is unusual, being dominated neither by Sunni nor Shia, but rather by the Ibadi sect of Islam (approximately 45–75 percent of the population).[132] Despite Oman's quiet image, the state has long dissuaded competition for legitimacy from religious groups, whether Sunni (the Muslim Brotherhood), Shia (based initially around the loose umbrella organization called The Prophet's Great Public Library in Muttrah), or Ibadi (organizations focusing on restoring the Imamate). All groups suffered from sporadic arrests typically from the 1990s onward.[133] Although sentences were often commuted, the groups understood the state's position, so the Omani Brotherhood followed the Qatari example to become an "intellectual community" only.[134]

GLOBALIZATION AND IDENTITY

No place in the world has transformed as rapidly as the Gulf monarchies. It may be a cliché to note that "within two generations, the peoples of Saudi Arabia, Kuwait, Bahrain, Qatar, the United Arab Emirates, and Oman have turned small desert towns and seaports into urbanized states" of central importance to the world economy, but that does not make it any less accurate.[135] Globalization in the Gulf provoked a backlash, not least as the process is often seen as synonymous with Westernization or quasi-colonialism.[136] There is nothing new about such pressures, as Princeton historian Leon Carl Brown succinctly argues:

> For roughly the last two centuries the Middle East has been more consistently and more thoroughly ensnarled in great power politics than any other part of the non-Western world. This distinctive political experience continuing from generation to generation has left its mark on Middle Eastern political attitudes and actions. Other parts of the world have been at one time or another more severely buffeted by an imperial power, but no area has remained so unremittingly caught up in multilateral great power politics.[137]

The word for globalization in Arabic (*awlama*) is a linguistically neutral derivation of the word for world (*'alm*). However, in its sociolinguistic usage, *awlama* tends to take on a range of negative, coercive connotations.[138] One regional scholar argues that it is about the opening of Arab markets to . . . Israeli science or American and European products. . . . It means trying to impose political, economic, social and cultural values on developing societies and underdeveloped societies. It is a process of destroying national identities not through invasion but saturation of invasive cultures.[139]

Azmi Bishara, a former member of the Israeli Knesset and subsequent éminence grise in Qatar, argues that it is "the tyranny of international exchange laws imposed by major industrial centres on the laws and needs of local economies."[140] Such definitions (which are indicative of the broader body of literature) suggest three key areas to address: the economic, political, and cultural aspects of globalization, which are interlinked.

The Gulf monarchies, relatively underdeveloped as they were before the advent of contemporary globalization, were not blank slates. Many of the Peninsula's towns and townspeople were involved in extensive trade and other exchanges, thanks to the importance of coastal entrepôts and the pilgrimage routes to Mecca and Medina.[141] This "natural state," as Al-Nakeeb termed it, fostered a competitive "capitalistic spirit" among traders on the coast of the Peninsula, driving their search for goods, markets, and profits as they engaged in international *tajribah al-mudarabah* (speculative trading).[142] Such commerce, along with Mecca- and Medina-oriented pilgrimage routes, comprised an earlier, if slower, form of globalization. Similarly, Oman's transnational colonial links, mostly with the West African coastline and spots on the modern-day Pakistani coast, are old and varied and have fundamentally shaped the nature of Oman today.[143]

The pace of change increased with the regional role of the Ottoman and the British empires. Their imposition of laws (such as those against piracy), institutions (such as rudimentary education systems), and norms (such as the abrogation of slavery) marked a new era of exchange. Traditional modes of commerce like *tajribah al-mudarabah* collapsed as traders privileged by empire were given priority and protection. This left local merchants to engage with empire on an unequal footing to act as local facilitators for their monopolies. The social impact of this was that trading classes were typically weakened. Consequently, there was a "transfer of the political centre of gravity in the region from commercial ports to the tribal interior."[144]

One of Western states' early and more significant impositions was the nation-state system. An invention that emerged from the heart of the European continent in 1648, it finds little resonance on the Peninsula. Chief among the disjunctures between this quintessentially Western concept of political geography and local understandings on the Peninsula are the issues of territory and control. Traditional understandings of delineating one area of political authority from another were fluid. The territory of a senior sheikh ebbed and flowed according to the movements of tribes that gave him tribute.[145] However, in the oil age, where each square meter of land was potentially valuable, a laissez-faire approach to delineating borders would not suffice. Thus, when the United Kingdom and the United States instigated the drawing of the Peninsula's borders, this not only triggered a litany of disputes between emerging governments but directly affected the social realities of tribes and people.

Passports became increasingly important, and the natural peripatetic lifestyles of the bedu, as discussed earlier, became incompatible with modern political geography. In turn, this meant that the identity of such groups proved to be increasingly incompatible with the emerging states.[146] With the upending of traditional economic practices resulting from the discovery and exploitation of oil (and later gas), the region's proto-states became exponentially wealthier, resulting in endemic changes across the sociocultural spectrum.[147] This dynamic is not unique to the Gulf, although it does find a particularly stark shift between old and new.[148] Globalization and the rentier economy foisted unprecedented social changes on the monarchies, shifting them to "the most racially, ethnically, religiously, and socially mixed [societies] to be found anywhere."[149] A large middle class emerged, particularly with the oil boom of the 1970s, as the states became ever-more-generous dispensers of largesse. This tended to undercut lingering protest movements based on socioeconomic rationales (as in the 1950s and 1960s), meaning that oppositional issues became increasingly centered on identity concerns and changes to social structures.[150] The tribe was replaced as "the guarantor of social welfare and honor . . . [and] as the primary political unit in Gulf society."[151]

The backlash against globalization-driven homogenization took various forms. Sultan Said bin Taimur in Oman (r. 1932–1970) isolated himself and his country to avoid modernization.[152] This led to the immiseration of Omani society as he refused to build schools and hospitals.[153] A more widespread reaction across the Gulf was to cantonize foreigners into compounds, keeping their illicit cultural ways away from local society.[154] A linked reaction is a vituperative one in the national press, bitterly criticizing the perfidious influence of the West—not a surprising response considering the changes wrought by globalization.[155]

Fuad Khuri, a pioneering Arab anthropologist, refers to the emergence of "petro-urbanism" to describe the nature of the cities that emerged in the Gulf.[156] The richer merchant and royal families often ghettoized themselves in exclusive communities away from others, the enriched middle classes left traditional neighborhoods, and peripheral communities emerged for sedentarianized bedu communities.[157] Moreover, there were visible changes in the towns and cityscapes as globalized versions of cities emerged. Elites sought to try to belong to the modern age by adopting Western architecture aesthetics.[158] All of this contributed to the deepening stratification of society. The tenor of cities transitioned from production centers to the centers of consumption, flipping traditional patterns.[159] The days where the ruler would host open majlis meetings multiple times per week and anyone could turn up for an audience dwindled. Farah Al-Nakib's 2016 book *Kuwait Transformed* is an ode to the transformative power of oil on the very fabric of Kuwaiti society via the medium of architectural change.[160] Across the Gulf, with shifts in architecture and the political economy, traditional societal realities changed. In a petro-urban life, families gathered less often, younger women had more freedom, there was more mixing of the sexes, women in droves took advantage of exponentially increased access to higher education, and traditional handicraft industries all but died out.[161] The basics of Gulf identity changed.

The expansion in the speed, accessibility, and reach of communication powers—another core aspect of globalization—is frequently seen, for a good reason, as another way through which cultures are homogenized, negating "cultural traits, practices, beliefs, and national identities."[162] Naomi Sakr argues that the major Gulf media firms have, because of financial incentives, been eager participants in the transmission of Western television shows into the Arab world, rather than providing a regionally rooted "alternative."[163] Such powerful vectors of communication and the increasing use of English as the business lingua franca mean that the Arabic language is changing. For Clive Holes, such changes must not be exaggerated, although he still argues that something profound is being lost amid such change.[164]

However, the tools of globalization have been marshaled to defend national and traditional societal identities by concerned states. Indeed, states emerged as the new core identity for the people on the Peninsula. This was done partly by dispensing opportunity and money, but also by meshing traditional sources of legitimacy like the pageantry, rituals, and symbols with modern, oil-fueled distributive powers.[165] The ease, speed, and breadth of communication enabled elites to benefit from the "banal advantages of public media and constant repetition" that reinforced a given message.[166] An entire "industry of nostalgia" emerged in art, architecture, museum gift shops, media, film, cinema, and radio, memorializing older economic modalities. Myths emerged, as with the near-invention of sports like camel racing as an ersatz link to an imagined communitarian past.[167]

Such tropes and industries are found across the monarchies. Indeed, with the formation of the GCC, made up of the six Gulf monarchies, in 1981, there emerged a formalized idea that something unique tied these states together. Indeed, the similarities of culture, religion, sociopolitical mores, and history among the monarchies are apparent, and certainly more prevalent than the differences. Additionally (at least theoretically), the GCC benefited from the pressures that came from being galvanized together against the large, ominous, and proven threats from Iran and Iraq. Nevertheless, profound problems developing a functioning security community, extensive intra-GCC economic links, and meaningful political coordination hint at abiding issues within the organization. Societally, more than three decades after the GCC's founding, the term *khaleeji*, referring to someone of the Gulf, remains undertheorized.[168] Despite familial links, there remains an aloofness between Gulf states. That a khaleeji can go into space but not take a train from one GCC capital to another speaks to the odd progress the region's states have made.[169] Mishaal Al Gergawi opined that "politics killed culture" in the Gulf.[170] Although he was mainly referring to the Qatar blockade, his sentiment speaks to enduring issues. With the invention of tradition in the young monarchies, state-driven politics forged ahead to create unique nation-states. However, the organic evolution of a khaleeji identity became collateral damage in the process. From the perspective of the states, this is a good thing: one fewer horizontal societal level identity about which to be concerned.

It is important to be mindful that globalization is not presented simply as modern or progressive ideas assailing monarchies and pressing them to evolve their backward practices toward contemporary international standards.[171] Cosmopolitan ideas and concepts of political representation and religious plurality are not alien to the monarchies. In Kuwait's early days, Kuwait City was a clearly cosmopolitan town hosting "Africans, Persians (both Sunni and Shi'i but mostly the latter), Hasawiyya, Bahrana, Zubaris, Beluchis, Jews, and Armenians . . . a handful of Arab and American Christian missionaries."[172] Kuwait became a haven for Jews fleeing sieges in Basra in 1776, to the extent that they founded their own cemetery and school, while the wealth of at least two Jewish families matched that of traditional Sunni merchants in the early twentieth century.[173] Al Ruwaih bookshop in Kuwait celebrated its centenary in 2020, which speaks to the long-term presence of an intellectual community in the developing state.[174] And as previously noted, emerging archival work indicates the presence of a thriving, critical intellectual scene in Bahrain, where local intellectuals fully engaged with contemporary debates, publishing commentary as they went.[175]

Discussion of the role of women in Gulf societies is also frequently skewed. Too often, women are reduced to a simplified pastiche of a group, downtrodden by religious and conservative forces and in need of saving by an enlightenment brought about by Western pressure. Clearly, aspects of these formulations reflect a certain reality, but overall, such cursory generalities contain many simplifications and obfuscations.

First, there is no single position in which women in the Gulf find themselves. Rather, their position is highly disaggregated. Geography plays a part, with different countries, regions, cities, towns, and suburbs all shaping sometimes vastly different experiences, allowing or constraining actions to differing degrees. Other shaping factors include different sociocultural backgrounds (e.g., hadar and bedu), those with or without a tribal background, or those who are descended from slaves (or not). A final factor to note is the often-critical role of socioeconomic power in emancipating women to a significant degree.[176]

Time is also a factor, with the realities changing for better and worse. For example, contrary to prevalent stereotypes of women as societally invisible and powerless, Bahrain and Oman have employed female police officers since the 1970s, and women make up approximately 10 percent of the Bahraini police force.[177] Such numbers are similar to those in some Western countries.[178] Although Saudi Arabia is reversing generations of misogynistic practice, such views have not always dominated. Calls emerged as early as 1926 for girls to be educated.[179] Similarly, the first Saudi weekly newspaper, *Akhbar al Dahran*, opened in 1954 and championed girls' education, even though this was controversial and was ultimately the final straw that led to the paper's closure in November 1956, after only forty-four issues.[180]

Second, as is often the case, it would be wrong to simply ascribe religion or tribalism as the cause for the apparently backward position of women on the Peninsula. Evidently, aspects of tribal norms, or perhaps Wahhabi doctrine as expressed in Saudi Arabia in much of the twentieth century, creates environments antagonistic to female emancipation. However, as these chapters continually highlight, the state's power is a critical variable. In other words, it is not some immutable characteristic of religious or tribal lore that produces a certain Overton window, delineating the limits of female empowerment and disempowerment in the Gulf. Rather, it is how the state chose to highlight and deploy certain approaches to women found in redolent cultural locations (be they religious or tribal), which are then folded into state nationalisms and development plans.[181] Indeed, Wahhabism as a core religious doctrine of both Qatar and Saudi Arabia allowed vastly different repertoires of experience for women in the two states. Clearly, therefore, Wahhabism in and of itself is not the causal variable shaping realities for women in these states. Rather, the shaping factors stem from the interpretation, the deployment, or simply the political choice to ignore its strictures by the state and elites.

Mirroring the nature of Gulf politics overall, where changes come typically from top-down direction instead of bottom-up grass-roots initiatives, or from parliamentary deliberation and then promulgation, key advances in women's rights in the Gulf have been decreed by male leaders. These directives take a variety of forms. King Abdullah in Saudi Arabia set a quota of 20 percent of seats for women in the state's Shura Council in 2013 and thirty women took their seats. Recent years have seen the increasing appointment of women as ministers in Gulf governments, and laws have, since Oman did so in 1994, increasingly been enacted giving women voting rights.[182] Equality in law is increasingly emerging in the Gulf for men and women, and support for women in the workplace is increasing. Paid parental leave in the private sector was introduced in the UAE in 2020.[183] Furthermore, increasingly new job categories are opening for women, such that, in the most extreme example, 28,000 applications were received for thirty positions as train drivers in Saudi Arabia in 2022.[184]

Indeed, various emancipatory moves in Saudi Arabia are understandably garnering a lot of headlines. There is little doubt that Mohammed bin Salman's directives have created a significant rupture from the past, ushering in a new era for women in the kingdom. The 2019 World Bank report "Woman, Business and the Law" saw Saudi Arabia jump by the largest number of points of any country that year, thanks to the unprecedented changes introduced by the Crown Prince:

> The reforms included increasing freedom of travel and movement by giving women the right to obtain passports on their own; enabling women to be heads of households in the same way as men and allowing them to choose a place of residency; a prohibition on the dismissal of pregnant women from the workplace; a mandate of non-discrimination based on gender in access to credit; the prohibition of gender-based discrimination in employment; the equalization of retirement ages between women and men; and a removal of the obedience provision for women. A year later, amendments to the Labor Law followed, which lifted restrictions on women's ability to work at night and opened all industries to women, including mining.[185]

The nature of these changes reinforces the centrality of states' decision-making in creating a milieu in which women's rights are or are not respected and enforced. The nature of Wahhabi doctrine has not changed. Rather, Mohammed bin Salman has increasingly decided not to acknowledge its importance anymore.[186] Equally, it would be remiss to ignore the effects of bottom-up action, stirring up small communities and groups to press issues and seek to influence policy.[187] Indeed, in Saudi Arabia, the potential influence of these kinds of subject-specific groupings is a concern for the elite. At first, the arrest of several female rights advocates does not seem to make sense, given that their demands are being met by the government to a surprising degree. However, the issue for Mohammed bin Salman and his government lies not in their message, but in the concept of a group corralling support on any subject and exerting influence. He is willing to instigate significant and tumultuous change, but only on his timetable, and only at his behest.

—— ∞∞∞ ——

Challenges to security and stability in a societal context tend to emerge along three lines: migration, horizontal competition from other similar often local projects, and vertical competition from broader regional projects, ideologies, and ideas. Challenges emerging in these three areas fundamentally shaped and indeed forged contemporary Gulf societies.

Vast migration was needed to sate the hydrocarbon-fueled desire to build and run modern states. With this immigration came waves of protests over conditions and the transmission of regional and international ideological causes. It took the monarchies decades to work out a recipe to neutralize these issues, where they ultimately swapped rambunctious Arab workers (in many arenas) for more pliant workers from Asia. At the same time, governments created contractual structures to make most workers temporary guests in order to inhibit their ability to stay in the monarchies ad infinitum, and to give national citizens profound levels of control over their often immensely cheap workforce. These measures significantly curtailed the threats of instability emanating from migrant workers.

What is new in more recent years are vociferous criticisms emerging from Western-based human rights organizations highlighting shoddy or often inhumane conditions under which foreign workers labor in the monarchies. Such headlines are acutely felt in states striving to leverage financial wealth to build soft power, often via sporting initiatives, like Qatar and the UAE. Against what can sometimes be a torrent of negative coverage, the monarchies react slowly (if at all) because control of migrant workers is one of the hot-button issues among Gulf citizens, who resent and resist the relaxation of controls on migrant workers. Indeed, even though the monarchies are in no way democracies, this is one of the areas where government policy is shaped (and notably slowed) by citizen concerns.

Equally, a paradox exists that is notably prevalent in Qatar, the UAE, and Bahrain, whereby segments of the political and economic elites are building vast residential developments that cater to numbers far in excess of any possible demand from citizens. In essence, these economic decisions mandate a de facto permanent population of foreigners in the state for the foreseeable future, guaranteeing that nationals in some monarchies will forever—or at least, for the foreseeable future—be a minority in their own lands. While cutting against popular sentiment, such policies are backed and driven by a strong alliance of interested parties with deep economic interests in their continuation. Such groups range from those in the construction industry, their financiers, their suppliers, and those companies that will service these vast numbers of foreigners. Even more potentially incendiary are creeping moves to offer citizenship to suitably qualified foreigners.[188] Presently, the numbers being discussed are suitably small that minimal popular reaction is visible. Nevertheless, as the broader economic bargains struggle as the hydrocarbon economy dwindles, arguments over who is and who is not a citizen, with all the rights and benefits that citizenship brings, will surely resurface.

In the face of these pressures, one might assume that nationals would reignite or otherwise revert to classical, older forms of societal cohesion, such as focusing on tribal lineages or Islam as an organizing principle. However, these spaces across the monarchies are instead either monopolized or increasingly controlled by the state. This is one significant difference between the early days of the monarchies and their contemporary instantiations. Indeed, elites have long seen other forms of horizontal competition for belonging as a challenge that, as noted earlier, often led to considerable strife for the governments. However, as states consolidated their power, thanks to the emergence and domination of hydrocarbon industries above all else, they increasingly countered and took control of these areas that posed challenges. This is seen especially conspicuously in Saudi Arabia in recent years. Certainly, there has long been an ebb and flow between religious and political centers of power in the state, with one side dominating whenever political currents allow. However, the domination of Mohammed bin Salman led to the sidelining of key religious actors. Institutionally, they were robbed of their formal powers so that, for example, the "once feared religious police"—as the collocation perennially has it—were stripped of their powers. As one former officer in the religious police put it, "Anything I should ban is now allowed, so I quit."[189] Similarly, key individuals—such as Salman Al Odah, with his 13 million Twitter followers—were jailed with no visible repercussions, something that would have been judged nearly impossible to occur until it transpired.

Similarly, states exerted more control over tribes. There is no question that tribes have lost potency as a core social organizing principle that shaped realities on the Peninsula. State power long encroached on traditional tribal roles, notably as a dispenser of socioeconomic aid and opportunity, as well as protection. This expansion has been slow but sure, and yet tribal politics retains a nontrivial importance. In Kuwait, tribal politics in the form of "tribal primaries" remains relevant.[190] Even in Qatar, one of the quietest Gulf states, tribally rooted concerns surface. In 2021, when the state finally promulgated its electoral laws, some tribal constituencies found themselves ineligible to vote, triggering consternation and public complaints.[191] Still, the art of the possible for the tribe has dwindled. In contrast, state elites have coopted and transitioned tribal sentiments into a form of mediated pageantry to project a new form of state-driven nationalism.

Vertical challenges, such as those emanating from regional or global ideological ideas, seem less salient and visible compared to the visceral and heady days of the 1960s and 1970s when leftist and nationalist winds buffeted and deeply concerned Gulf elites. Perhaps the key difference today is that Gulf governments are far stronger and less subject to the vicissitudes of regional or international challenges. Instead, today they are the states engaged in making the waves and generally pushing their own ideological ideas outward into the region and the wider international world.

A key clash here is between the broadly pro-Islamist line pushed by Qatar against the stoic anti-Islamist line of the UAE. Each state thinks that it understands what kind of governing principles are best for the Arab world, with Islamists playing a loose role and wielding influence in society and politics, as opposed to Islamists having no influence. With the resolution of the Qatar blockade in January 2021, an epic round of clashes, often rooted in this base difference, came to an end. Given how deeply both sides feel the respective convictions and how they have shaped each side's institutions, norms, and laws, it seems likely that the Al Ula cold peace, which brought about the end to the Gulf blockade in January 2021, is more a hiatus than an end of ideological hostilities.

Lastly, when it comes to the Gulf monarchies bending and swaying to international ideological winds, the past decade has seen the rise of a new challenger. Today, the Gulf monarchies remain in the thrall of the rising global antagonism between the United States and China. For the latter half of the twentieth century and well into the twenty-first century, the Gulf monarchies have felt pressure to democratize. The international states they were closest to—and from whom they sought protection—were democracies. Amid the end of the Cold War, the political organizing principle of democracy was widely seen as having won. Also, the dissolution of the Soviet Union coincided with the invasion of Kuwait and its liberation by a Western coalition of forces, where moves toward democracy were implicit in the agreement leading to the salvation of the state.

However, the rise of China proved that swift economic growth, the development of leadership roles in various technological fields, and the associated accumulation of power did not require democratization. China's model of authoritarian progress is attractive to the region's autocrats, who fear democratization. As the region's most democratic state, Kuwait has long been an advertisement for the perils of a powerful parliament that has strangled the development of the state. Otherwise, a core lesson of the Arab Spring is that moves toward democracy and the unseating of suboptimal but well-entrenched autocratic leaders lead to ructions or civil unrest. Overall, it seems likely that Gulf elites will reprise the times when their forefathers expertly played off colonial regimes in London and Constantinople as they strive to maximize the leverage they have and deals that they can make with Western powers while they follow a Chinese approach to autocratic development.

3

ECONOMIC SECURITY

The conflict between, on the one hand, advocates of the spontaneous extended human order created by a competitive market, and on the other hand those who demand a deliberate arrangement of human interaction by central authority based on collective command over available resources is due to a factual error by the latter about how knowledge of these resources is and can be generated and utilized. . . . Socialist aims and programmes are factually impossible to achieve or execute; and they also happen, into the bargain as it were, to be logically impossible.

HAYEK (1992)

Views on economic security or insecurity provided by a system or economic policy depend on political perspective. Consequently, discussions of economic security remain contentious when it comes to analyzing a given system and prescribing policies. A free marketer may see the demise of a state's traditional industries due to globalized market pressures as a necessary part of the creative destruction of a prospering economy. However, a socialist may reject such an interpretation, arguing that it is precisely the state's role to defend the weak against stronger powers.[1] Mindful of these many economic worldviews, this analysis is less rooted in any one international political economy theory, and no policy prescriptions follow a normative standpoint. Thus, when one of the persistent problems identified in the monarchies over the last century is a vast overreliance on public-sector jobs for nationals, this is not done on an ideological basis. Instead, this conclusion emerges from broader issues, such as growing state wage burdens and the inherent inefficiencies that this approach demonstrably creates. Ultimately, this chapter strives to be both descriptive, discussing the evolution of the region's economies, and analytical, in uncovering the impact that such changes have wrought on the principal referent object, Gulf citizens, whose lives have been thus shaped by the hydrocarbon political economy.

This chapter ultimately explores a core paradox at the heart of the Gulf political economy. It opens by reflecting on the development of the hydrocarbon industries and how elites swiftly parlayed the resulting fruits into funds to develop the state apparatus, with them firmly atop it, creating the distributive subsidy-driven "no taxation, no representation" ruling bargain. Elements of continuity are readily apparent in the formation and solidification of citizens' expectations about the role of the state in providing materially for subjects. Indeed, these are some of the most acute issues that the monarchies are dealing with today, pulling back—with some initial success—on parts of the ruling bargain with minimal democratic movement as compensation.

Gulf governments have long been aware of the need to diversify away from their hydrocarbon reliance, and plans have been promulgated for over half a century. Some of these approaches have partly worked. Dubai boasts the organic growth of one of the biggest, busiest, and most efficient ports globally. Several Gulf sovereign wealth funds (SWFs) are among the largest and most influential funds of their kind. Plans were (and often still are) written with considerable input from Western management consultancies, giving them a shiny veneer and a verisimilitude of real economic change. Foreign investments, creating SWFs, promulgating visions, and myriad iterations of megaprojects or even gigaprojects have been tried and tested. However, overall, any resulting diversification tends to be paltry compared to the soaring promised ambition. Ultimately, the paradox at the heart of the Gulf monarchies' political economy concerns states striving to use oil-derived wealth to extricate themselves from an oil economy that makes any such transition fiendishly tricky.

The first section of this chapter, "Rent and Subsidies," explains how the Gulf's rentier states were formed. Specifically, it follows the slow, and then ever-swifter emergence of the contemporary Gulf economies, and how the nature of the oil and broader hydrocarbon economies allowed an unusual emergence of state-society relations. In this deal, the states adopted a patronage-dispensing position, not least to retain their role at the apex of society with as few constraints as possible. However, this financially expensive bargain came under ever more pressure, and today's Gulf states are striving to pare back their benefits where possible. Indeed, as the second section, "Diversification and Development," notes, the monarchies have long sought ways to spend their oil and hydrocarbon wealth to drive economic diversification (at least ostensibly). All monarchies have plowed some often considerable monies into investments and SWFs, and all have published (usually multiple) documents espousing their visions. In reality, seldom have these plans really come to fruition. Nevertheless, elites continue to engage in epic megaprojects and gigaprojects, often underpinned by highly questionable logics, as explored in "Visions, Megaprojects, and Gigaprojects." The more recent trend in the monarchies is to (attempt to) forge knowledge economies and otherwise reform their labor markets, which are the subjects of the final section.

RENT AND SUBSIDIES

Before hydrocarbon industries dominated the political economy of the Gulf monarchies, much of the region's economy revolved around pearling and the economies that this industry drove: shipping, slaving, and associated trade.[2] Growing international demand for pearls in the late eighteenth and nineteenth centuries prompted the resettlement or founding, and then expansion, of towns like Kuwait, Abu Dhabi, and Zubara, Qatar.[3] In other words, Kuwait, Qatar, and the United Arab Emirates (UAE) were built and then expanded thanks to a naturally occurring, geographically specific, depletable natural resource subject to boom and bust economic cycles, which was lucrative enough to encourage mass immigration well over numbers that could be sustained locally.

Rising pearl prices drove innovation. New pearling beds were founded, the number of boats doubled in the nineteenth century, and the pearling season was extended. The size of the pearling economy shifted societal structures. Specialized jobs emerged, and immigration boomed, including the employment of the bedu and immigrants from Persia, Baluchistan, and Sind.[4] Coastal towns doubled revenues in the last decades of the nineteenth century. They expanded far beyond their natural ability for food production, drawing these settlements deep into regionalized food trade.[5] New financial mechanisms (e.g., tax systems, centralized governance, and loan systems) emerged. The nature of regional trade routes and centers of economic gravity meant that the ports of the Arabian Peninsula were more connected to Indian cities than to major Arab capitals. Indian Hindu merchants were a significant source of credit for the pearling industry. Around three-quarters of exports from the Trucial States and Bahrain went to India, and a majority of imports came back.[6] The Indian rupee (and from 1959, the India-issued Gulf rupee) were the most important currencies in the monarchies for much of the nineteenth and early twentieth centuries.[7] It remained dominant until the 1960s, with the launch of domestic currencies. The region prospered. For Bahrain, the value of pearl exports increased 600 percent from 1873 to 1906, reflecting both price and supply increases.[8] In the first decade of the twentieth century, swathes of the local population were involved in the pearling industry: 100 percent in Ajman, 69 percent in Dubai, 51 percent in Abu Dhabi, 48 percent in Qatar, 25 percent in Kuwait, and 31 percent in the Trucial States overall.[9]

These changes increased the region's vulnerabilities to shocks, and with such a profound dependency on one commodity, the Peninsula's political economy had a single point of failure. The region suffered egregiously when the demand for pearls plummeted as an alternative flooded the market in the 1920s—namely, Japanese cultured pearls. The Great Depression further slammed demand, and World War II interrupted international shipping, which was crucial for food supply, among other concerns. The overall effect on the region was seismic. The value of pearl harvests fell sevenfold, the number of pearling boats fell sixfold, and local population numbers fell dramatically as migrant workers left as did some nationals in search of opportunities.[10] The advent of the oil age from the 1950s onward killed the dwindling pearling industry thanks to better-paid, less-dangerous jobs. The lingering pearl markets became ceremonial, and when the last market closed in Kuwait in 2000, over 7,000 years of pearling commerce in the region ended.[11]

From the dire socioeconomic realities of the 1930s and 1940s, a near-miraculous recovery ensued, thanks to another naturally occurring, geographically specific, depletable, and nonrenewable resource. Oil discoveries allowed the proto-states in the Gulf to overcome their inherent natural unsustainability to support significant populations. The founding of this economic paradigm on the Peninsula started slowly. Kuwait discovered oil in its Burgan field on February 22, 1938. However, it was in Saudi Arabia where the larger story was to start, only ten days later. On March 4, 1938, a telegram was sent from the city of "Arabia," noting that what would come to be known as "Arabian Light" oil had emerged from well number seven in Saudi Arabia, at a rate of 1,585 barrels per day.[12] Up to this point, attempts to locate oil in Saudi Arabia struggled to find a reliable source. Nevertheless, U.S. companies persevered and, seventh time lucky, they struck black gold in such huge quantities and of such good quality that the concession they agreed to with Ibn Saud came to be worth well over $1 trillion.[13]

International firms had all the technical expertise. With only educated guesses that there would be oil found on the Peninsula, local sheikhs had to offer favorable terms to these companies to do the prospecting on their behalf. Thus, during the first era of prospecting, the proto-governments (in reality, the leading sheikhs' diwans, or ruling courts) were paid between 3 and 15 percent of royalties, as well as initial lump sums for the long-term right to prospect, by the international oil companies (IOCs).[14] The original, sixty-year-long Saudi concession that would be worth around $1 trillion was sold for under $1 million and comparatively small annual payments. It was a similar story across the monarchies.

As the size of the oil fields became apparent, IOCs made a fortune, but in an era of anticolonial nationalism in the 1950s and 1960s, their agreements became untenable. IOC heads tried to put off the inevitable by improving the terms of their deals in the 1960s and 1970s, but the leverage they once had over the monarchies diminished as the states developed. Iran, Iraq, Kuwait, Saudi Arabia, and Venezuela founded the Organization of Petroleum Exporting Countries (OPEC) in 1960 to exert more control over their industries and the later oil prices.[15] The typical narrative that, furious over Israel's policies and the U.S. support of Israel in the Yom Kippur War, Arab countries in 1973 increased the price of oil and cut production, causing chaos in Western states, is not entirely accurate. However, a mythology has undoubtedly built up promoting such logic.[16] Supplies to the United States and the Netherlands were halted, although no gasoline queues appeared in the Netherlands and oil shipments for the U.S. Sixth Fleet were mostly maintained.[17] So, while OPEC measures did engender a price increase of approximately 70 percent, broader market pressures arguably led to the price increasing 400 percent. This fostered a budgetary boom of near-unimaginable proportions. As Jim Krane notes, Saudi Arabia's state revenues increased 4,000 percent, going from $655 million in 1965 to $26.7 billion a decade later, while Gulf income increased 3,000 percent.[18] This was the era when the Gulf monarchies truly saw how linked their economy and gross domestic product (GDP) were to the oil price roller coaster, as figure 3.1 illustrates. Similarly, figure 3.2 shows how important oil income was as a percentage of GDP.

The states took advantage of this windfall, increasing stakes in their oil assets. Though there remained discussion in the late 1960s and 1970s about "participation, not nationalization," ultimately, most states took majority positions from IOCs.[19] Driven by domestic populism, Kuwait took full control of its oil concessions by 1965; Saudi Arabia took a 60 percent stake in Aramco in 1973, rising to 100 percent in 1980; Qatar took full control of its oil industry by 1977; and Bahrain took 60 percent in 1975 and 100 percent five years later, in 1980.

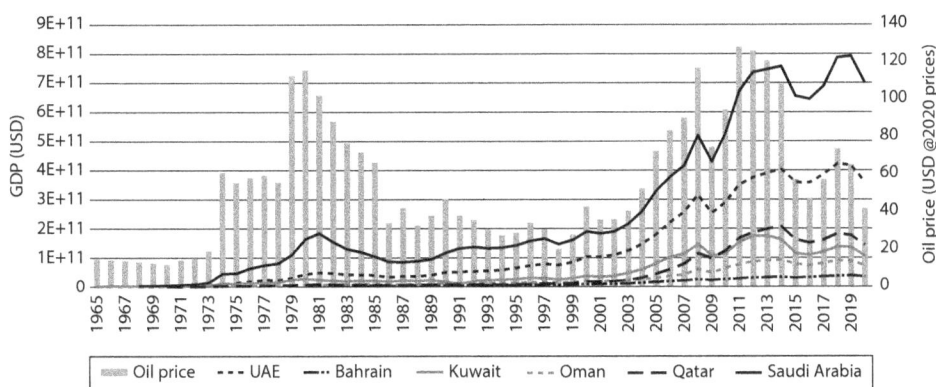

FIGURE 3.1 GDP and oil prices in the Gulf monarchies, 1965–2018.

Source: BP Statistical Review of World Energy (2020) and World Development Indicators, World Bank (2020).

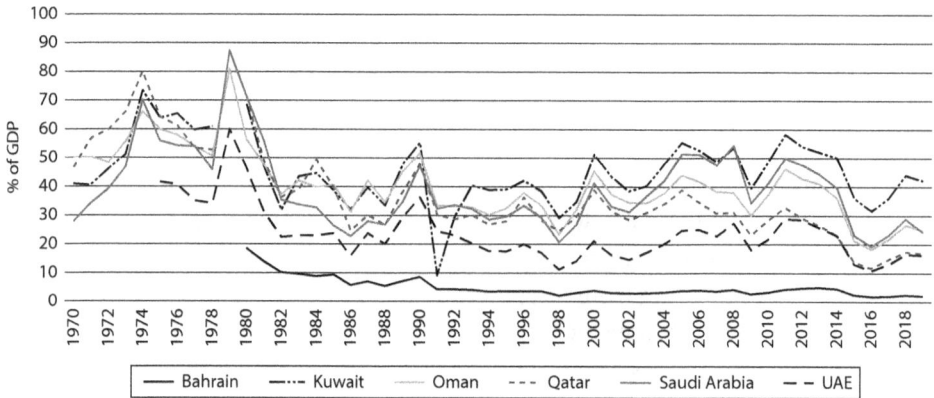

FIGURE 3.2 Oil rent as a percentage of GDP.

Source: World Development Indicators, World Bank (2020).

The oil boom of the 1970s is of seminal importance in shaping the very nature of the monarchies. The Gulf monarchies are often described as allocation or rentier states. Facilitated by oil- and gas-derived wealth, this form of development is characterized by "state-led development, wealth distribution, and limited emphasis on creating real economic assets."[20] Instead of taxing citizens or local businesses to derive most of its revenues, the state is broadly in the business of distributing oil and gas export revenues or "rents," often in the form of subsidies. Rent distribution, in turn, secures regime legitimacy and popular support instead of employing democratic means.[21] Naturally, this logic needs to be carefully applied. Rentierism did not instill a magic pacifying spell on Gulf nationals, and disgruntlement did sometimes emerge.[22] Nevertheless, overall, in such a modus operandi, the state is under minimal pressure to forge an efficient, productive national economy, and a rentier economy becomes entrenched. Then, it is widely argued that a "rentier mentality" among citizenry is forged and embedded that "is incompatible with hard work, discipline and risk-taking and embodies a disconnect in the work-reward relationship."[23]

The cumulative impact of over half a century of rentierism, where Gulf nationals have been relatively separated from how the states made their money, embedded to varying degrees this rentier mentality.

Despite differences in the source of state income and wealth, Mehran Kamrava, one of the region's leading scholars, concludes that "rentier economies remain firmly established across the Persian Gulf."[24] Artifacts of such processes have been abundantly apparent since the 1960s, when the Kuwaiti government launched its first study of the gross distortions of the labor market that its subsidies created, like the phenomenon of "masked unemployment," where employees do "no productive work."[25] Such problems remain. As Martin Hvidt notes, the monarchies demonstrably suffer from "low productivity, low job creation, lack of economic diversification, high volatility of state incomes, and lack of motivation and employability of the national workforce."[26]

It is not just an issue of mentality, though. The structure of Gulf labor markets is twisted by the prevalence of foreigners driving down wages, which often makes it uneconomical for Gulf nationals to compete.[27] Moreover, Gulf governments spend heavily on salaries for public servants to distribute the state's wealth, in order to secure popular support.[28] The Kuwaiti government has guaranteed jobs for citizens since at least the 1960s, while the Qatari and UAE governments provide similar implicit guarantees.[29] Approximately 40 to 60 percent of government budgets in the Gulf Cooperation Council (GCC) are spent on public-sector salaries and services.[30] The situation is acute in Kuwait, where compounded annual payroll growth increased 7.5 percent per year in the 2010s. The wages bill rose from 10 percent to nearly 20 percent of GDP by the end of the decade, comprising an astonishing 73 percent of public expenditures, alongside subsidies.[31] The International Monetary Fund (IMF) finds that when adjusted for skills and education, there is a vast premium on wages in the public sector compared to the private sector. It is approximately 250 percent in Kuwait, 225 percent in Bahrain, 175 percent in Qatar, and 160 percent in Saudi Arabia.[32] Unsurprisingly, Gulf nationals are eager for such well-remunerated positions in the government, where the demands are (rightly) perceived to be comparatively low and the job security high.[33] Indeed, the number of state employees is roughly double the global average.[34]

Particularly after the 1970s, subsidies became baked into Gulf ruling bargains, ripping up links between consumption and cost on a personal level. Structural factors contribute to the Gulf region's vast expansion in energy demand. The Gulf population rose from 8.2 million in 1971 to around 60 million in 2019, three times the world average. Citizen populations became much richer, and with the expansion of a middle class comes the demand for energy-consuming products. The arid, hot climate of the region mandates energy-intensive air conditioning.

Furthermore, deep subsidies for energy encourage consumption and induce profligate behavior at all levels of society.[35] The prices for electricity and fuel were reduced in the latter half of the twentieth century across the monarchies as governments sought to boost their popularity. Indeed, approximately half of the world's energy subsidies are spent in the Middle East and North Africa (MENA) region.[36] Ultimately, the typical Kuwaiti household consumes thirty-six times more energy than its German counterparts.[37]

Expectations of low fuel or electricity prices have been habitualized, and governments worry that cutting subsidies will affect this element of the ruling bargain. This is a wicked issue to remedy, but some subsidy reforms have continued since the 1990s. Dubai instituted some of the region's most successful reforms in 2009, where costs rose significantly, albeit far more for expatriates than residents.[38] Elsewhere, three of the four largest increases in gasoline prices anywhere in the world occurred in the Gulf. The average price worldwide increased 12 percent, but the largest increase of over 200 percent was in Saudi Arabia; the second largest was in Bahrain, at 87 percent; and the fourth largest was in the UAE, at 19 percent. Increases stemmed from policy choices, including reducing subsidies and the introduction of taxes.[39] Nevertheless, the absolute price remains among the lowest in the world, and the IMF calculated in 2021 that Saudi Arabia still has among the world's highest total subsidies per capita.[40]

As these subsidies are scaling down from an exalted high, the IMF classifies progress as contributing toward a gradual rebalancing of Gulf economies. The pace will have to increase considerably for some monarchies to meet medium- and long-term budget requirements.[41] However, ingrained behaviors are challenging to change, while whole industries have been established on the premise of cheap fuel sources. Such issues are acute in Saudi Arabia, the world's fifth-largest consumer of oil, but with only the world's forty-seventh-largest population.[42] Although alternatives are in the pipeline, there is a long way to go, with Saudi Arabia consuming approximately one-third of its production.[43] Back in 2011, when Saudi Arabia was consuming only one-quarter of its oil production, a Chatham House report spotted this unsustainable trend, noting that on a straight-line trajectory, it would become an oil importer by 2038.[44] This is not the likely outcome, as the authors note. However, if there is even a conversation whereby Saudi Arabia—a state where oil revenue frequently accounts for the majority of state income (68 percent in 2018, 64 percent in 2019, and 53.5 percent in 2020)—is consuming so much of its oil that it has none to export, then something is profoundly amiss.[45]

Across the monarchies, increasing progress is being made by cutting subsidies and introducing taxes if the developments have been unevenly distributed. Saudi Arabia has led the way, while Qatar and Kuwait lag, but this is unsurprising. Their fiscal situation is significantly better than that of their fellow monarchies. The rash of tax policies in the UAE and Saudi Arabia revolve around introducing a value-added tax (VAT). All six monarchies signed a 15 percent VAT framework on "most goods and services," but implementation dates differed.[46] Saudi Arabia increased its rate to 15 percent in 2020, Bahrain started with a 5 percent rate in 2019 and increased it to 10 percent in 2022, the UAE's and Oman's rates were both 5 percent, and Kuwait and Qatar had not implemented it at all. Thanks to the vast financial windfall resulting from the Russian invasion of Ukraine, energy prices peaked, and any sense of fiscal urgency was again undercut. Consequently, it would not be surprising if both states continued to demure in initializing VAT. Other than VAT, as Karen Young put it, in the face of mounting fiscal difficulty, there was

> experimentation in fiscal policy across the Gulf as governments make diverse decisions about where they can reduce spending on generous benefit programmes and employment opportunities for citizens and how they might capture savings from their expatriate populations in the form of new taxes and fees or by simply excluding them from certain sectors of the labour force.
>
> This slimmer, meaner form of fiscal management has also meant a renewed focus of the state (and its citizens) on value for money in investments and aid abroad.[47]

These measures will slowly increase, inter alia, the tax take in the monarchies, which has been broadly static for decades, except for Oman.

DIVERSIFICATION AND DEVELOPMENT

Development in the Gulf presents a puzzle. As Imad Salamey outlines, the basic premise of globalization holds that economic liberalization, driven by international institutions and the neoliberal system of globalized capital, engenders democratization:

> The removal of national trade barriers, the supremacy of global finance, the expansion of capital flow and foreign investment, the access of technological communication, the rise of global governance, the spread of mass culture, the massive population movements towards the centres, and the assertion of ethnic identities and cultural plurality are among the many global integration factors contributing to the liberal transformation and democratization of the nation state.[48]

Although the Gulf monarchies are deeply intertwined in a globalized economy, they are not democracies, nor are they in the process of becoming meaningfully democratic. Instead, ruling families control development and modernization projects—usually understood as drivers toward democratization—through state corporations.[49] Such "statist globalization" gives the monarchies greater control over the pace of change, empowering elites.[50] The dispensing of patronage in the form of contracts, grants, and opportunities for wealth creation created a thick protective crust of allied families, groups, institutions, and people around the monarchs. A further concentric circle of support usually comes from the majority of the state's citizens, who enjoy subsidies and benefits and hence are sated and comparatively apolitical.[51] Extensive subsidies remove a vector of concern that assailed many states in the MENA region and farther afield.[52] Such policies allow the Gulf monarchies to escape the king's dilemma, Samuel Huntington's argument that a government's granting of rights in a given sphere is a one-way street that can only ever engender demands for yet more rights.[53] Overall, Gulf economic strategies can be categorized in four broad ways: the promulgation of a long-term vision, the role of megaprojects, the creation of knowledge economies, and the founding of SWFs. Each has long been in evidence and undergirds state attempts to cheat traditional economics and escape the king's dilemma, maintain and strengthen its rentier economy, and simultaneously (and paradoxically) plan, usually in the most theoretical ways, for a post-oil future.

INVESTMENTS AND SOVEREIGN WEALTH FUNDS

Figure 3.3 highlights the close relationship between the price of oil and Saudi Arabia's revenues and expenditures: when the oil price rises, so do expenditures, and vice versa. This experience is reflective of the Gulf economies as a whole. The three black boxes cover periods of surplus, where the state squirreled away hundreds of billions of dollars of surplus rents, often in the form of investments. These reserves were useful during the two periods highlighted in the grey boxes, when expenditure outpaced revenues, leading to deficits.

This graph illustrates the roller-coaster ride that Gulf economies endure. Such volatility is harmful to long-term economic growth and stability. Focusing on long-term investments like SWFs is one way that states attempted—mostly unsuccessfully—to find methods to round off the peaks and troughs inherent to running an oil-rooted economy.

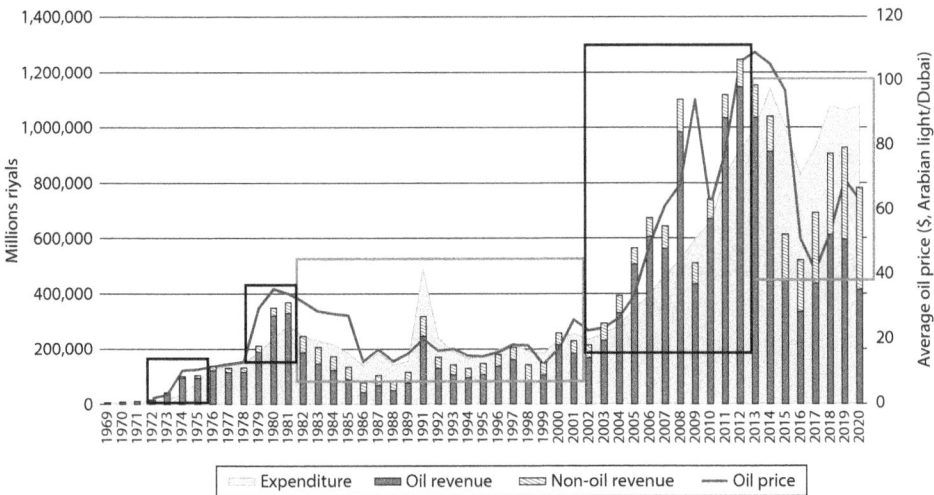

FIGURE 3.3 Saudi oil and non-oil revenues, expenditures, and historical oil prices. Note that revenues, expenditures, and oil prices are actual and not adjusted for inflation.

The emergence in recent decades of SWFs is a sign of shifting wealth patterns to developing states, with non-OECD countries now accounting for the majority of the world's SWFs, and a reassertion of state power in international financial markets.[54] SWFs are a long-employed tool in the Arab world. Their core rationales depend on the context of their formulation and range from a mechanism to compensate for oil price changes, a way to save hydrocarbon revenues for future generations, an investment mechanism, a tool to wield political influence abroad, a way to encourage domestic economic development and diversification, and a ploy to shore up domestic communities in eras of challenge and contestation.[55]

The Saudi Arabian Monetary Agency (SAMA) was created in 1952 to manage the state's wealth. Its role changed precipitously in the early 1970s as the budget soared into surplus, going from a deficit of −1.8 percent of GDP in 1969 to a surplus of 40.7 percent five years later.[56] Flush with cash, SAMA "turned to asset accumulation and management."[57] Because of Saudi Arabia's large population, it focused on "consumption smoothing and risk management [rather] than long term objectives like foreign asset accumulation and caring for future generations . . . [hence it had] a very conservative investment orientation, with heavy emphasis on bonds, thereby satisfying the demands for liquidity and safety."[58] SAMA and other Gulf SWFs emerged with Western help. In SAMA's case, the fund grew out of the Saudi Hollandi Bank—"the country's first bank"—which also stored the state's gold reserves.[59] SAMA is not an SWF in the traditional sense, and until recently, Saudi authorities denied that the state even needed one at all.[60] This changed with the rise to the power of Mohammed bin Salman, who wants to rebrand a relatively unknown Saudi development fund established in 1971, the Public Investment Fund (PIF), as the largest SWF globally.[61]

If Saudi Vision 2030 is the vehicle designed to catalyze the state's transformation to a self-sustaining, diversified, and competitive economy, then the PIF is the engine. From its original mandate as a low-profile, domestic "angel investor," it changed with the goal of becoming

> a global investment powerhouse and the world's most impactful investor, enabling the creation of new sectors and opportunities that will shape the future global economy, while driving the economic transformation of Saudi Arabia. . . . To actively invest over the long term to maximize sustainable returns, be the investment partner of choice for global

opportunities, and enable the economic development and diversification of the Saudi economy.[62]

In 2015, Mohammed bin Salman changed the structure of the PIF, taking it away from the Ministry of Finance and putting it under the control of the Council for Economic and Development Affairs (CEDA), which was under his jurisdiction.[63] This means that the PIF "is both the owner and manager of the fund's assets" and, from a wide-ranging board of individuals from different ministries and committees, it came under the sole direction of Mohammed bin Salman, who appointed the board himself.[64] Roll argues that this means that Mohammed bin Salman appointed people

> not due to their government positions, but rather to their personal proximity to the crown prince. This applies in particular to Khalid al-Falih (Energy) and Muhammad al-Jadaan (Finance) as well as Minister of State Muhammad al-Shaikh. It is striking that the Saudi central bank is no longer represented in the [board of directors (BoD)]. Its previous role as manager of the state's assets has thus been noticeably curtailed. Special powers have been granted to the managing director. Yasir al-Rumayyan, who is also a member of the fund's BoD and one of the crown prince's closest personal confidants, has held this position since September 2015. Al-Rumayyan has no political mandate but is part of the country's more informal key command and control centres.[65]

It is not unusual for Saudi Arabia to have fiscally strong parallel structures within the state. However, the scale of the PIF—with the potential to have an annual income exceeding the annual budgets of Saudi ministries—is a change. Roll cautions that the creation of such a gargantuan shadow budget is typically frowned upon as this has "not only potential to undermine the solidity of state fiscal policy and budgetary discipline, but . . . also [become] a gateway for political and administrative corruption."[66] Moreover, this entity remains firmly under the control of Mohammed bin Salman, who exerts "massive influence on the day-to-day business of the PIF," to the point where it is described as a "one-man investment vehicle."[67] The PIF expanded significantly in size. Press reports allege that several hundred billion dollars from central bank reserves and proceeds from the Ritz-Carlton anticorruption shakedown were channeled into the fund.[68]

Other funds came from the biggest shake-up in Saudi finances in decades. In January 2016, Mohammed bin Salman announced that Saudi Aramco would be partially privatized, and shares in the company would be sold on a major international stock exchange. Partly, this was to inject funds into the PIF to realize Saudi Vision 2030, but it would also indicate a new era of transparency in Saudi Arabia. This is because in order to list on an international exchange, Aramco's finances would have to be opened and disclosed to investors as never before. However, this venture was only partially successful. Ultimately, 1.5 percent of the company, not the intended 5 percent, was sold, and on the Saudi Bourse, not internationally. This raised approximately $30 billion for the PIF, not $500 billion.[69] The $2 trillion price was only aspirational. The Aramco prospectus was thin, lacking the usual pages and footnotes forensically outlining the company's accounts and related details (as expected for any significant deal on a reputable exchange).[70] This is not surprising. Until the initial public offering (IPO), Aramco finances were a de facto state secret, both in terms of the actual Saudi oil reserves and precisely how much income the company made. The floatation on the Saudi exchange went ahead without anything like the standard rigorous set of disclosures. Nevertheless, reports still indicate that Saudi banks and citizens and Kuwaiti and UAE investors were courted (or pressured) so that the fund would reach a pared-back target.[71] Overall, the editorial board of the *Financial Times* judged the floatation a "hollow victory," noting it was achieved only through "a mixture of coercion and stage management."[72]

The evolution of Aramco is inextricably intertwined with that of the PIF. This fund became a new behemoth in the Saudi state, thanks to restructuring the Aramco-state-PIF relationship. Previously, Aramco contributed heavily to the state budget via royalties, income taxes, and dividends. However, under Mohammed bin Salman's plans, the PIF received Aramco dividends directly, drastically cutting the state budget. Further, 2018 figures showed that the state budget received around a quarter of its revenue from a dividend of $58 billion, while part of the Aramco IPO had promised investors a dividend of at least $75 billion per year for five years.[73] Given that Aramco's profits dropped by 44 percent in 2020, to maintain the $75 billion, the company took on a range of debts, such as a bond sale and the $69.1 billion acquisition of 70 percent of Saudi Basic Industries Corporation (SABIC) from the PIF; cut capital expenditure; and delayed projects.[74]

The PIF is designed to underpin several gigaprojects in Saudi Arabia, including founding Qiddiya, a leisure-oriented, city-scale project near Riyadh; and the half-trillion-dollar NEOM project, on the northwest coast. Plans are also afoot to handmaiden the emergence of a local defense industry via Saudi Arabian Military Industries (SAMI), a PIF-owned conglomerate. The fund is also a dominant investor in Saudi banking, cement, chemicals, mining, and food companies. This prompted the IMF to comment that this domination could "lead to a strengthening of the government's role in the economy and push back the private sector," continuing the problematic statist approach to development evident since the 1970s.[75] The PIF also owns a vast international portfolio. Amid the COVID worldwide market crashes, the fund—like other Gulf SWFs— has been hunting for bargains in blue-chip companies like Shell, Total, Repsol, Boeing, Citigroup, and Eni. It acquired stakes in Disney, Facebook, and struggling cruise operator Carnival in the leisure sector. The PIF also invests in and works with funds to develop risky future technologies, such as partnerships with Blackstone and SoftBank.[76]

The scale of such Saudi foreign investments concerns some analysts, given that the mass withdrawal of funds from strategic sectors in a given state might cause widespread damage.[77] These concerns apply to all significant international investments. Of course, SWFs primarily exist to make money. However, given how controlled the PIF is as an engine of Mohammed bin Salman's vision, fearing the politicization of Saudi PIF investments is legitimate. However, there are arguably more salient concerns. As the principal architect and controller of the PIF, bin Salman is ramping up the risk given how centralized strategic decision making appears to be.

Kuwait was home to the world's first SWF in 1953, the British-run Kuwait Investment Board (KIB). Upon independence in 1960, the British managers were replaced, though the new organization, the Kuwait Investment Office (KIO), was still based in London.[78] With increasing oil revenues in the 1970s, a Future Generations Fund (FGF) was created in 1976. This fund looked to salt away 50 percent of the state's savings and at least 10 percent of all subsequent state revenues, almost all in international investments. The FGF was managed by the Kuwait Investment Authority (KIA).

The KIA was a cautious, shrewd investor, preferring smaller shareholdings and long-term returns and focusing, in the early years, on the United Kingdom (UK) and U.S. markets. By 1981, KIA holdings in London were

£1 billion, while in the United States, they were $4 billion in equities and $3 billion in bonds and short-term securities, which meant that for a time, Kuwait made more from its investments than its considerable oil revenues.[79] It is difficult to avoid linking the external nature of the KIA's investments to local pressure from influential merchant (and other) classes eager to ensure that some of the state's oil windfall wealth would be stashed away, safe from the clutches of the ruling family and from profligate spending on local subsidies. Similarly, the absence of the KIA's domestic mandate broadly fits the preferences of the influential local merchant elites, who wanted to protect their fiefdoms from being deluged with KIA money (and thus controlled by the state). The KIA intervened in the local market significantly only twice—to bail out those caught in the Souq al Manakh stock market meltdown in the early 1980s (discussed in more detail next) and to pay $80 billion to finance Operation Desert Storm in 1991 and the reconstruction of the Kuwaiti state.[80]

In Abu Dhabi's case, the British-run Abu Dhabi Investment Board (launched in 1967) was complemented upon independence in 1971 by the Abu Dhabi Investment Administration. By 1974, both were subsumed, and the Abu Dhabi Investment Authority (ADIA) emerged in 1976. From its inception, amid a weak local merchant class, ADIA was dominated by the ruling elite. Emiri decree appoints the board of directors, which mainly comprises senior governmental officials.[81] With its coffers filled by vast Abu Dhabi oil sales, ADIA concentrated on finance and real estate, with no development mandate "even within the UAE."[82] It continued to build a diversified international portfolio, rising to become the world's second-largest SWF.

Other SWFs emerged in the UAE, such as the International Petroleum Investment Corporation (IPIC), established in 1984; Mubadala, established in 2002; Dubai Holding, established in 2004; the Ras al Khaimah Investment Authority, established in 2005; the Investment Corporation of Dubai, established in 2006; the Abu Dhabi Investment Council (ADIC), established in 2007; the Emirates Investment Authority, established in 2007; and Sharjah Asset Management Holding, established in 2008. While they all invested internationally, Mubadala and ADIC also pivoted and focused their efforts domestically in order to nurture the diversification and development of a local economy.[83] Because of a low oil price environment, IPIC merged with Mubadala in 2017, and that new company then merged with ADIC in 2018.

Qatar founded an investment board in 1972 upon achieving independence, which was run with external assistance from Manufacturers Hanover, the First National Bank of Chicago, and Lord James Crichton Stuart.[84] Few initial records of Qatari investments are available, aside from the perennial desire to acquire property in London.[85] As a contemporary investor, Qatar emerged to burgeoning prominence with the founding of the Qatar Investment Authority (QIA) in 2005. Its approach was hybrid: amid a range of high-profile international investments, it also has a domestic focus. It owns half of the state's largest bank, Qatar National Bank, and a subsidiary within QIA, Hassad Foods, concentrates on boosting Qatar's food security via international and domestic investments. Although the QIA is approximately only the eleventh largest SWF globally, its media coverage is much more extensive. This is neatly shown in figure 3.4, translating the searches for the world's four largest SWFs (from Norway, the

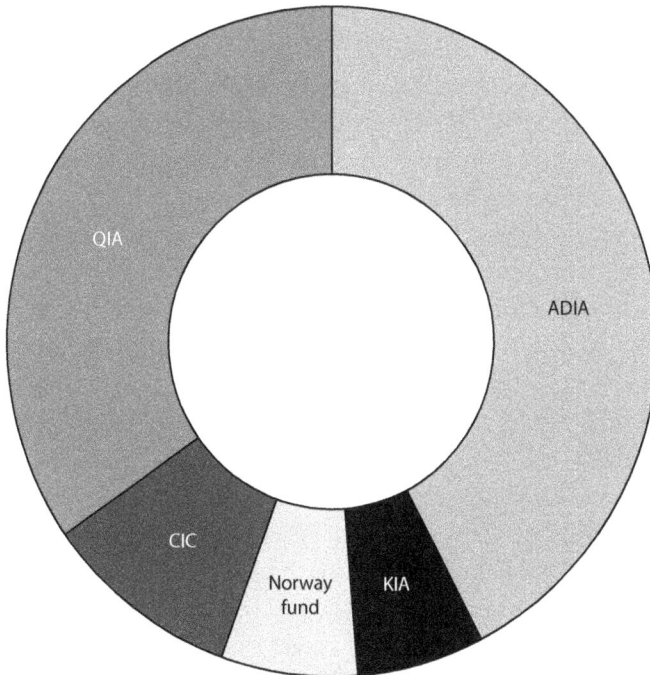

FIGURE 3.4 Google Trends search term (2004–2020).

Source: Google Trends, https://www.google.com/trends.

UAE, China, and Kuwait) and the QIA. The much smaller Qatari SWF grabs a disproportionate amount of search interest.

This extra interest has not come about by chance. Instead, the QIA's investment choices are rooted in a mixture of goals, many of which revolve around securing a certain amount of visibility. The first goal is securing long-term value—something that investing in the bluest of blue-chip companies definitively does. The second is boosting the Qatari brand as an exclusive player at the top tier of international finance via investments in major financial institutions like Credit Suisse. The third is raising the visibility of Qatar, such as by using sports as a soft-power tool to accentuate the state's appeal via investing in Paris St. Germain and acquiring regional screening rights for major sporting tournaments for Al Jazeera (i.e., BeInSport). The fourth is acquiring stakes in institutions like the London Stock Exchange or Heathrow Airport that are of strategic significance to essential allies like the United Kingdom. The fifth is investing in recognizable, top-end institutions like Harrods, Tiffany, and Porsche in order to telegraph to domestic audiences in Qatar that their money is being spent visibly and ostensibly wisely.[86]

Most Qatari investments make up a mix of rationales, and many have a political aspect. This was mainly in evidence under the SWF stewardship of Hamad bin Jassim Al Thani, Qatar's "Metternich of the Gulf," who ran the Qatari foreign portfolio from 1992 to 2013, shaping the state as he went. Although the QIA strove to offer a more traditional approach after his retirement, the 2018 appointment of Foreign Minister Abdulrahman bin Mohammed Al Thani as chair of the QIA signals something of a return to the Hamad bin Jassim days, when Qatari investment was aligned with Qatari foreign policy.[87] Signs of a $15 billion, QIA-linked investment in Turkey in 2018 and 2019 are the more obvious examples of this move.[88]

Bahrain and Oman, by contrast, are states with much less spare financial capital owing to their much smaller hydrocarbon reserves and revenues. Consequently, their furrows in the SWF world are more limited. Bahrain instead concentrated on establishing itself as the Arab world's leading financial center, with some success.[89] In 2006, the Bahraini government launched Mumtalakat (whose name means "assets") as an SWF. Twenty-nine key domestic assets, like Gulf Air, Aluminium Bahrain, and Bahrain Telecommunications Company, were transferred to its

ownership, along with approximately $13 billion. Consequently, Mumta-
lakat focuses on developing these businesses with allied investments to
transparently demonstrate Bahrain's financial maturity.[90]

In 1980, Oman established the State General Reserve Fund (SGRF) as
a savings- and stability-focused SWF.[91] After initially receiving 15 percent
of oil revenues, this was downgraded to 5 percent by 1986, and by the
late 1990s, the fund received only the "oil revenue in excess of the refer-
ence oil price set in the annual budget."[92] The Oman Oil Fund was then
established in 1993, primarily to focus on investment in the energy sector
under the auspices of the Ministry of Finance. This fund was replaced by
the Oman Investment Fund (OIF) in 2006 to combine local investments
(in tourism and infrastructure development) and the usual international
portfolio building. In 2020, under Sultan Haitham, the OIF and the SGRF
combined to form the Oman Investment Authority. With funds of around
$18 billion, the OIF is designed to stabilize government revenues, a critical
issue in 2020 given that the oil crash and the COVID crisis left the state
with a 17 percent budget deficit.[93]

The literature argues that SWFs can be used by elites to consolidate
power. In this way, Mohammed bin Salman's control of the PIF can be
seen as a mechanism to "purchase the loyalty of politically important
factions within the elite . . . [and] to 'buy' international support for his
political goals."[94] Given the elite domination of SWFs in the UAE, Qatar,
and Oman, similar motives can be imputed. There is also something of a
divide in terms of age. The older the SWF—notably the KIA and ADIA—
the more traditional the approach. The newer the SWF—notably QIA and
PIF—the riskier and more high profile the strategies that are employed.
Both newer funds lack the layers of bureaucratic and institutional oversight associated with the likes of the KIA.[95] There are reasonable concerns that the more a fund becomes personalized and politicized, the less
fiscally effective it may become.[96] Moreover, the politicization of SWF
investment can be harmful. Reputational concerns can affect investments,
as happened when the U.S. Congress engaged in an "unrelenting biparti-
san attack" on the prospect of Dubai Ports World acquiring six U.S. ports
in 2006, based on little more than prejudice.[97]

This is significant. Remember that SWFs are not merely luxury institutions. Their reserves have been important—critical, even, in some cases—
during oil price collapses that created budget deficits, as well as during

other periods of unrest. The combination of the 2008 financial crash and the 2010 Arab Spring emptied approximately $350 billion from Gulf SWFs, around 25 percent of their known value.[98] Saudi Arabia spent an extra $130 billion domestically. Qatar invested the equivalent of 6.6 percent of its GDP in its banking sector. Kuwait approved a $105 billion package. Abu Dhabi granted Dubai a $20 billion bailout, and the monarchies banded together to offer multibillion-dollar packages for Oman and Bahrain.[99] Externally, finance was used to prop up regional allies. Around $25 billion of investment was channeled toward Egypt by the UAE and Saudi Arabia, amounting to 49 percent of all inward investment.[100]

Therefore, there is an emerging difficulty in the role and utility of SWFs. Theoretically, they are long-term investment tools. However, as they become used for immediate political ends—necessary as they may be—the funds become emptier and the opportunities to top them off are winnowing, not least as the number of "magic" decades, as Young put it, where the oil price soars to $100 per barrel and the monarchies can top off their coffers, is surely dwindling.[101]

VISIONS, MEGAPROJECTS, AND GIGAPROJECTS

The Gulf region has long been awash with five-year plans, ten-year plans, visions, megaprojects, and now gigaprojects. Initially, these plans were bluntly successful: cities, national infrastructure, and industries were built where none existed previously. Given the importance of establishing efficient oil industries as the central (and at times nearly the only sizable) source of state revenue and the practically impossible complexities involved for states with no ministries and minimal formal education apparatus, IOCs led the way. As noted, they raked in a good deal for themselves initially, often forging so-called islands of efficiency in the monarchies. Aramco became a state within a state; it even had its own intelligence service and took on broader roles on behalf of the government, like eradicating malaria in nearby regions.[102] Similar dynamics are found across the monarchies, even into the 1990s. When Qatar wanted to build a liquified natural gas (LNG) industry, even though the state was relatively developed, its leadership knew that it could not lead such a project.

It thus assigned lead roles to IOCs to manage projects that ultimately saw Qatar become the world's largest LNG exporter.[103]

Kuwait was an early starter along the development planning route. In the 1950s, a British officer was asked by Shaikh Abdallah to lead development projects, with a budget of £400 million. It was disastrous. The efforts stoked local inflation, ignored local demands, oversaw shoddy work, and engaged in preposterous projects like a contraption where a sheep went in one end and hot mutton sandwiches were supposed to come out of the other.[104] A planning board was subsequently formed in 1962, and the state's first five-year plan materialized in 1967.[105]

In transforming Oman from what is often described as medieval levels of development under Sultan Qaboos' predecessor, the nascent Omani government called on the expertise of an IOC, Shell, to provide "talent for the new government."[106] The first of several five-year plans was promulgated in 1976. These projects were successful. A modern nation-state emerged that the United Nations (UN) categorized as having undergone the most significant development worldwide from 1970 to the millennium.

The Trucial States—the forerunner of the UAE—instituted a series of five-year plans starting in 1955, focusing on the basic needs of its population, the first two of which were paid for by the United Kingdom. By the third plan in 1965, a Trucial States Development Office was founded in Dubai, whose aim was to "increase the aid spent on the northern sheikhdoms."[107] In 1966, Shaikh Zayed, the ruler of Abu Dhabi, contributed £500,000 to this fund, matching what the United Kingdom gave previously, which mirrored the desire in Abu Dhabi to take a leading role across the Emirates.[108] Contributions of finance and expertise also came from Qatar, Bahrain, Kuwait, and the Arab League, under the sway of Nasserism.

Aside from these formal plans, development abounded, particularly in Abu Dhabi, Dubai, and Sharjah. Each competed against the others to develop a regional reputation as the most modern, largest, and most efficient trading hub, port, airport, and tourist destination.[109] Sharjah also hosted the region's most prominent school, Choueifat, and a campus of the University of Maryland.[110] Dubai led the way with a 3,000-foot-long underwater tunnel, and even back in the 1970s, it suffered from the region's worst traffic jams.[111] From the 1970s onward,

Dubai's leadership, flush with small oil deposits but more important, with a real non-oil economy as well, handmaidened the foundation of strategic infrastructural clusters in the city. Michael Porter describes these clusters as

> geographic concentrations of interconnected companies and institutions in a particular field. Clusters encompass an array of linked industries and other entities important to competition. They include, for example, suppliers of specialized inputs such as components, machinery, and services, and providers of specialized infrastructure. Clusters also often extend downstream to channels and customers and laterally to manufacturers of complementary products and to companies in industries related by skills, technologies, or common inputs. Finally, many clusters include governmental and other institutions—such as universities, standards-setting agencies, think tanks, vocational training providers, and trade associations—that provide specialized training, education, information, research, and technical support.[112]

Relentlessly pushed by Rashid bin Saeed Al Maktoum and then his son, Mohammed bin Rashid Al Maktoum, this commerce-focused, grandiose modus operandi is often dubbed the "Dubai model."[113] By the mid-1970s, Dubai was leading the region amid fierce competition, in what Christine Osborne describes as the monuments race for "who can build the tallest building, the fastest flyover, the splashiest fountain, the biggest conference centre, the largest roundabout and ultimately, the most expensive earth station?"[114] The visit of Queen Elizabeth II to Dubai in 1979 was a "momentous" occasion for the statelet, and she inaugurated "some of the most ambitious engineering projects the world had ever seen."[115] This included opening the Middle East's tallest building, the thirty-nine-story World Trade Center complex, and inaugurating various port projects, including the world's largest excavation and construction project, which some claimed would be visible from space.[116] Shaikh Rashid also used the megaproject that created the Jebal Ali port to delineate Dubai's borders with Abu Dhabi and to undercut the commercial rationale of any future port projects founded by Abu Dhabi.[117] Clearly, this was a commercial project with an overt rationale—to carve out as much political autonomy as possible.

King Faisal undertook the first systematic modernization campaign in Saudi Arabia, and the Economic Development Committee was founded in 1958.[118] This organization had a broad remit—namely, to coordinate initiatives and to found rudimentary organizations (like a statistical body) with advice from the United Nations, the IMF, and the Research Institute of Stanford University.[119] Saudi Arabia produced the first of nine five-year development plans in 1970.[120] Some of the aims of these plans were met as living standards climbed. Nevertheless, attempts to diversify the economy failed nearly universally.[121] The numbers involved in Saudi budgets and aspirational plans bounced around. With an expenditure of $140 billion, the second five-year plan (1975–1980) was fourteen times as large as the first one (1970–1975), and thirteen times as large as the entire national income in 1973.[122]

Across the Gulf, American and British private consultants like Stanford Research Institute and Arthur D. Little Consultants often provided "extensive help" writing these plans.[123] Government-to-government assistance through foreign military sales, training, or the U.S. Corps of Army Engineers' formative role was also significant in the military realm (but not exclusively so).[124] Subsequently, the likes of McKinsey and Booz Allen Hamilton would form a near-symbiotic relationship with Gulf institutions engendering the creation of the mocking term, the Ministry of McKinsey.[125] Indeed, the familiarity between the Saudi Vision 2030 and McKinsey's 2015 report *Moving Saudi Arabia Beyond Oil* is striking.[126] At least in the Saudi case, these nascent industries were also staffed by the tens of thousands of citizens who received a higher education in the United States.[127]

Elsewhere in the Gulf, Bahrain's modest oil production (figure 3.5) and minimal expectation of finding more reserves prompted the state to make a more concerted effort to diversify its economy.

Having been the region's most advanced state, Bahrain had a "fifty-year start" when it came to formally educating its population compared to its neighbors.[128] Amid the 1975 Lebanon civil war, it became the preferred Middle East offshore banking center. Even its fellow monarchies headquartered their jointly owned Gulf International Bank in Manama. Supplying international financiers, Gulf Air—the airline then jointly owned by Bahrain, Qatar, Oman, and the UAE—expanded its routes, some of which were the most luxurious in the sky, with planes that had "a lounge,

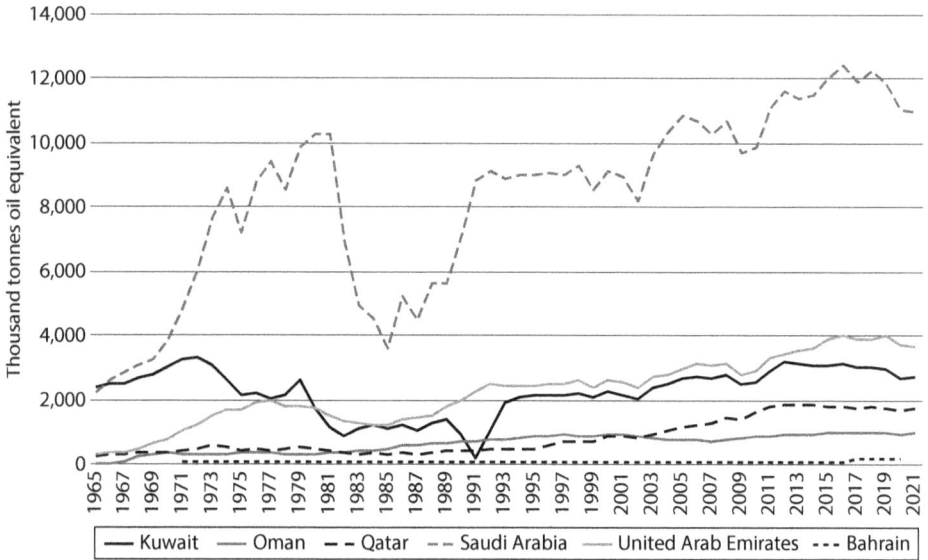

FIGURE 3.5 Crude oil production of the Gulf monarchies (1965–2021).

library, shop, radio-ground telephones and wide-berth tables with swivel chairs."[129] Despite fears of a severe drop-off in Bahrain's oil exports, as is often the case, new oil finds and better technology that resulted in reduced costs of exploration kept production steady. There was, thus, enough pressure on the government to oversee the emergence of a relatively stable financial sector, but not enough pressure to force a more widespread change in the state's rentier mentality.

Peaking oil prices in the 1970s and early 1980s swelled government coffers, reducing the incentives to institute painful but necessary policies to rebalance economies across the Gulf. Budget surpluses were invested in local industries and abroad into the early 1980s. They also fueled one of the world's most spectacular stock market bubbles. Flush with cash from the boom in the 1970s, a parallel stock exchange in Kuwait emerged in 1978, the Souq Al Manakh. Located in an air-conditioned parking garage "built over the old camel trading market," the Souq Al Manakh was an unregulated market from which new financial instruments emerged, like postdated checks.[130] It was phenomenally successful, taking on forty non-Kuwaiti stocks and with prices rising 200 percent in 1980 and 1981, to become the third-largest stock market in the world (in terms of capital traded) after the United States and Japan.[131] However, the convoluted system of (often multiple) postdated checks and lack of regulation meant that the system could not deheat slowly. Consequently, the 1982 crash was sudden and spectacular. In a seismic event in Kuwait, the government ultimately stepped in, shoring up public losses of $90 billion, or around $180,000 per citizen.[132]

Oil revenues tanked with the oil price crash from 1984. Capital spending on projects was slashed from 21 percent of GDP from 1981–1985 to 13 percent from 1985–1989, deficits were run, and states borrowed externally.[133] Iraq's invasion of Kuwait in 1990 exacerbated issues. Enduringly low oil prices led to minuscule growth rates of 2 percent, expanding budget deficits and external borrowing, and an overall decline in real GDP per capita.[134] Saudi Arabia, Kuwait, and Oman launched new plans to balance their budgets by the millennium, promising the usual litany of goals like private-sector growth and the development of local human capital.[135]

Contemporary plans acted as only visions, with generic long-term goals where the path to achieving them was underspecified.[136] Each monarchy has its longer-term vision project that contains some aspirational mix of building a knowledge-based economy, economic development, and diversification.[137] Saudi Arabia's King Abdullah (regent 1996–2005; r. 2005–2015) attempted to launch a Saudi non-oil economy by founding six new cities. Theoretically, this was to provide over a million jobs, house four and a half million people, and, by 2020, contribute a GDP of $150 billion.[138] Set against these ambitions, this project was a failure. Only one of the cities—King Abdullah Economic City—came to fruition, and today it has a population of under 10,000.[139]

Mohammed bin Salman reprised this approach from his multihatted perch as crown prince and head of the Saudi Vision 2030 plan to restructure the Saudi economy, which promised not megaprojects but "giga-projects."[140] Plans aimed at "cutting unemployment from 12 percent to 7 percent, raising women's participation in the workforce from 22 percent to 30 percent, increasing the private sector contribution to GDP from 40 percent to 65 percent, and boosting non-oil government revenues from SR163 billion ($44 billion) to SR 1 trillion."[141] In accompanying interviews, Mohammed bin Salman unrealistically asserted in 2016 that "I think in 2020 we can live without oil."[142] The core mechanisms through which Vision 2030 would transform the state are deeply neoliberal.[143] Thus, privatization of government assets from hospitals to schools to airports, public-private partnerships (PPPs), a fundamental embrace of international financial markets, and a hoped-for increase in Saudi competitiveness would lead the way.[144] The National Transformation Programme 2020 was delivered in June 2016 as a plan unpacking how the vision would be met. The *Financial Times*'s long-serving Gulf correspondent Simeon Kerr summed up the program as "Saudi Thatcherism."[145] As previously noted, the most stunning development, hinted at for months but confirmed in the Vision 2030, was a plan to privatize part of Aramco to fund PIF investment. The centerpiece of the proposed gigaprojects is a half-trillion dollar new city on Saudi Arabia's northwest coast, NEOM.[146] This futuristic city will be thirty-three times larger than New York City, it will rely on cloud seeding to alter its weather, "holographic teachers" will lead the education system, and there will be a Jurassic Park–style theme park with robotic dinosaurs. There are also plans for NEOM to be lit by a "giant artificial moon at night" and for "glow-in-the-dark" sand to be added to the region's beaches, and people will get around in flying taxis, naturally.[147] Another project under the NEOM banner was dubbed "the Line," a car-less, 105 mile long, 500 meter tall city encased in mirrored glass for up to 9 million residents.

Aside from the extravagant fripperies, much of Saudi Vision 2030 sounds familiar. The language, tools, and plans deployed are replete with neoliberal and state capitalist tropes and ideas peddled by Western consultants.[148] These kinds of arch neoliberal policies, like driving privatization of state assets and PPPs, are far from limited to Saudi Arabia.[149] Instead, they are core components of Qatar's National Development Strategy, Bahrain's health strategy, and Oman's ninth five-year plan (2016–2020), and they are widely employed across the Gulf, notably in the UAE and, amid much controversy, in Kuwait.[150]

The fact that the Gulf monarchies are home to many of the world's most audacious megaprojects is no surprise. Frequent financial windfalls periodically from peaking oil prices created fiscal surpluses. Such fiscal realities mean that spending several billion dollars building the world's tallest building, creating a mini-city of world-class university campuses, or building new cities from whole cloth is a plausible notion.[151] However, such ventures require the specific type of governance that exists in the Gulf, that of "enlightened despots," as Kamrava terms it.[152] Unelected but often enlightened and broadly benevolent leaders can be found around the Gulf, and they have grandiose visions for the future of their states, and many enjoy minimal fiscal or political impediments. Moreover, and quite crucially, plowing many billions of dollars into the local economy from either soft loans or straightforward hydrocarbon wealth is an ideal way to channel funds to loyal client groups in the state. Local construction magnate families are the most obvious—though far from the only—beneficiaries of the megaproject craze in the Gulf. Consequently, although these relations are not simplistic and these groups are not rendered inert or pliant drones of elites, the groups that benefit so handsomely from government contracts become vital supporters.[153]

Another reoccurring feature of Gulf visions and megaprojects is the scale of duplication. In the 1960s and 1970s, each monarchy gravitated toward industries that enjoyed a comparative advantage. This typically meant starting energy-intensive industries where cheap hydrocarbons could be used as fuel stock to leverage advantage, such as petrochemicals, aluminum, and steel production.[154]

If the 1970s and 1980s were the decades of industrial duplication, then the 2000s and 2010s were the eras of aviation and logistics duplication.[155] At one stage, the UAE alone hosted six international airports, and it continues to host two world-spanning airlines and other lower-cost regional aviation companies.[156] Such a concentration transcends the advantages of operating a regional cluster in a given industry, considering that Qatar Airways, Gulf Air in Bahrain, Etihad in Abu Dhabi, and Emirates Airlines in Dubai compete with each other—not to mention global airlines—for market share.[157] Although Saudi Arabia's airlines are seldom considered in the same category as other Gulf carriers, domestic business in the kingdom is significant. Jeddah's King Abdulaziz International Airport alone was the third busiest in the world in the early 1980s because of the pilgrimage passenger business.[158] The broader argument is not that duplication automatically means that these industries are failures or some such notion. World-spanning airlines can be real fillips to a state's visibility and tourism at the very least. Instead, the duplication critique is one of deep inefficiency in allocating regional resources.

Elsewhere in the transport infrastructure sectors, Dubai's Jebel Ali had a first-mover advantage in port logistics. The genesis of Dubai as a world-spanning port goes back to its entrepôt history and concerted efforts, noted earlier, to develop the scale of the venture from the 1970s. Jebal Ali, Dubai's principal port, was the eleventh busiest port in the world in 2022 measured in shipping volume. The next-biggest Middle Eastern port is Jeddah, coming in forty-fourth in 2022, indicating Dubai's grip on the local market.[159] DP World has a global portfolio of approximately eighty shipping terminals on six continents, and in 2019, its profits grew more than 10 percent despite being affected by the Qatar blockade.[160] Despite this domineering position, Kuwait, Oman, Qatar, and Abu Dhabi launched port projects, each one nibbling away at Dubai's share, driving down profits for one and all.[161]

KNOWLEDGE ECONOMIES AND LABOR MARKET REFORMS

Gulf leaders have long sought to encourage knowledge economies, which strive to root economic success on "intangible assets such as knowledge, skills, and innovative."[162] Leaders reason that the resulting jobs might be higher paying and more likely to attract Gulf nationals, given the strong taboos about what jobs are and are not suitable for a Gulf national to do.[163] Developing such an economy involves investing heavily in education and research and development and encouraging entrepreneurship, all for long-term payback.[164] The significant capital costs of launching such an economy are not that relevant in the Gulf oil context. The monarchies are eager to follow Singapore's path of a tiny, resource-poor state that nevertheless emerged to real prosperity by focusing on its human capital.[165] Moreover, there is an argument that capitalist economies are irreversibly shifting from value being derived from mass production by labor to "productivity and economic growth [derived from] knowledge and intellectual capabilities."[166] As such, the Gulf monarchies are striving to invest in economic models of the future, not the past. Indeed, knowledge economies are seen as a central step toward shifting the economic center of gravity in the monarchies toward a sustainable, posthydrocarbon economic model.

Many facets of knowledge economies are inherently intangible and difficult to ascertain. The successes of Silicon Valley in the United States and the rise to prominence of a state like Singapore are linked to the fruitful emergence and growth of knowledge economies, but precisely ascertaining their secrets is difficult. Various initiatives and structures underpinning their successes can be replicated, but the secret sauce is often elusive.

Gulf monarchies have certainly invested in the infrastructure underpinning a knowledge economy. With a reliable education system long assumed to be a critical factor in building a knowledge economy, many monarchies have invested heavily in this sector. Foreign higher-education institutions have been seen around the Gulf for decades. Sharjah, as already noted, hosted Maryland University and the Choueifat School decades ago. However, today Qatar is the region's leading example in this area. At the tertiary level, its Education City complex is an unquestionably impressive establishment hosting faculties of world-class institutions like Georgetown University and Texas A&M University. Around two thousand students have graduated from these institutions as of 2020, approximately 15 percent of whom are Qatari. Qatar has also invested in the widest-ranging educational reform processes in the Gulf. Led by the RAND Corporation under the emirship of Hamad bin Khalifah, he sought a root-and-branch reform of the Qatari education system to point it toward fostering more of a knowledge economy.[167] However, Qatar is not alone. Abu Dhabi has a clutch of top-tier foreign universities—including the Sorbonne and New York University—and Dubai, Bahrain, Kuwait, and Oman are peppered with lower-ranked institutions or outposts. The Qatar Science and Technology Park (QSTP), clusters in Dubai and Abu Dhabi (like Dubai Internet City and Masdar), and Saudi Arabia's King Abdullah University of Science and Technology (KAUST), are well-funded entities that strive to attract investment and enable research.[168]

Overall, research rooted in qualitative and quantitative data covering a range of metrics finds that Qatar leads the Gulf in terms of its readiness for a knowledge economy future.[169] Nevertheless, the Gulf monarchies lag far behind leaders like Finland and Singapore regarding networked readiness

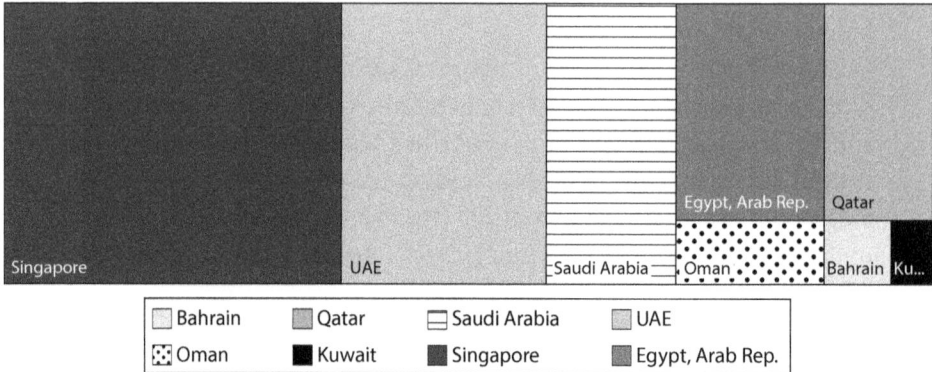

FIGURE 3.6 Research and development spending (% of GDP). Data is the latest available as of 2020: Bahrain 2014, Qatar 2015, Saudi Arabia 2013, UAE 2018, Oman 2018, Kuwait 2018, Singapore 2016, Egypt 2018.

Source: World Development Indicators, World Bank (2020).

and research and development spending for such comparatively wealthy states. As figure 3.6 shows, investment figures for Kuwait are exceptionally poor in terms of percentage of GDP.

Other indicators, like the Global Innovation Index, paint a similarly middling picture, with Qatar sixty-fifth in the world, the UAE thirty-sixth, and Kuwait sixtieth.[170] Such data does not, of course, provide a complete picture. Indeed, intangible aspects of knowledge economy creation are potentially even more important than infrastructure, policy change, or investment alone. Success ultimately depends on developing a cultural mindset that utilizes the tools and resources available to drive invention or innovation.[171] Indeed, in the context of forging a knowledge economy, Joseph Stiglitz emphasizes the importance of changing mindsets and beliefs and how such changes need to be intrinsic instead of coerced, induced, or incentivized.[172] Such an admonition could have been written specifically for the Gulf context, where leaders so often strive to direct change from above.

It remains to be seen how the more recent moves to forge a knowledge economy in the Gulf will turn out. However, the track record is not compelling. Instead, the pervasive influence of decades of distributive policies that forged the region's rentier bargain maintain a viselike grip across the labor markets for Gulf nationals. As Hvidt simply puts it,

> Only a very limited segment of GCC citizens actually work, many are uneducated or poorly educated and the incentive structures have emphasized employment in the public sector, where working hours are short, the demands few and the pay high compared with the private sector.[173]

Gulf citizen participation in the workforce (i.e., taking into account those not looking for work and those older or younger than working age) is notably low, at approximately 52 percent of men and 25 percent of women in the late 2000s.[174] Such figures are exacerbated by structures that allow, for example, certain Kuwaiti civil servants to retire on full pay after twenty years of service in their late thirties.[175]

This bargain is deeply institutionalized. Article 41 of the Kuwait constitution notes that "the State shall make work available to citizens." Pay in the public sector is often significantly higher than that in the private sector (for instance, by over 150 percent in Saudi Arabia and 245 percent in Kuwait); small wonder, then, that 80 percent of Qataris and 84 percent of Kuwaitis are employed in the public sector.[176] This results in notably low levels of labor productivity. The IMF and the Conference Board's Total Economy Database provide data attesting to generally poor levels of labor productivity in the public sectors in the Gulf monarchies, which have only worsened in recent decades.[177] Indeed, it must not be forgotten that salaries can be highly (or even entirely) unlinked to productivity, with wages being interpreted by all parties as a fundamental part of the state ruling bargain.[178] In this sense, the concept of employment and remuneration starts from a different epistemological premise in the Gulf, at least in its classic formulation.

This is a Gordian knot of a problem. Generations of practice inculcating the right that nationals have to a job with the government, minimal pressure in such work, and a de facto (if not de jure) inability to be fired from their positions coalesce to reify the ruling bargain. Governments worry about altering only one end of this expectation (i.e., removing benefits from citizens without rebalancing the bargain via forms of political representation).

Governments control their workforces primarily by hiring, firing, and expelling expatriates. Amid the COVID-induced economic crashes, all states have cut back on foreigners. Oman announced that 70 percent of foreign consultants working in the civil service would not have their contracts renewed.[179] Saudi Arabia expected to lose up to 1.2 million foreigners in 2020 after 445,000 already left in 2019.[180] Kuwait's prime minister Sheikh Sabah Al-Khalid Al-Sabah announced plans to reduce the state's expatriate population by more than 50 percent.[181] Slower approaches to rebalancing the labor force come from the "Saudization" programs and similar variants across the monarchies, which mandate specific percentages of nationals be employed in certain sectors. Such programs in the 1990s were toothless, but now they are becoming increasingly impactful.[182] Many obstacles remain. The fact that Gulf nationals refuse to do certain types of menial labor or want to move directly into more senior management positions is a regional reality, but that is changing slowly.[183] Nevertheless, one need not be a Friedrich Hayek devotee to worry about the impact of such significant state-driven interference in local markets and the distorting effects it brings.

Historically as well as today, difficult decisions are made during economic crises (e.g., cutting subsidies or increasing taxes), which are typically reversed when the oil pendulum delivers surpluses. The COVID pandemic and its initially cratering effects on oil prices slammed the monarchies. Oil revenue dropped 24 percent and non-oil revenue dropped 17 percent, causing Saudi Arabia to tap into its foreign reserves.[184] Qatar's export revenues were down nearly half from April 2019 to April 2020.[185] Kuwait ran a 40 percent budget deficit, which, combined with lawmakers' refusal to accept subsidy cuts, prompted the government to consider tapping into its SWF for funds.[186] One Gulf-focused consultancy calculated that the monarchies' combined fiscal deficit might reach a quarter of a trillion dollars (around 20 percent of GDP) in 2020–2021.[187]

Yet just as the fiscal situation was pressuring Gulf governments, forcing meaningful cutbacks, and a serious prioritization in spending, as has happened on numerous occasions in the past, the oil price rebounded swamping state coffers. Precipitated largely by the Russian invasion of Ukraine in 2022, the oil price (which is de facto linked to the gas price) spiked to $120 barrel, while gas prices in Europe skyrocketed to unprecedented levels. The IMF calculated that energy producing states in the

Middle East, which are predominantly found in the Gulf region, are in line for a $1.3 trillion windfall from 2022 to 2026. Gulf budgets surged into surpluses for the first time in years in some cases, and economic growth for the monarchies is expected to jump from 2.7 percent to 6.4 percent in 2022.[188] While a crucial boon for the Gulf economies, such sporadic surges in the oil price undercut the case for the urgency of economic diversification and change.

———— ✇ ————

The central thread of this book is rooted in this chapter and the nature of the political economy that underpinned the emergence, growth, and modernization of the Gulf monarchies in a particular image. For many regional states, the economy that has taken hold today replaced a remarkably similar political economy. The pearling industry shaped society around the search for, extraction, processing, and trade of a basically nonrenewable, finite, and locally occurring resource. In many cases, these statelets became wholly dependent upon this single commodity. From the structure of the day, season, and year being dictated by the needs of the industry to the ebb and flow of demand for mass immigration making locals a minority in their own lands, the pearling economy shaped the fabric of sociopolitical life.

With the swift extinction of this entire paradigm in the early twentieth century came a ruinous period for these smaller states and their societies. However, salvation appeared within a generation. Pearling was replaced across much of the Peninsula by the emergence of the oil industry. This economy was wildly more lucrative, so its shaping powers were even more dramatic. No element of the monarchies remained unchanged by the swift changes wrought by the necessities, realities, and results of expanding oil industries. While there are important differences among the monarchies, with the hydrocarbon paradigm being significantly larger and more dominant in some states, the overall effect of having this kind of extractive industry underpin the early stages of development created a critical path dependency for the states. Elites enjoyed unusual levels of control over the state's revenue compared to a more normal and organically diversified economics. They thus entrenched their positions and, building on customary norms, created some of the most generous welfare states on Earth.

This, in turn, created expectations for citizens who abrogated political rights for economic comfort, knowing full well that their endeavor, diligence, and efforts mattered comparatively little to the prosperity of their state and of themselves.

Nevertheless, for much of the last century, and with increasing concern, the Gulf monarchies strove to diversify their economies. It has long been known an axiomatic reality that the oil and wider hydrocarbon paradigm will dwindle someday, meaning that just as with the death of the pearling markets, states would be left in a calamitous economic position unless there were non-oil- and non-gas-related elements to national economies. However, despite generations of leaders being aware of this reality, no state has managed to meaningfully disentangle itself from the hydrocarbon paradigm and develop an unlinked non-oil economy, but this is not without trying.

Regional governments amassed some of the largest SWFs in the world. This gives Kuwait, Qatar, and the UAE substantial income, while Saudi Arabia is in the process of retrofitting its economy to power the foundation of the PIF, a mega-SWF that it hopes will similarly contribute to its future economy. However, as well endowed as these funds are, the IMF concluded that the region's saved wealth could be depleted by 2034. It seems odd that such immense savings—some $700 billion, in the case of Kuwait—could be eaten up in such a short time frame, especially when many monarchies will still receive substantial hydrocarbon receipts for years yet. However, to continue with the Kuwait example, the typical citizen is the beneficiary of state largesse and that is, via the parliament representing the views of their constituents, the key blockage to change. In 2020–2021, 74 percent of the government's budget was spent on salaries, allowances, and subsidies, a figure that has more than doubled since 2013.[189]

Within the monarchies, a range of world-leading companies emerged. However, they have almost always benefited from adjacency to the hydrocarbon industry, and thus cheaper fuel and the associated raw materials. Moreover, they are conspicuous by their very rarity in the Gulf. In essence, most Gulf companies are simply not as well run and profitable as they should be. As Tarek Fadlallah incisively notes, excluding financial firms and Aramco, the profits of the Gulf's top 600 companies have been "essentially flat" for the past fifteen years, despite the regional economy growing by around 140 percent.[190]

Recent history shows that the lavish spending on megaprojects and gigaprojects in the Gulf presents mixed results at best. Although these ventures initially have been a bonanza for local contractors, most of whom are by definition among the state's elite, the longer-term benefits are harder to deduce. Significant examples like the supposed creation of several new cities under the auspices of King Abdullah failed almost entirely to reach their own goals. Contemporary versions of this project under Mohammed bin Salman—NEOM, a city dubbed "the Line," and so on—look like similarly unnecessarily grandiose projects. It remains difficult to see how and why these ventures on a similarly colossal scale will work when others failed.

Otherwise, some of these glitzier projects hide progress elsewhere. For instance, female participation in the Saudi labor force is rising nicely, up to 25 percent from 18 percent, and privatizations are swiftly expanding the private sector.[191] Perhaps more significantly, a genuine shift in mentality is noted by essentially all researchers who visit the kingdom, with more and a wider range of jobs being undertaken by Saudis. This suggests that although concerns about the rentier mentality or citizen expectations of the ruling bargain are hurdles, they are not as unsurmountable as once feared.

4

MILITARY SECURITY

REG: We're the Peoples' Front of Judea!
LORETTA: Oh. I thought we were the Popular Front?
REG: Peoples' Front! C-huh.
FRANCIS: Whatever happened to the Popular Front, Reg?
REG: He's over there.
ALL TOGETHER: Splitter!

SCENE FROM *MONTY PYTHON'S LIFE OF BRIAN*

For Barry Buzan, Ole Wæver, and Jaap de Wilde, military security revolves tightly around states. Their logic runs that states are the primary referent object in the military realm because "states generally command far greater military resources than other actors but also because governing elites have evolved legally and politically as the prime claimants of the legitimate right to use force both inside and outside their domain."[1] As every liberal arts student knows, Max Weber grounded statehood in the ability of the state to uphold a monopoly on the use of violence within its borders.[2] Some modern doctrines (such as of the responsibility to protect) are nibbling at the edges of state sanctity and leaders' ability to use force.[3] Nevertheless, given the basis of contemporary sociopolitical organization, which fundamentally starts from the premise of the state and its rights, it is little wonder that states remain dominant in international affairs in the military realm.

The military sector thus puts mostly—though not exclusively—a focus on the state's role and its use of military means to defend itself from internal and external aggression. Internally, leaders consider the maintenance of civil order. States whose nationals are heavily outnumbered by foreigners, such as the United Arab Emirates (UAE) and Qatar, where the ratio is approximately 9:1 as a consequence of their political economies, are obliged to focus on this issue, as are governments where coups are a potential concern. Externally, the Gulf monarchies face an acute dose of the usual trials and tribulations that afflict states. Threats to territorial integrity like invasion and irredentist causes have plagued the Gulf, as have threats emanating from ideological roots, all of which may require the use of the military as a tool of state policy.

Toward this end, states, many of which have considerable hydrocarbon assets, might be considered to have an advantage. A comparatively or absolutely strong financial position allows them to develop high-end military equipment to shore up national security in a region that has seen one major conflict every decade throughout the lifetimes of most regional leaders. Indeed, the Gulf monarchies have certainly deployed their financial resources in the military realm, just not quite in the expected fashion.

Militaries can be used in different ways. The standard approach assumes that a state recruits its forces, trains its troops, and procures equipment to protect its territorial integrity and sovereignty and the national interest. According to Majid Khadduri, Middle Eastern states display a "keen interest . . . in organizing well-disciplined national armies along European lines," and the Gulf militaries certainly look the part.[4] The monarchies possess various land forces, militarized police forces, special operations forces, navies, coast guards, air forces, air defense forces, and offensive missile forces. Some monarchies are developing cyberwarfare capabilities. National day parades are an impressive sight, and the monarchies equip their forces with the best equipment that money can buy. In total, these states have spent over $1.5 trillion of their hydrocarbon-derived wealth on procurement and military base construction. Conscription was introduced in Qatar in 2014 and the UAE in 2015, and Kuwait brought it back in 2017. Moreover, the UAE and Saudi Arabia launched a large-scale series of military operations in Yemen in 2015, and Qatar and the UAE joined the North Atlantic Treaty Organization (NATO) forces in the alliance's operations in Libya in 2011. One might think that none of this is that unusual for states that have invested so assiduously in military forces.

However, as explored in this chapter, though replete with artifacts of militarism, the monarchies have tended not to use their military forces. Other rationales linked to developing relationships with security-providing allies better explain much Gulf military procurement than a more traditional desire to build a capable armed force. In this context, the war in Yemen challenges the status quo, which is why it is explored in detail here to ascertain what it means for the role of the military in the monarchies henceforth.

———— ✸ ————

The first section of this chapter, "Emerging and Evolving," surveys the founding of the modern security and defense forces in the Gulf monarchies. Advice from Western states extensively shaped the nascent forces in all the monarchies, who usually eagerly sought to diversify their security concerns to Western states, particularly with the uptick of regional spats. The second section, "Modernization and Threat Proliferation," continues chronologically, examining the breakout of conflict, notably on the south of the Arabian Peninsula in Oman and particularly Yemen. Flush with oil receipts in the 1970s, most monarchies significantly increased their military inventories. However, a growing difficulty emerged as the scale and complexity of military procurement increasingly outmatched the rate at which the monarchies could meaningfully use their forces. The final section, "Protection Curses and Moral Hazards," examines how the Gulf monarchies sought to square this difficult circle in recent decades. It analyzes how the monarchies increasingly vested security in the hands of the United States (and to a lesser degree, other Western states), notably after the liberation of Kuwait in 1991, which led to the installation of vast amounts of U.S. equipment on the Peninsula. Cocooned in the feeling that the United States was protecting the monarchies, elites continued to buy equipment more to maintain the protective status quo than to build actual, meaningfully effective military forces. The UAE and its role in the war in Yemen is then examined as an interesting counterpoint to this logic, signaling that elite direction can create genuine pockets of effective forces.

EMERGING AND EVOLVING

In the first decades of the twentieth century, Ibn Saud reconquered his family's ancestral lands by raising a shock troop of bedouin warriors known as the Ikhwan.[5] These camel-mounted troops were rudimentary but effective. However, their zealotry got the better of them. They railed against Ibn Saud's insufficiently puritanical policies, such as his tolerance of the sale of tobacco, and regional political agreements, and they refused to heed political borders. They attacked Iraq, which was under British protection, and nearly absorbed Kuwait into the growing Saudi territories in the early 1920s.[6] Such antagonistic behavior was precisely the reason for the Ottoman-led backlash that ended the first Saudi state. By 1930, a combination of other troops raised by Ibn Saud and the British destroyed the mutinying Ikhwan forces.[7] Foundational to Saudi Arabia's experience, therefore, was the specter of leaders whipping up religiously motivated forces that eventually ignored orders, struck out alone, incurred the wrath of powerful actors, and jeopardized the state's integrity.

The Saudi state remained aware of what it saw as its bedouin "problem"—poor, martially minded groups of tribes unhappy with the speed of change around them that curtailed their traditional ways of life—and Ibn Saud needed to find a way to control this latently powerful segment of society.[8] His approach was to institutionalize them into a new organization that depended on state largesse, in order to lower their likelihood of posing another internal security problem and give him a military force should he need one. The remnants and successors of the Ikhwan were thus folded into the Saudi Arabia National Guard (SANG), also known as the White Army "since its members wore no uniforms and reported for duty, rather haphazardly in those [early] days, in their white thobes [the long, flowing, often white, ankle and arm length garments traditionally worn by men on the Peninsula]."[9] Ibn Saud felt confident enough about the loyalty of the SANG forces to deploy them in 1934 to secure the Saudi claim on Najran and Jizan on the Yemeni border. One Saudi formation "marched in . . . from Najran and heading for Sana'a, made some progress before becoming bogged down in the [Yemeni] mountains."[10] Still, Ibn Saud managed to ensure acquiescence to his claim to the Asir region, on the Saudi side of today's Yemen border.

Subsequently, the SANG became a distinct "fourth force," existing outside traditional military structures and understood primarily as a praetorian guard for the Al Saud family (or parts thereof) until the rise of Mohammed bin Salman, who reintegrated it into the Ministry of Defence.[11] Initially, it maintained a bedouin approach, consisting of "a uniformed element called fedayin and a tribal element called mujahidin," overseen by bedouin sheikhs.[12] However, by the 1960s and 1970s, foreign forces were shaping regional armies according to Western doctrine. British-trained Jordanian officers were some of the initial trainers, while British and American teams were soon set up to shape and modernize the force.[13] The SANG grew to be a separate force based between regular armed forces stationed in Saudi's periphery and the main population centers, reinforcing the sentiment of a praetorian guard.[14]

While the Ministry of Defence was established in 1944, Saudi military structures other than the SANG emerged only from the late 1940s under British and then mostly U.S. tutelage.[15] The impact of British aircraft mowing down Ibn Saud's rebelling Ikhwan forces in the late 1920s and early 1930s bequeathed a heavy focus on airpower. Ibn Saud relied on a motley array of British, Italian, American, French, and Russian pilots, planes, and mechanics, with minimal indigenous capability into the 1950s and beyond.[16]

Mirroring Lugardian approaches elsewhere in the empire,[17] police forces and militaries in the smaller monarchies were created, trained, staffed, supplied, and overseen by the British. The goal was to strengthen the coercive capacities of local proxies to defend themselves against the vicissitudes of local politics.[18] A secondary factor—but one of growing importance from the 1930s onward—was the use of these forces for external protection against Ibn Saud.[19]

The first armed force organized in a fashion that would be recognized today was created in Sharjah in 1951 by the British, working with rulers of the Trucial States. The Trucial Oman Levies (renamed the Trucial Oman Scouts on March 19, 1956) were designed "for the maintenance of law and order and the protection of the shaikhdoms against eternal aggression."[20] Out of this British organized force emerged the Dubai Police in 1956, the Abu Dhabi Defence Force in 1965, the Ras Al Khaimah Mobile Force in 1969, the Dubai Defence Force in 1971, and the Sharjah National Guard in 1972.[21] The Trucial Oman Scouts were renamed the Union Defence Force upon the founding of the UAE in 1971.

The Trucial Oman Levies played a direct role in defending the territorial integrity and interests of the Trucial States and Oman in 1952 in the Buraimi Oasis dispute with Saudi Arabia. Contested by Oman and the would-be UAE, supported by the United Kingdom on the one side against Saudi Arabia on the other, this dispute contained elements of irredentism, resource competition (i.e., oil), tribal dynamics, and the shifting and diminishing powers of Britain as an arbiter.[22] Ultimately, after arbitration proved unsuccessful, the Trucial Oman Levies deployed in 1955 to drive out the Saudis. The next year, the Trucial Oman Scouts (as they became), over 10 percent of whom were British, fought counterinsurgency campaigns in Oman supporting local forces, foreshadowing further British involvement in the 1960s.

By the time independence arrived in 1971, intra-UAE competition had stoked the expansion of separate military commands. There was a notional state force, the Union Defence Force (approximately 2,500 strong), and the Abu Dhabi Defence Force (whose figures vary from 4,000 to 9,500 strong), and Dubai, Sharjah, Ras Al Khaimah, and Ajman all had or were developing forces.[23] Border skirmishes in living memory of leaders, tribal envy, and personal animosities—Shaikh Saqr of Ras al Khaimah evidenced an "almost pathological . . . fear and hatred of Shaikh Zayed"[24]—militated against the efficient decision to pool the separate forces.

In Qatar, the deputy commander of the British Land Forces Gulf outlined plans to Shaikh Khalifah, the de facto ruler from the late 1960s, for a Qatari military of 1,850 men.[25] A British special forces team began training Qatari forces soon afterward. Bahrain's leader, Shaikh Isa bin Salman Al Khalifah, wanted to model his forces on Saudi Arabia's White Army—that is, more of a bedouin-rooted army as opposed to a force with broader recruitment. Britain shaped the structure of the force, and in 1968 a Jordanian training team arrived and the Jordanian colonel Rushdi commanded the Bahrain Defence Force (BDF). Bahraini forces—of whom no more than 25 percent could be Shia, and neither could a Shia ever rise to become an officer—were trained in Jordan, the United Kingdom, and Iraq.[26]

British military leadership was retained for a few years after independence in most UAE-based military forces.[27] Elsewhere, the Omanis kept British leadership of their army until 1987, and their navy and air force until 1990.[28] In Bahrain and Qatar, armed forces emerged from British-run police forces. In Qatar, the armed police were overwhelmingly foreign:

British, Pakistani, and Yemeni, with only three Qataris in the ranks in the early 1960s. This reflected the reality of having a small population with a negligible history of martial training, the foreign-oriented nature of the force, and the ruler's desire to keep weapons out of the hands of locals.[29]

In a region with several looming threats—Saudi Arabia, the People's Democratic Republic of Yemen (PDRY), Iran, and Iraq—and generally only comparatively small, atomized defense forces, it seemed self-evident that the smaller sheikhdoms would band together. Initial Qatari plans for a nine-state federation came to be known as the Dubai Agreement and combined the Trucial States (Abu Dhabi, Dubai, Ras Al Khaimah, Sharjah, Umm Al Quwain, Ajman, and Fujairah) with Bahrain and Qatar. This idea was discussed, but it never materialized. The historiography on this putative federation offers various reasons for this failure. Long-term Qatar-Bahraini animosity played a part, as did popular sentiment in Bahrain for the formation of an independent state. Also, a 1970 United Nations (UN) visit to Bahrain that resulted in an official dismissal of long-standing Iranian claims to the archipelago encouraged Bahrain to go it alone.[30] Qatar followed Bahrain's declaration a few weeks later.

Having gone it alone, Bahrain's leaders were beset with security concerns. Shaikh Isa could scarcely fathom whether the threats to his rule came from his BDF or his police. The former was almost entirely Bahraini, and the latter was almost entirely foreign. This confusion resulted in Isa's undercutting of the BDF's capabilities by reducing its strength and blocking the reenlisting of soldiers beyond one three-year term.[31]

Upon independence in 1961, Kuwait's forces were approximately 4,500 strong, with only a modest armored component and a small air force.[32] However, the shock of Iraqi forces amassing at the border upon Kuwait's independence announcement prompted UK forces to return swiftly by launching Operation Vantage. Within months, the United Kingdom amassed substantial forces in Kuwait (approximately 7,000 troops strong), deterring an Iraqi invasion.[33] A British Kuwait Liaison Team (KLT) expanded continually from its inception in 1961 and spent the 1960s working with Kuwaiti forces. British officers throughout the Kuwaiti military were judged by the UK ambassador at the time to be "a valued and almost irreplaceable prop to the Kuwait Armed Forces."[34] A sense developed that the Kuwait Armed Forces were deeply dependent on foreign assistance, whether it be British forces or Pakistani pilot trainers and mechanics.

Even as local political sentiment led to the winnowing of the scope of the UK role in the KLT, in practice, Kuwait's military leadership wanted the UK role to continue. For example, when Kuwait founded its navy, it automatically turned to a Royal Navy officer, Commander Lofton Edward Peton-Jones, to establish and lead the force, which was shot through with former Royal Navy officers.[35]

After Operation Vantage in July 1961, British forces were replaced by a weaker Arab League force, prompting the British to base a high-readiness parachute battalion in Bahrain to develop Operation Sodabread, an intervention plan.[36] This vignette encapsulates the realities of the defense of the wider region: namely, defending Kuwait was of prime interest to the United Kingdom, Kuwait alone was incapable of defending itself, and even a multinational Arab force was not sufficient to defend the state.

Nowhere was the British military commitment greater in the Gulf than in Oman. A local insurgency morphed into a civil war between Dhofar and the sultanate of Muscat and Oman, where the British armed and trained Omanis and took part in the war on the side of Muscat. The United Kingdom supported, and perhaps even directed, the 1970 coup against the sultan, driving his replacement by his son, Qaboos. From the mid-1950s until 1975, Britain committed around 700 soldiers, including Special Air Services (SAS), engineers, and Royal Air Force (RAF) personnel.[37] British and Iranian support (the shah of Iran had contributed at least 5,000 men by 1975) was critical to putting down the insurgency, maintaining Qaboos in power, and safeguarding the integrity of Oman as a nation.[38] British influence would continue, such that there were more British than Omani officers in Omani forces until 1982.[39]

MODERNIZATION AND THREAT PROLIFERATION

The dynamics that had characterized the military sphere in the first half of the twentieth century did not shift precipitously as the century wore on. Internal threats to rulers continued, most of which—as discussed in chapter 1—revolved around ideological winds that stirred up discontent and challenge. External threats to territorial integrity were deeply salient as well. Oman's very existence was in question during its war against internal secessionists in the late 1960s and 1970s. The UAE lost three of its islands when Iran seized them in 1971, and neither the United Kingdom nor local forces could do anything about it. Lingering mistrust over Saudi Arabia's irredentist tendencies, precipitated primarily by the Buraimi Oasis incident, pervaded regional politics for decades. Kuwait had a profound shock in 1961 when, as previously noted, Iraqi forces massed on its border upon its independence. Qatar and Bahrain, two tiny nations, looked pensively at these machinations, realizing that they would be relatively ineffectual at deterring attack or defending themselves. Saudi Arabia, as the Peninsula's largest and most prominent state, faced a demonstrably hostile wider region. In 1962, Saudi forces faced Egyptian and Yemeni units, and in 1969 and 1973, PDRY forces attacked Saudi forces.[40] Threats animated by communist ideology proliferated. Thousands of Cuban, East German, and Czech military personnel appeared in Yemen. Indeed, Soviet influence grew across the region in Iraq, Egypt, Afghanistan, and the PDRY. This influence was manifested in the stationing of twenty naval ships in the Indian Ocean and the construction of twelve submarine pens in Aden and anchorages on Socotra Island.[41]

Accordingly, the monarchies continued to take twin approaches to state security, striving both to secure external alliances and develop their militaries. Against the multifaceted Egyptian/UAR/Yemeni/communist threats from southern Yemen in the early 1960s, the U.S. Air Force was deployed by President John F. Kennedy to defend Saudi airspace.[42] Moreover, the work of the United States to build up and train Saudi military forces continued apace, ranging from vast infrastructural works to a fundamental rebuilding of the Saudi navy to the reorganization of entire forces.[43]

The oil bonanza of the 1970s came at the right time. As the British withdrew in 1971 and the United States was at best lukewarm about replacing London's presence, the monarchies ramped up their military spending.[44] From 1973 to 1980, Gulf militaries grew in personnel by 35 percent, or over 40,000: Bahrain went from 1,100 to 2,500; Kuwait from 10,000 to 12,400; Qatar from 2,200 to 4,700; Oman from 9,600 to 14,200; Saudi Arabia from 42,500 plus 3,500 in the SANG to 47,000 plus 20,000 in the SANG; and the UAE from 11,150 to 21,150.[45]

However, the core change in the region's security dynamic in the latter half of the twentieth century was not internal, but external with the blooming of U.S. engagement throughout the region. The Nixon

Doctrine of the 1970s, spearheaded by U.S. president Richard Nixon, encouraged local powers to defend themselves, albeit with increased defense procurement from the United States. The Carter Doctrine of the 1980s declared that the United States was willing to use force if it had to defend its "national interests" in the Gulf region. During the 1984–1988 Tanker War, the U.S. navy entered the region at scale reflagging Gulf commercial shipping to protect them from attack from the belligerents in the 1980–1988 Iran-Iraq war. The United States took the lead role in an international coalition protecting Saudi Arabia and the other Gulf monarchies after Iraq invaded Kuwait in 1990 with Operation Desert Sheild. Some 600,000 U.S. troops were positioned throughout the Arabian Peninsula and led the liberation of Kuwait in 1991 with Operation Desert Storm. These two military operations, which were stunning military successes easily routing a vaunted, experienced, and feared Iraqi army, transformed the U.S. role in the Gulf. It moved from somewhere between a sizable but comparatively silent security partner for Saudi Arabia and Bahrain, and with a minimal security presence in Kuwait, Qatar, Oman, and the UAE, to taking a highly visible and preeminent security role across the entire Peninsula.

Of course, foreigners playing a variety of roles in the security sphere was not unusual in the course of Gulf history. British and Pakistani pilots continued to fly for the Royal Saudi Air Force in 1969, while the UAE and Pakistan "jointly owned" French Mirage III jets that were "purchased by the UAE but flown and maintained . . . by Pakistanis."[46] This situation was replicated elsewhere, with Pakistani servicemen being found throughout the militaries of the Gulf monarchies, not least with 1,500 in Saudi Arabia alone.[47]

Foreign support was required for several reasons. First, the smaller monarchies lacked sufficient population sizes. Yemeni, Jordanian, and Pakistani officers and troops made up for this fundamental deficiency in human resources. Second, even in Saudi Arabia, with its far-larger population, the challenges of forging capable fighting forces using modern (usually Western) technology and doctrine were legion. These organizations were new and foreign. The professionalism of foreign services could not simply be replicated and imported. This is not a value judgment, just a reflection of the reality that bedouin warfare was more of a raiding mentality than a day-to-day job with structured training.[48] The technical requirements of modern equipment, even in the 1960s and 1970s, were problematic considering that the talent pool of recruits suffered from poor schooling. Lest it be forgotten, ministries of education were barely a decade old and were rooted in rote-learning pedagogy.[49] Unsurprisingly, studies into military capability development noted that it took "twice as long" to train Gulf forces than those in the United States.[50] Ultimately, foreign forces were needed across the board—from trainers to logisticians to officers to commanders to pilots—to staff these complex, burgeoning militaries.[51] Third, a healthy smattering of foreigners throughout the militaries enhanced government control, given that foreigners were deemed more likely to be loyal to their paymasters rather than to vestiges of tribal or other domestic groups of alternative belonging.[52]

Reliable figures for the number of foreigners in Gulf military forces are lacking. In the 1980s, Laura Guazzone stated that one-sixth of the forces in Oman and Saudi Arabia consisted of foreigners, while it was approximately a third in the UAE.[53] In addition to the role of foreigners in Gulf forces, from what open-source information is available, Oman and the UAE sought and received defensive agreements from the United Kingdom until at least 1986 (despite considerable British concerns about their putative role in a crisis).[54]

However, such foreign interaction and presence stressed bilateral relations. Before the Iraqi invasion, because of its feisty parliament, Kuwait exhibited an anti-American stance rooted in Arab anger about U.S. support for Israel against the Palestinians. Such sentiments were sporadically apparent across the Gulf. Saudi Arabia was the region's aspiring hegemon whose founding raison d'état was rooted in a conservative form of Islamism that sat uncomfortably with increasingly close U.S. relations in an era of anticolonial and anti-Western sentiment. Consequently, the presence of foreigners was problematic. Leaders had to manage the paradox that building forces to counter internal threats based so heavily on the influence and requirement for ever-more foreigners might ironically provoke internal discontent. Indeed, regionally, at a time of bubbling Arab nationalism and anti-Western sentiment, the presence of foreigners creating "the appearance, and perhaps the reality, of dependence" was something to be avoided at all costs.[55]

Also playing into this was the fear of foreigners as transmission sources of radical ideas. As noted already, this was a concern going back decades, with coup attempts against Ibn Saud in the early 1940s believed to have been led by Italian officers and coup attempts in the 1950s and 1960s led by officers under the sway of Arab nationalism.[56] A consequent desire not to have too many of any one foreign nationality in a segment of their forces (for appearances' sake and lest they get too influential) prompted Gulf leaders to diversify the foreigners they employed. However, this just worsened the broader situation. Employing different nationalities in training or commanding roles meant instituting various doctrines, training regimens, and procurement paths, which bedeviled interoperability.[57] In the mid- to late-twentieth century, decisions created multidecade path dependencies that plague interoperability at all levels (i.e., within an army, between service arms, and between countries) to this day.

PROTECTION CURSES AND MORAL HAZARDS

Most literature examining the monarchies' militaries concludes that there is a fundamental lack of seriousness in military affairs and, as Richard Russell puts it, the states are "long on hardware, short on power."[58] The overall record offers a sobering tally. Time and again, regional military forces struggled to defend state interests when required. Omani forces needed significant British and Iranian assistance in the Dhofar conflict in the 1960s and 1970s.[59] During the 1984–1988 Tanker War, hostile actions from Iran (and Iraq on occasion) targeted the monarchies' economic lifeline—their oil tanker fleets. Unable to do anything about this, the Gulf monarchies called for international support and the reflagging of their tankers for protection.[60] Logically, the Gulf monarchies ought to have had (and still ought to have), pound for pound, some of the strongest navies on Earth, given their near-complete dependence on seaborne oil exports. However, this was not—and still is not—the case.[61]

The starkest example of the failure of Gulf militaries came in 1990, with the Iraqi invasion of Kuwait. It is not surprising that a small state like Kuwait could pose little more than a speed bump for an invasion from a much larger state. However, Saudi Arabia also needed to call for international help. This failure cannot be glossed over. Saudi Arabia was a substantial state, with aspirations of regional hegemony, and it spent hundreds of billions of dollars on its forces. Nevertheless, it was unprepared to face an evident and fairly predictable challenge to state sovereignty, something typically seen as the core job of an armed force. Indeed, Saudi Arabia, a state with profound qualms about its decades of close relations with the United States, had to call for protection from over half a million foreign men and women, mostly Americans.

In the aftermath of the invasion and liberation of Kuwait, the monarchies immediately looked for external protection. A 1988 proposal by Egyptian president Hosni Mubarak for the stationing of up to 15,000 troops to secure the Gulf monarchies in return for financial support was revived.[62] Later, a proposed Damascus Declaration was to base Syrian and Egyptian troops in the monarchies to protect them, in return for financial support.[63] However, this declaration "dwindled into nothingness," as Gulf leaders did not trust their fellow Arab leaders, and they got a better offer.[64] The invasion transformed Kuwait from a state once prickly toward the United States to its biggest champion. A local petition calling for the U.S. base to stay in Kuwait gathered more signatories than voters. Despite initial denials about foreign bases in Kuwait—"mere pie in the sky," said Shaikh Jaber al-Ahmad Al-Sabah[65]—this is precisely what transpired. Such was the transforming nature of the invasion.

Arguments as to the incapability of Gulf militaries are damning, but the critique must be tempered. The monarchies suffer from a lack of analysis, and their military and security affairs even more so.[66] This reflects difficulties in researching sensitive topics in autocracies. Moreover, since the Arab Spring, there has been a regionwide narrowing of the intellectual space for such conversations, further stifling research.[67] Accordingly, it is more likely that long-held assumptions, correct or otherwise, may reverberate around academic or policy communities. Nevertheless, keeping such limitations in mind, two baskets of critiques can be identified: one finds explanatory variables in political decisions, the other in culture.

The first explanation argues that leaders make political decisions to weaken their military forces or, to put it slightly differently, choose not to put in the required effort to forge capable military forces. For example, the literature exploring the topic of coup proofing argues that leaders, usually in autocratic states, make political decisions to introduce measures to undercut the effectiveness of their military forces (or large segments thereof) so that they do not pose as much of a threat to the leader's rule.

Indeed, autocratic leaders, the statistical record shows, should rationally fear usurpation by competitors from the military or political rivals using military force.[68] Modern militaries are powerful institutions, corralling thousands of individuals inculcated to follow orders from a small group of leaders.[69] Florence Gaub notes that "as little as 2 percent of the armed forces can execute a successful coup," and barely more than a few dozen people at leadership levels.[70] Such regional lessons were not lost on the monarchs of the Gulf, and the record is full of instances where leaders took measures to weaken their forces, fearing they might become too potent.

Saudi Arabia long employed a range of coup-proofing methods. The SANG was, as noted previously, a fourth force loyal to the leadership, to check the power of the regular armed forces that were historically the focus of coup-proofing concerns.[71] Levels of centralization in regular forces were such that spare parts and ammunition were controlled at strategic levels, limiting core resources to inhibit their ability to mobilize and revolt.[72] Control in the armed forces was exerted through appointments on the basis of loyalty rather than merit. This led to an overpromotion of royals throughout the monarchies (except in Oman), which harmed efficiency.[73] This culture of heavily centralized decision-making mingles within a highly stratified society and proves to be particularly problematic.[74] Centralized leadership fosters a competitive atmosphere at elite levels and creates fiefs that undermine interservice and intraservice coordination. Risa Brooks argues that this means "these militaries will be at a systematic disadvantage in maneuver warfare," the standard approach to warfighting for much of the last one hundred years.[75] Indeed, modern militaries prioritize jointery or jointness—the joint operation of different services—to leverage the added value and unique skill sets of each force to achieve a given task.[76] Gulf militaries typically took precisely the opposite approach, atomizing their forces, actively keeping forces and parts of forces apart, and keeping them unpracticed in working together in order to lessen any putative threat they might pose. It would, for example, make sense to intertwine the air force and air defense forces, given that both are inter alia tasked with defending a state's airspace. However, in Saudi Arabia, they were kept distinct and remain apart.[77]

None of these policies prevented the monarchies from engaging in large procurement programs. The six monarchies have spent over $1.5 trillion on weapons since records began, which, if anything, is an underestimation, given the dozens of years of data not available.[78] By comparison, China only spent 8.5 percent more ($1.6 trillion).[79] The point here is not to make exact comparisons. Instead, it points to the colossal scale of expenditure that conventional conceptions of military power argue means that the military forces of the Gulf monarchies are strong. Instead, procurement in the monarchies was often (if not usually) whimsical and clearly not the result of a sober assessment of the state's requirements. Anthony Cordesman, the most prolific author focusing on the Gulf militaries writing in Arabic or English, describes procurement as too often driven by leaders' desire for the "glitter factor" rather than for meaningful operational and strategic rationales.[80] Alternatively, at the very least, other strategic priorities played outsized roles in procurement logic, like channeling funds to certain parts of the ruling family as another way of shoring up elite support.[81] Other scholars argue that procurement is undertaken "based on the military commanders' preference rather than on the nation's need for these specific arms or the armed forces' ability to maintain them."[82] Indeed, it has been suggested that the monarchies buy equipment from specific international allies according to what might be termed the "protection racket theory of procurement."[83] This logic runs that a $10 billion purchase is more about the implicit political guarantees that are believed to come with such a large investment rather than the actual military capabilities acquired.[84]

This is not to say that similar logics never appear for procurement decisions elsewhere.[85] Instead, the argument is that the literature finds such logics notably persuasive in the Gulf region. This approach is still arguably in evidence in some monarchies, as with Qatar's acquisition of three models of advanced fast jets from France, the United States, and the United Kingdom. This decision is militarily illogical. No procurement board would choose to obtain three exquisitely complex, different types of fast jets from three different suppliers. This odd approach creates unnecessary and expensive complexities in training, interoperability, logistics, doctrine, and facilities management, including basic issues like the three jets often needing unique sets of tools and different fuels.

Moreover, Qatar's military requirements egregiously outstrip the numbers that its population can provide. This is not a new problem, but today's recruitment issues are far more significant than in the past. With a native population of approximately 300,000, there is minimal room to expand organically. Encouraging ex-Jordanian military officers to sign up (and other such approaches) will be the only viable way to fill the spots.[86] This kind of approach asks difficult questions about the future role of Qatar's military if it is stuffed full of foreigners. In such a light, the state's strategy of using its military as a diplomatic tool rather than a defensive force per se makes more sense. Indeed, the standing-up of a Typhoon fast jet and a Hawk training jet squadron with the United Kingdom is a smart way to get the British deeply involved in Qatari affairs.[87]

A linked phenomenon is leaders making political decisions not to strive to forge capable military forces because they simply do not feel the need to do so. In this conceptualization, the Gulf monarchies suffer profoundly from a "protection curse" unintentionally foisted upon them by the United States.[88] The resource curse, a concept familiar to those examining the Gulf monarchies,[89] argues that an overabundance of an ostensible benefit, such as the presence of vast amounts of hydrocarbon wealth, confoundingly reliably leads to a range of weak socioeconomic and democratic indicators. It is much the same with the protection curse. The presence of an ostensible benefit—in this case the presence of abundant implicit guarantees of U.S. protection for the Gulf monarchies—leads reliably to unusually and surprisingly weak levels of domestic Gulf military effectiveness. In essence, the United States created a moral hazard for the monarchies. In such a situation, actors are enticed to act in a way that otherwise might be harmful "because it—in this case, the state—is insulated from the risks of its actions."[90] The simple but powerful kernel of logic underpinning the protection curse argues that regional *perceptions* of solid international security and defense guarantees allowed Gulf leaders to continue implementing deleterious cultural methodologies and take an unserious approach to creating military power.

It started innocently enough. After the Iraqi invasion, Kuwait purged up to three-quarters of its armed forces through a mix of retribution for their failure and fear that stateless soldiers and officers (i.e., the bidoon) could not be trusted. Kuwait did this reassured by the knowledge that U.S. forces would, perhaps for a decade, provide the state's ultimate defense.[91] However, the curse deepened and widened. Today, with vast U.S. military command and logistical bases in Kuwait, Qatar, Bahrain, and the UAE—and smaller but not insignificant bases in Oman from which the United States conducted operations from Afghanistan to the coast of Somalia—the Gulf region is a core part of the *pax Americana*.[92] Saudi Arabia also used to host regionally critical U.S. military facilities. While there are no legal defensive agreements in place whereby the United States promises to defend a Gulf state if attacked, the explicit security guarantee made by President Jimmy Carter in the 1970s has been upgraded with shows of force by subsequent leaders.[93] The United States does not preposition entire brigades, equipment, a fleet, multiple air wings, and a special operation command in the Gulf because it lacks space within its continental borders; it does so because that guards the status quo in the region from external aggression, for the time being at least.

Thus, as with the resource curse, the vast presence of something beneficial brings with it a range of unforeseen detrimental externalities. The pernicious mechanism at play with both curses is the removal of pressure on leaders to make necessarily difficult choices, whether in the sociopolitical or the military sphere. If leaders feel secure thanks to— what they, perhaps erroneously, feel to be—external implicit protection agreements, they do not need to focus on forging capable domestic armed forces, so they do not need to carefully match military means to political ends. This means that states can procure whatever they want. This is surely the reason why the monarchies have long purchased the leading fast jets available but seldom invested in any meaningful sense in, for example, minesweeping capabilities.[94] The former is as eye-catching as military technology gets, showcasing the state's prowess through its ability to fly the same jets as the superpowers. The latter—minesweepers—are defensive, slow, and hardly set pulses racing. Yet the Gulf monarchies are critically dependent on the seaways for most of their imports and almost all of their hydrocarbon exports.[95] Moreover, the monarchies argue that Iran is a menacing state in the Gulf that has long threatened to shut down the Strait of Hormuz.[96] Despite being a strategic fixation of the security establishments in the monarchies for generations, minesweepers—the critical equipment required in such an eventuality—are noticeable by their relative rarity in local navies.

Other scholars offer culturally rooted explanations for the lack of military effectiveness of the monarchies' militaries despite vast outlays on equipment. Kenneth Pollack, who has written over half-a-million words on the subject, concludes that Arab military forces overall have consistently evidenced debilitating issues of poor tactical leadership, poor information management, poor weapons handling, and poor maintenance.[97] This is because, he argues, there are a range of Arab cultural "patterns and predilections"—things like conformity, centralization of authority, and manipulation of information—that inhibit military effectiveness.[98] Similarly, Novell De Atkine, a former U.S. Army colonel with decades of experience working with and training military forces in the Arab world, argues that fundamentally different cultural approaches of Western and Arab military forces mean that "decades of western-led military training on western military kit has been—and will be—an exercise in 'pounding square pegs into round holes.' "[99]

However, recent research suggests that such essentialist explanations that rely on culture as the master variable are wide of the mark.[100] The UAE, in its 2015 war in Yemen, undertook successful amphibious landings in Aden and Mukalla, into hostile territory far from its home bases, using jointness and coalition forces that allowed operational goals to be reached.[101] This was not a perfect operation, some goals were not met, and there were real setbacks along the way. However, such a large-scale, broadly successful operation challenges Orientalist-oriented explanations that see, explain, and predict that Arab forces will inherently struggle in modern warfare for cultural reasons. The UAE has also consistently evidenced regionally atypical capabilities in recent years when it comes to its special operations forces and its Joint Aviation Command (JAC), the unit in charge of most of its aircraft and helicopters, in both of which foreigners play important leadership roles.[102]

Nevertheless, UAE military successes in aspects of its Yemen campaign are the only documented outlier of a Gulf military force performing demonstrably above expectations. According to the scholarly commentary, Saudi forces in Yemen performed as poorly as expected. Otherwise, commentary is broadly agnostic on the military effectiveness of the Kuwaiti, Qatari, Bahraini, and Omani military forces, as there are few opportunities for evaluation. Nevertheless, interviews with NATO military officers and academics with extensive experience working in Gulf military institutions continue to offer robust critiques of local forces, with only a few notable exceptions (usually to be found in each state's special operations personnel).[103]

The two explanations for this underperformance—political choice in the form of coup proofing or cultural (Orientalist) rationales—can be reconciled. Culture is real, it exists, and it has widespread effects. At the 2018 FIFA World Cup, for example, Japanese soccer fans picked up their litter in Russian stadiums after matches not because they were instructed to, but because this was a culturally imbued element of their behavior. Similarly, it is perfectly reasonable to posit that different cultures engage with military training differently. Some cultures, states, and people may be better or worse at adhering to training methodologies. Ultimately, it is not irrational to think that culture affects military effectiveness. However, there is no reason to think that culture is an implacable obstacle. The UAE case study in Yemen demonstrates vignettes where UAE forces evidenced levels of proficiency that negate to no small degree the generalized cultural exhortations cautioning that Arab states cannot succeed in modern military environments.

Cultural impediments, to the degree that they are indeed impediments in the Gulf, can be overcome by political decision-making, at least on a smaller scale. Mohammed bin Zayed Al Nahyan, the key UAE leader in question, chose to pursue the active creation of large pockets of military effectiveness in the UAE's armed forces, having decided that coup-proofing concerns were not as relevant an issue. The story of the UAE highlights that a longer-term political strategy to actually develop capable forces yields results. The contrasting Saudi story reconfirms much of the criticism directed at Gulf militaries. The Saudi war in the north of Yemen was intrinsically difficult. Nevertheless, it was in Saudi control when to start the conflict, and the state benefited from decades of procurement of top-of-the-range equipment. Plus, the war was well within the Saudi state's operation ambit near its border with Yemen, and the Saudis had fought (and struggled) in an analogous, if smaller, conflict against the Houthis in 2009–2010.[104] Lessons ought to have been learned. With such advantages, the fact that Saudi forces struggled so badly in this conflict offers a staunch critique of their military effectiveness.

The UAE provides a pathway for other monarchies to follow. However, it is unclear whether Emirati lessons are that translatable. For example, one essential facet of the UAE approach was to empower foreigners within their forces meaningfully, to the point where the former head of Australia's Special Air Service (SAS), Mike Hindmarsh, was tasked with setting up and then running the UAE presidential guard. This would be a difficult (virtually impossible) approach to take in Saudi Arabia, to have such a large country admit that it needed a foreigner to professionalize its forces. Indeed, this concept—outsourcing the lead role in their state's presidential guard (or equivalent)—draws a flat, unequivocal rejection even in the smaller monarchies.

However, it may be necessary for the Gulf monarchies to develop higher levels of military self-sufficiency. Fundamental shifts are transpiring in the Gulf with the protection curse. The implicit U.S. security guarantees that have acted as the bedrock of Gulf security for generations are waning. The September 2019 attacks on Saudi Arabia's Abqaiq and Khurais oil facilities by drones and cruise missiles launched by Iran and its proxies (or so it is widely believed) was a stunning moment in Gulf history.[105] Moreover, these attacks came after several incidents of Iran boarding and holding ships hostage and mine attacks on shipping in the Gulf, also seemingly conducted by Iran.[106]

The central point of the U.S. interest in the region—the reason for the decades of difficult but close relations and the hundreds of billions of dollars of investment in the politico-military-industrial complex—is arguably above all else to prevent precisely these kinds of attacks on the world's most important oil infrastructure. U.S. deterrence was supposed to stop these attacks. Then, in the event of an attack, U.S. military technology, acquired at vast expense, was supposed to intercept missiles from Iran, a state comparatively impoverished and generations behind the latest U.S. technologies. However, the offending missiles and drones whistled unperturbed through expensively assembled U.S. defenses, with neither interception nor much warning. The U.S. reaction was then the opposite of reassuring. Amid general bluster from President Donald Trump, eventually, he relocated some U.S. forces to the region, but this was scarcely more than a run-of-the-mill force redeployment. Then, within a few months, the extra U.S. Patriot antimissile batteries that were deployed (to cover U.S. forces) were withdrawn because the forces were only ever meant to be on a short tour, and they returned home.[107]

If the concern were just a spate of attacks, there would be more room for reconciliation. However, there has been a burgeoning, lingering disenchantment with the United States growing over several years in the Gulf.[108] It started with a lack of support for regional strongmen during the Arab Spring. Despite Hosni Mubarak's three decades of close U.S. relations, when there were a few protests in Cairo (at least from the perspective of the Gulf monarchies), U.S. support was nowhere to be seen. There was also a feeling of minimal Arab Spring solidarity with the Al Khalifah in Bahrain. Then the United States spearheaded the Joint Comprehensive Plan of Action (JCPOA)—the Iran nuclear deal—which was interpreted in the Gulf as the United States dealing with the devil. This move began the fulfillment of long-held, fatalistic assumptions in the Gulf that the United States would eventually sell out their interests in favor of an Iranian rapprochement. This deal compounded regional disillusionment with U.S. president Barack Obama's administration, which was perceived to be aloof, too pro-Iranian, and insufficiently pro–Gulf monarchies. Obama's pivot to Asia policy was seen as a slight by those in the Gulf as further evidence of the drifting U.S. focus from the Gulf to elsewhere (in reality, it was more a pivot from Europe, and there was no meaningful U.S. force drawdown from the Gulf itself until the withdrawal from Afghanistan in 2021). Then the Abqaiq attack happened.

Unless there is a conventional attack by Iran or U.S. citizens are killed quite demonstrably by Iran in an attack, U.S. disengagement is likely to increase fast. The United States will not disappear from the Gulf. Generations of procurement and training have bequeathed a path dependency of doctrine, norms, and equipment that will last decades in some cases. However, with the implicit protection from the United States now explicitly questioned, shifts can be expected as leaders realize they are increasingly on their own.[109] Certainly, there will be considerably more diversification away from the United States as a core arms supplier. Indeed, long exacerbating this issue is the U.S. (and wider Western) adherence to the Missile Technology Control Regime (MCTR), which places limits on the kinds of technologies that can be sold. Of particular relevance recently has been the traditional U.S. refusal to sell armed drones, despite considerable entreaties from the Gulf monarchies. President Trump relaxed restrictions to allow some limited sales, but Chinese drones have filled this potential U.S. market gap for years.[110]

The UAE's leadership saw decades ago that Uncle Sam's guarantees might be useful against a conventional Iranian threat but would likely be minimal help against ideational challenges to political order at the substate level. They were correct. Most recently, in the 2015 war in Yemen, the monarchies were displeased to see that the United States would offer only grudging logistical assistance. This was despite the view in the Gulf that this was a war of necessity against imminent dangers posed by the Zaydi Houthi rebels who, the monarchs maintain, are little more than an Iranian proxy force.

Linked to these developments, it is noticeable that the military's role is changing in different monarchies. In the UAE, the presidential guard and the air power component of the military (under the control of the JAC) are genuinely potent. This is a change from the recent history of the monarchies and their militaries. Moreover, at least temporarily, with an increasing military footprint in the Horn of Africa, the UAE is emerging as a regional power.[111] The war in Yemen demonstrated a willingness to launch an offensive campaign for the first time in the Gulf's recent history, putting Gulf nationals in harm's way. Saudi Arabia crossed the same threshold to colaunch the war with the UAE, indicating a new relationship between military and state.

In the hands of an iconoclastic leader like Mohammed bin Salman, who witnessed the UAE's comparatively more successful campaign, significant changes are to be expected. Moreover, seeing Iranian and Houthi missiles whistling through critical missile defenses must challenge deeply held certainties, both in the role of the United States and the utility of Saudi forces. Some structural changes in the Ministry of Defence have already occurred.[112] However, changing cultures and institutional practices seldom occurs quickly. Saudi leaders revived the mirage of establishing some kind of Arab NATO, possibly linked to a similarly reanimated Gulf Cooperation Council (GCC) military force.[113] However, the participants would need a historical lobotomy for such an organization to succeed—such are the levels of intra-alliance difficulties consistently evidenced in recent generations.

The military sector plays a comparatively smaller role in daily political discourse in Kuwait, Bahrain, and Oman. These states are neither concentrating on redeveloping their forces as the UAE and Saudi Arabia have done nor fastidiously and extravagantly bolstering long-held international alliances like Qatar. Instead, they take a middle road, continuing to work closely with international allies with whom they have bonded for generations. Oman reengaged with the United Kingdom, signing a significant defense agreement in 2019 that provided, at the very least, an uptick in joint training and the opening of a UK naval base in Duqm, on the Arabian Sea. Similarly, the United Kingdom made permanent a preexisting naval base in Bahrain in 2018. In Kuwait, meanwhile, discussion abounded about the opening of a UK military base, although this idea has fizzled out for the moment.[114] Such commitments fit with the broad tenor of a downturn in trust in the United States and a slight hedging toward the United Kingdom, reflecting a deep continuity in an era of change.

The military sector of security is in many ways the simplest to grasp. It typically concerns the protection of state sovereignty from physical attack and destabilization, whether from internal or external sources, and the use of military and related security forces in this endeavor. Moreover, a region like the Gulf would seem to be a natural home for these concerns. It is important not to see the region as a backwater, dominated by a Hobbesian logic until the advent of the age of empire. Equally, the historical record is quite clear that tribes engaged in frequent and repeated squabbles among themselves. And the arrival of empires did quieten regional conflict, especially littoral ones, as that was the primary concern of the British at the time.

These foreign empires were often not imposed at the point of force from abroad. Some local leaders sought out foreign powers, so long as they could be leveraged to their advantage to augment a leader's security and position. With the freezing of ruling families in the topmost positions due to their engagements with foreign powers, so territorial boundaries became ever more solidified. The need to maximize one's land amid the search for oil challenged boundaries, and some changed, but typically local and external power reinforced borders, as they were sometimes drawn by treaty.

Securing the proto-state then saw the foundation and development of professional armed forces in a broadly Western image. Western equipment was procured, and Western officers established most of the region's force structures and led the training of local soldiers, with increasing help over the years from officers from the likes of Jordan, Iraq, and Pakistan. Many Gulf leaders supplied their forces with high-end military equipment. There are three reasons for this. First, this can be explained as a reaction to the sizable latent threat posed by Iran and Iraq, as well as (for the smaller monarchies) Saudi Arabia. Second, such purchases were part of the intraregional "monuments race," whereby leaders sought to boast of their level of advancement by building the biggest bridge or building or acquiring the latest weaponry. Third, these acquisitions often included embedding foreign advisers in local forces, linking Gulf forces to their Western counterparts. At the same time, commercial imperatives became self-reinforcing. Life maintenance, logistical support, and training created a stream of income from the ever-richer monarchies to (usually) Western states engaged in an often-bitter competition to secure these lucrative contracts.

Procurement was often infamously whimsical in the monarchies, particularly in the twentieth century. Leaders repeatedly made conscious political choices to inhibit the effectiveness of their armed forces, even in the face of a clearly dangerous region. Such decisions are partly explained by leaders engaging in coup-proofing practices whereby they feared that genuinely powerful armed forces might be used to topple them from power, as happened dozens of times in the twentieth century in autocratic states. However, remotely rational leaders would realize that in denuding their own forces of potency, they were increasing the vulnerabilities of their states—and their own position therein—potentially significantly. While some might have simply seen this as a reasonable wager, one could argue that Gulf leaders increasingly fell into a U.S.-created protection curse. This allowed many regional leaders to take a fundamentally unserious approach to securing their states in any meaningful way.

Indeed, many harder-edged discussions of Gulf security will likely be split into pre- and post-Abqaiq eras. Before the stunningly successful drone and missile attacks on the world's most important oil refining facility in September 2019, the Gulf monarchies luxuriated in a protection curse–driven fiction about the role of the United States and what it means for their security. With the Abqaiq attacks, these myths dissolved. The might of the U.S. military was not enough to prevent the attacks. Then it was seen that U.S. military technology did not stop comparatively cheaply assembled drones and Iranian-designed missiles, winging their way unopposed through air defenses to strike one of the most important critical national infrastructure sites on the Peninsula with unerring accuracy. Compounding these concerns, the U.S. reaction lacked any real redress.

In this new era, Gulf leaders are reconceptualizing how to secure their states. There has been a noticeable shift from the monarchies toward Iran and the JCPOA discussions. Shorn of the U.S. security blanket, which long clouded their calculations and gave them a profoundly false sense of security, even hawkish regional leaders sought to deescalate tensions with Iran and supported the JCPOA negotiations. Given the approach to defense evidenced in the past century or two, it is unsurprising to see Gulf leaders reflexively seek to root security in international alliances or agreements. Indeed, there has been an uptick in engagement with lesser powers like the United Kingdom, including opening a second UK military base in the region in Duqm, Oman joining Al Jufair in Bahrain, and Turkey and France also having a regional presence. It seems, therefore, that the region is shifting from the domination of the security environment by a single country, the United States. Instead, hedging against ever more U.S. drawdown from the region, some monarchies are actively seeking to forge significant indigenous military capability of their own. Meanwhile, the wider trend is toward a mosaic approach to security, with the proliferation of more, if smaller, security and defense engagements with lesser powers.

5

ENVIRONMENTAL SECURITY

Growing . . . cereals at an exorbitant cost in the desert makes about as much sense as planting bananas in Alaska.

JOHN BLOCK, FORMER U.S. SECRETARY OF AGRICULTURE,
OPINING ON SAUDI ARABIA'S AGRICULTURAL SUBSIDIES IN 1985
(QUOTED IN JONES [2010])

Barry Buzan, Ole Wæver, and Jaap de Wilde identify five broad environmental concerns: disruption of ecosystems (climate change, desertification, pollution); energy and water problems (depletion of natural resources, disaster management, scarcities); food problems (poverty, overconsumption, epidemics); economic problems (unsustainable production modes, societal instabilities, inequalities); and civil strife (from conflict-related environmental degradation).[1] Many of these issues are empirical concerns. Average temperatures are rising or not. Water resources are coming under more significant stress or not. Most agree that humans play a central role in this dynamic, nicely captured in the iPat formula ($i = P \times A \times T$), which illustrates how environmental impact (i) results from population (P) multiplied by affluence (A) multiplied by technology (T).[2] In the Gulf context, with a population rising from approximately 5 million in 1900 to nearer 60 million a century later, and with soaring affluence, including the world's most generous cradle-to-grave welfare states, this formula succinctly reveals how and why environmental concerns in the monarchies are so apparent.

The political will to accept scientific facts and conclusions is as important as establishing the facts and conclusions themselves.[3] Yet the nature of environmental threats makes such endeavors especially difficult. Many impacts are not localized; rather, they are regionalized or globalized in hidden ways so that cause and effect are hard to parse. Moreover, it can be difficult to translate how an environmental issue (e.g., marine habitat loss or dwindling biodiversity) becomes an environmental security concern, and how this becomes an "instability-inducing" factor indirectly affecting political concerns or directly fostering conflict.[4] Sometimes, as with the "first climate conflict" in Darfur in the 2000s, a direct case can be made between the climate-driven search for scarce water resources and the resulting civil conflict.[5] However, links usually are less obvious. There is yet to emerge anything like a critical mass of pressure to deal with environmental concerns in the Gulf.

Humans have always sought to shape and mold the environment to their advantage.[6] The Gulf monarchies are no exception, save for the reality that they have engaged in more far-reaching molding more recently than most others. Consequently, the monarchies are mired in an inherently unsustainable paradigm like many states. Mari Luomi's 2012 monograph remains the touchstone in this regard.[7] She frames her investigation around the concept of "natural unsustainability," which she sees as inherently built into the sociopolitical economies of the monarchies.[8] Building from this approach, this study examines the contemporary nature of this unsustainability in the monarchies and links it to securitization. This is undertaken against the backdrop of the concept of risk.[9] The point is not to prove that any facet of natural unsustainability exacerbated by climate change caused or is likely to cause a given security issue. Instead, the goal is to offer evidence that "supports (or challenges) the plausibility of a linkage, suggesting a degree of likelihood that the linkage may recur."[10]

Consequently, this chapter discusses a range of environmental concerns and their translation (or not) up the security agenda. As always, choices need to be made as to what issues are prioritized. Taking the lead from the literature, water and food security concerns are among the most discussed environmental issues in the Gulf context. Indeed, from the early days of the expansion of the Gulf monarchies, some of the first, most visible, and impactful changes to the environment were wrought in the areas of agriculture and associated water usage. This is not a surprise.

Given the inherent difficulties of engaging in large-scale agriculture in such a relatively arid region, questions have long been asked about the Arabian Peninsula's ability to ensure food security.

⸺ ◦◦◦ ⸺

The opening section of this chapter, "Expansion and Natural Unsustainability," explores the evolution of the monarchies, as their populations expanded, toward challenging the ability of local resources to cater to their needs. These concerns have always troubled the monarchies, given how inhospitable much of the land is, meaning that trade has long been a critical facet of the economy. But the swift expansion of the population driven by oil economies drove these concerns to another level. The introduction of new technologies helped, but their impact seldom matched the hyped claims. The next section, "Ecosystems and Climate Change," takes a broadly data-driven approach to assessing the core environmental challenges assailing the monarchies in an era of severely worsening climate change. The data presents a grim picture. The final section, "Risk and Reality," focuses on the critical water-food-subsidy nexus that, in essence, lies at the heart of the environmental security paradigm. Yet again, this analysis highlights the pervasive and pernicious influence of how oil and hydrocarbon economies have shaped citizen norms and expectations to realities that are increasingly expensive to maintain for the state.

EXPANSION AND NATURAL UNSUSTAINABILITY

It did not take much expansion to reveal the natural unsustainability of life on the Qatari peninsula in a brutal fashion. Pearling induced the population on the peninsula to increase to the tens of thousands at the turn of the twentieth century. However, with a hyperarid climate and a topography inimical to anything like large-scale traditional agriculture, high dependence on food imports from neighbors and international markets emerged.[11] With the end of Ottoman protections of the Qatari hinterland, Qatar's leaders became vulnerable to influence from Wahhabi powers from the interior of the Peninsula. Simultaneously, the worldwide Great

Depression took hold in the 1930s, followed by World War II, which severed international food supply lines. Qatar was plunged into famine as Saudi Arabia cut off supplies and Bahrain launched a blockade.[12] An estimated third of its 10,000 residents died in the 1940s, and thousands more migrated.[13] Such environmentally rooted issues grew from a worry to a political issue to a severe security concern.

Qatar's case may be a more extreme example, but its experience was a microcosm of regional struggles. It typically took external intervention for comparatively large-scale agricultural projects to be undertaken on the Peninsula. Led by the British in the 1930s and 1940s, expansion in agriculture was inextricably linked to boosting water resources, while both ventures were ultimately "part and parcel" of oil exploration initiatives.[14] With one of the world's largest and thirstiest navies dependent on oil, the United Kingdom was keenly interested in the region's resources.[15] Indeed, such were the British interest and need to engage in the region, London changed its fundamental approach. Frederick Lugard's indirect approach—the "orthodox colonial philosophy"[16]—originally applied in the Gulf, meaning the British seldom involved itself in domestic affairs, ruling instead at arm's length, via proxies.[17] However, shifting with the promise of oil, a far more direct approach emerged, with food and water projects leading the way.[18] Therefore, a strong link between developing the local environment and broader political issues was set from the outset. For example, in Sharjah in the Trucial States, the British wanted to use water and agricultural projects to appease locals to boost "our general influence over them" and use these projects to demarcate and reinforce existing geographic boundaries.[19]

The same logic was apparent up and down the Peninsula. The Buraimi Oasis dispute in the 1940s and 1950s between Saudi Arabia and the United Kingdom (and Oman and the Trucial States, under trusteeship) energized British policy. Retaking the oasis in 1955 after three years of Saudi occupation, the British worried that they had created a "definitive frontier line" where none existed previously. Consequently, Britain feared subsequent Saudi attempts to penetrate the region to "undermine the loyalty of the inhabitants . . . [which might] in the end threaten the security of the area."[20] Environmentally focused water and food production initiatives were one way that Britain sought to forge a "hearts and minds" impact on the ground to shore up local support.

The development of an agricultural trials station at Digdagga in Ras Al Khaimah in 1955 came directly from the fallout of the Buraimi Oasis dispute and vociferous Saudi critiques that the British was doing nothing for locals in the Trucial States, despite nominally ruling for the better part of a century.[21] The core goal of the trial was to import new technologies and showcase their benefits for local farmers to encourage them to "abandon traditional subsistence agriculture in favor of commercial farming."[22] In 1957, Bahrain boasted a "first in the Persian Gulf" agricultural show that 14,000 people visited, demonstrating the latest technologies tested at its "Experimental Station" including "modern spraying machinery and extensive 'anti-pest' measures."[23] This annual festival acted as a public event, reminiscent of quintessential English summer fetes, with musical horse displays and tent pegging.[24] Around the same time, Britain engaged in prospecting for water for local rulers in Bahrain, in return for the right to prospect for oil.[25]

In the 1950s, Oman was deemed one of the more promising locations on the Peninsula, agriculture-wise. Monies were set aside for investment (i.e., £6,000 per year and £15,000 for capital investment) to set up an agricultural station hub in Jameh in central Oman that featured four satellite stations to test new approaches. The location for the station was driven both by agricultural pragmatism—where the more suitable soils may be found—and for political advantage related to expanding British influence in central Oman.[26] Reports about the British role in bringing new technologies and approaches to Omani agriculture are pregnant with the political subtext of the United Kingdom seeking ways to demonstrate its utility to the ruler. Meanwhile, in turn, the ruler used such mechanisms to shore up local support when Oman was far from a centralized state.[27] The Political Resident in the Gulf sought to hurry the setup of these projects, bearing in mind "the political desirability of making a splash soon."[28] Such concerns reflect precisely the securitization logic of an issue (agricultural trials) being moved up the ladder toward a political and a near-security concern in the context of a precarious state that was far from unitary and not under the control of the (British-supported) leader.[29]

Agriculture was not the only focus. Water surveys and aligned conservation plans, the mapping out of the beginnings of local formalized education systems, public health campaigns, capital contributions to the ongoing construction and expansion of projects like the El Maktum

Hospital in Dubai, and the establishment of local police forces and judicial systems were all undertaken.[30] Also, these agricultural projects had a broader political impact. The proliferation of British agricultural and development advisers in the 1950s (and thereafter) induced Egypt's *Sawt Al Arab* (*Voice of the Arabs*) to broadcast that a British official who arrived in Muscat was a spy using agricultural expertise as a way to "undermine the nationalist movement."[31]

These activities continued as the smaller monarchies approached and then gained independence. From 1969 to 1974, the Environment Research Lab at the University of Arizona worked on an advanced, multimillion-dollar power-, water-, and food-producing project on Abu Dhabi's Saadiyat Island.[32] This project fits Shaikh Zayed's reputation as an early pioneer of environmentalism. Once again, however, a political purpose behind an environmental idea can be discerned. One of Zayed's early successes was instituting a local irrigation system (*falaj*) in Al Ain, a town in the Trucial States with a unique historical resonance, which he used to buttress his claims to political power.[33] Moreover, Zayed went on to tie environmentalism to his appeal, harking back to Islamic precepts.[34] Pragmatic proof of his greening policies is the estimated 200 million trees planted under his direction (something that might displease some academics, who see such activities as "an obsession of postcolonial environmental governance"[35]). Nor was his recognition in this regard only local. In 2005, the United Nations (UN) Environment Programme granted him the posthumous title of "Champion of the Earth."[36]

Progress continued at the same peripatetic pace as new technologies were adopted. In the United Arab Emirates (UAE), for example, borehole pumps allowed more efficient irrigation and there was a winnowing of less fruitful practices of small-scale agriculture.[37] Despite these advances, agriculture remained only a national enterprise. It comprised just 0.5 percent of the UAE's gross domestic product (GDP) in 1975. By the millennium, it peaked at 2.3 percent, and by 2020, it had shrunk to 0.9 percent.[38]

Across the Gulf, developments were catalyzed by the soaring oil revenues of the 1970s. Subsidies ramped up, and, as noted, whole population segments were sedenterized (i.e., made to transition from a nomadic to a settled lifestyle) and inculcated into the state as civil servants.[39] Nowhere was this clearer than in Saudi Arabia, where subsidies induced the heavily desertified state to become, at its peak, the world's sixth-largest wheat producer; from the 1970s onward, it has spent upward of $85 billion subsidizing wheat production.[40] In 1983, Joseph Kraft interviewed a Saudi businessman for the *New Yorker*, who commented on the opportunities that subsidies had brought:

> Agriculture, he said, was the field he would like to enter. He said land could be bought with long-term government loans at no interest. Seed and equipment were practically free. Loans were available for water desalinization. The government then bought the produce at highly subsidized prices. Wheat was purchased at about two thousand dollars per ton—or about fifteen times the going price in international markets. He said, "Agriculture is the best business in the Kingdom. The government wants to become self-sufficient. You can even import livestock by plane and make money."[41]

Many subsidies were phased out in the 2000s. However, the distortions they created—industries that they fed—remain such that, for example, Saudi Arabia has one of the world's largest dairy industries. Consequently, to maintain this industry, Saudi Arabia has become the world's second-largest importer of U.S. alfalfa to feed its dairy herds, while the expansion of agriculture and dairy farming built tremendous pressure on scarce water resources into the system.[42]

A central trope and concern of contemporary environmentalism in the Gulf is the inherently unsustainable use of finite hydrocarbon resources at highly subsidized rates. Indeed, discussion of energy diversification options in the monarchies has a surprisingly long history. As today, there were concerns about the long-term viability of fossil fuels as a source of income and a consequent interest—if not an overly strong one—in options for diversification. At the same time, given the backdrop of contestation and competition among the monarchies, there is often an element of one-upmanship about engaging in projects, which speaks to a political form of rivalry.

The available records suggest that Qatar was the first Gulf monarchy to dabble in the concept of nuclear energy as far back as 1974. Khalifah bin Hamad Al Thani (r. 1972–1995) was cementing his role in the state and boosting his legitimacy and popularity among citizens in order to relieve himself of the onerous demands of his family.[43] This is the context in which he asked the British ambassador (and likely the French one as well) for help in building a nuclear power station in Qatar.[44] As with many such requests, the proposal went nowhere, but it is arguably indicative of a desire to use one of the totems of twentieth-century modernism—nuclear power—as a token of political prestige. More serious inquiries on the same subject came from the other monarchies.

Kuwait undertook a full appraisal—feasibility studies, tendering, proposals, and so on—of launching a nuclear power industry, but the Council of Ministers balked at the cost of the venture in 1977.[45] This induced the Saudis to research alternative sources of energy, principally nuclear energy and solar projects. Saudi leaders wanted to "keep in step with the Kuwaitis" in the mid-1970s, with inquiries to the French about facilitating some kind of nuclear facility.[46] The UAE also expressed a similar interest at that time, further hinting at the politics of reputation tied up in these quintessentially modernist ventures.[47]

The 1980s saw Gulf nuclear aspirations continue. Egypt offered to build two nuclear power stations in Saudi Arabia in 1981, and Oman engaged in discreet discussions in 1985 as to whether the United Kingdom could develop nuclear power with or for Oman.[48] In announcements that mirror myriad contemporary communiqués, a range of agreements were signed on a visit to the Gulf by the French president Valéry Giscard d'Estaing in 1980. They included notes on solar cooperation and agricultural development in Qatar and the establishment of a renewable energy research institute, with a solar and desalination focus, in Abu Dhabi.[49] D'Estaing also promised cooperation with the UAE to explore nuclear power for their after-oil future for electricity, research, and desalination purposes.[50] The Arab world's first nuclear power plant opened in the UAE in 2020 in a large-scale joint venture with South Korea.

ECOSYSTEMS AND CLIMATE CHANGE

The changing regional seascape is perhaps the most visible sign of climate and ecosystem change in the Gulf monarchies.[51] All the monarchies have engaged in colossal dredging projects of their coastlines. Bahrain, by far the smallest of them, has been reclaiming land for decades. Originally, the state had an area of 668 square kilometers, but dredging and land reclamation added approximately 100 square kilometers, while the causeway linking Saudi Arabia and Bahrain dredged around 60 square kilometers of sediment in itself.[52] Qatar preferred to reclaim land rather than build its new airport amid its thousands of empty kilometers of hinterland. Dubai has undoubtedly the most famous reclamation project—its attempt to re-create "the world" in mini-islands. Overall, the Gulf monarchies have developed over 40 percent of their coastlines, all of which affects the coastal marine environment.[53] Whole mini-ecosystems have been wiped out, such as reefs that used to thrive between Dubai and Ras Ghanoot on the Emirati coast, while Bahrain's mass dredging wiped out at least 153 square kilometers of marine habitat.[54] In Qatar, whole reefs have died from climate change, and Saudi Arabia dredged a reef as an innovative way to resolve a territorial dispute between Qatar and Bahrain.[55]

Any natural balance between the monarchies and their coastal fisheries is long gone. Over 40 percent of Gulf shorelines are covered by urban, industrial, and residential developments, while the coastline has doubled in several regional cities.[56] Two-thirds of the Gulf's sabkhas (coastal mudflats) have been destroyed by reclamation and dredging, vast swathes of the region's mangroves have been killed, and over 70 percent of the region's coral reefs are considered "effectively lost."[57] Climate change concerns are measurably exacerbating these issues.[58]

Unsurprisingly interlinked to these myriad concerns, Gulf fisheries suffer from overfishing, pollution, and the destruction of nurseries. Kuwaiti fishermen's landings (or rather, the foreign fishermen doing the work for Kuwaiti fishing boat owners) have consistently decreased in recent decades, down by half in 2007 from 1995 levels.[59] In the UAE, fish stocks were down approximately one-fifth from 1978 to 2002, while recent studies note that at least twelve species "have been harvested beyond sustainable levels."[60] Extensive heavy metal poisoning of Gulf waters from various sources linked to industry exacerbates these issues, as does the discharge from desalination plants.[61] Gulf waters are considered some of the most at risk in the world from these multiple threats.[62] Assessing the overall impact of these various construction projects on the Gulf is difficult. Authorities tend to be secretive about commissioned impact assessments.

It is challenging to ascertain a baseline from which to measure an impact, due to the level of development over recent decades.[63]

More generally, much of the regional environmental scholarship focuses on Saudi Arabia, for good reason. The state covers nearly 80 percent of the whole Peninsula and over 90 percent of the Gulf monarchies. Much of the basic data edges in a dangerous direction. Temperature variations and extremes in Saudi Arabia and overall average temperatures have increased significantly in recent decades, and these changes are accelerating.[64] Across the whole Peninsula, from 1879–1992, the temperature increased by 0.63 Celsius, while the heating up has increased faster in more recent decades.[65] Studies suggest that the Peninsula is among the world's most vulnerable regions to climate extremes, with incidences of deadly heat waves becoming ever more normalized.[66]

Temperature increases are linked to decreases in rainfall. As before, these trends are only getting faster in recent decades. Average rainfall in Saudi Arabia fell by half from 1979–2009, from 250 millimeters to less than 100 millimeters.[67] The majority of Oman, the UAE, and all Qatar and Bahrain enjoy less than 100 millimeters of rain per year, classifying these areas as hyperarid.[68] Overall, a 2015 modeling study argued that under a business-as-usual approach, temperature extremes around the Arabian Gulf are likely "to approach and exceed" levels likely to "severely impact human habitability in the future."[69]

As the iPat formula suggests, overcoming the region's hyperaridity and high-temperature climate amid a rising population with rising affluence inevitably results in a higher energy footprint. However, the use of energy and water is not just above average—it is among the highest in the world, as figure 5.1 demonstrates referring to the per capita energy usage of the Gulf monarchies.

There are three interlinked reasons why the monarchies' per capita energy consumption is so high. Energy subsidies induce care- and (often nearly) cost-free approach to energy, which leads to endemic wastefulness. This is in terms of personal lack of discipline in energy use, societal indifference to energy costs (in both senses of the word), and a commercial lack of urgency to address energy efficiency issues. Regulation is improving such issues around the edges, as with evolving building codes for energy-efficient buildings. There is also increasing education focus on these issues, alongside incentive programs to rebalance from egregious

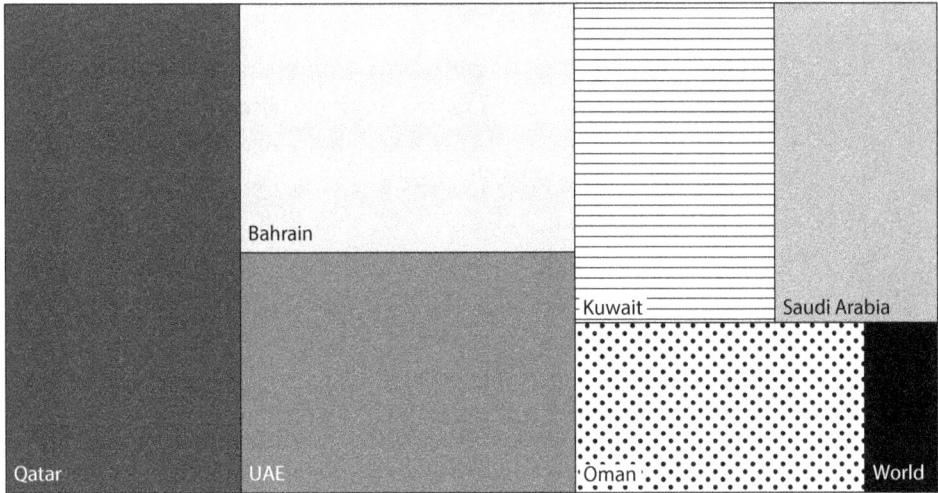

FIGURE 5.1 Gulf monarchies' per capita energy use.

Note: Energy consumption per capita (kWh). These figures are the latest available: 2019 for all the monarchies except Bahrain, where the data is from 2016.

Source: Our World in Data based on BP and Shift Data Portal.

energy use.[70] Equally, local populations do not tend to see climate concerns as overly important, while it is also questionable whether elites give climate change concerns the deference and concern they deserve.[71] For example, in the UAE's 2021 articulation of its core principles to guide its next fifty years, climate concerns and any sense of environmental awareness are simply absent.[72]

Second, the economies of the monarchies are deeply intertwined with energy-intensive industries in the wider hydrocarbon sector, such as aluminum smelting. Combined with their comparatively small populations, their per capita carbon footprint is consequently conspicuously high. Third, the region is hot and arid, which mandates high levels of air conditioning use and the desalination of most consumable water.[73]

Energy use per se is not the problem. Rather, the concern is that the Gulf's energy comes from mostly nonrenewable fossil fuels, which belch out emissions. Such emissions and related externalities exacerbate localized climate change concerns and contribute to broader, transboundary, climate-related problems.

Such myriad issues are self-compounding and exacerbating; each makes the other worse. David Wallace-Wells notes that some regions may find upsides to the multiplying effects of climate change. Scandinavia or Russia might benefit from "a more temperate climate for agriculture and unlocking natural resources locked in permafrost," whereas for the Gulf region, "there are no discernible upsides to the climate change outlook. It simply makes myriad issues worse to a greater or a much greater degree."[74]

RISK AND REALITY

Environmental changes directly affect state security. Michael McCormick and colleagues argue that the rise and fall of ancient Rome was highly correlated with climatic changes. More recently, the Darfur conflict of the early 2000s is typically recognized as precipitated by drought.[75] In the contemporary Middle East and North Africa (MENA) region, there are a range of scenarios where environmental concerns exacerbate (or at least are poised to exacerbate) security concerns. The 2020 *Routledge Handbook on Middle East Security* dedicates six chapters to "energy, resource issues and climate change as security issues in the Middle East."[76] However, the Gulf monarchies get minimal mention. This reflects scholarly opinion that although the monarchies are facing multiple environmental concerns, they are assumed to have the finances to overcome them. Nevertheless, just because the monarchies have hitherto threaded the environmental needle forging states in inherently inhospitable climes is not to say that their mix of luck, good management, and fiscal prowess will forever inure them from environmentally rooted security concerns.

When pondering areas most likely to be the root of environmental security issues for the monarchies, the literature invariably alights on the water-food-subsidy nexus as the Achilles' heel. Even after a century of increasing local agricultural practice, the monarchies are still at a comparative disadvantage in the field. Revealed comparative advantage (RCA) is a method of assessing the relative advantages for a given country making a product, rooted in observing trade flows. An RCA of less than one demonstrates a comparative disadvantage, more than one indicates a comparative advantage, and two or more shows a competitive advantage. The data in figure 5.2 demonstrates both the small role that agriculture plays locally and just how disadvantaged the monarchies are when it comes to agricultural production.

Given the brittleness of Gulf agriculture, it is tempting to opine that it was a matter of time before food and water provision ascended the securitization ladder from technical matters to political issues to security concerns. Andy Spiess argues that food security in a modern guise first demonstrably concerned the leadership in the Gulf monarchies when, in 2008, the world endured sharp food price spikes owing to an array of droughts.[77] Qatar, for example, founded two organizations in 2008, the Qatar National Food Security Programme (QNFSP) and Hassad Foods. The former strives to understand and remedy the state's food security vulnerabilities, while the latter invests in agronomics for the state's sovereign wealth fund (SWF), the Qatar Investment Authority (QIA).

The central end or goal of the food and water security paradigm is for a state to enjoy adequate and resilient supplies to meet its peoples'

	Share of Agriculture in GDP	Share of Agriculture in Employment	RCA
Qatar	0.3	3	0.00
Kuwait	0.4	1.7	0.03
Saudi Arabia	3.4	6.3	0.14
UAE	1.3	6.9	1.43
Bahrain	0.4	7.6	0.35
Oman	1.6	7.6	0.28
Upper-Middle-Income MENA	6	15.8	0.82
Lower-Middle-Income MENA	27.5	49.5	3.6

FIGURE 5.2 Agriculture in the Gulf.

Note: These figures reflect the latest available data for 2010–2014.

Source: Alejandro Nin-Pratt et al., Agriculture and Economic Transformation in the Middle East and North Africa: A Review of the Past with Lessons for the Future, International Food Policy Research Institute (2018), 18.

needs now and in the near future.[78] With Gulf populations rising from approximately 5 million to 60 million in the last one hundred years, there are many more mouths to feed to sustain the states. There are two basic ways or strategies to achieve the central end of realizing food and water security. Food can be imported or it can be grown locally. Similarly, water needs to be imported or found locally, and in much greater quantities, if a country plans to grow food within its borders. Each approach comes with different benefits and concerns.

The Gulf monarchies have improved, securing several aspects of their food and water security. From the 1990s to the late 2000s, Kuwait and Saudi Arabia made some of the largest improvements worldwide in combating hunger.[79] Today, given how financially secure the Gulf monarchies are (even Oman and Bahrain), it is not surprising that the Gulf monarchies barely feature as states of concern when assessed by the Global Hunger Index.[80]

Self-sufficiency is not about growing all food consumed in a state domestically. A more pragmatic definition of self-sufficiency focuses on domestic production and what percentage this could cover of a state's consumption.[81] The Food and Agriculture Organization (FAO) of the United Nations estimates the dependency ratio (i.e., imports compared to domestic consumption) for grain is 90 percent in Oman and more than 95 percent in Kuwait, Saudi Arabia, and the UAE.[82] The monarchies are even highly dependent on imports for fish, even though they are coastal countries.[83] Progress has been made on some fronts, and some data is relatively old. However, not much has changed in a macro sense. At the start of the Gulf blockade of Qatar in 2017, despite the QNFSP having been in operation for over a decade, Qatar was still reliant on imports for 90 percent of its food needs, with 40 percent coming over its only land border, which is with Saudi Arabia.[84] In reaction to the blockade, local agriculture in Qatar increased 400 percent.[85] This provided a partial answer to the blockading states that stopped the transshipments of food to Qatar via regional ports like Dubai and the Saudi border's closure.

Qatar's response was symbolized by the Baladna company, whose name translates as "our country." Mirroring Saudi Arabia's approach in the 1980s, as noted in the *New Yorker* interview mentioned earlier in this chapter, Qatar airlifted thousands of Holstein milking cows from Australia to start indigenous production.[86] Otherwise, with concerted government intervention, Qatar produced more than it needed of dairy and chicken, while it significantly improved local production of vegetables, red meat, and fish.[87]

Elsewhere in the Gulf, the long-heralded use of modern technology continued to be a promoted solution to age-old problems. Aside from Qatar, the UAE led the way in promoting agritech initiatives, with a $272 million incentive package to support futuristic approaches to agriculture in Abu Dhabi and a range of hydroponic farms supported by Dubai-based foundations and funds.[88] Aside from these ventures, given the inherently difficult (and worsening) climactic conditions on the Peninsula, the reality remains that all states still rely heavily on imports. Buying up foreign farmland, signing long-term contracts for supply, and taking out "virtual imports" options are all methods of securing supply. Buying or leasing foreign fields as a practice came to the fore particularly with the 2008 acquisition by South Korea's Daewoo of a ninety-nine-year lease for around one-third of the arable land in Madagascar. This highlighted this trend and led to regime change in Madagascar and the cancellation of the deal.[89] Nevertheless, despite this and associated bad press labeling such moves as neocolonial land grabs, Gulf monarchies remain active with institutions like QNFSP and the King Abdullah Initiative for Saudi Agricultural Investment Abroad leading the way.

Securing an array of imports is no panacea, though. Rising commodity prices in the 2000s boosted import bills and challenged subsidy regimes worldwide, leading to increased food prices, instigating as many as twenty-five "food riots" between September 2007 and April 2008.[90] Importers are vulnerable to supplies becoming interrupted because of droughts, civil strife, or warfare. With climate change promising to shift weather patterns fostering drought in traditional exporting countries like Sudan, the prospect of interrupted supplies increases. Diversification of supply can mitigate this concern but not eliminate it, and prices may still follow the trend upward, as happened in 2007–2008.

Otherwise, as one RAND report notes, much of the imported grain for the Gulf monarchies passes through one (or often more) of the world's great maritime choke points. Around 90 percent of the UAE's wheat imports, 80 percent of Qatar's, and nearly all of Bahrain's and Kuwait's goes through the Strait of Hormuz.[91] Although the extended closure of any choke points is unlikely, and considerable international military and political energies are focused on preventing such eventualities, it must be factored in as a low-probability but high-impact concern.

Nevertheless, all states need a healthy mix of food importers. The Economist Intelligence Unit (EIU) created the Global Food Security Index to track a range of related metrics. The monarchies do reasonably well considering the intrinsic inhospitability of their climate, thanks mainly to the highly subsidized nature of the Gulf water, food, and importing nexus. This financially rooted attribute allows the monarchies to overcome conspicuously low rankings in the "Natural Resources and Resilience" aspect of the EIU rankings, as seen in figure 5.3.

The point is not to suggest that these metrics scientifically reveal a definitive truth. Instead, they are considered as metrics that tell an interesting story. Until hydroponics or a similar technology matures (or Gulf populations drastically plummet), the monarchies will be as highly dependent on external suppliers to meet their food security needs as they are on continuing fiscal strength to overcome these myriad, interlinked difficulties that prevent them from building resilience in these areas.

At the core of the monarchies' hamartia in local agriculture is the reality that they suffer from some of the world's most stressed water resource situations.[92] Various metrics are used to gauge a state's wealth or paucity in terms of water resources (i.e., precipitation, rivers, aquifers, and so on). "Water stress" is the mildest term for water shortage, signaling under 1,700 square meters of water available per capita. Other measures include

	Overall Food Security Rank	Natural Resource and Resilience Ranking
Qatar	24	91
Kuwait	30	93
UAE	35	88
Oman	40	76
Bahrain	43	107
Saudi Arabia	44	84

FIGURE 5.3 The Economist Intelligence Unit ranking of food security facets.

Source: Global Food Security Index (2021).

"sufficient water," over 1,250 square meters per capita; "water scarcity," under 1,000 square meters; and worst of all, "absolute water scarcity," at under 500 square meters. All of the Gulf monarchies are in the last camp, as indicated by figure 5.4.[93]

Water supply can be split into "big" and "small." The former refers to the vast quantities of water used in industrial agriculture; the latter concerns surface water and groundwater and their provision to urban and other industrial and energy sectors. Unsurprisingly, big water is a problem throughout the MENA region, with low basic water availability (Egypt is an exception because of the Nile).[94] Consequently, for the Gulf monarchies to engage in anything like large-scale agriculture—as Saudi Arabia did from the 1970s with wheat—Herculean efforts are required to overcome this natural unsustainability.

As noted previously, Saudi Arabia emerged to become the world's sixth-largest wheat exporter at its height in the 1990s.[95] However, a cost-benefit analysis of this project indicates that it must rank as one of the most disastrously wasteful policies ever undertaken. In total, Elhadj calculates that between direct and indirect subsidies plus capital investments, the state spent $83.6 billion subsidizing agriculture for "foodstuffs that could have been imported for less than US$40 billions" between 1984 and 2000.[96] This accounted for 18 percent of Saudi's oil revenue during this time.[97] The cost in water from (mostly nonreplenishable) acquirers

World Ranking	Level of Baseline Water Stress
Qatar	1
Kuwait	7
Saudi Arabia	8
UAE	10
Bahrain	12
Oman	15

FIGURE 5.4 World rankings of baseline water stress.

Source: World Resources Institute, Aqueduct, https://www.wri.org/applications/aqueduct/country-rankings/?indicator=bws.

is estimated to be a similarly gargantuan 300 billion cubic meters—the equivalent of six years' flow of the Nile.[98] In 2008, the FAO estimated that Saudi aquifers would run dry within twenty-five years, and reports by King Faisal University concurred. Moreover, this is a Gulf-wide problem. The available domestic water resources have fallen dramatically in the monarchies per capita, reflecting the population booms in recent decades. From 1972 to 2014, they fell 96 percent in Qatar, 80 percent in Kuwait, 94 percent in the UAE, and 93 percent in Saudi Arabia.[99]

Qatar's postblockade agricultural approach has mirrored (albeit in a smaller way) these inefficiencies and problems. The Qatar Airways in-flight magazine used to boast that Qatar is the world's only "100 percent desertified country," with no rivers or lakes. So 92 percent of the water that the state uses for agriculture comes from aquifers, which are provided free of charge for farming, leading to high wastage.[100] The state subsidizes the Baladna venture at all stages—land availability, water use, electricity tariffs, taxes, and other areas—so the company, and its shareholders, can turn a profit. In a postblockade era, this is seen, not unreasonably, as a necessary expense for the Qatari state to have its own dairy industry. However, for Baladna then to look to export its product makes little sense. The cost for Baladna does not reflect the hidden subsidies. Thus, if the company sells milk at internationally competitive prices (as it plans to do), the Qatari state will be in effect subsidizing Turkey or the United Kingdom purchasing Qatari milk, while depleting their mostly nonrenewable, scarce water resources.[101]

Indeed, water resources are shrinking in the Gulf. To make sure that their taps do not run dry, Gulf monarchies long ago moved past traditional water procurement measures (i.e., digging wells).[102] Using oil-, gas-, or solar-powered plants to remove the brine from seawater (i.e., desalination) to create potable water has long been seen as the answer. Although figures vary, approximately half of the world's desalination plants are found in the MENA region, with Saudi Arabia running at 15.5 percent, the UAE at 10.1 percent, and Kuwait at 3.7 percent of the world's total.[103] Saudi Arabia is the world's largest producer of desalinated water and is home to several of the world's largest plants.[104]

However, desalinating on such a large scale and with no end in sight brings a series of costs and risks of its own.[105] As Molly Walton notes, "Two-thirds of the water produced from seawater desalination in the

[MENA] region today is from fossil fuel–based thermal desalination, while the rest . . . relies heavily on electricity produced using natural gas. Overall, the Middle East accounts for roughly 90 percent of the thermal energy used for desalination worldwide, led by the United Arab Emirates and Saudi Arabia."[106] The UAE, for example, released nearly 5 million metric tons of carbon dioxide per year, fueling its desalination plants. Desalination accounts for almost 20 percent of Saudi Arabia's electricity generation.[107] Various initiatives are underway throughout the Peninsula to add in renewable energy sources to power desalination plants, but there is a long way to go. Otherwise, the desalination process produces brine as a by-product. The Gulf monarchies alone produce 55 percent of the world's brine, with the top producers being Saudi Arabia (22.2 percent), the UAE (20.2 percent), Qatar (6.6 percent), and Kuwait (5.8 percent).[108] Given that the brine is typically returned directly to the Persian Gulf, this means that the waters become warmer, saltier, and polluted with other desalinated by-products.[109] Warming temperatures are likely to adversely affect fish stocks, biodiversity, and coral reefs, which may directly affect those dependent on fishing for income.[110] Desalination plants also provide an ideal target for adversaries, something that the U.S. Central Intelligence Agency (CIA) recognized back in 1983.[111] The largest plant in the world, the $7.2 billion Ras Al Khair desalination facility, supplies the Saudi capital of Riyadh with water and eastern parts of Saudi with electricity. Concern for its safety took on greater salience in the aftermath of the Abqaiq and Khurais energy facility attacks in September 2019, which saw the world's most important oil-processing center, one of the most heavily defended installations in the Gulf, attacked by drones and missiles that sailed unopposed through expensively assembled defenses.[112]

There are few alternatives to desalination. In 1989, Qatar initiated discussions with Iran about the possibility of importing freshwater from Iran. Although the discussions lasted many years, they came to nothing, nor are there any meaningful prospects of a similar project being revived.[113] The monarchies thus need to use desalination. However, an appreciation of the risks it brings is needed.

Indeed, Gökçe Günel describes how the monarchies unreflectingly base their daily sociocultural, economic, and political existence on the provision of an "infinity of water."[114] Water emerges at usually negligible cost, offering the false image of bountiful supplies of water. This finds form in the region's enormous fountains and thousands of kilometers of palms and grasses alongside regional roads. The latest sally in this regard is an outdoor street in Dubai where artificial rain cools shoppers when it gets hot.[115] In normalizing such indications of an abundance of water, states obscure its inherent and profound scarcity, effacing "the 'natural' characteristics of this resource."[116] This hiding of the true precipitous nature of water scarcity is dangerous, as is the sublimation of the real financial costs of obtaining water through subsidies. It means that the monarchies, some of the most water-stressed states globally, have nearly twice the residential water consumption figures of other high-income countries.[117]

It was only in January 2015 that Emirati nationals began paying for water for the first time, while expatriates have been paying since 1997.[118] Minimal charges were introduced for water and electricity in Qatar for Qataris in the deficit years of the mid-1980s. However, these were rescinded soon afterward, and Qataris still pay no charge for water (or electricity) at their primary residences.[119] By contrast, much later in 2014, Dubai introduced water tariffs that matched production costs in 2011, but this remains a regional outlier.[120]

Although it has been broached, the idea of cutting subsidies and introducing fees for water and electricity tends to induce panic in regional leaders, fearing that the subject is the fourth rail of the ruling bargain where change will not be countenanced. These fears are not entirely unfounded. Occasionally, when subsidies have been cut in recent years, there have been outcries at the rising prices, such as with Saudi Arabia and the price of milk, Kuwait and the price of fish, and Bahrain with the price of meat.[121] In these instances, the governments swiftly relented, forcing companies to keep their prices artificially below cost and revisiting subsidy cuts. Similarly, in 2016, Abdullah Al Hasin, the Saudi minister for water and electricity, was dismissed after overseeing cutbacks that raised prices.[122]

These instances highlight how issues intimately linked to food, water, and energy security can translate directly into the security sphere. A fiscally rooted decision to change the price of a commodity swiftly gained political salience with outcries from the population, which, in the case of Kuwait and Bahrain, took on security-oriented elements. Opposition elements in parliament took on the government in both cases, defending constituents' proclivities and using the opportunity to make political hay of the controversy. As Ulrichsen notes, similar issues caused riots, mass mobilizations, protests, and strikes in Egypt in 1977, Morocco in 1981, Tunisia in 1984, Algeria in 1988, and Yemen in 2005.[123] As noted in chapter 3, subsidies have been cut. However, the point is that the monarchies are facing economic strains and stresses that tax their subsidy regimes, but environmental stresses and strains are exacerbating these dynamics.

There is no definitive answer when assessing the risks associated with environmental concerns precipitating political and security crises. As Luomi shows, compiling metrics from international organizations can provide a smorgasbord of comparable information.[124] Figure 5.5 highlights a range of concerning data. The Yale Environmental Performance Index provides a detailed ranking of various issues worldwide, including environmental health, air quality, water and sanitation, biodiversity and habitat, fishery stock vitality, carbon dioxide emissions, air pollution, and an assessment of water resources.[125] The Ocean Health Index focuses on countries' relations with their water resources, from issues of biodiversity to coastal protection to assessing the sense of place of a state's relations with the sea or ocean.[126] And the Sustainable Development Index focuses on a more holistic concept of development, encompassing

	Yale Environmental Performance Index 2020	Ocean Health Index 2021	Sustainable Development Report 2021
Bahrain	56	71	100
Kuwait	47	75	113
Oman	110	74	73
Qatar	122	78	94
Saudi Arabia	90	69	98
UAE	42	80	71

FIGURE 5.5 World rankings: Gulf monarchies in international environmental and sustainability indexes.

Source: https://dashboards.sdgindex.org/rankings; https://oceanhealthindex.org/global-scores/; and https://epi.yale.edu/epi-results/2020/component/epi.

issues ranging from poverty, quality education, and gender equality to clean water, sustainable cities, climate action, and "life below water."[127] Such metrics show, quite unequivocally, that the monarchies are in poor shape when it comes to raw levels of environmental stress, often coming easily in the bottom third.

However, as a rule, these issues remain comparatively unsecuritized in the monarchies. They remain in the realm of normal politics, with rulers and bureaucracies striving to find ways to overcome natural unsustainabilities. The core problem is that climate change extenuates all environmental difficulties, exacerbating the state's job in maintaining the illusion of plenty. In this political rut where leaders ignore regional unsustainabilities, duped into imagining a world of infinite solutions to growing problems, harmful policies are still being undertaken that trade short-term for long-term risk.

⸻ ∞ ⸻

Security in the environmental sector revolves around the interplay of empirical factors and the political awareness and acceptance of such issues. At the base, assessments need to be made regarding the level of disruption affecting ecosystems and habitats. Climate change is a huge factor in these debates, as is pollution and desertification. The knock-on effects are keenly felt within water and food security dynamics, which in turn can deeply and adversely affect broader economic security concerns that in some cases lead to civil strife. These varied environmental security concerns are no longer on the fringe. Instead, environmental awareness is increasingly a mainstream issue, whether prompted by increasingly common extreme weather events, significant coverage of the annual Conference of the Parties (COP) series of conferences held under UN auspices, or the concerns of younger generations. However, this awareness does not translate into an overly effective groundswell for action, as myriad stymied international agreements can attest.

Many of these issues are found in extremis in the Gulf. The region suffers palpably from a harsh and worsening climate. Whatever natural balance had once existed has long gone. The region's intrinsic ability to support a small local population was put under strain by the advent of the pearling industry. The needs of that industry mandated that the population increase significantly, mostly with migrant workers, as the seasonal work demanded. This drove the expansion of long-established interregional trade, notably with the Indian coast, to sate the expanded local demands for various goods, but most important was food. Equally, a heavy burden was placed on local resources (water, fisheries, and other important materials). With the subsequent founding and expansion of the oil industries across the region, the same dynamics took hold once more, only in a souped-up fashion, with an even greater dependence on trade and the exploitation of finite local resources. Under empire and the influence of foreign states, and comparatively flush with cash, local leaders sought technological solutions to age-old problems. A litany of expensive solutions promising to make the desert bloom were offered and purchased.

The first-order reactions to ensuring regional food and water security have been, as already noted, resoundingly successful in the Gulf. Supermarkets are full at all price points, and water flows unabated. Modern technological developments have allowed huge, world-leading cities to sprout up in the most unlikely places, at least from a climate suitability perspective. Furthermore, Saudi Arabia's desert indeed bloomed with wheat for decades on end. However, these technologies were blunt, simply bludgeoning development onto the Peninsula and creating mighty externalities in the process. The promise of smart technologies that allow development without wrecking the environment and pushing untold costs onto future generations remains perpetually unrealized. However, the technofetishistic allure of simple solutions to wicked problems remains to this day an unsinkable rubber duck in the region that keeps bobbing back up no matter how many times similar solutions have failed in the past.

Moreover, in establishing societies and economies that are deeply naturally unsustainable, a litany of escalating second- and third-order risks are produced. Even diversified imports can suffer from interruptions, price spikes, or other factors—such as blockades—that choke off needed supplies. Similarly, desalination technologies are a (or perhaps even *the*) central facilitating factor underpinning life on the Peninsula. But these critical industries have acute costs in terms of pollution, which is invisible to most citizens, and act in some cases as a single point of failure.

Aside from black swan events that can strike at any time, the master variable for the monarchies is money. If the monarchies can pay their litany of subsidies across the food, water, and energy spectra, luxuriating in the illusion that the monarchies are not some of the hottest, most arid places on Earth, most problems can be vanquished. More water can be desalinated. Brine can be expensively recycled or dealt with. Food can be imported, even flown in, in great quantities. Yet more roads can be adorned with verdant grass verges and palm trees. Energy can still be wasted on a colossal scale as nuclear and solar plants slowly come online. However, this fanciful, Peter Pan logic is coming under ever more pressure. Accordingly, deescalation is required. However, given how intertwined such dynamics are with the social contract, institutional design, and decades of experience, there is little in the Gulf's history suggesting that leaders will faithfully and successfully be able to pursue such policies.

CONCLUSION

Unless we ourselves take a hand now, they'll foist a republic on us. If we want things to stay as they are, things will have to change.

THE LEOPARD, DI LAMPEDUSA (2007)

The Gulf monarchies look like they have changed more than almost anywhere else in the world in the past one hundred years. They rose from struggling fishing villages and towns to become futuristic-looking states with missions to Mars while their populations expanded more than tenfold, going from some of the poorest to some the richest on Earth. Nevertheless, as the twenty-first century trundles through its third decade, leaders face similar challenges to their grandfathers' generation, even if the scale of the problems has changed. Such tropes of change amid continuity do not arise by chance. The perpetual centrality of the region's oil paradigm consecrated a hamartia that instituted path dependencies delineating how the region would grow and prosper. Simultaneously, it baked into the regional DNA delicate structures, relations, and processes that the states have been successfully but uneasily reconciling for generations. Oil greased these many complicated interactions and aided the monarchies in overcoming numerous difficulties. However, as the oil paradigm dwindles, it is right to ponder whether the machinery of the Gulf monarchies might begin to seize up.

Such a broad perspective reflecting on a century of development across six different states inevitably elides some detail and nuance. It is vital to resist reflexively seeing oil as a Western-facilitated development tool used to lift backward regions out of poverty. While there are realities to be dealt with—oil plainly drove the transformation and enrichment of the monarchies—such encapsulations run the risk of denuding local actors of nuance, agency, and influence. Initially, workers who came to the Gulf were not politically neutral or pliant. Migrants transmitted ideas, instigated protests, and shaped emerging states, reflecting contemporary arguments of how such groups—so often relatively voiceless in colonial and Gulf histories—genuinely enjoyed influence and impact. Similarly, cogent arguments can be made for the abiding importance of these myriad "others" in the Gulf as foils against which local identities were forged. Nor should the agency of Gulf nationals and leaders be elided. Local publications in the 1950s and 1960s demonstrated dynamism, open-mindedness, so-called modern ideas of equality, and nuanced and skeptical approaches to the role of religion in state-society relations. Real social engagement in political matters existed. Too often, such realities disappear in histories that focus on colonial archives and implicitly (or even explicitly) paternalistic Western sentiments toward regional development. Gulf leaders, meanwhile, were also real agents of change, often deftly manipulating external powers and directly shaping the destiny of their states.

It is a curiosity of the region that oil was not the first locally found, naturally occurring, finite resource that catalyzed and bent the monarchies to its needs. Pearls, as oil would do later, dominated parts of the region, mandating the complete reshaping of its demography, with myriad knock-on social effects. Pearls, and then oil, meant that thousands, hundreds of thousands, and then millions of foreigners migrated to the region, bequeathing it one of its more distinctive characteristics—population imbalances hardly seen anywhere else in the world. The oil (and broader hydrocarbon) political economy definitively and enduringly shaped what it means to be a Gulf citizen, with the accompanying roles, rights, and expectations. Preexisting complexities—tribes, religions, and other forms of belonging—were neither erased nor simply replaced. However, they were diminished in importance and influence by the nature of the oil-fueled ruling bargain that vastly empowered states.

Although the presence of a disproportionately large number of foreigners is a constant in the past century, important aspects of their roles
changed. Foreigners played a large constructive role in building infrastructure, running key bureaucracies, and advising elites. As has been
noted, initially foreigners agitated far more. They acted as the transmission
source for radical ideas from the heart of the Middle East (and far beyond)
to the politically less active monarchies. Gulf governments consistently
struggled to deal with ensuing protests. However, as concepts of citizenship became ever more secure, the distinctions between foreigner and
national widened and stricter controls over immigration emerged.

Today, the Gulf's foreign workers are far more *homo economicus* and
significantly less politically active than in the past. Otherwise, recent
changes saw governments build industries and economic sectors—as
with the mountains of real estate that far outstrip any possible demand
from native populations—premised on the de facto permanent presence
of hundreds of thousands of foreigners. The slow expansion of permanent
visas and the opening of new paths for citizenship are also significant new
developments. These policies strive to attract economically successful
migrants in order to diversify the state's economic base. However, none
of these policies enjoyed any kind of public consultation. If history is a
guide, which it often can be, policies cutting against Gulf citizenship's
uniqueness and special status will continue to be unpopular.

Politically, Gulf rulers secured themselves by exponentially expanding
their role at the apex of society as a revenue-dispensing mechanism, in
exchange inter alia for minimal pressure for real democratic accountability. In a sense, this role was presaged by earlier conceptions of local
hierarchies, although oil wealth secured leading families as never before.
However, in an example of how oil clearly did *not* determine everything,
pre-oil structures had a lasting impact. For example, Kuwait's rambunctious political culture, established when the Al Sabah was on a far more
equal footing with other domestic actors, set a tenor of institutionalized consultation genuinely countering elites that remains to this day.
Similarly, the rising oil price tide of the 1970s did lift all Gulf boats, and
regional welfare states blossomed. However, significant difference in
wealth between (as well as within) the monarchies is clear to see.

The oil-shaped nature of Gulf ruler–dominated politics that emerged
coalesced to produce a litany of socioeconomic problems. Chief among

such issues was the removal of Gulf nationals from the need to perform productive work to receive financial recompense. In the 1960s, the issue of masked unemployment was widely known, and it plagues the region still. The point is not that Gulf citizens are innately locked into this mentality; instead, they respond to structured incentives like everyone else. If, in an internationalized economy with relatively easy entry for expatriates, a foreigner will take a professional job for a fifth of a Gulf citizen's salary expectation, then the company will hire the foreigner, and the Gulf citizen will look elsewhere.

Accordingly, local nonoil economies struggled to emerge, given the scale of government domination, the grossly distorted (oil-rooted) labor market, and the removal of economic pressure from education systems because of the generosity of the welfare state. Also, because the monarchies' chief export was energy, levels of intra-Gulf trade were (and remain) exceptionally low. Alongside special relations with nations like the United States and the United Kingdom, this arguably meant that intra-Gulf rivalries were prolonged without a more traditional organic growth of trade links and interdependencies. Associated with this was a lack of financial, political, or security pressure to overcome the usual litany of regional differences. Qatar's 2017–2021 blockade by the United Arab Emirates (UAE), Saudi Arabia, Bahrain, and Egypt mimicked Saudi blockades of Kuwait, Qatar, and the UAE generations ago. Indeed, it seems like a policy from another age.

Various factors allowed this aberration to transpire. Low levels of interdependence played a part, as did small-group, elite dynamics. Both allowed drastic decisions to be made with minimal pushback. A broader, fundamental lack of seriousness in defense and security affairs due to the region's U.S. domination also facilitated the blockade. Overall, there was simply a low cost for such grandiose political posturing.

With close relations to Western governments, and with state coffers sporadically full of fiscal reserves (especially after an oil windfall), tendencies emerged for monarchies to seek quick, often expensive solutions from consultants peddling what they touted as "modern" ideas. This kind of "technofetishistic allure" is long evidenced, for example, in water and agricultural sectors, where solutions have been sought to age-old, complex issues, overcoming an inherent inhospitability.[1] A heady mix of oil-fueled financial largesse, political leaders striving to entrench their

power and embed the social contract, and thoughtless wielding of technology has led to Herculean wastage with Saudi Arabia's wheat subsidies
in the 1980s and 1990s. For many of the same reasons, Gulf leaders persistently engaged in the "monument race" to outcompete neighbors in
expensive, grandiose projects to contribute to the formation of national
pride and unique identities, as well as to demonstrate modernity.[2] This is
also why Gulf monarchies compete so often in the same industrial sectors.
With the perennial notion of an oil windfall around the corner and bud-
geting consequently less stringently focused on economic rationales,
establishing four world-spanning airlines within a forty-minute flight of
each other—but no rail links—is seen as a good idea. Gulf leaders have
tried for generations to buy a knowledge-focused economy in the education sector. In the 1970s, Dubai hosted the Choueifat School and the
University of Maryland. In the 2000s, it was Qatar building world-class
universities when its education system was a decade or two away from
filling even half the places.

Indeed, decades along the track of educational reform, diversification,
sovereign wealth funds (SWFs), and various visions and development
plans; in a world of climate change, renewable fuels, and decreasing oil
demand; and even with states like Bahrain and Oman exporting minimal
oil, a century after the oil paradigm's foundation, it retains a viselike grip,
with nonoil revenues averaging just 17 percent of gross domestic product (GDP) across the monarchies in 2019.[3] In trying to escape the grav-
itational pull of oil, attempts to diversify in the monarchies succumb to
Friedrich Hayek's critique by engaging in a "fatal conceit" that political
elites can forge a "deliberate arrangement of human interaction . . . [to]
command . . . available resources."[4] Extensive nationalization policies—
deeply intervening to mandate a percentage of nationals working in various sectors—are a prime example of government intervention striving to
rebalance the labor market in the wake of the realities shaped by oil.

Pockets of regionally (and sometimes globally) competitive businesses
have emerged. However, they are notable for their rarity. Dubai's status as
a world-ranking port city is rooted in a necessity that drives commerce-
oriented leaders to forge productive sectors without the direct fallback
of significant hydrocarbon wealth. Elsewhere, world-ranking companies, mainly in the hydrocarbon or adjacent sectors, emerged to real
prominence and profitability. This was thanks to an atypically low level

of governmental interference and leveraging the region's core, cheap asset—oil. Realizing the critical importance of these firms, political leaders tended to avoid interfering (until recently), leaving them instead to experienced professionals to shape.

At the heart of Gulf politics, it is important not to overemphasize the freedom of action of Gulf leaders, as institutions have long retained an ability to affect decisions. Nevertheless, one of the more consistent tropes in Gulf history is the emergence of young leaders to upset the status quo (often radically). Mohammed bin Salman is far from the first Saudi or regional leader to slay preciously guarded, oft-repeated, and deeply entrenched shibboleths. Ibn Saud raised an army to take back ancestral lands, and then, with the help of the British, he killed them. Faisal bin Abdulaziz Al Saud deeply cut against social mores by supporting girls' education and the expansion of various media, shocking swathes of Saudi society. Furthermore, when terrorists took hold of the Holy Mosque in Mecca in 1979, Khalid bin Abdulaziz Al Saud called in foreign (and not even Muslim) special operations forces to regain control. These decisions scandalized segments of society at the time, but needs must when the devil drives.

Ibn Saud was twenty-two years old when he began to reforge Saudi Arabia. Oman would be inconceivable today—and quite likely would be more than one country—were it not for Sultan Qaboos galvanizing the state and dragging it into the twentieth century when he took power in 1970 as a thirty-year-old. In Qatar, Hamad bin Khalifah Al Thani transformed the fundamental character of the state in his early forties, transitioning it from, as the *Lonely Planet* guide used to put it, "the most boring place in the Gulf" to a hub of intrigue and, for a time, the center of politics in the Arab world. Mohammed bin Salman's apparent iconoclasm is exacerbated in contrast with recent octogenarian and nonagenarian leadership in Saudi Arabia. However, it is not at all unique in a broader Gulf context.

What is different with Mohammed bin Salman in the Saudi context is the centralization of power in his hands in a manner unseen since the days of Ibn Saud. This approach represents a shift from the typically more consultative and collaborative forms of decision-making at elite levels in Saudi Arabia. Given his control over the Public Investment Fund (PIF) and the way that it has absorbed the state's crown jewels like Saudi Aramco and SABIC, as well as ever-larger shares of the state's dwindling foreign reserves, he is transposing his success onto the broader state's success. The corollary of this is that were he to fail in directing the PIF, then to a greater extent, the Saudi state would fail along with it. His level of control represents a potential single choke point for the kingdom.

Leadership has played a decisive role in recent developments in the UAE. In a departure from the regional norm, Mohammed bin Zayed drove the creation of sizable pockets of international-standard military forces. He then tested these forces in foreign conflicts of increasing scale and danger—a development without precedent for the Gulf monarchies. Some of the UAE's amphibious operations in southern Yemen must count as the most successful and complex expeditionary warfare by Arab military forces in contemporary history.

Elsewhere, however, continuity remains in the military realm. Mohammed bin Salman's Saudi forces engaged in yet another fruitless border conflict in Yemen. Like Ibn Saud's forces generations ago, they became supremely bogged down as they ventured farther south into Yemen. Moreover, the U.S. military retains an overarching role in the monarchies, much as British forces did before them. This oversized presence is encouraged by all the monarchies. The protection curse that it foists is arguably in evidence across the region. Other than the presidential guard and Joint Aviation Command (JAC) in the UAE, there are no prominent examples of Gulf military forces breaking the mold in an effort to develop demonstrably capable forces. Instead, Kuwait, Bahrain, and Qatar seem to vest their security quite transparently in U.S. protection. Qatar's recent approach of procuring three different fast jets from the United States, the United Kingdom, and France is a case in point: evidently the Qatari government felt quite secure that Uncle Sam was de facto protecting the state allowing them to ignore any semblance of a joined-up and sensible procurement approach, but instead to go for a truly whimsical strategy. No procurement expert would wish upon their nation the exquisite expense and boggling complexity that comes from such an approach. Instead, first and foremost, this venture seems aimed at engendering security-oriented attention by powerful states instead of meaningfully striving to build an actual military capability. This example is the zenith of the consistently fuzzy martial thinking evidenced in the recent history of the Gulf monarchies, where military ends, ways, and means have so reliably been wildly out of kilter.

There is debate about the secret sauce that allowed the monarchies to escape the various waves of democratization, remaining autocratic in a changing world. The most persuasive factors come down to a relative abundance of financial resources to buy acquiescence, extensive foreign support, and the elusive element of leaders making the correct decisions from a stability point of view.[5] It is not possible to gaze into the future to assert whether today's important decisions by Gulf leaders are or are not correct. The PIF might become the largest SWF in the world, providing a long-term income catalyzing the Saudi domestic economy. The resolution of the Qatar blockade may set the stage for a sincere reconciliation in the future. However, amid this uncertainty, there are several realities with which the monarchies will have to contend.

The glory days of the oil industry are surely over. The monarchies have gone through withdrawal before. Pearling was a single point of failure for much of the economy on the coast of the Arabian Peninsula, and it was especially dominant in Bahrain, Qatar, and the Trucial States. When demand withered in a few short years, the states stagnated under a colossal depression. Even though the COVID crisis hints at how even today's complex, modern economy can be brought to a juddering halt, the drop-off in oil demand will be less precipitous than it was for pearls. Nevertheless, between mounting pressures to shift to a posthydrocarbon world, acute climate change threats, and renewable fuel costs dropping in price, any further magic decades of high oil prices are increasingly unlikely. The days of splashing tens of billions, or even a hundred billion dollars, to overcome local disenchantment are dwindling.

A last key facet of continuity is the ongoing, outsized role of influential international states. The Gulf monarchies were hardly pried open by colonialism; they have always been internationalized states. Early development was predicated on cheek-by-jowl relations with India and the Horn of Africa region, and, in the oil era, the monarchies' internationalization was embedded. Day-to-day support was often critical. However, long experienced with empire, from the Portuguese to the Ottomans to the British, the monarchies developed nimble relations with their lurching, slow-footed overseers. External powers have a mixed record for local leaders. Gulf leaders often got what they wanted, from demanding that one son or brother was or was not officially recognized as the crown prince to securing twelve-gun salutes to boost local pride. External intermediaries of empire just wanted an easy life. Often this involved striking up a modus vivendi with a local leader. These moves entrenched the leader's power and that of his family, privileging particular political elites and ultimately giving them an edge (and then massively overbearing power in the oil era) when it came to securing power.

Nevertheless, external powers repeatedly proved singularly unable to do their job in critical moments. In the late-nineteenth century, the Ottomans in Qatar were unable to preserve the Qatari Peninsula from Wahhabi (i.e., proto-Saudi) influence emerging from the interior of the Arabian Peninsula. While under nominal British protection, Kuwait lost two-thirds of its territory to Saudi Arabia in 1922. In the 1950s, the British only just held on in Buraimi against the Saudis on behalf of Omani and Trucial States clients. British guarantees and promises proved to be worth nothing when Aden was handed over in 1967 to the world's only avowedly Arab Marxist regime. And in 1971, Britain abandoned its protectorates and was unable to defend three Emirati islands from Iranian invasion. Even the mighty United States, a world superpower, lost its most important regional ally after the Iranian Revolution in 1979, forcing a huge, awkward pivot to further supporting Saudi Arabia. History demonstrates that external protection is not always good to its word.

However, the embrace of the United States proved to have a wooing allure. After the United States proved itself seemingly invincible, smashing Saddam Hussein's substantial armed forces and much-feared Republican Guard out of Kuwait in 1991, the monarchies nuzzled and courted Uncle Sam. When a good chunk of the U.S. military relocated to massive bases on the Peninsula from the 1990s onward, most monarchies de facto abrogated working to build their own military forces in any meaningful way. Kuwait and Bahrain wondered what the point would be, given that they are so small. Qatar barely bothered at all in the 1990s and early 2000s to build an armed force. Saudi Arabia continued to build up their forces, but they proved incapable when they were humiliated by the Houthis in 2008–2009. Oman continued discreetly building its forces. For its part, the UAE feared that Uncle Sam would protect it against Iran, a state threat, but not against substate threats. This intuition proved correct when state and substate threats comingled in Yemen in the mid- and late-2010s, with Iranian proxy forces working closely with the Houthis.

Amid continuity, a sense of change in the military arena is in the offing. Barring a black swan event like a state-on-state war with Iran, the U.S. era in the Gulf is past its peak. U.S. presidents Barack Obama, Donald Trump, and Joe Biden all evidenced a fundamental skepticism about why thousands of U.S. troops continue de facto defending autocratic monarchies 10,000 kilometers away. Obama refused to mire the United States in the war in Yemen, enraging Saudi Arabia and the UAE. Trump turned the American role into a "pay-for-play" venture, demanding compensation for U.S. services. Moreover, in 2019, the most critical oil installation in the world, at Abqaiq, Saudi Arabia, was struck multiple times by what is nearly universally regarded to have been Iranian missiles and drones. Trump's reaction to this brazen attack that undermined the absolute core of the raison d'être of the entire U.S. presence in the region was minimal. Biden hardly reassured Gulf monarchs, and the drawdown from Afghanistan has further lightened the U.S. presence in the Gulf.

Ernest Hemingway wrote in *The Sun Also Rises* that bankruptcy happens "gradually, then suddenly."[6] So too it is with the U.S. role in the Gulf. After more than half a century of engagement in some states, with the attack on Abqaiq, Gulf elites realized with some horror that the U.S. role was far more ephemeral than they thought. Their presence did not deter, their technology did not protect, and their reaction was nearly nonexistent; the American emperor swiftly lost his clothes.

There are, of course, persuasive reasons for U.S. forces to remain in the Gulf. However, the fundamental elastic in the logic of the supposed U.S. protection of the region is broken. Nevertheless, the downslope of U.S. engagement in the Gulf will be long. Michel Foucault coined the term *dispositif* to refer to the grand panoply of a given subject's rules, ideas, norms, experiences, laws, and practices. In the Gulf, the security and defense *dispositif* is predominantly shaped in an American image. This means that the legacy of U.S. equipment, training, logistics, and basing will take at least a generation to work through. However, as the United States dials down its focus across the Gulf, the British and others have returned, in a classic example of continuity. The Gulf monarchies are increasingly developing a mosaic approach to their security. This is signified by the opening of permanent British bases in Bahrain and Oman and the comparatively recent installation of French (2009) and Turkish (2016) bases in the region.

It is more than a quirk that Gulf history repeats itself with such alacrity. Instead, it is a signal that the underpinning structures and dynamics in the region retain continuity amid change. Oil bequeathed finances that shaped a ruling bargain and heavily involved external powers, which shepherded the monarchies through some of the swiftest development changes in the world. However, as the oil paradigm slowly sloughs away, the monarchies will face more of the same challenges. They will do so with the legacy, demands, and expectations that oil created, but increasingly without the benefits the oil political economy bestowed.

There is no one single day when the oil economy will fall, just as there is no single day when climate change will be seen as a genuine and imminent threat. Both realities are too diffuse and complex to be simplified in such a way. Moreover, both situations require significant levels of societal consensus that a potentially existential problem is real and that concerted, difficult action needs to be taken years, if not decades, in advance. Spoilers abound. Amelioratory actions, like reducing subsidies or greenhouse gas emissions, cut against a welter of norms and baked-in structures, processes, expectations, and ways of doing business. Ultimately, each requires little less than the fundamental reimagining of daily life.

The monarchies are relatively well armed to meet these challenges. Together, they have comparatively significant financial reserves, well-developed infrastructures, embedded identities, and a range of important allies. What the monarchies do not have is anything approaching consensus on the scale or imminence of the problems. Consequently, piecemeal and incremental changes are liable to be implemented and repealed. However, the monarchies have transformed themselves before, faster than most. The oil paradigm will not end suddenly as the pearling one did. The warning signs—like longer-term stagnant oil prices—will become increasingly apparent across the region before the real changes in the Gulf begin.

NOTES

INTRODUCTION

1. *BP Statistical Review of World Energy* (London: British Petroleum, 2021).
2. "Marmore: Gulf Cooperation Council (GCC) Sovereign Wealth Funds Experience Asset Growth," *Soveriegn Wealth Fund Institute* (June 4, 2019), https://www.swfinstitute.org /news/73342/marmore-gulf-cooperation-council-gcc-sovereign-wealth-funds-dominate -in-asset-growth; and Claire Milhench, "Global Sovereign Fund Assets Jump to $7.45 Trillion—Preqin," *Reuters* (April 12, 2018), https://tinyurl.com/yb2rbfvf.
3. Reem Salim, "طي الكتمان: اتجاهات الفقر في دول مجلس التعاون الخليجي" ("Untold: Trends in Poverty in the GCC"), مركز البديل للتخطيط والدراسات الاستراتيجية (*Al Badeel Centre for Planning and Strategic Studies*), https://tinyurl.com/y9cd6tut.
4. *Human Development Report 2010*, United Nations Development Programme (Basingstoke, UK: Palgrave Macmillan, November 2010), 29.
5. *Human Development Report 2010*, 29.
6. Marc Owen Jones, *Political Repression in Bahrain* (Cambridge: Cambridge University Press, 2020); Kristian Coates Ulrichsen, *Qatar and the Gulf Crisis: A Study of Resilience* (New York: Oxford University Press, 2020); Abdulrahman Alebrahim, *Kuwait's Politics before Independence: The Role of the Balancing Powers* (Berlin: Gerlach, 2019); Omar AlShehabi, *Contested Modernity: Sectarianism, Nationalism, and Colonialism in Bahrain* (London: One World Academic, 2019); Farah Al-Nakib, *Kuwait Transformed: A History of Oil and Urban Life* (Stanford, CA: Stanford University Press, 2016); Jim Krane, *Energy Kingdoms* (New York: Columbia University Press, 2019); Mark C. Thompson, *Being Young, Male and Saudi: Identity and Politics in a Globalized Kingdom* (Cambridge: Cambridge University Press, 2019); Adam Hanieh, *Money, Markets, and Monarchies: The Gulf Cooperation Council and the Political Economy of the Contemporary Middle East*

(Cambridge: Cambridge University Press, 2018); and Mehran Kamrava, *Troubled Waters: Insecurity in the Persian Gulf* (Ithaca, NY: Cornell University Press, 2018).

7. Rosemarie Said Zahlan, *The Making of the Modern Gulf States: Kuwait, Bahrain, Qatar, the United Arab Emirates and Oman* (Reading, UK: Ithaca, 1998); Gregory Gause III, *Oil Monarchies: Domestic and Security Challenges in the Arab Gulf States* (New York: Council on Foreign Relations, 1994); Kristian Coates Ulrichsen, *Insecure Gulf* (London: Hurst, 2011); Rory Miller, *Desert Kingdoms to Global Powers* (London: Yale University Press, 2016); Omar AlShehabi, تصدير الثروة واغتراب الإنسان: تاريخ الخلل الإنتاجي في دول الخليج العربية (*Exporting Wealth and Alienating the Citizen: History of Production in the GCC*) (Beirut: Centre for Arab Unity Studies, 2018); and Omar AlShehabi and Hamad Al Rayes, الثابت والمتحول 2020: الاستدامة في الخليج (*Change and Continuity 2020: Sustainability in the Gulf*), 8th ed. (Kuwait: مركز الخليج لسياسات التنمية [Gulf Centre for Development Policies], 2020). The main exceptions to this rule are Miller's 2016 book, which is readable but less rooted in the literature, and AlShehabi's 2018 book and annual edited collections, which are excellent resources, but as both are in Arabic, their readership is limited.

8. Ric Neo, "Religious Securitisation and Institutionalised Sectarianism in Saudi Arabia," *Critical Studies on Security* 8, no. 3 (2020): 203–222; Jennifer Carol Heeg, *Seeing Security: Societal Securitization in Qatar* (PhD dissertation, Georgetown University, 2010); Toby Matthiesen, "Sectarianization as Securitization: Identity Politics and Counter-Revolution in Bahrain," in *Sectarianization: Mapping the New Politics of the Middle East*, ed. Nader Hashemi and Danny Postel (London: Hurst, 2017), 199–214; Keith Smith, "Realist Foreign Policy Analysis with a Twist: The Persian Gulf Security Complex and the Rise and Fall of Dual Containment," *Foreign Policy Analysis* 12, no. 3 (2016): 315–333; Harry Verhoeven, "The Gulf and the Horn: Changing Geographies of Security Interdependence and Competing Visions of Regional Order," *Civil Wars* 20, no. 3 (2018): 333–357; and Kamrava, *Troubled Waters*, 22–32.

9. Nadav Safran, *Saudi Arabia: The Ceaseless Quest for Security* (Ithaca, NY: Cornell University Press, 1991), 58–59; and *Future of: Royal Family. Probable Happenings on the Death of Ibn Saud*, Coll 6/16, India Office Records and Private Paper, British Library and Qatar Digital Library, https://www.qdl.qa/archive/81055/vdc_100000000555.0x00026c.

10. Rosemarie Said Zahlan, *The Creation of Qatar* (London and New York: Croom Helm 1979), 59.

11. Safran, *Saudi Arabia*, 87; and Robert Lacey, *Inside the Kingdom* (London: Arrow, 2010), 318–326.

12. *U.S. Interests in and Policy toward the Persian Gulf*, U.S. House of Representatives (1972), 146; and *HM Government Policy in Persian Gulf*, Foreign and Commonwealth Office, London (January 1–December 31, 1971).

13. Jeremy Jones and Nicholas Ridout, *A History of Modern Oman* (New York: Cambridge University Press, 2015), 99–195.

14. Gregory Gause III, *The International Relations of the Persian Gulf* (New York: Cambridge University Press, 2010), 45–136.

15. Russell E. Lucas, "Monarchical Authoritarianism: Survival and Political Liberalization in a Middle Eastern Regime Type," *International Journal of Middle East Studies* 36, no. 1 (2004): 104.

16. Samuel P. Huntington, *Political Order in Changing Societies* (New Haven, CT and London: Yale University Press, 1968). This proved an enduring concern for academics focusing on the Arab world. Marina Ottaway and Michele Dunne, *Incumbent Regimes and the "King's Dilemma" in the Arab World: Promise and Threat of Managed Reform* (Washington, DC: Carnegie Endowment for International Peace, 2007), https://carnegie endowment.org/2007/12/10/incumbent-regimes-and-king-s-dilemma-in-arab-world -promise-and-threat-of-managed-reform-pub-19759.

17. Samuel P. Huntington, "Democracy's Third Wave," *Journal of Democracy* 2, no. 2 (1991): 12–34.

18. Sean Yom, "Understanding the Durability of Authoritarianism in the Middle East," *Arab Studies Journal* 13/14, no. 2/1 (Fall 2005/Spring 2006): 227.

19. Lucas, "Monarchical Authoritarianism," 108; and Lisa Anderson, "Absolutism and the Resilience of Monarchy in the Middle East," *Political Science Quarterly* 106, no. 1 (1991): 1–2.

20. It should also be noted that the invasion of Kuwait precipitated speculation as to whether a post-invasion Gulf or Middle East might be more democratic. See Michael C. Hudson, "After the Gulf War: Prospects for Democratization in the Arab World," *Middle East Journal* 45, no. 3 (1991): 407–426. For examples of the kinds of texts that were preoccupied with democratization and the Arab world, see Rex Brynen, Bahgat Korany, and Paul Noble, eds., *Political Liberalization and Democratization in the Arab World: Theoretical Perspectives*, vol. 1 (Boulder, CO: Lynne Rienner, 1995); Augustus Richard Norton, ed., *Civil Society in the Middle East* (Leiden, Netherlands: Brill, 1996); and Ghassan Salame, ed., *Democracy without Democrats? The Renewal of Politics in the Muslim World* (London and New York: I. B. Tauris, 1994).

21. Gregory Gause III, "Kings for All Seasons: How the Middle East's Monarchies Survived the Arab Spring," *Brookings Doha Center Analysis Paper* 8 (2013), https://www.brookings. edu/research/kings-for-all-seasons-how-the-middle-easts-monarchies-survived-the -arab-spring/; and Hassan A. Barari, "The Persistence of Autocracy: Jordan, Morocco and the Gulf," *Middle East Critique* 24, no. 1 (2015): 99–111.

22. Victor Menaldo, "The Middle East and North Africa's Resilient Monarchs," *Journal of Politics* 74, no. 3 (2012): 707–722.

23. Fawaz A. Gerges, ed., *The New Middle East: Protest and Revolution in the Arab World* (New York: Cambridge University Press, 2014). Also see Kristian Coates Ulrichsen, "Bahrain's Uprising: Domestic Implications and Regional and International Perspective," in *The New Middle East: Protest and Revolution in the Arab World*, ed. Fawaz A. Gerges (New York: Cambridge University Press, 2014), 332–352. The Bahrain chapter in this edited collection is one of the better chapters focusing on the small-state Arab Spring experience.

24. Holger Albrecht and Oliver Schlumberger, " 'Waiting for Godot': Regime Change without Democratization in the Middle East," *International Political Science Review* 25, no. 4 (2004): 371.

25. Emma C. Murphy, "Institutions, Islam and Democracy Promotion: Explaining the Resilience of the Authoritarian State," *Mediterranean Politics* 13, no. 3 (2008): 459 (italics in original).

26. Murphy, "Institutions, Islam and Democracy Promotion," 459.

27. Lucas, "Monarchical Authoritarianism," 103.

28. E. P. Thompson, *The Making of the English Working Class* (New York: Penguin, 2013 [1963]), 12; and Herbert Butterfield, *The Whig Interpretation of History* (New York and London: W. W. Norton, 1965), 12. On this wider argument, see Jonas Grethlein, "'Future Past': Time and Teleology in (Ancient) Historiography," *History and Theory* 53 (October 2014): 309–315, 324–327.

29. ISS is not a universally recognized term. Some scholars discuss similar concepts under categories like "international security," "security studies," and "peace studies." Barry Buzan and Lene Hansen, *The Evolution of International Security Studies* (Cambridge: Cambridge University Press, 2010), 1.

30. Emma Rothschild, "What Is Security?," *Daedalus* 124, no. 3 (1995): 53–98.

31. Buzan and Hansen, *The Evolution of International Security Studies*, 22–32, 156–184; Pinar Bilgin, "Individual and Societal Dimensions of Security," *International Studies Review* 5, no. 2 (2003): 203–222; and David A. Baldwin, "Security Studies and the End of the Cold War," *World Politics* 48, no. 1 (1995): 120.

32. See Walt's history of ISS for a clear summation of the field from a realist standpoint. Stephen M. Walt, "The Renaissance of Security Studies," *International Studies Quarterly* 35, no. 2 (1991): 211–239. For critiques of Walt's approach, see Edward A. Kolodziej, "Renaissance in Security Studies? Caveat Lector!," *International Studies Quarterly* 36, no. 4 (1992): 421–438; and Keith Krause and Michael Charles Williams, "From Strategy to Security: Foundations of Critical Security Studies," in *Critical Security Studies*, ed. Keith Krause and Michael Charles Williams (Minneapolis: University of Minnesota Press, 1997), 36–39.

33. Buzan and Hansen, *The Evolution of International Security Studies*, 87–98; Ole Wæver, "The History and Social Structure of Security Studies as a Practico-Academic Field," in *Security Expertise: Practice, Power, Responsibility*, ed. Trine Villumsen Berling and Christian Bueger (Oxford, UK: Routledge, 2015), 76–106; and Ole Wæver, *Aberystwyth, Paris, Copenhagen: New "Schools" in Security Theory and Their Origins between Core and Periphery*, presented at the annual meeting of the International Studies Association, Montreal, March 17–20, 2004.

34. Baldwin, "Security Studies," 123; and Joseph S. Nye and Sean M. Lynn-Jones, "International Security Studies: A Report of a Conference on the State of the Field," *International Security* 12, no. 4 (1988): 8–9.

35. Nye and Lynn-Jones, "International Security Studies," 9–10; and Baldwin, "Security Studies," 124.

36. Steve Smith, "The Increasing Insecurity of Security Studies: Conceptualizing Security in the Last Twenty Years," *Contemporary Security Policy* 20, no. 3 (1999): 72–101.

37. Buzan and Hansen, *The Evolution of International Security Studies*, 1–2.

38. Buzan and Hansen, *The Evolution of International Security Studies*, 10–13.

39. For instance, Walt ignores this entire segment of security debates in his overview article; see Walt, "Renaissance of Security Studies."

40. Wæver, *New "Schools" in Security Theory and Their Origins*, 3–6.

41. Jef Huysmans, "Revisiting Copenhagen: Or, on the Creative Development of a Security Studies Agenda in Europe," *European Journal of International Relations* 4, no. 4 (1998): 482. See Buzan and Hansen, *The Evolution of International Security Studies*, 187–225, for reflections on the widening and deepening of the security debate.

42. On the evolution of these five sectors in the Copenhagen School, see Huysmans, "Revisiting Copenhagen," 486–491.

43. Matt McDonald, "Securitization and the Construction of Security," *European Journal of International Relations* 14, no. 4 (2008): 565. For key critiques of the Copenhagen School, see Bill McSweeney, "Identity and Security: Buzan and the Copenhagen School," *Review of International Studies* 22, no. 1 (1996): 81–93; Lene Hansen, "The Little Mermaid's Silent Security Dilemma and the Absence of Gender in the Copenhagen School," *Millennium Journal of International Studies* 29 (2000): 285–306; and Michael Williams, *Culture and Security: Symbolic Power and the Politics of International Security* (London: Routledge, 2007).

44. Huysmans, "Revisiting Copenhagen," 490.

45. On the widespread influence of leaders, see Margaret G. Hermann and Joe D. Hagan, "International Decision Making: Leadership Matters," *Foreign Policy*, no. 110 (1998): 124–137. And for a specific discussion of leaders' influence in the Gulf context, see Marwan Kablan, "سياسة قطر الخارجية: النخبة في مواجهة الجغرافيا" ("Qatari Foreign Policy: Elites Versus Geography"), *Siyasat Arabiya*, no. 28 (September 2017), 7–24, https://www.dohainstitute .org/ar/Lists/ACRPS-PDFDocumentLibrary/Siyassat28_kablan_Qatar%27s_Foreign _Policy_Elite_Versus_Geography.pdf.

46. Lewis W. Snider, "Comparing the Strength of Nations: The Arab Gulf States and Political Change," *Comparative Politics* 20, no. 4 (1988): 461; Gregory Gause III, "Understanding the Gulf States," *Democracy Journal*, no. 36 (Spring 2015): 31; John Willoughby, "Segmented Feminization and the Decline of Neopatriarchy in GCC Countries of the Persian Gulf," *Comparative Studies of South Asia, Africa and the Middle East* 28, no. 1 (2008): 184; and Abubakr M. Suliman and Rehana Hayat, "Leadership in the UAE," in *Leadership Development in the Middle East*, ed. Beverly Dawn Matcalfe and Fouad Mimouni (Cheltenham, UK: Edward Elgar, 2012), 111–115.

47. Raymond Hinnebusch, "Foreign Policy in the Middle East," in *The Foreign Policies of Middle East States*, ed. Raymond Hinnenusch and Anoushiravan Ehteshami (Boulder, CO: Lynne Rienner, 2014), 1.

48. Hinnebusch, "Foreign Policy in the Middle East"; and Gerd Nonneman, "Analyzing Middle East Foreign Policies: A Conceptual Framework," in *Analyzing Middle East Foreign Policies and the Relationship with Europe*, ed. Gerd Nonneman (Abingdon, UK: Routledge, 2005), 6–18.

49. Hinnebusch, "Foreign Policy in the Middle East," 1, 3.

50. Edward A. Kolodziej, *Security and International Relations* (New York: Cambridge University Press, 2005), 26–27.

51. Arnold Wolfers, "'National Security' as an Ambiguous Symbol," *Political Science Quarterly* 67, no. 4 (1952): 481–502. For a lucid discussion of Wolfers and his contribution to the delineation of these kinds of questions, see David A. Baldwin, "The Concept of Security," *Review of International Studies* 23, no. 1 (1997): 12.

52. Barry Buzan, *People, States and Fear: An Agenda for International Security Studies in the Post-Cold War Era*, 2nd ed. (Colchester, UK: ECPR, 1991), 157–188.

53. Barry Buzan, Ole Wæver, and Jaap de Wilde, *Security: A New Framework for Analysis* (Boulder, CO: Lynne Rienner, 1998), 201 (italics in original).

54. Buzan, *People, States and Fear*.

55. Gregory Gause III, "Gulf Regional Politics: Revolution, War and Rivalry," in *The Dynamics of Regional Politics: Four Systems on the Indian Ocean Rim*, ed. W. Howard Wriggins (New York: Columbia University Press, 1992); Gause, *The International Relations of the Persian Gulf*; Henner Fürtig, "Conflict and Cooperation in the Persian Gulf: The Interregional Order and US Policy," *Middle East Journal* 61, no. 4 (2007): 627–640; and Kristian Coates Ulrichsen, *Insecure Gulf* (London: Hurst, 2011).

56. *Economic Prospects and Policy Challenges for the GCC Countries*, Internatioal Monetary Fund (Riyadh, October 26, 2016); and Anthony DiPaola, "Middle East's $2 Trillion Wealth Could Be Gone by 2034, IMF Says," *Bloomberg* (February 6, 2020), https://www.bloombergquint.com/technology/middle-east-s-2-trillion-wealth-could-be-gone-by-2034-imf-says.

1. POLITICAL SECURITY

1. Caitlin Dewey and Max Fisher, "Meet the World's Other 25 Royal Families," *Washington Post* (July 22, 2013), https://www.washingtonpost.com/news/worldviews/wp/2013/07/22/meet-the-worlds-other-25-royal-families/.

2. Lisa Anderson, "Dynasts and Nationalists: Why Monarchies Survive," in *Middle East Monarchies: The Challenge of Modernity*, ed. Joseph Kostiner (Boulder, CO: Lynne Rienner, 2000), 53.

3. J. E. Peterson, "The Arabian Peninsula in Modern Times: A Historiographical Survey," *American Historical Review* 96, no. 5 (1991): 1435, http://www.jstor.org/stable/2165280.

4. Barry Buzan, Ole Wæver, and Jaap de Wilde, *Security: A New Framework for Analysis* (Boulder, CO: Lynne Rienner, 1998), 141.

5. Buzan, Wæver, and Wilde, *Security*, 141.

6. Buzan, Wæver, and Wilde, *Security*, 142–144.

7. Buzan, Wæver, and Wilde, *Security*, 144–145.

8. Omar AlShehabi, تصدير الثروة واغتراب الإنسان: تاريخ الخلل الإنتاجي في دول الخليج العربية (*Exporting Wealth and Alienating the Citizen: History of Production in the GCC*) (Beirut: Centre for Arab Unity Studies, 2018), Loc. 7069–8057.

9. Gail Buttorff, Bozena Welborne, and Nawra al-Lawati, "Measuring Female Labor Force Participation in the GCC," *Issue Brief* 1 (2018): 4.

10. John Chalcraft, "Migration and Popular Protest in the Arabian Peninsula and the Gulf in the 1950s and 1960s," *International Labor and Working-Class History* 79, no. 1 (2011): 30.

11. File 35/3, the Divers' Riot of May 1932 (British Library and Qatar Digital Library).

12. File 35/3, the Divers' Riot of May 1932.

13. Helen Lackner, *A House Built on Sand* (London: Ithaca, 1978), 90.

14. Fred Halliday, *Arabia without Sultans*, 2nd ed. (London: Saqi, 2002), Loc 3425; and Chalcraft, "Migration and Protest," 30.

15. Chalcraft, "Migration and Protest," 29.

16. File 6/18 I, Arab and Persian Schools in Bahrain (Qatar Digital Library).

17. Ian J. Seccombe, "Labour Migration to the Arabian Gulf: Evolution and Characteristics 1920–1950," *British Journal of Middle Eastern Studies* 10, no. 1 (1983): 6–10.

18. Timothy Mitchell, *Carbon Democracy: Political Power in the Age of Oil* (London: Verso, 2011), 104.

19. Khaldoun Hasan al-Naqeeb, *Society and State in the Gulf and Arab Peninsula: A Different Perspective* (London: Routledge, 1990), 92–93.

20. Rosemarie Said Zahlan, *The Making of the Modern Gulf States: Kuwait, Bahrain, Qatar, the United Arab Emirates and Oman* (Abingdon, UK: Routledge, 1989), 37.

21. Michael Herb, *All in the Family* (Albany: State University of New York, 1999), 140–141; and Abdullah Omran Taryam, *The Establishment of the United Arab Emirates* (Abingdon, UK: Routledge, 1987), 14–15.

22. Christopher Davidson, *The United Arab Emirates: A Study in Survival* (Boulder, CO: Lynne Rienner, 2005), 36; and Jim Krane, *Energy Kingdoms* (New York: Columbia University Press, 2019), 40.

23. David B. Roberts, "Kuwait," in *Power and Politics in the Persian Gulf Monarchies*, ed. Christopher Davidson (London: Hurst, 2011), 93.

24. Anthony B. Toth, "Tribes and Tribulations: Bedouin Losses in the Saudi and Iraqi Struggles over Kuwait's Frontiers, 1921–1943," *British Journal of Middle Eastern Studies* 32, no. 2 (2005): 145–167; and Mary Cubberly Van Pelt, "The Sheikhdom of Kuwait," *Middle East Journal* (1950): 12–26.

25. Chalcraft, "Migration and Protest," 38; Khaldoun Hassan al-Nakeeb and L. M. Kenny (trans.), *Society and State in the Gulf and Arab Peninsula: A Different Perspective*, Routledge Library Editions (Abingdon, UK: Routledge, 2012); and Jill Crystal, *Oil and Politics in the Gulf: Rulers and Merchants in Kuwait and Qatar* (Cambridge: Cambridge University Press, 1995). On the wider influence of such migrants on Saudi politics and state formation, see Rosie Bsheer, "A Counter-Revolutionary State: Popular Movements and the Making of Saudi Arabia," *Past and Present* 238, no. 1 (2018): 233–277.

26. Chalcraft, "Migration and Protest," 38.

27. Mitchell, *Carbon Democracy*, 106.

28. Emile A. Nakhleh, *Bahrain* (New York: DC Heath, 1976), 78–79.

29. Malcolm Byrne, "CIA Confirms Role in 1953 Iran Coup," *National Security Archive Electronic Briefing Book* 435, no. 19 (2013), https://nsarchive2.gwu.edu/NSAEBB/NSAEBB435/.

30. Chalcraft, "Migration and Protest," 32.

31. David B. Roberts, *Qatar: Securing the Global Ambitions of a City-State* (London: Hurst, 2017), 18–19.

32. Crystal, *Oil and Politics in the Gulf*, 81–83.

33. Crystal, *Oil and Politics in the Gulf*, 81.

34. Farah Al-Nakib, *Kuwait Transformed: A History of Oil and Urban Life* (Stanford, CA: Stanford University Press, 2016), 91–149.

35. Crystal, *Oil and Politics in the Gulf*, 141–145.

36. Toby Matthiesen, "Sectarianization as Securitization: Identity Politics and Counter-Revolution in Bahrain," in *Sectarianization: Mapping the New Politics of the Middle East*, ed. Nader Hashemi and Danny Postel (London: Hurst, 2017), 204.

37. Hasan Tariq Alhasan, "The Role of Iran in the Failed Coup of 1981: The IFLB in Bahrain," *Middle East Journal* 65, no. 4 (2011): 604.

38. Tariq Alhasan, "Failed Coup," 604.

39. Nadav Safran, *Saudi Arabia: The Ceaseless Quest for Security* (Ithaca, NY: Cornell University Press, 1991), 90–91.

40. Safran, *Saudi Arabia*, 92.

41. Stephane Lacroix, "Understanding Stability and Dissent in the Kingdom," in *Saudi Arabia in Transition: Insights on Social, Political, Economic and Religious Change*, ed. Bernard Haykel, Thomas Hegghammer, and Stephane Lacroix (Cambridge: Cambridge University Press, 2015), 169.

42. Lacroix, "Understanding Stability and Dissent," 173.

43. For a forensic account of the tacit and explicit state support for such ideas, see Saud Al Sarhan, "The Struggle for Authority: The Shaykhs of Jihadi-Salafism in Saudi Arabia, 1997–2003," in *Saudi Arabia in Transition: Insights on Social, Political, Economic and Religious Change*, ed. Bernard Haykel, Thomas Hegghammer, and Stephane Lacroix (Cambridge: Cambridge University Press, 2015), 181–205.

44. Courtney Freer, *Rentier Islamism: The Influence of the Muslim Brotherhood in Gulf Monarchies* (New York: Oxford University Press, 2018), chapter 4.

45. For a clear overview of this early history, see Marc Valeri, "Oman," in *Power and Politics in the Persian Gulf Monarchies*, ed. Christopher Davidson (London: Hurst, 2011), 135–138.

46. Marc Valeri, *Oman: Politics and Society in the Qaboos State* (London: Hurst, 2017), 50–52; and Jeremy Jones and Nicholas Ridout, *A History of Modern Oman* (New York: Cambridge University Press, 2015), 122–131.

47. Safran, *Saudi Arabia*, 94.

48. Chalcraft, "Migration and Protest," 33–35.

49. Halliday, *Arabia without Sultans*, Loc. 6323.

50. Toby Matthiesen, "Red Arabia: Anti-Colonialism, the Cold War, and the Long Sixties in the Gulf States," in *Routledge Handbook of the Global Sixties* (London: Routledge, 2018), 98.

51. Nakhleh, *Bahrain*, 77–81.

52. Matthiesen, "Red Arabia," 97.

53. Matthiesen, "Red Arabia," 101.

54. *Future of: Royal Family. Probable Happenings on the Death of Ibn Saud*, Coll 6/16, India Office Records and Private Paper, British Library and Qatar Digital Library, https://www.qdl.qa/archive/81055/vdc_100000000555.0x00026c.

55. Safran, *Saudi Arabia*, 58–59; *Future of: Royal Family. Probable Happenings on the Death of Ibn Saud*; Michel G. Nehme, "Saudi Arabia 1950–80: Between Nationalism and Religion,"

Middle Eastern Studies 30, no. 4 (1994): 930–931; and Ellen Wald, *Saudi Inc.: The Arabian Kingdom's Pursuit of Profit and Power* (New York and London: Pegasus, 2018), 112–116.

56. Mai Yamani, *Changed Identities: The Challenge of the New Generation in Saudi Arabia* (London: Royal Institute of International Affairs, 2000), 30.

57. David B. Roberts, "Breaking the Saudi Rules of Succession," *Washington Post* (May 27, 2015), https://www.washingtonpost.com/news/monkey-cage/wp/2015/05/27/breaking-the-saudi-rules-of-succession/.

58. Nabil Mouline, "Enforcing and Reinforcing the State's Islam," in *Saudi Arabia in Transition: Insights on Social, Political, Economic and Religious Change*, ed. Bernard Haykel, Thomas Hegghammer, and Stephane Lacroix (Cambridge: Cambridge University Press, 2015), 53–56.

59. Joseph Kraft, "Letter from Saudi Arabia," *New Yorker* (July 4, 1983), 43.

60. Mouline, "State's Islam," 56–57.

61. Abdulrahman Alebrahim, *Kuwait's Politics before Independence: The Role of the Balancing Powers* (Berlin: Gerlach, 2019), 1–58.

62. Crystal, *Oil and Politics in the Gulf*, 44–83.

63. Jane Kinninmont, "Bahrain," in *Power and Politics in the Persian Gulf Monarchies*, ed. Christopher Davidson (London: Hurst, 2011), 30–33.

64. Omar AlShehabi, *Contested Modernity: Sectarianism, Nationalism, and Colonialism in Bahrain* (London: One World Academic, 2019), chapter 1.

65. Anita L. P. Burdett, ed., *British Resident E.F. Henderson, Doha, to JL Beaven Arabian Department, FCO London, "Qatar Internal" February 21, 1972*, vol. IV: 1970–1971, Records of Qatar 1966–1971 (Slough, UK: Archive Editions Limited, 2006), 714.

66. Crystal, *Oil and Politics in the Gulf*, 155.

67. Valeri, "Oman," 139–156.

68. Christopher Davidson, *Abu Dhabi: Oil and Beyond* (New York: Columbia University Press, 2009), 44–64.

69. *U.S. Interests in and Policy toward the Persian Gulf*, U.S. House of Representatives (1972), 145–147.

70. AlShehabi, تصدير الثروة واغتراب الإنسان: تاريخ الخلل الإنتاجي في دول الخليج العربية (*Exporting Wealth and Alienating the Citizen: History of Production in the GCC*), Loc. 4463, chapter 5.

71. Gerd Nonneman, *Political Reform in the Gulf Monarchies: From Liberalisation to Democratization*, Sir William Luce Fellowship Paper (Durham, UK: University of Durham, Institute for Middle Eastern and Islamic Studies, 2006), 3.

72. Nonneman, *Political Reform*, 3–4; and Valeri, *Oman*, 62–64.

73. This sentiment is superbly brought to life in Kuwait's case by Al-Nakib, *Kuwait Transformed*, 43–91.

74. Christine Osborne, *The Gulf States and Oman* (Abingdon, UK: Routledge, 2017), 17.

75. Mehran Kamrava, "The Political Economy of Rentierism in the Persian Gulf," in *Political Economy of the Persian Gulf*, ed. Mehran Kamrava (New York: Columbia University Press, 2012), 54.

76. Eran Segal, "Political Participation in Kuwait: Dīwāniyya, Majlis and Parliament," *Journal of Arabian Studies* 2, no. 2 (2012): 129.

77. Kohei Hashimoto, Jareer Elass, and Stacy Eller, "Liquefied Natural Gas from Qatar: The Qatargas Project," Baker Institute Energy Forum, Rice University (Stanford, CA: December 2004), 10; and Colin Brant, *Valedictory from Qatar: A Land of Promise*, Foreign and Commonwealth Office, London (July 9, 1981), 3.

78. Steffen Hertog, *Princes, Brokers, and Bureaucrats: Oil and the State in Saudi Arabia* (Ithaca, NY: Cornell University Press, 2011), 78–82.

79. Toby Jones, *Desert Kingdom: How Oil and Water Forged Modern Saudi Arabia* (Cambridge, MA: Harvard University Press, 2010), 84.

80. Jones, *Desert Kingdom*, 63, 83–89.

81. Jones, *Desert Kingdom*, 85.

82. Jones, *Desert Kingdom*, 15.

83. Sarah G. Phillips and Jennifer S. Hunt, " 'Without Sultan Qaboos, We Would Be Yemen': The Renaissance Narrative and the Political Settlement in Oman," *Journal of International Development* 29, no. 5 (2017): 645–660.

84. Hertog, *Princes, Brokers, and Bureaucrats*, 80; and Sarah Yizraeli, "Al Sa'ud: An Ambivalent Approach to Tribalism," in *Tribes and States in a Changing Middle East*, ed. Uzi Rabi (New York: Oxford University Press, 2016), 99–101.

85. Hertog, *Princes, Brokers, and Bureaucrats*, 80; and Yizraeli, "Al Sa'ud," 100–101.

86. Abdulaziz Al Fahad, "Raiders and Traders: A Poet's Lament on the End of the Bedouin Heroic Age," in *Saudi Arabia in Transition: Insights on Social, Political, Economic and Religious Change*, ed. Bernard Haykel, Thomas Hegghammer, and Stephane Lacroix (Cambridge: Cambridge University Press, 2015), 261–262.

87. Abdulaziz Al Fahad, "Rootless Trees: Genealogical Politics in Saudi Arabia," in *Saudi Arabia in Transition: Insights on Social, Political, Economic and Religious Change*, ed. Bernard Haykel, Thomas Hegghammer, and Stephane Lacroix (Cambridge: Cambridge University Press, 2015), 276–279.

88. Kamrava, "Political Economy," 55–62; and AlShehabi, تصدير الثروة واغتراب الإنسان: تاريخ الخلل الإنتاجي في دول الخليج العربية (*Exporting Wealth and Alienating the Citizen: History of Production in the GCC*), Loc. 8447–10158.

89. Gregory Gause III, *Oil Monarchies: Domestic and Security Challenges in the Arab Gulf States* (New York: Council on Foreign Relations, 1994), 44–54.

90. AlShehabi, *Contested Modernity*; and Marc Owen Jones, *Political Repression in Bahrain* (Cambridge: Cambridge University Press, 2020).

91. Hertog, *Princes, Brokers, and Bureaucrats*, 78–79.

92. David Leigh and Rob Evans, "Secrets of Yamamah," *The Guardian*, https://www.theguardian.com/baefiles/page/0,,2095831,00.html.

93. Herb, *All in the Family*; F. Gregory Gause, "The Persistence of Monarchy in the Arabian Peninsula: A Comparative Analysis," in *Middle East Monarchies: The Challenge of Modernity*, ed. Joseph Kostiner (Boulder, CO: Lynne Rienner, 2000); Madawi Al Rasheed, "Circles of Power: Royals and Saudi Society," in *Saudi Arabia in the Balance*, ed. Gerd Nonneman and Paul Aarts (New York: New York University Press, 2005), 185; and Adam Hanieh, *Money, Markets, and Monarchies: The Gulf Cooperation Council and the Political Economy of the Contemporary Middle East* (Cambridge: Cambridge University Press, 2018), 114–131.

94. AlShehabi, تصدير الثروة واغتراب الإنسان: تاريخ الخلل الإنتاجي في دول الخليج العربية (*Exporting Wealth and Alienating the Citizen: History of Production in the GCC*), Loc. 6123–6206.

95. Hertog, *Princes, Brokers, and Bureaucrats*, 78–82, 86–98.

96. Marc Valeri, "Liberalization from Above: Political Reforms and Sultanism in Oman," in *Constitutional Reform and Political Participation in the Gulf*, ed. Abdulhadi Khalaf and Giacomo Luciani (Dubai: Gulf Research Center, 2006), 187.

97. Valeri, "Liberalization from Above," 187.

98. Valeri, *Oman*, 136.

99. Valeri, *Oman*, 136.

100. Jill Crystal, "Tribes and Patronage Networks in Qatar," in *Tribes and States in a Changing Middle East*, ed. Uzi Rabi (New York: Oxford University Press, 2016), 45–46.

101. Crystal, "Tribes and Patronage Networks in Qatar," 46–50; and Hadi Alshawi and Andrew Gardner, "Tribalism, Identity and Citizenship in Contemporary Qatar," *Anthropology of the Middle East* 8, no. 2 (2013): 51–57.

102. Al-Nakib, *Kuwait Transformed*, 121–149, 175–199.

103. Andrea B. Rugh, "Backgammon or Chess? The State of Tribalism and Tribal Leadership in the United Arab Emirates," in *Tribes and States in a Changing Middle East*, ed. Uzi Rabi (New York: Oxford University Press, 2016), 67–69, 74–75.

104. Rugh, "Backgammon," 68.

105. Rugh, "Backgammon," 68–69.

106. Tariq Alhasan, "Failed Coup," 604–605.

107. Tariq Alhasan, "Failed Coup," 605–609.

108. Tariq Alhasan, "Failed Coup," 606–613.

109. See also the specter of Hezbollah operating, as described in Ghassan AlShehabi, "حزب الله البحرين".. قصة متجذرة شائكة" ("Hezbollah Bahrain: A Deep Rooted Thorny Story"), *Al Majallah* (October 14, 2013), https://gulfpolicies.org/2019-05-18-07-14-32/92-2019-06-25-12-45-40/765-2019-06-26-09-01-59.

110. Matthiesen, "Sectarianization as Securitization," 204–205.

111. J. C. B. Richmond, *Despatch No. 42* (Kuwait: Foreign and Commonwealth Office, London, August 14, 1960), https://www.agda.ae/en/catalogue/tna/fo/371/148912/n/4.

112. Richmond, *Despatch No. 42*.

113. *Past and Present Problems of Iraq's Boundaries with Kuwait and Saudi Arabia* (Washington, DC: Central Intelligence Agency, August 1975), 2, https://www.cia.gov/readingroom/document/cia-rdp86t00608r000600140013-8.

114. E. T. Davies, *Codewords under Operation Sodabread* (Manama: Foreign and Commonwealth Office, London, November 2, 1961).

115. Michael Herb, "A Nation of Bureaucrats: Political Participation and Economic Diversification in Kuwait and the United Arab Emirates," *International Journal of Middle East Studies* 41, no. 3 (2009): 380.

116. Roberts, "Kuwait," 93.

117. Roberts, "Kuwait," 94.

118. A. T. Lamb, *First Impressions of Kuwait* (Kuwait: Foreign and Commonwealth Office, August 1, 1974).

119. Roberts, "Kuwait," 94.

120. Bradley L. Glasser, "External Capital and Political Liberalizations: A Typology of Middle Eastern Development in the 1980s and 1990s," *Journal of International Affairs* 49, no. 1 (1995): 72–73.

121. Robert Strayer, "Decolonization, Democratization, and Communist Reform: The Soviet Collapse in Comparative Perspective," *Journal of World History* 12, no. 2 (2001): 375–406.

122. Lisa Anderson, "Arab Democracy: Dismal Prospects," *World Policy Journal* 18, no. 3 (2001): 54–55; and Michael C. Hudson, "After the Gulf War: Prospects for Democratization in the Arab World," *Middle East Journal* 45, no. 3 (1991): 424–426.

123. Lawrence Freedman and Efraim Karsh, *The Gulf Conflict, 1990–1991: Diplomacy and War in the New World Order* (London: Faber and Faber, 1993), 85–94, 299–330.

124. May Seikaly, "Kuwait and Bahrain: The Appeal of Globalization and Internal Constraints," in *Iran, Iraq, and the Arab Gulf States*, ed. Joseph A. Kechichian (New York: Palgrave, 2001), 179, 183.

125. Ghanim Al Najjar, "Struggle over Parliament in Kuwait," Sada, Washington, DC: Carnegie Endowment for International Peace, August 18, 2008, https://carnegieendowment.org/sada/20845. On the nature of Kuwait's participatory culture, see Hussein Ismail Mirza, "أسباب العزوف عن المشاركة السياسية في الإنتخابات في الكويت : دراسة مسحية" ("Reasons for Not Participating in Political Elections in Kuwait: A Survey"), المركز الديمقراطي العربي (Arab Democratic Centre) (May 2017).

126. Kristin Smith Diwan, "Divided Government in Kuwait: The Politics of Parliament since the Gulf War," *Domes* 8, no. 1 (1999): 4.

127. Smith Diwan, "Divided Government in Kuwait," 4–5.

128. Seikaly, "Kuwait and Bahrain," 183.

129. Smith Diwan, "Divided Government in Kuwait," 7.

130. Mouline, "State's Islam," 63–65.

131. Gilles Kepel, *The War for Muslim Minds* (Cambridge, MA: Harvard University Press, 2006), 181.

132. Andrzej Kapiszewski, "Elections and Parliamentary Activity in the GCC States: Broadening Political Participation in the Gulf Monarchies," in *Constitutional Reform and Political Participation in the Gulf*, ed. Abdulhadi Khalaf and Giacomo Luciani (Dubai: Gulf Research Center, 2006), 91.

133. Khalid Al Dakhil, *2003: Saudi Arabia's Year of Reform*, Sada (Washington, DC: Carnegie Endowment for International Peace, August 22, 2008).

134. Kapiszewski, "Elections and Parliamentary Activity," 92.

135. Kapiszewski, "Elections and Parliamentary Activity," 95–96.

136. Lacroix, "Stability and Dissent," 178–180.

137. Matthiesen, "Sectarianization as Securitization," 205.

138. Matthiesen, "Sectarianization as Securitization," 205–206.

139. Abdulhadi Khalaf, *Bahrain's Parliament: The Quest for a Role*, Sada (Washington, DC: Carnegie Endowment for Middle East Peace, 2004), https://carnegieendowment.org/sada/21282.

140. Valeri, "Liberalization from Above," 188.

141. Valeri, "Liberalization from Above," 189.

142. Valeri, "Liberalization from Above," 191–195.

143. Roberts, *Qatar: Securing the Global Ambitions*, 22.

144. Amna Al Marri, "المستجدات في دولة قطر" ("New Developments in the State of Qatar"), in الثابت والمتحول 2020: الاستدامة في الخليج (*Change and Continuity 2020: Sustainability in the Gulf*), ed. Omar AlShehabi and Hamad Al Rayes (Kuwait: مركز الخليج لسياسات التنمية [Gulf Centre for Development Policies], 2020).

145. Justin Gengler and Majed Al Ansari, "Qatar's First Elections since 2017 Reveal Unexpected Impact of GCC Crisis," *Al Monitor* (April 24, 2019), https://www.al-monitor.com/originals/2019/04/qatar-first-elections-reveal-unexpected-impact-gcc-crisis.html.

146. David B. Roberts, "News from Qatar Protest," *TheGulfBlog.com* (March 16, 2011), http://thegulfblog.com/2011/03/16/news-from-qatar-protest/. One Qatari was arrested and sentenced for writing abusive poems about the emir and his immediate family. But the very fact that it was one individual alone speaks to Qatar's quietism.

147. Ali Khalifah Al-Kuwari, ed., الشعب يريد الإصلاح في قطر أيضا (*The People Want Reform in Qatar Too*) (Beirut: The Knowledge Forum, 2012).

148. Freer, *Rentier Islamism*, chapter 6.

149. Fawaz A. Gerges, "The Obama Approach to the Middle East: The End of America's Moment?," *International Affairs* 89, no. 2 (2013): 307–310.

150. Guido Steinberg, *Leading the Counter-Revolution: Saudi Arabia and the Arab Spring* (Berlin: German Institute for International and Security Affairs, 2014), https://www.swp-berlin.org/publications/products/research_papers/2014_RP07_sbg.pdf.

151. David B. Roberts, "Qatar and the Muslim Brotherhood: Pragmatism or Preference?," *Middle East Policy* 21, no. 3 (2014): 84–94.

152. Birol Baskan and Steven Wright, "Seeds of Change: Comparing State-Religion Relations in Qatar and Saudi Arabia," *Arab Studies Quarterly* 33, no. 2 (Spring 2011): 96–111.

153. Roberts, "Qatar and the Muslim Brotherhood."

154. Roberts, *Qatar: Securing the Global Ambitions*, 123–149.

155. It was called the Al Udeid base even though it is not in Al Udeid itself, which is a Qatari village located in the southeast corner of the country where it meets Saudi Arabia, and where it used to meet the United Arab Emirates (UAE) before a border change in the late 1960s. The reason for misnaming the base in this way is that, should the Saudis claim Al Udeid as their own—not an unlikely concern given myriad irredentist wranglings in the Gulf and recent grim Qatari regional relations—then, at least at the very beginning, this would sound to the Americans as unequivocally wrong: Al Udeid (the air base) is obviously Qatari.

156. Justin Gengler, "Qatar's Ambivalent Democratization," *Foreign Policy* (November 1, 2011), http://mideast.foreignpolicy.com/posts/2011/11/01/qataris_lesson_in_revolution.

157. David B. Roberts, "Is Qatar Bringing the Nusra Front in from the Cold?," *BBC* (March 6, 2015), http://www.bbc.co.uk/news/world-middle-east-31764114.

158. Freer, *Rentier Islamism*, chapters 2 and 3.

159. Shadi Hamid, "The Tragedy of Egypt's Mohamed Morsi," *The Atlantic* (June 18, 2019), https://www.theatlantic.com/ideas/archive/2019/06/mohamed-morsi-and-end-egyptian-democracy/591982/.

160. Robert F. Worth, "Mohammed Bin Zayed's Dark Vision of the Middle East's Future," *New York Times* (January 2, 2020), https://www.nytimes.com/2020/01/09/magazine/united -arab-emirates-mohammed-bin-zayed.html.

161. Worth, "Mohammed Bin Zayed's Dark Vision."

162. David B. Roberts, "Qatar and the UAE: Exploring Divergent Responses to the Arab Spring," *Middle East Journal* 71, no. 4 (2017): 544–561.

163. Shadi Hamid, *Temptations of Power: Islamists and Illiberal Democracy in a New Middle East* (New York: Oxford University Press, 2014), chapter 7.

164. David B. Roberts, "Mosque and State: The United Arab Emirates' Secular Foreign Policy," *Foreign Affairs* (March 18, 2016), https://www.foreignaffairs.com/articles/united-arab -emirates/2016-03-18/mosque-and-state.

165. On the background of this history, see Amna Al Marri and Miriam Al Hajri, "المستجدات السياسية في دولة قطر" ("Political Developments in the State of Qatar"), in التنمية يف هامش الخليج :2018 الثابت واملتحول (*Change and Transformation: Development at the Margins of the Gulf*), ed. Omar AlShehabi, Ahmed Al Owfi, and Khalil Bohazza (Kuwait: مركز الخليج لسياسات التنمية [Gulf Centre for Development Policies], 2018); and Roberts, *Qatar: Securing the Global Ambitions*, 151–153.

166. Roberts, *Qatar: Securing the Global Ambitions*, 149–157.

167. David B. Roberts, "A Dustup in the Gulf," *Foreign Affairs* (June 13, 2017), https://www .foreignaffairs.com/articles/middle-east/2017-06-13/dustup-gulf.

168. Habib Toumi, "Qatari Plots against Bahrain Revealed," *Gulf News* (August 22, 2017), https://gulfnews.com/world/gulf/qatar/qatari-plots-against-bahrain-revealed -1.2078073. Ignore the editorializing: this just reflects Bahraini perspectives. Few, however, doubt that the workshop described here and other similar meetings took place.

169. *A Survey of Global Terrorism and Terrorist Financing* (Washington, DC: U.S. Government, April 22, 2015), 29, https://www.govinfo.gov/content/pkg/CHRG-114hhrg95059 /html/CHRG-114hhrg95059.htm.

170. Alex Emmons, "Saudi Arabia Planned to Invade Qatar Last Summer," *The Intercept* (August 1, 2018), https://theintercept.com/2018/08/01/rex-tillerson-qatar-saudi-uae/; and Juan Cole, "David and Goliath: How Qatar Defeated the Saudi and UAE Annexation Plot," *The Nation* (February 16, 2018), https://www.thenation.com/article/archive/david -and-goliath-how-qatar-defeated-the-saudi-and-uae-annexation-plot/.

171. See *The Impact of the Blockade on Families in Qatar* (Doha, Qatar: Hamad Bin Khalifah University Press, 2018), https://www.difi.org.qa/wp-content/uploads/2018/07/Blockade -English-FINAL.pdf.

172. Anas El Gomati, "The Libyan Revolution Undone—the Conversation Will Not Be Televised," in *Divided Gulf: The Anatomy of a Crisis*, ed. Andreas Krieg (Singapore: Palgrave Macmillan, 2019), 184–195; Benoit Faucon, Jared Maslin, and Summer Said, "U.A.E. Backed Militia Leader's Bid to Take Control of Libyan Oil Exports," *Wall Street Journal* (July 13, 2018), https://www.wsj.com/articles/u-a-e-backed-militia-leaders -bid-to-take-control-of-libyan-oil-exports-1531474200; and Frederic Wehrey, *The Burning Shores: Inside the Battle for the New Libya* (New York: Farrar, Straus and Giroux, 2018), 262–266.

173. Simon Tisdall, "Sudan: How Arab Autocrats Conspired to Thwart Reformists' Hopes," *The Guardian* (June 3, 2019), https://www.theguardian.com/world/2019/jun/03/sudanese-crackdown-comes-after-talks-with-egypt-and-saudis; and Mehran Kamrava, "The Arab Spring and the Saudi-Led Counterrevolution," *Orbis* 56, no. 1 (2012): 96–101.

174. On the importance of structures in bureaucracies, see Bence Nemeth, *How to Achieve Defence Cooperation in Europe? The Subregional Approach* (Bristol, UK: Bristol University Press, 2022), chapter 6.

175. Lewis W. Snider, "Comparing the Strength of Nations: The Arab Gulf States and Political Change," *Comparative Politics* 20, no. 4 (1988): 460.

176. Snider, "Strength of Nations," 461.

177. Stig Stenslie, "Salman's Succession: Challenges to Stability in Saudi Arabia," *Washington Quarterly* 39, no. 2 (2016): 117.

178. Gary Samuel Samore, quoted in Stenslie, "Salman's Succession," 119.

179. Roberts, "Saudi Rules of Succession."

180. "When Kings and Princes Grow Old," *The Economist* (July 15, 2010), https://www.economist.com/briefing/2010/07/15/when-kings-and-princes-grow-old.

181. Nathan J. Brown, "The Remaking of the Saudi State," Washington, DC: Carnegie Endowment for International Peace, November 9, 2017, https://carnegieendowment.org/2017/11/09/remaking-of-saudi-state-pub-74681.

182. Bruce Riedel, "The Prince of Counter-Terrorism," *Brookings Essay* (September 29, 2015), http://www.brookings.edu/research/essays/2015/the-prince-of-counterterrorism.

183. Brown, "The Remaking of the Saudi State."

184. "محمد بن سلمان على جبهة الحرب" ("Mohammed Bin Salman on the War Front"), *Elaph* (July 10, 2015), https://elaph.com/Web/News/2015/7/1025189.html; and Simeon Kerr, "New Monarch and Yemen Offensive Spark Wave of Saudi Nationalism," *Financial Times* (May 24, 2015), https://www.ft.com/content/3b9358b4-feee-11e4-84b2-00144feabdc0.

185. For an informed reflection on this topic, see Noora Al Daaiji, "قراءة في تحولات الحركة النسوية السعودية: من الهامش إلى المركز" ("A Reading on the Saudi Feminist Movement from the Periphery to the Center"), in الثابت والمتحول 2018: التنمية في هامش الخليج (*Change and Continuity 2018: Developments in the Margins of the Gulf*), ed. Omar AlShehabi, Esraa Al Muftah, and Khalil Buhazza (Kuwait: مركز الخليج لسياسات التنمية [Gulf Centre for Development Policies], 2018).

186. Katherine Zoepf, "Talk of Women's Rights Divides Saudi Arabia," *New York Times* (May 31, 2010), https://www.nytimes.com/2010/06/01/world/middleeast/01iht-saudi.html.

187. Zoepf, "Women's Rights."

188. Ben Hubbard, "Saudi Arabia Agrees to Let Women Drive," *New York Times* (September 26, 2017), https://www.nytimes.com/2017/09/26/world/middleeast/saudi-arabia-women-drive.html.

189. Ben Hubbard and Vivian Yee, "Saudi Arabia Extends New Rights to Women in Blow to Oppressive System," *New York Times* (August 2, 2019), https://www.nytimes.com/2019/08/02/world/middleeast/saudi-arabia-guardianship.html.

190. Ben Hubbard, "Saudi Arabia Lightens up, Building Entertainment Industry from Scratch," *New York Times* (March 17, 2018), https://www.nytimes.com/2018/03/17/world/middleeast/saudi-arabia-entertainment-economy.html.

191.   Simeon Kerr, "Saudi King Stamps His Authority with Staff Shake-up and Handouts," *Financial Times* (January 30, 2015), https://www.ft.com/content/8045e3e0-a850-11e4-bd17 -00144feab7de.

192.   "Kingdom of Saudi Arabia Budget Report 2019," *KPMG* (December 21, 2018), https:// home.kpmg/sa/en/home/insights/2018/12/kingdom-of-saudi-arabia-budget-report .html.

193.   "Saudi Aramco to Be Separated from the Oil Ministry," Economist Intelligence Unit, London (May 4, 2015), http://country.eiu.com/article.aspx?articleid=583135242.

194.   Leanna Garfield, "Saudi Arabia Is Building a $500 Billion Mega-City That's 33 Times the Size of New York City," *Business Insider* (February 22, 2018), https://www.businessinsider .com/saudi-arabia-mega-city-jordan-egypt-oil-2017-10.

195.   Andrew Ross Sorkin, "In the Saudi Desert, World's Business Leaders Follow the Money," *New York Times* (October 23, 2017), https://www.nytimes.com/2017/10/23/business /dealbook/in-the-saudi-desert-worlds-business-leaders-follow-the-money.html.

196.   Thomas Friedman, "Saudi Arabia's Arab Spring, at Last," *New York Times* (November 23, 2017), https://www.nytimes.com/2017/11/23/opinion/saudi-prince-mbs-arab-spring.html.

197.   @anhistorian (Abdullah Al Arian), "In Honor of Thomas Friedman's . . ." Twitter (November 24, 2017), https://twitter.com/anhistorian/status/934080718816399361.

198.   Ben Hubbard, "Saudi Arabia Says Detainees Handed over More Than $100 Billion," *New York Times* (January 30, 2018), https://www.nytimes.com/2018/01/30/world /middleeast/saudi-arabia-corruption.html; and David D. Kirkpatrick, "Saudis End Purge That Began with Hundreds Locked in the Ritz-Carlton," *New York Times* (January 31, 2019), https://www.nytimes.com/2019/01/31/world/middleeast/saudi-arabia-corruption -purge.html.

199.   Simeon Kerr, "Saudi Investors Check out after Hotel Turned into Luxury Prison," *Financial Times* (November 17, 2017), https://www.ft.com/content/4cb6a472-caf5-11e7 -ab18-7a9fb7d6163e.

200.   Saudi-focused conference (Cadenabbia, Italy: June 15–17, 2019).

201.   Ben Hubbard, "One Year on, Shadow of Khashoggi's Killing Stalks Saudi Prince," *New York Times* (October 2, 2019), https://www.nytimes.com/2019/10/02/world/middleeast /khashoggi-killing-mbs-anniversary.html.

202.   Andrew England, "Female Activists Swept up in Saudi Crackdown," *Financial Times* (August 1, 2018), https://www.ft.com/content/ef8fcaf2-959d-11e8-b747-fb1e803ee64e.

203.   Stephane Lacroix, "Saudi Arabia Finally Let Women Drive. Don't Mistake It for Democratic Reform," *Washington Post* (October 5, 2017), https://www.washingtonpost.com/news /monkey-cage/wp/2017/10/05/saudi-arabia-finally-let-women-drive-dont-mistake-it -for-democratic-reform/.

204.   Anne Barnard and Maria Abi-Habib, "Why Saad Hariri Had That Strange Sojourn in Saudi Arabia," *New York Times* (December 24, 2017), https://www.nytimes.com/2017/12/24 /world/middleeast/saudi-arabia-saad-hariri-mohammed-bin-salman-lebanon.html.

205.   Eman Al Hussein, *Saudi First: How Hyper-Nationalism Is Transforming Saudi Arabia*, European Council on Foreign Relations (June 2019), 3.

206. Ben Hubbard, "Saudi King Unleashes a Torrent of Money as Bonuses Flow to the Masses," *New York Times* (February 19, 2019), https://www.nytimes.com/2015/02/20/world/middleeast/saudi-king-unleashes-a-torrent-as-bonuses-flow-to-the-masses.html.

207. Al Hussein, *Saudi First*, 2–13.

208. Al Hussein, *Saudi First*, 3–15.

209. Simon Henderson, *A Fifty-Year Reign? MBS and the Future of Saudi Arabia* (Washington, DC: Washington Institute for Near East Policy, April 2019), 1–5.

210. "Sabah Takes over as Kuwaiti Parliament Shows Its Muscle," *Gulf States Newsletter* 774 (January 27, 2006), https://www.gsn-online.com/downloadable/1203.

211. "Kuwaiti Succession Gets Clearer, but Disappoints Next Generation," *Gulf States Newsletter* 775 (February 10, 2006), https://www.gsn-online.com/downloadable/2084.

212. Ali Al Zameea, "جدلية التنمية المستدامة وبنية الدولة وسياساتها العامة" ("The Dialectic of Sustainable Development, State Structure and Public Policies"), in الثابت والمتحول 2020: الاستدامة في الخليج (*Change and Continuity 2020: Sustainability in the Gulf*), ed. Omar AlShehabi and Hamad Al Rayes (Kuwait: مركز الخليج لسياسات التنمية [Gulf Centre for Development Policies], 2020), 80–99.

213. Simon Henderson and Kristian Coates Ulrichsen, *Kuwait: A Changing System under Stress* (Washington, DC: Washington Institute for Near East Policy, October 2019), 4–6, https://www.washingtoninstitute.org/policy-analysis/kuwait-changing-system-under-stress-sudden-succession-essay-series.

214. *Oman: Domestic Forces and the Succession* (Washington, DC: Central Intelligence Agency, March 1985), 4–9.

215. Judith Miller, "Creating Modern Oman: An Interview with Sultan Qabus," *Foreign Affairs* 76 (May/June 1997), https://www.foreignaffairs.com/articles/oman/1997-05-01/creating-modern-oman-interview-sultan-qabus.

216. Georges Malbrunot, "Oman: La Succession de l'inamovible Sultan Qabus Plane Sur Le Pays" ("Oman: The Sucession of the Irremovable Sultan Qabus Hovers Over the Country"), *Le Figaro* (March 19, 2019), https://www.lefigaro.fr/international/2019/03/18/01003-20190318ARTFIG00164-oman-la-succession-de-l-inamovible-sultan-qabus-plane-sur-le-pays.php.

217. Simeon Kerr, "Oman Swears in New Sultan Following Death of Qaboos," *Financial Times* (January 11, 2020), https://www.ft.com/content/b274993a-3444-11ea-a6d3-9a26f8c3cba4.

218. Cinzia Bianco, "Meet Oman's New Sultan. How Will He Navigate the Region's Turmoil?," *Washington Post* (January 15, 2020), https://www.washingtonpost.com/politics/2020/01/15/meet-omans-new-sultan-how-will-he-navigate-regions-turmoil/.

219. Wadha Shams, " المستجدات في سلطنة عمان" ("Developments in the Sultanate of Oman"), in الثابت والمتحول 2019: المواطنة يف تيارات الخليج (*Change and Continuity 2019: Citizenship Currents in the Gulf*), ed. Omar AlShehabi and Khalil Buhazza (Kuwait: مركز الخليج لسياسات التنمية [Gulf Centre for Development Policies], 2019), 261–263.

220. Shams, " المستجدات في سلطنة عمان" ("Developments in the Sultanate of Oman"), 261–263.

221. "Qaboos Bequeaths a Smooth Succession as Haitham Bin Tariq Takes over in Oman," *Gulf States Newsletter* 1096 (January 23, 2020), https://www.gsn-online.com/news-centre/article/qaboos-bequeaths-smooth-succession-haitham-bin-tariq-takes.

222. الثابت والمتحول 2017: الخليج ("المستجدات السياسية في دولة الإمارات" ("Political Developments in the UAE"), in والإصلاح الاقتصادي في زمن أزمة النفطية (*Change and Continuity 2017: The Gulf and Economic Reform in a Time of Oil Crisis*), ed. Omar AlShehabi, Ahmed Al Owfi, and Khalil Bohazza (Kuwait: مركز الخليج لسياسات التنمية [Gulf Centre for Development Policies], 2017), 50.

223. Kamrava, *Troubled Waters*, 101–104.

224. David B. Roberts, "Bucking the Trend: The UAE and the Development of Military Capabilities in the Arab World," *Security Studies* 29, no. 2 (2020): 301–334.

225. Roberts, "Bucking the Trend."

226. Khalid S. Almezaini, *The UAE and Foreign Policy: Foreign Aid, Identities and Interests* (London: Routledge, 2012), 45–47.

227. Arno Maierbrugger, "Domain Grabber Registers Burj Khalifa's Web Address," *Gulf News* (January 6, 2010), https://gulfnews.com/business/domain-grabber-registers-burj-khalifas-web-address-1.563400.

228. Almezaini, *UAE and Foreign Policy*, 45–47.

229. Kristian Coates Ulrichsen, *The United Arab Emirates: Power, Politics, and Policymaking* (Oxford, UK: Routledge, 2017), 1997.

230. Worth, "Mohammed Bin Zayed's Dark Vision."

231. It remains to be seen how much this changes amid contemporary pressures. See Andrew England and Simeon Kerr, "US Sanctions Put Chill on Iranian Trade with UAE," *Financial Times* (July 26, 2019), https://www.ft.com/content/bbe3c99a-aee9-11e9-8030-530adfa879c2.

232. Adam Taylor, "The Once Flourishing Iranian Community in Dubai Faces Pressure amid Persian Gulf Tensions," *Washington Post* (August 13, 2019), https://www.washingtonpost.com/world/middle_east/the-once-flourishing-iranian-community-in-dubai-faces-pressure-amid-gulf-tensions/2019/08/12/450dfb88-afa7-11e9-9411-a608f9d0c2d3_story.html; and Shayerah Ilias, *Iran's Economic Conditions: U.S. Policy Issues* (Washington, DC: Congressional Research Service, June 15, 2009), 23.

233. Calvert W. Jones documents this process extensively in her book *Bedouins into Bourgeois: Remaking Citizens for Globalization* (Cambridge: Cambridge University Press, 2017).

234. Jon B. Alterman and Margo Balboni, *Citizens in Training: Conscription and Nation-Building in the United Arab Emirates* (Doha, Qatar: Center for International and Regional Studies, 2017), 19–21, https://www.csis.org/analysis/citizens-training-conscription-and-nation-building-united-arab-emirates.

235. Alterman and Balboni, *Citizens in Training*, 2.

236. Eleonora Ardemagni, *Gulf Monarchies' Militarized Nationalism* (Washington, DC: Carnegie Endowment for International Peace, February 28, 2019), https://carnegieendowment.org/sada/78472; "Museum to Commemorate UAE's Martyrs to Be Built," *The National* (September 7, 2015), https://www.thenationalnews.com/uae/government/museum-to-commemorate-uae-s-martyrs-to-be-built-1.132202; and Eleonora Ardemagni, "Icons of the Nation: The Military Factor in the UAE's Nation-Building," *LSE Blogs* (February 1, 2019), https://blogs.lse.ac.uk/mec/2019/02/01/icons-of-the-nation-the-military-factor-in-the-uaes-nation-building/.

237. Emmons, "Saudi Arabia Planned to Invade Qatar Last Summer"; and Cole, "David and Goliath: How Qatar Defeated the Saudi and UAE Annexation Plot."

238. Courtney Freer, "Social Effects of the Qatar Crisis," *IndraStra Global* 10 (October 3, 2017), https://www.indrastra.com/2017/10/Social-Effects-of-Qatar-Crisis-003-10-2017-0013. html; and Justin Gengler, "Society and State in Post-Blockade Qatar: Lessons for the Arab Gulf Region," *Journal of Arabian Studies* 10, no. 2 (2020): 238–255.

239. Freer, "Social Effects of the Qatar Crisis."

240. Al Marri and Al Hajri, "المستجدات السياسية في دولة قطر" ("Political Developments in the State of Qatar"), 74075.

241. Louise Pyne-Jones, *Thousands of Al Ghofran Tribesmen Stripped of Their Qatari Citizenship Fight for Their Rights* (London: International Observatory of Human Rights, May 13, 2019).

242. "Bahrain/Qatar: Tribes' Mass Show of Allegiance," *Gulf States Newsletter* 1086 (August 1, 2019).

243. Gerd Nonneman, "European Policies towards the Gulf: Patterns, Dynamics, Evolution, and the Case of the Qatar Blockade," *Journal of Arabian Studies* 10, no. 2 (2020): 278–304.

244. David B. Roberts, *Securing the Qatari State* (Washington, DC: Arab Gulf States Institute Washington, June 2017).

245. Henry Jones, "Joint UK-Qatari Typhoon Squadron Stands Up," *UK Defence Journal* (July 25, 2018), https://ukdefencejournal.org.uk/joint-uk-qatari-typhoon-squadron-stands-up/.

246. Bülent Aras and Pınar Akpınar, "Turkish Foreign Policy and the Qatar Crisis," Istanbul Policy Center–Sabanci University–Stiftung Mercator Initiative (2017), 2–7.

247. Anwar Al Khatib, "دراسة: 66% من القطريين يؤيدون استمرار العضوية في مجلس التعاون الخليجي" ("Study: 66 Percent of Qataris Support Continued Membership in the Gulf Cooperation Council"), *Al Arab* (February 26, 2018), https://tinyurl.com/y8cwpkt2.

248. "Qatar 'Fake News' Law Signals 'Worrying Regression': Rights Group," *Al Jazeera* (January 24, 2020), https://www.aljazeera.com/news/2020/01/qatar-fake-news-law-signals -worrying-regression-rights-group-200122071721600.html.

249. Al Marri, "المستجدات في دولة قطر" ("New Developments in the State of Qatar"), 278–285.

250. Imad Murad, "عرضة أهل قطر.. الحصار يلمّ شمل القبائل" ("The Dance of the Qatari People . . . the Siege Unifies the Tribes"), December 18, 2018, https://tinyurl.com/y7hd7sss; "أنا قطر وقبيلتي قطرية" شعار القبائل في عرضة هل قطر" ("I Am Qatar and My Tribe Is Qatari: The Slogan of Tribes 'Welcome Qatar'"), *Al Sharq* (December 18, 2017), https://tinyurl.com/y7klj9g4; and Al Marri, "المستجدات في دولة قطر" ("New Developments in the State of Qatar").

251. Mahmoud Cherif Bassiouni et al., *Report of the Bahrain Independent Commission of Inquiry* (Manama, Bahrain: Bahrain Independent Commission of Inquiry, November 23, 2011), http://www.bici.org.bh/BICIreportEN.pdf.

252. Kylie Moore-Gilbert, "Sectarian Divide and Rule in Bahrain: A Self-Fulfilling Prophecy?," *Middle East Institute* (January 19, 2016), 166–170, https://www.mei.edu/publications /sectarian-divide-and-rule-bahrain-self-fulfilling-prophecy.

253. "The King's Risky Move," *The Economist* (November 26, 2011), https://www.economist.com/middle-east-and-africa/2011/11/26/the-kings-risky-move.

254. Bassiouni et al., *Report of the Bahrain Independent Commission of Inquiry*; and "Bassiouni Commission Report Is Released," Economist Intelligence Unit, London (December 13, 2011), http://country.eiu.com/article.aspx?articleid=1838675968&Country=Bahrain&topic =Politics&subtopic=_6.

255. *One Year Later: Assessing Bahrain's Implementation of the BICI Report*, Project on Middle East Democracy (November 2012), https://pomed.org/one-year-later-assessing-bahrains -implementation-of-the-bici-report/; and *Steps Taken by the Government of Bahrain to Implement the Recommendations in the 2011 Report of the Bahrain Independent Commission of Inquiry*, Washington, DC: U.S. Department of State (June 21, 2016).

256. Ronald Neumann, "Bahrain's Rulers Last Chance to Save Their Country," *National Interest* (June 20, 2019), https://nationalinterest.org/feature/bahrains-rulers-last-chance-save -their-country-63532.

257. Neumann, "Bahrain's Rulers."

258. Neumann, "Bahrain's Rulers."

259. Ali Faris, "المستجدات في مملكة البحرين" ("Developments in the Kingdom of Bahrain"), in الثابت والمتحول 2020: الاستدامة في الخليج (*Change and Continuity 2020: Sustainability in the Gulf*), ed. Omar AlShehabi and Hamad Al Rayes (Kuwait: مركز الخليج لسياسات التنمية [Gulf Centre for Development Policies], 2020), 235–238.

260. Emile A. Nakhleh, "Could Bahrain's New Prime Minister Chart a New Path toward Reform?," *Responsible Statecraft* (November 19, 2020), https://responsiblestatecraft .org/2020/11/19/could-bahrains-new-prime-minister-chart-a-new-path-toward-reform/.

261. Simeon Kerr, "UAE Pushes Merchant Families to Open up to Competition," *Financial Times* (December 26, 2021), https://www.ft.com/content/116b083a-1811-4501-ad9b -2f6a3183db3e.

262. Graham Allison, *Essence of Decision* (New York: HarperCollins, 1971); and Irving L. Janis, *Victims of Groupthink: A Psychological Study of Foreign-Policy Decisions and Fiascoes* (Boston: Houghton Mifflin, 1972).

2. SOCIETAL SECURITY

1. Barry Buzan, Ole Wæver, and Jaap de Wilde, *Security: A New Framework for Analysis* (Boulder, CO: Lynne Rienner, 1998), 119.

2. Buzan, Wæver, and Wilde, *Security*. 123.

3. Simon Mabon, "Sovereignty, Bare Life and the Arab Uprisings," *Third World Quarterly* 38, no. 8 (2017): 1783.

4. Eric Hobsbawm and Terence Ranger, *The Invention of Tradition* (Cambridge: Cambridge University Press, 2010); and Mohammed Ayoob, "Defining Security: A Subaltern Realist Perspective," in *Critical Security Studies: Concepts and Cases*, ed. Keith Krause and Michael C. Williams (London: Routledge, 1997), 36–39.

5. Andrew M. Gardner, "Gulf Migration and the Family," *Journal of Arabian Studies* 1, no. 1 (June 2011): 5.

6. Hisham Al Awadhi, تاريخ العبيد في الخليج العربي (*The History of Slaves in the Arabian Gulf*) (Beirut and Cairo: دار التنوير للطباعة والنشر [House of Enlightnment for Printing and Publishing], 2021), Loc. 68.; and Ian J. Seccombe, "Labour Migration to the Arabian Gulf: Evolution and Characteristics 1920–1950," *British Journal of Middle Eastern Studies* 10, no. 1 (1983): 4.

7. For more on the concept of a "natural states" thesis, see Khaldoun Hasan al-Naqeeb, *Society and State in the Gulf and Arab Peninsula: A Different Perspective* (London: Routledge, 1990), 6–24.

8. John Chalcraft, "Monarchy, Migration and Hegemony in the Arabian Peninsula," *Kuwait Programme on Development, Governance and Globalization in the Gulf States* 12 (2010): 1–4.

9. Christopher S. Browning and Pertti Joenniemi, "From Fratricide to Security Community: Re-Theorising Difference in the Constitution of Nordic Peace," *Journal of International Relations and Development* 16, no. 4 (2013): 496; Catarina Kinnvall, *Globalization and Religious Nationalism in India: The Search for Ontological Security* (London: Routledge, 2007); and for a discussion of such broad matters in the Gulf, see David B. Roberts, "Ontological Security and the Gulf Crisis," *Journal of Arabian Studies* 10, no. 2 (2021): 221–237.

10. John Chalcraft, "Migration and Popular Protest in the Arabian Peninsula and the Gulf in the 1950s and 1960s," *International Labor and Working-Class History* 79, no. 1 (2011): 28–30.

11. Chalcraft, "Migration and Protest," 29.

12. Chalcraft, "Monarchy, Migration and Hegemony," 11.

13. Chalcraft, "Monarchy, Migration and Hegemony," 8. For more on the cosmopolitan attitudes of Bahrain's intelligentsia, see emerging research like Wafa Al Sayed, "Sawt Al-Bahrain: A Window onto the Gulf's Social and Political History," *LSE Blogs* (July 1, 2020), https://blogs.lse.ac.uk/mec/2020/07/01/sawt-al-bahrain-a-window-onto-the-gulfs-social-and-political-history/.

14. Sharon Stanton Russell, "Politics and Ideology in Migration Policy Formulation: The Case of Kuwait," *International Migration Review* 21, no. 1 (1989): 30–31.

15. Sir John Richmond, *An Evaluation of Kuwait as a Welfare State*, Foreign and Commonweath Office (June 16, 1963), 5, https://www.agda.ae/en/catalogue/tna/fo/371/168780/n/4.

16. Russell, "Politics and Ideology," 36.

17. On this broader subject, see Shafeeq Ghabra, النكبة ونشوء الشتات الفلسطيني في الكويت (*The Nakhba and the Emergence of the Palestinian Diaspora in Kuwait*) (Doha, Qatar: Arab Centre for Research and Policy Studies, 2018).

18. Russell, "Politics and Ideology," 31; and Chalcraft, "Monarchy, Migration and Hegemony," 10.

19. Russell, "Politics and Ideology," 32.

20. Russell, "Politics and Ideology," 35.

21. Paul Dresch, "Debates on Marriage and Nationality in the UAE," in *Monarchies and Nations: Globalization and Identity in the Arab States of the Gulf*, ed. Paul Dresch and James Piscatori (New York: I. B. Tauris, 2013), 142.

22. Dresch, "Marriage and Nationality," 142.

23. Russell, "Politics and Ideology," 36–37; and Nazli Choucri, "Asians in the Arab World: Labor Migration and Public Policy," *Middle Eastern Studies* 22, no. 2 (1986): 252–269.

24. Chalcraft, "Monarchy, Migration and Hegemony," 15.

25. Dresch, "Marriage and Nationality," 149, 155.

26. Andrzej Kapiszewski, "Arab Labor Migration to the GCC States," in *Arab Migration in a Globalized World* (Geneva: International Organization for Migration, 2004), 121.

27. Chalcraft, "Monarchy, Migration and Hegemony," 21.

28. Chalcraft, "Monarchy, Migration and Hegemony," 23.

29. Chalcraft, "Monarchy, Migration and Hegemony," 29.

30. Christine Osborne, *The Gulf States and Oman* (Abingdon, UK: Routledge, 2017), 34.

31. Michael Field, "Tree of the Al Attiyah," *Arabian Charts* (v. 1), http://arabiancharts .wordpress.com/about/.

32. "Saudi Royal Wealth: Where Do They Get All That Money?," *Wikileaks* (November 30, 1996), https://www.aftenposten.no/norge/i/LAvE9/30111996saudi-royal-wealth-where-do -they-get-all-that.money.

33. Nicholas Kulish and Mark Mazzetti, "Saudi Royal Family Is Still Spending in an Age of Austerity," *New York Times* (December 27, 2016), https://www.nytimes.com/2016/12/27 /world/middleeast/saudi-royal-family-money.html.

34. Malise Ruthven, "The Saudi Trillions," *London Review of Books* 39, no. 17 (September 7, 2017), https://www.lrb.co.uk/the-paper/v39/n17/malise-ruthven/the-saudi-trillions; and Omar AlShehabi, "Show Us the Money: Oil Revenues, Undisclosed Allocations and Accountability in Budgets of the GCC States," LSE Research Online Documents on Economics 84521, London School of Economics and Political Science, LSE Library (2017), 5–29.

35. I use the term "Caucasian" here on purpose, given myriad anecdotal incidents across the monarchies of non-Caucasian British, American, and Canadian citizens facing racism, sometimes even codified into pay scales, based on the color of their skin. More generally, nationality is a widely known differentiator of salary in the Gulf. Colin Simpson, "Good Salary, Depending on Where You're Coming From," *The National* (April 26, 2012), https://www.thenationalnews.com/uae/good-salary-depending-on-where-you -re-coming-from-1.574113. See also chapters 2 and 5 in Amélie Le Renard, *Western Privilege: Work, Intimacy, and Postcolonial Hierarchies in Dubai* (Stanford, CA: Stanford University Press, 2021).

36. Omar AlShehabi, تصدير الثروة واغتراب الإنسان: تاريخ الخلل الإنتاجي في دول الخليج العربية (*Exporting Wealth and Alienating the Citizen: History of Production in the GCC*) (Beirut: Centre for Arab Unity Studies, 2018), 7606–7834, 8016.

37. Personal interview of anonymous Qatar University lecturer, November 5, 2012.

38. On the fluctuating number of Arab immigrants going to the Gulf, see Omar AlShehabi, "تاريخه واسبابه ومعوقات مواجهته تفاقم الخلل السكاني في دول مجلس التعاون" ("The Population Imbalance in the GCC Countries: Its History and Its Causes and Impediments to Confronting It"), paper presented at دول مجلس التعاون الخليجي في سياسات وآليات لمواجهة الخلل السكاني المتفاقم (Policies and Mechanisms to Address the Growing Population Imbalance in the Gulf Cooperation Council), 2013.

39. Alicia Buller, "Are You Paid According to Your Skin Colour?," *Gulf Business* (March 5, 2013), https://gulfbusiness.com/are-you-paid-according-to-your-skin-colour/.

40. Gardner, "Gulf Migration," 7.

41. Gardner, "Gulf Migration," 7–9.

42. Zahra R. Babar, "The Cost of Belonging: Citizenship Construction in the State of Qatar," *Middle East Journal* 68, no. 3 (Summer 2014): 414–420.

43. Babar, "Cost of Belonging," 411–414; and Gardner, "Gulf Migration," 8.

44. Abdoulaye Diop, Kien Trung Le, Trevor Johnston, and Michael Ewers, "Citizens' Attitudes towards Migrant Workers in Qatar," *Migration and Development* 6, no. 1 (2017): 144–160.

45. Emilie J. Rutledge, "Labor Markets in the Gulf and the South Asian Migration," in *South Asian Migration in the Gulf*, ed. Mehdi Chowdhury and S. Irudaya Rajan (Cham, Switzerland: Palgrave Macmillan, 2018).

46. AlShehabi, " الخلل السكاني في دول مجلس التعاون " ("The Population Imbalance in the GCC Countries).

47. AlShehabi, " الخلل السكاني في دول مجلس التعاون " ("The Population Imbalance in the GCC Countries).

48. AlShehabi, " الخلل السكاني في دول مجلس التعاون " ("The Population Imbalance in the GCC Countries).

49. AlShehabi, " الخلل السكاني في دول مجلس التعاون " ("The Population Imbalance in the GCC Countries).

50. Gregory Gause III, *Oil Monarchies: Domestic and Security Challenges in the Arab Gulf States* (New York: Council on Foreign Relations, 1994), 10.

51. Gause III, *Oil Monarchies*, 10.

52. Abdulaziz Al Fahad, "Raiders and Traders: A Poet's Lament on the End of the Bedouin Heroic Age," in *Saudi Arabia in Transition: Insights on Social, Political, Economic and Religious Change*, ed. Bernard Haykel, Thomas Hegghammer, and Stephane Lacroix (Cambridge: Cambridge University Press, 2015), 238–241.

53. For the key refutation of the wider British critique of the rampant piracy in the Persian Gulf in the eighteenth and nineteenth centuries, see Muhammad al-Qasimi, *The Myth of Arab Piracy in the Gulf*, 2nd ed. (London: Routledge, 1988).

54. J. E. Peterson, "Tribes and Politics in Eastern Arabia," *Middle East Journal* 31, no. 3 (Summer 1977): 297–298.

55. C. D. Matthews, "Bedouin Life in Contemporary Arabia: Preliminary Remarks," *Rivista Degli Studi Orientali* 35 (1960): 32–33.

56. Donald P. Cole and Soraya Altorki, "Was Arabia Tribal? A Reinterpretation of the Pre-Oil Society," *Journal of South Asian and Middle Eastern Studies* 15, no. 4 (Summer 1992): 71–73. See also Sheila Carapico, "Arabia Incognita: An Invitation to Arabian Peninsula Studies," in *Counter-Narratives: History, Contemporary Society and Politics in Saudi Arabia and Yemen*, ed. Madawi Al Rasheed and Robert Vitalis (New York: Palgrave Macmillan, 2004), 14–30.

57. Al Fahad, "Raiders and Traders," 231–262.

58. Al Fahad, "Raiders and Traders," 250–254.

59. Al Fahad, "Raiders and Traders," 233.
60. Al Fahad, "Raiders and Traders," 252.
61. Khaldoun Hassan al-Nakeeb and L. M. Kenny (trans.), *Society and State in the Gulf and Arab Peninsula: A Different Perspective*, Routledge Library Editions (Abingdon, UK: Routledge, 2012, 91; and Mohammed Obaid Ghobash, في السلطة مفاهيم خمسة:الخليجية الدولة" "الخليج - محمد عبيد غباش ("Gulf States: Five Concepts of Power in the Gulf"), *Al Jazeera* (October 3, 2004), https://tinyurl.com/ya6jd9u9.
62. Donald P. Cole, "Where Have the Bedouin Gone?," *Anthropological Quarterly* 76, no. 2 (Spring 2003): 242, 248–250.
63. Farah Al-Nakib, *Kuwait Transformed: A History of Oil and Urban Life* (Stanford, CA: Stanford University Press, 2016), 12, 133–137.
64. Al Fahad, "Raiders and Traders," 253–254.
65. Cole, "Where Have the Bedouin Gone?," 251.
66. Cole, "Where Have the Bedouin Gone?," 249–250.
67. Cole, "Where Have the Bedouin Gone?," 255–257.
68. Hobsbawm and Ranger, *The Invention of Tradition*.
69. Cole, "Where Have the Bedouin Gone?," 255–258.
70. Ghobash, "الخليج في سلطة" ("Power in the Gulf"), https://gulfpolicies.org/2019-05-18-07-14 -32/92-2019-06-25-12-45-40/794-2019-06-26-09-34-45.
71. Cole, "Where Have the Bedouin Gone?," 255–258.
72. Miriam Cooke, *Tribal Modern: Branding New Nations in the Arab Gulf* (Berkeley: University of California Press, 2014), 16–64, 99–138; and Karen Exell and Trinidad Rico, "'There Is No Heritage in Qatar': Orientalism, Colonialism and Other Problematic Histories," *World Archaeology* 45, no. 4 (2013): 674–676.
73. John C. Wilkinson, "Traditional Concepts of Territory in South East Arabia," *Geographical Journal* 149, no. 3 (1983): 301–315.
74. Political Resident, *Secret Telegram from the Political Resident to the Secretary of State for India* (August 30, 1935); Jacob Goldberg, *The Foreign Policy of Saudi Arabia: The Formative Years, 1902–1918* (Cambridge, MA: Harvard University Press, 1986), 66; and J. B. Kelly, *Eastern Arabian Frontiers* (London: Frederick A. Praeger, 1964), 243.
75. Al-Nakib, *Kuwait Transformed*, 142–143.
76. Al-Nakib, *Kuwait Transformed*, 202.
77. Anh Nga Longva, "Nationalism in Pre-Modern Guise: The Discourse on Hadhar and Badu in Kuwait," *International Journal of Middle East Studies* 38 (2006): 171–187; and Farah Al-Nakib, "Revisiting Hadar and Badu in Kuwait: Citizenship, Housing, and the Construction of a Dichotomy," *International Journal of Middle East Studies* 46, no. 1 (2014): 5–30.
78. Chase Untermeyer, "Qatar: Update on Nationality Issue," *Wikileaks* (Doha, Qatar, May 10, 2005), https://wikileaks.org/plusd/cables/05DOHA845_a.html. In early 2006, reports emerged that 5,266 members of the Al Murrah tribe had had their Qatari passports restored. Mariam Al Hakeem, "Citizenship Restored to 5,266 Qataris," Gulf 2000 Archives, *Gulf News* (February 3, 2006), https://gulfnews.com/world/gulf/qatar /citizenship-restored-to-5266-qataris-1.223912.

79. Mehran Kamrava, *Qatar: Small State, Big Politics* (Ithaca, NY: Cornell University Press, 2013).

80. "عشيرة الغفران "تشكو قطر إلى مجلس حقوق الإنسان" ("Al-Ghafran Clan Complains About Qatar to Human Rights Council"), *BBC Arabic* (March 9, 2018), http://www.bbc.com/arabic/middleeast-43342736.

81. "Qatar: Al-Murrah Return, 'Seeking Mercy,'" *Gulf States Newsletter* 1078 (April 4, 2019).

82. "Citizenship Revoked to Stifle Dissent," *Gulf States Newsletter* 976 (September 5, 2014), https://www.gsn-online.com/news-centre/article/citizenship-revoked-stifle-dissent.

83. "Bahrain/Kuwait: More Citizenships Revoked," *Gulf States Newsletter* 978 (October 2, 2014).

84. "Bahrain/Kuwait."

85. Jane Kinninmont, "Citizenship in the Gulf," in *The Gulf States and the Arab Uprisings*, ed. Ana Echagüe (Spain: FRIDE, 2013), 52–54.

86. Atossa Araxia Abrahamian, "Who Loses When a Country Puts Citizenship up for Sale?," *New York Times* (January 5, 2018), https://www.nytimes.com/2018/01/05/opinion/sunday/united-arab-emirates-comorans-citizenship.html.

87. Hootan Shambayati, "The Rentier State, Interest Groups, and the Paradox of Autonomy: State and Business in Turkey and Iran," *Comparative Politics* 26, no. 3 (1994): 329.

88. Hassan Hamdan Al Alkim, *The GCC States in an Unstable World* (London: Saqi, 1994), 34.

89. John Duke Anthony, "Aspects of Saudi Arabia's Relations with Other Gulf States," in *State, Society and Economy in Saudi Arabia*, 3rd edition, ed. Tim Niblock (Abingdon, UK: Routledge, 2015), 164.

90. "النظام الأساسي" ("The Statute"), Gulf Cooperation Council, http://www.gcc-sg.org/ar-sa/AboutGCC/Pages/Primarylaw.aspx.

91. David Commins, *The Wahhabi Mission and Saudi Arabia* (London: I. B. Tauris, 2009).

92. Mohammed Ayoob, "Political Islam: Image and Reality," *World Policy Journal* 21, no. 3 (2004): 3–6.

93. Stephane Lacroix, "Understanding Stability and Dissent in the Kingdom," in *Saudi Arabia in Transition: Insights on Social, Political, Economic and Religious Change*, ed. Bernard Haykel, Thomas Hegghammer, and Stephane Lacroix (Cambridge: Cambridge University Press, 2015), 169.

94. Lacroix, "Understanding Stability and Dissent," 169.

95. David B. Roberts, "Qatar and the Muslim Brotherhood: Pragmatism or Preference?," *Middle East Policy* 21, no. 3 (2014): 84–94; and Courtney Freer, *Rentier Islamism: The Influence of the Muslim Brotherhood in Gulf Monarchies* (New York: Oxford University Press, 2018), 62–63.

96. Talal Al-Rashoud, "From Muscat to the Maghreb: Pan-Arab Networks, Anti-Colonial Groups, and Kuwait's Arab Scholarships (1953–1961)," *Arabian Humanities* 12, no. 12 (2019).

97. Afshan Ahmed, "The UAE's History Lesson," *The National* (November 8, 2011), https://www.thenationalnews.com/uae/the-uae-s-history-lesson-1.460608.

98. Joseph Kraft, "Letter from Saudi Arabia," *New Yorker* (July 4, 1983), 43.

99. Stephane Lacroix and George Holoch (trans.), *Awakening Islam* (Cambridge, MA: Harvard University Press, 2011), 38–80.

100. Lacroix, "Understanding Stability and Dissent," 170–171. On the fundamentally misogynistic nature of the traditional clerical approach to women in Saudi Arabia, see Madawi Al Rasheed, "Caught between Religion and State: Women in Saudi Arabia," in *Saudi Arabia in Transition: Insights on Social, Political, Economic and Religious Change*, ed. Bernard Haykel, Thomas Hegghammer, and Stephane Lacroix (Cambridge: Cambridge University Press, 2015).

101. Yaroslav Trofimov, *The Siege of Mecca* (London: Penguin, 2007), 198–218.

102. Lacroix, "Understanding Stability and Dissent," 172–174.

103. James Piscatori, "Managing God's Guests: The Pilgrimage, Saudi Arabia and the Politics of Legitimacy," in *Monarchies and Nations: Globalization and Identity in the Arab States of the Gulf*, ed. Paul Dresch and James Piscatori (New York: I. B. Tauris, 2013), 222–247.

104. Timothy Niblock, *Saudi Arabia: Power, Legitimacy and Survival* (London: Routledge, 2006), 145–151.

105. Lacroix and Holoch (trans.), *Awakening Islam*, 1352–1442.

106. Buzan, Wæver, and Wilde, *Security*, 119.

107. For the definitive account of these emergent relationships, see Jason Burke, *Al Qaeda: The True Story of Radical Islam* (London: I. B. Tauris, 2003).

108. Ann M. Lesch, "Osama Bin Laden: Embedded in the Middle East Crises," *Middle East Policy* 9, no. 2 (2002): 85.

109. Geoffrey F. Gresh, *Gulf Security and the U.S. Military: Regime Survival and the Politics of Basing* (Stanford, CA: Stanford University Press, 2015), 104–105; and "Defend Us Discretely," *The Economist* (June 6, 1981).

110. Gerd Nonneman, "Political Reform in the Gulf Monarchies: From Liberalization to Democratization? A Comparative Perspective," in *Reform in the Middle East Oil Monarchies*, ed. Anoushiravan Etheshami and Steven Wright (Reading, UK: Ithaca, 2011), 8–13.

111. Saud Al Sarhan, "The Struggle for Authority: The Shaykhs of Jihadi-Salafism in Saudi Arabia, 1997–2003," in *Saudi Arabia in Transition: Insights on Social, Political, Economic and Religious Change*, ed. Bernard Haykel, Thomas Hegghammer, and Stephane Lacroix (Cambridge: Cambridge University Press, 2015), 183–186.

112. Al Sarhan, "Struggle for Authority," 183–186.

113. Paul Aarts and Carolien Roelants, *Saudi Arabia: A Kingdom in Peril* (London: Hurst, 2015), 21.

114. Robert F. Worth, "Leftward Shift by Conservative Cleric Leaves Saudis Perplexed," *New York Times* (April 4, 2014), https://www.nytimes.com/2014/04/05/world/middleeast/conservative-saudi-cleric-salman-al-awda.html; and Madawi Al Rasheed, *Muted Modernists: The Struggle over Divine Politics in Saudi Arabia* (London: Hurst, 2015), 8.

115. Geneive Abdo, *The New Sectarianism: The Arab Uprisings and the Rebirth of the Shi'a-Sunni Divide* (New York: Oxford University Press, 2017), chapter 3; Worth, "Leftward Shift."

116. Cooper Smith, "These Are the Most Twitter-Crazy Countries in the World, Starting with Saudi Arabia (!?)," *Business Insider* (November 7, 2013), https://www.businessinsider.com/the-top-twitter-markets-in-the-world-2013-11?r=US&IR=T.

117. Ben Hubbard, "Why Spy on Twitter? For Saudi Arabia, It's the Town Square," *New York Times* (November 7, 2019), https://www.nytimes.com/2019/11/07/world/middleeast

/saudi-arabia-twitter-arrests.html; and Iyad El Baghdadi, "How the Saudis Made Jeff Bezos Public Enemy No. 1," *Daily Beast* (February 25, 2019), https://www.thedailybeast .com/how-the-saudis-made-jeff-bezos-public-enemy-1?source=twitter&via=desktop.

118. "عام / أمر ملكي: يكون يوم (22 فبراير) من كل عام يوماً لذكرى تأسيس الدولة السعودية باسم (يوم التأسيس) ويصبح إجازة رسمية", ("General/Royal Decree: The Day [February 22] of Each Year Shall Be a Day to Commemorate the Founding of the Saudi State under the Name [Foundation/Founders Day] and It Becomes an Official Holiday"), *Saudi Press Agency* (January 27, 2022), https:// www.spa.gov.sa/2324646.

119. Nuance here is important. This is not to suggest that he converted Qatar's institutions toward becoming active members of the Muslim Brotherhood. Rather, the tone of his doctrinal approach is perhaps better described as being loosely affiliated with Brotherhood logics, and this is the change that he instituted in Qatar. David H. Warren, *Rivals in the Gulf: Yusuf Al-Qaradawi, Abdullah Bin Bayyah, and the Qatar-UAE Contest over the Arab Spring and the Gulf Crisis* (Abingdon: Routledge, 2021), 7, 19–35.

120. Warren, *Rivals in the Gulf*, 30–32.

121. Warren, *Rivals in the Gulf*, 2, 32; and Bettina Gräf and Jakob Skovgaard-Petersen, *Global Mufti: The Phenomenon of Yusuf Al-Qaradawi* (London: Hurst, 2009).

122. Warren, *Rivals in the Gulf*, 2, 32.

123. Kristin Smith Diwan, "Who Is Sunni? Chechnya Islamic Conference Opens Window on Intra-Faith Rivalry," Washington, DC: Arab Gulf States Institute Washington, September 16, 2016, https://agsiw.org/who-is-a-sunni-chechnya-islamic-conference-opens -window-on-intra-faith-rivalry/.

124. Smith Diwan, "Who Is Sunni?"

125. David B. Roberts, "Mosque and State: The United Arab Emirates' Secular Foreign Policy," *Foreign Affairs* (March 18, 2016), https://www.foreignaffairs.com/articles/united-arab -emirates/2016-03-18/mosque-and-state.

126. Courtney Freer, "The Changing Islamist Landscape of the Gulf Arab States," Washington, DC: Arab Gulf States Institute Washington (November 21, 2016), 3, https://agsiw .org/wp-content/uploads/2016/11/Freer_ONLINE-1.pdf.

127. Freer, "Changing Islamist Landscape," 18–21.

128. Courtney Freer, *Challenges to Sunni Islamism in Bahrain since 2011* (Beirut: Carnegie Middle East Center, March 2019), https://carnegie-mec.org/2019/03/06/challenges-to -sunni-islamism-in-bahrain-since-2011-pub-78510.

129. "Kuwaiti Islamists Take a Hit in Parliament," *Arab Weekly* (March 24, 2019), https:// thearabweekly.com/kuwaiti-islamists-take-hit-parliament.

130. Freer, "Changing Islamist Landscape," 1–22.

131. Freer, "Changing Islamist Landscape," 16–17.

132. Kenneth Katzman, *Oman: Politics, Security, and U.S. Policy*, Congressional Research Service (June 17, 2020), 7.

133. Saeed Al Hashemi, "الحركات الإسلامية في عُمان قراءةٌ في معالم طريقٍ غامض" ("Islamic Movements in Oman: Reading the Mysterious Milestones Along the Road"), in الحركات الاسلامية في الوطن العربي (*Islamic Movements in the Arab World*) (Beirut: Centre for Arab Unity Studies, 2013).

134. Al Hashemi, "الحركات الإسلامية في عُمان" ("Islamic Movements in Oman").

135. John W. Fox, Nada Mourtada-Sabbah, and Mohammed Al Mutawa, "The Arab Gulf Region," in *Globalization and the Gulf*, ed. John W. Fox, Nada Mourtada-Sabbah, and Mohammed Al Mutawa (Abingdon, UK: Routledge, 2006), 16.

136. Robert E. Looney, "Review: The Arab World's Uncomfortable Experience with Globalization," *Middle East Journal* 61, no. 1 (Spring 2007): 341; Fareed Zakaria, *The Future of Freedom: Illiberal Democracy at Home and Abroad* (New York: W. W. Norton, 2007), 139; and Mark C. Thompson, *Being Young, Male and Saudi: Identity and Politics in a Globalized Kingdom* (Cambridge: Cambridge University Press, 2019), 172–185.

137. Quoted in Robert Springborg and Clement Moore Henry, *Globalization and the Politics of Development in the Middle East* (Cambridge: Cambridge University Press, 2010), 3.

138. Gaber Asfour, "An Argument for Enhancing Arab Identity within Globalization," in *Globalization and the Gulf*, ed. John W. Fox, Nada Mourtada-Sabbah, and Mohammed Al Mutawa (Abingdon, UK: Routledge, 2006), 288–289, 292–293.

139. Ayoob Al Dakhallah, التربية ومشكلات المجتمع في عصر العولة (*Education and Societal Problems in the Age of Globalization*) (Beirut: Dar Al Kotob Al Imiyah, 2015), 81.

140. Al Dakhallah, التربية ومشكلات المجتمع في عصر العولة (*Education and Societal Problems in the Age of Globalization*), 81.

141. Pascal Menoret, "Cities in the Arabian Peninsula: Introduction" *City* 18, no. 6 (2013): 698–670; and Oystein S. LaBianca and Sandra Arnold Scham, *Connectivity in Antiquity: Globalization as a Long-Term Historical Process* (Abingdon, UK: Routledge, 2016), 62–70.

142. al-Nakeeb and Kenny (trans.), *Society and State*, 16–17.

143. Madawi Al Rasheed, "Transnational Connections and National Identity: Zanzibari Omanis in Muscat," in *Monarchies and Nations: Globalization and Identity in the Arab States of the Gulf*, ed. Paul Dresch and James Piscatori (New York: I. B. Tauris, 2013), 96–113.

144. al-Nakeeb and Kenny (trans.), *Society and State*, 51.

145. Wilkinson, "Traditional Concepts of Territory."

146. Paul Dresch, "Introduction: Societies, Identities and Global Issues," in *Monarchies and Nations: Globalization and Identity in the Arab States of the Gulf*, ed. Paul Dresch and James Piscatori (New York: I. B. Tauris, 2013), 9–16.

147. J. E. Peterson, "Change and Continuity in Arab Gulf Society," in *After the War: Iraq, Iran and the Arab Gulf*, ed. Charles Davies (Chichester, UK: Carden, 1990), 288–290.

148. B. Al Ammari and M. H. Romanowski, "The Impact of Globalization on Society and Culture in Qatar," *Pertanika Social Sciences and Humanities* 24, no. 4 (2016): 1137–1139.

149. Although this quote specifically refers to the United Arab Emirates (UAE), it applies to all of the monarchies. Frauke Heard-Bay, "The United Arab Emirates: Statehood and Nation-Building in a Traditional Society," *Middle East Journal* 59, no. 3 (2005): 360.

150. Lacroix and Holoch (trans.), *Awakening Islam*, 17; and David Held and Kristian Coates Ulrichsen, "Introduction: The Transformation of the Gulf," in *The Transformation of the Gulf: Politics, Economics, and the Global Order*, ed. David Held and Kristian Coates Ulrichsen (Abingdon, UK: Routledge, 2012), 23.

151. Peterson, "Change and Continuity," 290.

152. Jeremy Jones and Nicholas Ridout, *A History of Modern Oman* (New York: Cambridge University Press, 2015), 99–131.

153. Al-Rashoud, "From Muscat to the Maghreb."

154. Georg Glasze and Abdallah Al Khayyal, "Gated Housing Estates in the Arab World: Case Studies in Lebanon and Riyadh," *Environment and Planning* 29, no. 3 (2002): 325; and Georg Glasze, "Segregation and Seclusion: The Case of Compounds for Western Expatriates in Saudi Arabia," *GeoJournal* 66 (2006), 83–87.

155. Levon H. Melikian, "Gulf Reactions to Western Cultural Pressures," in *The Arab Gulf and the West*, ed. B. R. Pridham (Beckenham, UK: Croom Helm, 1985), 210–211.

156. Sulayman Khalaf, "The Evolution of the Gulf City Type, Oil, and Globalization," in *Globalization and the Gulf*, ed. John W. Fox, Nada Mourtada-Sabbah, and Mohammed Al Mutawa (Abingdon, UK: Routledge, 2006), 504.

157. Khalaf, "Gulf City," 492–518.

158. Richard Anderson and Jawaher Al Bader, "Recent Kuwaiti Architecture: Revionalism vs. Globalization," *Journal of Archiectural and Planning Research* 23, no. 2 (Summer 2006): 135–144.

159. Khalaf, "Gulf City," 492–518; and Pascal Menoret, *Joyriding in Riyadh: Oil, Urbanism, and Road Revolt* (New York: Cambridge University Press, 2014), 61–101.

160. Al-Nakib, *Kuwait Transformed*.

161. Peterson, "Change and Continuity," 290–291, 299–301.

162. Asfour, "An Argument for Enhancing Arab Identity within Globalization," 289.

163. Naomi Sakr, "Channels of Interaction: The Role of Gulf-Owned Media Firms in Globalization," in *Monarchies and Nations: Globalization and Identity in the Arab States of the Gulf*, ed. Paul Dresch and James Piscatori (New York: I. B. Tauris, 2013), 34–51.

164. Clive D. Holes, "Language and Identity in the Arabian Gulf," *Journal of Arabian Studies* 1, no. 2 (2011), 129–145.

165. Peterson, "Change and Continuity," 290–291.

166. Neil Partrick, "Nationalism in the Gulf States," in *The Transformation of the Gulf: Politics, Economics, and the Global Order*, ed. David Held and Kristian Coates Ulrichsen (Abingdon, UK: Routledge, 2012), 59.

167. Wanda Krause, "Gender and Participation in the Arab Gulf," in *The Transformation of the Gulf: Politics, Economics, and the Global Order*, ed. David Held and Kristian Coates Ulrichsen (Abingdon, UK: Routledge, 2012), 97; Paul Dresch, "The Place of Strangers in Gulf Society," in *Globalization and the Gulf*, ed. John W. Fox, Nada Mourtada-Sabbah, and Mohammed Al Mutawa (Abingdon, UK: Routledge, 2006), 413–415; and Suzi Mirgani, "Consumer Citizenship: National Identity and Museum Merchandise in Qatar," *Middle East Journal* 73, no. 4 (2019): 555–572.

168. Nermin Allam and Magdalena Karolak, "Introduction," in *Gulf Cooperation Council Culture and Identities in the New Millennium*, ed. Nermin Allam and Magdalena Karolak (Singapore: Palgrave MacMillan, 2020), 1–10.

169. UAE astronaut Hazza Al Mansouri went to the International Space Station in September 2019, but although some plans have been floated for regional train links, concrete steps have yet to be taken.

170. Mishaal Al Gergawi, "Death of the Khaliji," *Gulf News* (August 22, 2017), https://gulfnews
.com/opinion/op-eds/death-of-the-khaliji-1.2078355.

171. Asseel Al-Ragam, "'Denial of Coevalness': Discursive Practices in the Representation of
Kuwaiti Urban Modernity," *Traditional Dwellings and Settlements Review* 28, no. 2 (2017):
7–20.

172. Al-Nakib, *Kuwait Transformed*, 74.

173. Al-Nakib, *Kuwait Transformed*, 28, 74–75.

174. Fathia El Haddad, "مكتبة الرويح.. 100 عام من القراءة" ("Al Ruwaih Bookshop . . . 100 Years of
Reading"), *Al Qabas* (July 8, 2020), https://www.alqabas.com/article/5785299.

175. Al Sayed, "Sawt Al-Bahrain."

176. Amélie Le Renard, *A Society of Young Women: Opportunities of Place, Power, and Reform
in Saudi Arabia* (Stanford, CA: Stanford University Press, 2014), 10–13.

177. Staci Strobl, "Progressive or Neo-Traditional? Policewomen in Gulf Cooperation Council
(GCC) Countries," *Feminist Formations* 22, no. 3 (2010): 52.

178. Strobl, "Progressive or Neo-Traditional?," 54–58.

179. Madawi Al Rasheed, *A Most Masculine State: Gender, Politics and Religion in Saudi
Arabia* (Cambridge: Cambridge University Press, 2013), 78.

180. Toby Jones, *Desert Kingdom: How Oil and Water Forged Modern Saudi Arabia* (Cambridge, MA: Harvard University Press, 2010), 149–150.

181. Al Rasheed, *A Most Masculine State*, 15–18; and Le Renard, *Young Women*, 2.

182. Thuraiya Alhashmi, "Cracking the Glass Ceiling: Gulf Women in Politics," Washington, DC: Arab Gulf States Institute Washington, July 6, 2018, https://agsiw.org
/cracking-glass-ceiling-gulf-women-politics/.

183. Issam Abousleiman, "Gender in the GCC—the Reform Agenda Continues," *Opinion: The
World Bank* (February 24, 2021), https://www.worldbank.org/en/news/opinion/2021/02/24
/gender-in-the-gcc-the-reform-agenda-continues.

184. "Women Apply in Their Thousands to Drive Trains in Saudi Arabia," *The Guardian*
(February 17, 2022), https://www.theguardian.com/world/2022/feb/17/women-apply-in
-their-thousands-to-drive-trains-in-saudi-arabia.

185. Abousleiman, "Gender in the GCC."

186. Hassan Hassan, "The 'Conscious Uncoupling' of Wahhabism and Saudi Arabia," *New
Lines Magazine* (February 22, 2022), https://newlinesmag.com/argument/the-conscious
-uncoupling-of-wahhabism-and-saudi-arabia/.

187. Saudi-focused conference, Konrad-Adenauer-Stiftung (Cadenabbia, Italy: June 15–17,
2019); and Andrew Michael Leber and Charlotte Lysa, "Onwards and Upwards with
Women in the Gulf," *Middle East Report* (January 11, 2018), https://merip.org/2018/01
/onwards-and-upwards-with-women-in-the-gulf/.

188. Mira Al Hussein, "The Economic Contracts of New Gulf Citizenships," *Orient*
(December 30, 2021), https://orientxxi.info/magazine/the-economic-contracts-of-new
-gulf-citizenships,5265.

189. "Changing Times for Saudi's Once Feared Morality Police," *France 24* (January 14,
2022), https://www.france24.com/en/live-news/20220114-changing-times-for-saudi-s-once
-feared-morality-police?ref=tw.

190. Courtney Freer and Andrew Leber, "The 'Tribal Advantage' in Kuwaiti Politics and the Future of the Opposition," *Brookings Institution* (April 19, 2021), https://www.brookings .edu/blog/order-from-chaos/2021/04/19/the-tribal-advantage-in-kuwaiti-politics-and -the-future-of-the-opposition/.

191. David B. Roberts, "Qatar's Shura Council Elections: Incrementally Strengthening Local Politics," Washington, DC: Arab Gulf States Institute Washington, October 7, 2021, https:// agsiw.org/qatars-shura-council-elections-incrementally-strengthening-local-politics/.

3. ECONOMIC SECURITY

1. Barry Buzan, Ole Wæver, and Jaap de Wilde, *Security: A New Framework for Analysis* (Boulder, CO: Lynne Rienner, 1998), 95–97.

2. Ian J. Seccombe, "Labour Migration to the Arabian Gulf: Evolution and Characteristics 1920–1950," *British Journal of Middle Eastern Studies* 10, no. 1 (1983): 3.

3. Robert Carter, "The History and Prehistory of Pearling in the Persian Gulf," *Journal of the Economic and Social History of the Orient* 48, no. 2 (2005): 152–153.

4. Carter, "Pearling in the Gulf," 157, 179, 183–184.

5. Carter, "Pearling in the Gulf," 157, 177–181.

6. Fahad Ahmad Bishara et al., "The Economic Transformation of the Gulf," in *The Emergence of the Gulf States: Studies in Modern History*, ed. J. E. Peterson (London: Bloomsbury, 2016), 191, 197.

7. Alexander Jabbari, "The Ancient Word Linking Oman, Thailand and Aboriginal Australia," *The National* (n.d.), https://www.thenationalnews.com/opinion/comment/the-ancient-word -linking-oman-thailand-and-aboriginal-australia-1.1247153.

8. Bishara et al., "Economic Transformation," 196.

9. Carter, "Pearling in the Gulf," 199; and Bishara et al., "Economic Transformation," 189.

10. Carter, "Pearling in the Gulf," 184–185.

11. Carter, "Pearling in the Gulf," 140.

12. Ed Crooks, "The Most Momentous Telegram of the 20th Century? Western Union Brings the News That Oil Has Been Found in Saudi Arabia, 80 Years Ago This Week, #CERAWeek18," Twitter (accessed March 20, 2019), https://twitter.com/Ed_Crooks /status/971039511244361730.

13. Jim Krane, *Energy Kingdoms* (New York: Columbia University Press, 2019), 32–33.

14. Krane, *Energy Kingdoms*, 39–40.

15. Krane, *Energy Kingdoms*, 43–55.

16. For the traditional arguments, see Daniel Yergin, *The Prize: The Epic Quest for Oil, Money and Power* (New York: Simon and Schuster, 2011), 570–614. And for a contemporary rebuttal and recasting, see Robert Vitalis, *Oilcraft: The Myths of Scarcity and Security That Haunt U.S. Energy Policy* (Stanford, CA: Stanford University Press, 2020), 61–64.

17. Victor McFarland, *Oil Powers: A History of the U.S.-Saudi Alliance* (New York: Columbia University Press, 2020), 143.

18. Krane, *Energy Kingdoms*, 49.

19. Valeris Marcel, "National Oil Companies in the Middle East," in *Oil Titans*, ed. Valeris Marcel (Washington, DC: Brookings, 2005), 19–31.

20. Martin Hvidt, *Economic Diversification in GCC Countries: Past Record and Future Trends*, London School of Economics (January 2013), 189.

21. Mehran Kamrava, "The Political Economy of Rentierism in the Persian Gulf," in *Political Economy of the Persian Gulf*, ed. Mehran Kamrava (New York: Columbia University Press, 2012), 52–55.

22. Jessie Moritz, "Reformers and the Rentier State: Re-Evaluating the Co-Optation Mechanism in Rentier State Theory," *Journal of Arabian Studies* 8, no. 1 (2018), https://doi.org/10.1080/21534764.2018.1546933; and Jocelyn Sage Mitchell and Justin J. Gengler, "What Money Can't Buy: Wealth, Inequality, and Economic Satisfaction in the Rentier State," *Political Research Quarterly* 72, no. 1 (2019), https://doi .org/10.1177/1065912918776128.

23. Hazem El Beblawi, "Gulf Industrialization in Perspective," *Industrialization in the Gulf: A Socioeconomic Revolution* (2010); quoted in Hvidt, *Economic Diversification*, 190.

24. Kamrava, "Political Economy," 40.

25. Michael Herb, *The Wages of Oil: Parliaments and Economic Development in Kuwait and the UAE* (Ithaca, NY: Cornell Univestity Press, 2014), Loc. 503.

26. Martin Hvidt, "Planning for Development in the GCC States: A Content Analysis of Current Development Plans," *Journal of Arabian Studies* 2, no. 2 (2012): 190.

27. Omar AlShehabi, تصدير الثروة واغتراب الإنسان: تاريخ الخلل الإنتاجي في دول الخليج العربية (*Exporting Wealth and Alienating the Citizen: History of Production in the GCC*) (Beirut: Centre for Arab Unity Studies, 2018), 7206.

28. Herb, *Wages of Oil*, chapter 1.

29. Herb, *Wages of Oil*, Loc. 495–531.

30. Antonio Carvalho, Jeff Youssef, and Nicolas Dunias, *Maximizing Employment of Nationals in the GCC*, Oliver Wyman, Marsh and McLennan (October 2018), https://www .oliverwyman.com/content/dam/oliver-wyman/v2/publications/2018/october/maximizing -employment-of-nationals-in-the-gcc.pdf.

31. "Budget Deficit Drops by 60 Percent on Back of Higher Revenues," *Kuwait Times* (July 29, 2019), https://www.kuwaittimes.com/budget-deficit-drops-by-60-on-back-of -higher-revenues/; and *Kuwait Selected Issues* (Washington, DC: International Monetary Fund, January 2018), 11–14.

32. Natalia Tamirisa and Christoph Duenwald, *Public Wage Bills in the Middle East and Central Asia* (Washington, DC: International Monetary Fund, 2018), 6.

33. *The Jobs Agenda for the Gulf Cooperation Council Countries* (Washington, DC: World Bank Group, 2018), https://openknowledge.worldbank.org/handle/10986/29741.

34. Adeel Malik, *The Political Economy of Macroeconomic Policy in Arab Resource-Rich Countries*, Working Papers 1117, Economic Research Forum, revised June 7, 2017, 7.

35. Krane, *Energy Kingdoms*, 74–76.

36. Malik, *Political Economy*, 7.

37. Krane, *Energy Kingdoms*, 71.

38. Tim Boersma and Steve Griffiths, *Reforming Energy Subsidies: Initial Lessons from the United Arab Emirates*, Brookings Institution and Masdar Institute (January 19, 2016),

4–11, https://www.brookings.edu/research/reforming-energy-subsidies-initial-lessons
-from-the-united-arab-emirates/.

39. *World Energy Prices: An Overview*, International Energy Agency Statistics (2019), 8,
https://iea.blob.core.windows.net/assets/567bac7c-5b6f-4aab-8e88-90af3e464d97/
World_Enery_Prices_2019_Overview.pdf.

40. Ian Parry, Simon Black, and Nate Vernon, *Still Not Getting Energy Prices Right: A Global
and Country Update of Fossil Fuel Subsidies*, Working Paper (Washington, DC: International Monetary Fund, 2021), 38, https://www.imf.org/en/Publications/WP/Issues
/2021/09/23/Still-Not-Getting-Energy-Prices-Right-A-Global-and-Country-Update-of
-Fossil-Fuel-Subsidies-466004.

41. Tokhir N. Mirzoev, Ling Zhu, Yang Yang, Tian Zhang, Erik Roos, Andrea Pescatori, and
Akito Matsumoto, *The Future of Oil and Fiscal Sustainability in the GCC Region*, Departmental Paper (Washington, DC: International Monetary Fund, 2020), 17–30, https://
www.imf.org/en/Publications/Departmental-Papers-Policy-Papers/Issues/2020/01/31
/The-Future-of-Oil-and-Fiscal-Sustainability-in-the-GCC-Region-48934.

42. Krane, *Energy Kingdoms*, 69.

43. *BP Statistical Review of World Energy* (London: British Petroleum, 2019).

44. Glada Lahn and Paul Stevens, *Burning Oil to Keep Cool: The Hidden Energy Crisis in
Saudi Arabia*, Chatham House Research Paper (London: Royal Institute of International
Affairs, 2011), 2, https://www.chathamhouse.org/sites/default/files/public/Research/Energy,
%20Environment%20and%20Development/1211pr_lahn_stevens.pdf.

45. *The Saudi Economy in 2019*, Jadwa Investment, Riyadh (February 2019), 21; and "Kingdom
of Saudi Arabia Budget Report 2019," *KPMG* (December 21, 2018), https://home.kpmg
/sa/en/home/insights/2018/12/kingdom-of-saudi-arabia-budget-report.html.

46. "Country-Specific Updates—Gulf Cooperation Council (GCC)," *DLA Piper* (February 3,
2020), https://www.dlapiper.com/en/belgium/insights/publications/2020/01/vat-alert-january
/country-specific-updates-gcc/#0.

47. Karen E. Young, "Sovereign Risk: Gulf Sovereign Wealth Funds as Engines of Growth
and Political Resource," *British Journal of Middle Eastern Studies* 47, no. 1 (2020): 97.

48. Imad Salamey, "Middle Eastern Exceptionalism: Globalization and the Balance of
Power," *Democracy and Security* 5, no. 3 (2009): 251.

49. Kamrava, "Political Economy," 59–66.

50. Jerry Harris, "Statist Globalization in China, Russia and the Gulf States," in *The Nation in
the Global Era*, ed. Jerry Harris (Leiden, Netherlands: Brill, 2009), 30–40.

51. Justin Gengler, "Qatar's Ambivalent Democratization," *Foreign Policy* (November 1, 2011),
http://mideast.foreignpolicy.com/posts/2011/11/01/qataris_lesson_in_revolution.

52. Robert Springborg and Clement Moore Henry, *Globalization and the Politics of Development in the Middle East* (Cambridge: Cambridge University Press, 2010), 318–319.

53. Samuel P. Huntington, *Political Order in Changing Societies* (New Haven, CT and
London: Yale University Press, 1968), 177–191; and Marina Ottaway and Michele
Dunne, *Incumbent Regimes and the "King's Dilemma" in the Arab World: Promise and
Threat of Managed Reform* (Washington, DC: Carnegie Endowment for International
Peace, 2007), 10, https://carnegieendowment.org/2007/12/10/incumbent-regimes-and
-king-s-dilemma-in-arab-world-promise-and-threat-of-managed-reform-pub-19759.

54. Juergen Braunstein, "Domestic Sources of Twenty-First-Century Geopolitics: Domestic Politics and Sovereign Wealth Funds in GCC Economies," *New Political Economy* 24, no. 2 (2019): 197.

55. Sara Bazoobandi and Jeffrey B. Nugent, *Political Economy of Sovereign Wealth Funds in the Oil Exporting Countries of the Arab Region and Especially the Gulf*, Working Papers 1143, Economic Research Forum (2017), 1.

56. *Annual Statistics 2018*, Saudi Arabian Monetary Authority (May 29, 2019), 5–2, https://tinyurl.com/y7gzl783.

57. Bazoobandi and Nugent, *Political Economy of Sovereign Wealth Funds*, 6.

58. Bazoobandi and Nugent, *Political Economy of Sovereign Wealth Funds*, 6.

59. Bazoobandi and Nugent, *Political Economy of Sovereign Wealth Funds*, 6.

60. "Saudi Finance Minister Says No Need to Create Sovereign Wealth Fund," *Reuters* (December 26, 2014), https://www.reuters.com/article/us-saudi-sovereign-funds/saudi-finance-minister-says-no-need-to-create-sovereign-wealth-fund-idUSKBN0K40 A820141226.

61. Stephan Roll, "A Sovereign Wealth Fund for the Prince: Economic Reforms and Power Consolidation in Saudi Arabia," Research Paper, 8 (Berlin: Stiftung Wissenschaft und Politik, 2019), 5.

62. "About the PIF," https://www.pif.gov.sa/en/Pages/About-PIF.aspx.

63. Roll, "SWF for the Prince," 11.

64. Roll, "SWF for the Prince," 11.

65. Roll, "SWF for the Prince," 11.

66. Roll, "SWF for the Prince," 17.

67. Roll, "SWF for the Prince," 12.

68. Roll, "SWF for the Prince," 12–13; and Andrew England and Simeon Kerr, "Saudi Foreign Reserves Fall as Sovereign Wealth Fund Spends Overseas," *Financial Times* (June 1, 2020), https://www.ft.com/content/6825366f-92db-4473-b5b2-cacda032d8ee.

69. Anjli Raval, "Saudi Aramco Stretches away as Top IPO after Extra Sale," *Financial Times* (January 12, 2020), https://www.ft.com/content/6ecc8978-3524-11ea-a6d3-9a26f8c3cba4.

70. Interview with an anonymous Gulf-focused fund manager, June 26, 2020.

71. Young, "Sovereign Risk," 110.

72. "Saudi Aramco's Public Debut Is a Hollow Victory," *Financial Times* (December 12, 2019), https://www.ft.com/content/db9cb912-1cf4-11ea-9186-7348c2f183af.

73. Stephan Roll, "Aramco's IPO and Bin Salman's Fiscal Takeover," Sada (Washington: DC: Carnegie Endowment for International Peace, December 2, 2019), https://carnegieendowment.org/sada/80463; and "Saudi Aramco Reports Strong 2019 Results despite Difficult Macro Environment," *Saudi Aramco* (March 15, 2020), https://www.saudiaramco.com/en/news-media/news/2020/saudi-aramco-full-year-2019-results#:~:text=Total %20dividend%20payments%20were%20%2473.2,%2C%20through%20December%2031 %2C%202019.

74. Anjli Raval, "Saudi Aramco Sticks by $75bn Dividend despite Sharp Profit Fall," *Financial Times* (March 21, 2021), https://www.ft.com/content/b91097a9-c554-4e5c-9b89-a8abec354a55.

75. Quoted in Roll, "SWF for the Prince," 20.

76. Andrew England and Arash Massoudi, "'Never Waste a Crisis': Inside Saudi Arabia's Shopping Spree," *Financial Times* (May 25, 2020), https://www.ft.com/content/af2deefd -2234-4e54-a08a-8dbb205f5378.

77. Roll, "SWF for the Prince," 26.

78. Sara Bazoobandi, *The Political Economy of the Gulf Sovereign Wealth Funds: A Case Study of Iran, Kuwait, Saudi Arabia and the United Arab Emirates* (Abingdon, UK: Routledge, 2013), 15–16, 33–35.

79. K. J. Passmore, *Visit to the UAE and Kuwait by Puss Transport*, Ministerial Visit from the UK to the Persian Gulf, General, Foreign and Commonwealth Office, London (December 15, 1981).

80. Bazoobandi, *Sovereign Wealth Funds*, 34.

81. Braunstein, "Domestic Politics and SWFs," 205.

82. A. H. K. Slater, *United Kingdom/United Arab Emirates (UAE) Joint Committee*, Foreign and Commonwealth Office, London, FCO 8/3143 (October 3, 1978), https://www.agda .ae/en/catalogue/tna/fco/8/3142.

83. Braunstein, "Domestic Politics and SWFs," 4–16.

84. Ragaei El Mallakh, *Qatar: Development of an Oil Economy* (London: Croom Helm, 1979), 126, 131; and J. F. Slater, *Mr Barratt's Visit to Qatar*, Foreign and Commonwealth Office, London (November 27, 1974).

85. R. D. Gordon, *Qatar Investment in UK Property*, Foreign and Commonwealth Office, London (October 28, 1974).

86. Roberts, *Qatar: Securing the Global Ambitions*, 81–101.

87. David B. Roberts, "Qatar Shuffles Back to the Future" (Washington, DC: Arab Gulf States Institute Washington, December 13, 2018), https://agsiw.org/qatar-shuffles-back-to-the -future/.

88. "Qatar to Invest $15 Billion in Turkey; Source Says Banks the Focus," *Reuters* (August 15, 2018), https://uk.reuters.com/article/us-turkey-currency-qatar-investments/qatar-to -invest-15-billion-in-turkey-source-says-banks-the-focus-idUKKBN1L01P7.

89. Braunstein, "Domestic Politics and SWFs," 213.

90. Braunstein, "Domestic Politics and SWFs," 199.

91. Gawdat Bahgat, "Sovereign Wealth Funds in the Gulf: An Assessment," in *The Transformation of the Gulf: Politics, Economics and the Global Order*, ed. David Held and Kristian Coates Ulrichsen (London: Routledge, 2012), 27.

92. Jeffrey Davis, Rolando Ossowski, James A. Daniel, and Steven Barnett, "Stabilization and Savings Funds for Nonrenewable Resources: Experience and Fiscal Policy Implications," in *Fiscal Policy Formulation and Implementation in Oil-Producing Countries*, ed. J. M. Davis, R. Ossowski, and A. Fedelino (Washington, DC: International Monetary Fund, 2001), 307; and Bazoobandi and Nugent, *Political Economy of Sovereign Wealth Funds*, 8.

93. Dominic Dudley, "Oman Sets up $18 Billion Sovereign Wealth Fund Even as Economy Shrinks," *Forbes* (June 5, 2020), https://www.forbes.com/sites/dominicdudley/2020/06/05 /oman-sovereign-wealth-fund/.

94. Roll, "SWF for the Prince," 6.

95. Bahgat, "SWFs in the Gulf," 5; and Young, "Sovereign Risk," 96.

96. Bazoobandi and Nugent, *Political Economy of Sovereign Wealth Funds*, 10–14.
97. David Sanger, "Under Pressure, Dubai Company Drops Port Deal," *New York Times* (March 10, 2006), https://www.nytimes.com/2006/03/10/politics/under-pressure-dubai-company-drops-port-deal.html.
98. Bahgat, "SWFs in the Gulf," 23.
99. Simeon Kerr, "Dubai Fears the End of Its 'Build It and They Will Come' Model," *Financial Times* (April 1, 2019), https://www.ft.com/content/4d169d0c-4be4-11e9-8b7f-d49067e0f50d; Steffen Hertog, "The Costs of Counter-Revolution in the GCC," *Foreign Policy* (May 31, 2011), http://foreignpolicy.com/2011/05/31/the-costs-of-counter-revolution-in-the-gcc/; and Bahgat, "SWFs in the Gulf," 23–24.
100. Bazoobandi and Nugent, *Political Economy of Sovereign Wealth Funds*, 12.
101. Young, "Sovereign Risk," 108.
102. Jones, *Desert Kingdom*, 97, 102–103.
103. Roberts, *Qatar: Securing the Global Ambitions*, 47–53.
104. Rosemarie Said Zahlan, *The Making of the Modern Gulf States: Kuwait, Bahrain, Qatar, the United Arab Emirates and Oman* (Reading, UK: Ithaca, 1998), 41–45.
105. Gregory Gause III, *Oil Monarchies: Domestic and Security Challenges in the Arab Gulf States* (New York: Council on Foreign Relations, 1994), 62.
106. John E. Peterson, "Oman: Three and a Half Decades of Change and Development," *Middle East Policy* 11, no. 2 (2004): 125–137.
107. Kristian Coates Ulrichsen, *The United Arab Emirates: Power, Politics, and Policymaking* (Oxford, UK: Routledge, 2017), 1437.
108. Coates Ulrichsen, *The United Arab Emirates*, 1437.
109. Christine Osborne, *The Gulf States and Oman* (Abingdon, UK: Routledge, 2017), 105–113.
110. Osborne, *Gulf States and Oman*, 111–112.
111. Osborne, *Gulf States and Oman*, 96–97.
112. Michael E. Porter, "Clusters and the New Economics of Competition," Harvard Business Review (November–December 1998), https://hbr.org/1998/11/clusters-and-the-new-economics-of-competition. Also see Stephen J. Ramos, *Dubai Amplified: The Engineering of a Port Geography* (Farnham, UK: Ashgate, 2010), 92.
113. Ramos, *Dubai Amplified*, 89–93. On the "Dubai model" concept, see Martin Hvidt, "The Dubai Model: An Outline of Key Development-Process Elements in Dubai," *International Journal of Middle East Studies* 41, no. 3 (2009), https://doi.org/doi:10.1017/S0020743809091120.
114. Osborne, *Gulf States and Oman*, 15, 97.
115. Ramos, *Dubai Amplified*, 102.
116. Ramos, *Dubai Amplified*, 102–103.
117. Ramos, *Dubai Amplified*, 108–109.
118. David G. Edens and William P. Snavely, "Planning for Economic Development in Saudi Arabia," *Middle East Journal* 24, no. 1 (1970): 22.
119. Edens and Snavely, "Planning for Economic Development in Saudi Arabia," 27.
120. Adel Abdel Ghafar, "A New Kingdom of Saud?," *Cairo Review of International Affairs*, no. 45 (Winter 2018), https://www.thecairoreview.com/essays/a-new-kingdom-of-saud/.

121. Ghafar, "A New Kingdom of Saud?"
122. Joseph Kraft, "Letter from Saudi Arabia," *New Yorker* (October 20, 1975), 112.
123. Kraft, "Letter from Saudi Arabia," 128; Hvidt, "Planning for Development," 192; and Bruce D. Grant, *U.S. Military Expertise for Sale: Private Military Consultants as a Tool of Foreign Policy*, USAWC Strategy Research Project (Pennsylvania: US Army War College, 1998), https://citeseerx.ist.psu.edu/viewdoc/download?doi=10.1.1.466.5983&rep =rep1&type=pdf.
124. Laleh Khalili, "The Infrastructural Power of the Military: The Geoeconomic Role of the U.S. Army Corps of Engineers in the Arabian Peninsula," *European Journal of International Relations* 24, no. 4 (2018): 911–933.
125. Calvert W. Jones, "Adviser to the King: Experts Rationalization, and Legitimacy," *World Politics* 71, no. 1 (2019): 11–20; Andrew Leber, "@Mckinsey Advising #Saudi on Gov't Reform Way Back in 1980. Cc @Adelaghafar," Twitter (June 21, 2016), https://twitter.com /AndrewMLeber/status/745337286758379520; and Salem Saif, "When Consultants Reign," *Jacobin* (May 9, 2016), https://jacobin.com/2016/05/saudi-arabia-aramco-salman-mckinsey -privatization/.
126. "Moving Saudi Arabia's Economy Beyond Oil," *Mckinsey* (December 1, 2015), https:// www.mckinsey.com/featured-insights/employment-and-growth/moving-saudi-arabias -economy-beyond-oil.
127. Jones, *Desert Kingdom*, 22.
128. Osborne, *Gulf States and Oman*, 23.
129. Osborne, *Gulf States and Oman*, 33.
130. Ben R. Craig, *The Souk Al-Manakh Crash*, Economic Commentary (Cleveland, OH: Federal Reserve Bank of Cleveland, 2019), https://www.clevelandfed.org/en/newsroom -and-events/publications/economic-commentary/2019-economic-commentaries /ec-201920-kuwait-souk-al-manakh.aspx.
131. Craig, *The Souk Al-Manakh Crash*.
132. Patrick Clawson, "Sometimes the Grass Is Indeed Greener: The Successful Use of Energy Revenues," in *Beyond the Resource Curse*, ed. Brenda Shaffer and Taleh Ziyadov (Philadelphia: University of Pennsylvania Press, 2011), 78.
133. *Policy Challenges in the Gulf Cooperation Council Countries* (Washington, DC: International Monetary Fund, May 1996), Section II.
134. *Policy Challenges*, II.
135. Sarah Moser, Marian Swain, and Mohammed H. Alkhabbaz, "King Abdullah Economic City: Engineering Saudi Arabia's Post-Oil Future," *Cities* 45 (2015): 71–80; and *Policy Challenges*, II.
136. Hvidt, "Planning for Development," 192.
137. Hvidt, "Planning for Development," 193–195.
138. *Saudi Arabia's Economic Cities*, Saudi Arabian General Investment Authority (n.d.), https://www.oecd.org/mena/competitiveness/38906206.pdf.
139. Ahmed Al Omran, "Saudi Arabia's Sleepy City Offers Prince a Cautionary Tale," *Financial Times* (May 27, 2018), https://www.ft.com/content/ae48574c-58e6-11e8-bdb7-f6677d2e1ce8.
140. "Saudi Arabia: MBS Promises 'Giga-Projects'," *Gulf States Newsletter* (November 2, 2017).

141. "Saudi Arabia Sets Itself up for a Fall with Ambitious Economic Reform Plan," *Gulf States Newsletter* 40, 1014 (May 5, 2016).

142. "Saudi Arabia Sets Itself up".

143. Jones, "Adviser to the King," 13.

144. Adam Hanieh, *Money, Markets, and Monarchies: The Gulf Cooperation Council and the Political Economy of the Contemporary Middle East* (Cambridge: Cambridge University Press, 2018), 202–204.

145. Quoted in Hanieh, *Money, Markets, Monarchies*, 204.

146. "NEOM" is a name comprising "Neo," as in "new," and "Mustaqbal," Arabic for "future."

147. Bill Bostock, "Everything We Know About Neom, a 'Mega-City' Project in Saudi Arabia with Plans for Flying Cars and Robot Dinosaurs," *Business Insider* (September 23, 2019), https://www.businessinsider.in/miscellaneous/everything-we-know-about-neom-a -mega-city-project-in-saudi-arabia-with-plans-for-flying-cars-and-robot-dinosaurs /slidelist/71232419.cms.

148. Jones, "Adviser to the King," 13.

149. Mark Mazzetti et al., "Consulting Firms Keep Lucrative Saudi Alliance, Shaping Crown Prince's Vision," *New York Times* (November 4, 2018), https://www.nytimes .com/2018/11/04/world/middleeast/mckinsey-bcg-booz-allen-saudi-khashoggi .html; Adel Abdel Ghafar, "Saudi Arabia's McKinsey Reshuffle," Brookings Institution (May 11, 2016), https://www.brookings.edu/blog/markaz/2016/05/11/saudi-arabias -mckinsey-reshuffle/; Anjli Raval and Neil Hume, "Saudi Aramco Listing Presents Challenge for Investors," *Financial Times* (January 10, 2016), https://www.ft.com/content /of331bde-b784-11e5-b151-8e15c9a029fb; and Salem Saif, "When Consultants Reign," *Jacobin* (May 9, 2016), https://www.jacobinmag.com/2016/05/saudi-arabia-aramco -salman-mckinsey-privatization/.

150. Hanieh, *Money, Markets, Monarchies*, 213–214; and Courtney Trenwith, "Kuwait's New PPP Law Is 'Selling' the Country, Says MPS," *Arabian Business* (July 1, 2014), https:// www.arabianbusiness.com/kuwait-s-new-ppp-law-is-selling—country-says-mps-556260 .html.

151. Although Dubai did not benefit significantly in the same way from rising oil prices owing to its small supplies, its economy remained entangled with the wider UAE ascendency during the oil boom years.

152. Kamrava, "Political Economy," 61.

153. Kamrava, "Political Economy," 60–64.

154. Hvidt, *Economic Diversification*, 40.

155. Osborne, *Gulf States and Oman*, 14–15; and Hvidt, *Economic Diversification*, 40–41.

156. Clawson, "Sometimes the Grass Is Indeed Greener," 78.

157. Hvidt, *Economic Diversification*, 40–41.

158. Kraft, "Letter from Saudi Arabia."

159. "One Hundred Ports 2021," *Lloyds List*, https://lloydslist.maritimeintelligence.informa .com/-/media/lloyds-list/images/top-100-ports-2021/top-100-ports-2021-digital -edition.pdf.

160. Simeon Kerr, "DP World Profits Rise by a Tenth despite 'Geopolitical Challenges,'" *Financial Times* (March 14, 2019), https://www.ft.com/content/2f339cfc-4628-11e9-a965 -23d669740bfb.

161. Rafeef Ziadah, "Constructing a Logistics Space: Perspectives from the Gulf Cooperation Council," *Environment and Planning D: Society and Space* 36, no. 4 (2018): 666–682.

162. The Economic and Social Research Council in the United Kingdom, quoted in Kristian Coates Ulrichsen, "Knowledge-Based Economies in the GCC," in *The Political Economy of the Persian Gulf*, ed. Mehran Kamrava (New York: Columbia University Press, 2012), 97.

163. Martin Hvidt, "The Role of 'Lavish Construction Schemes' in 'Late-Late-Late' Developing Societies: The Case of the Arab Gulf States," in *Under Construction: Logics of Urbanism in the Gulf Region*, ed. Steffen Wippel, Katrin Bromber, Christian Steiner, and Birgit Krawietz (Farnham, UK: Ashgate, 2014), 33. The acceptability of jobs evolves over time and differs across the monarchies. For instance, a Bahraini or Omani taxi driver is common; a Qatari taxi driver is unheard of. Similarly, Saudis working as front-of-house staff in hotels or shop assistants was comparatively rare before, say, the late-2010s, but it is an increasingly common sight today. Martin Hvidt, "The State and the Knowledge Economy in the Gulf: Structural and Motivational Challenges," *Muslim World* 105, no. 1 (2015): 24–45.

164. Mahfouz E. Tadros, "The Arab Gulf States and the Knowledge Economy: Challenges and Opportunities" (Washington, DC: Arab Gulf States Institute Washington, 2015), 4, https://agsiw.org/wp-content/uploads/2015/07/Tadros_Knowledge-Economy_Rev1 .pdf.

165. John Curtis Perry, *Singapore: Unlikely Power* (New York: Oxford Univeristy Press, 2017), xx–xxv.

166. Richard Florida and Martin Kenney, "The New Age of Capitalism: Innovation-Mediated Production," *Futures* 25, no. 6 (1993): 637. Quoted in Hvidt, "Knowledge Economy," 27.

167. Joy S. Moini, Tora K. Bikson, Richard Neu, and Laura DeSisto, *The Reform of Qatar University* (Santa Monica, CA: RAND Corporation, 2009); and Gail L. Zellman et al., *Education for a New Era: Design and Implementation of K-12 Education Reform in Qatar* (Santa Monica, CA: RAND Corporation, 2007).

168. Tadros, "The Arab Gulf States and the Knowledge Economy," 5.

169. Wolfgang G. Stock, Julia Barth, and Julia Gremm, "The Era after Oil: Knowledge-Intensive Cities on the Arabian Gulf," in *Knowledge-Intensive Economies and Opportunities for Social, Organizational, and Technological Growth*, ed. Miltiadis Lytras, Linda Daniela, and Anna Visvizi (Hershey, PA: IGI Global, 2019), 65–82, https://doi .org/10.4018/978-1-5225-7347-0.

170. Soumitra Dutta, Bruno Lanvin, and Sacha Wunsch-Vincent, *Global Innovation Index 2019* (Ithaca, NY, Fontainebleau, France, and Geneva, Switzerland: Cornell University, INSTEAD, and World Intellectual Property Organization, 2019).

171. Hvidt, "Knowledge Economy," 24–27.

172. Joseph Stiglitz, "Public Policy for a Knowledge Economy," *Remarks at the Department for Trade and Industry and Center for Economic Policy Research* 27, no. 3 (1999): 3–7.

173.   Hvidt, "The Role of 'Lavish Construction Schemes,'" 34. On the local perception of this
       social contract, see Mark C. Thompson, *Being Young, Male and Saudi: Identity and Poli-*
       tics in a Globalized Kingdom (Cambridge: Cambridge University Press, 2019), 59–70.
174.   Hussein Abdulmutallab Al Assaraj, "اشكالية البطالة فى دول مجلس التعاون الخليجي" ("The Paradox of
       Unemployment in the GCC Countries"), *Munich Personal RePEc Archive* 54600 (March
       2014), 6.
175.   AlShehabi, تصدير الثروة واغتراب الإنسان: تاريخ الخلل الإنتاجي في دول الخليج العربية (*Exporting Wealth and*
       Alienating the Citizen: History of Production in the GCC), 7316.
176.   Tamirisa and Duenwald, *Public Wage Bills*, 7–9.
177.   *Labor Market Reforms to Boost Employment and Productivity in the GCC—an Update*
       (Washington, DC: International Monetary Fund, October 25, 2014), 21–23; and *Outlook*
       for Producer Economies 2018, International Energy Agency, Paris (2018), 28.
178.   AlShehabi, تصدير الثروة واغتراب الإنسان: تاريخ الخلل الإنتاجي في دول الخليج العربية (*Exporting Wealth and*
       Alienating the Citizen: History of Production in the GCC), 7395.
179.   "In Latest Spending Cut, Oman Not Renewing Majority of Foreign Consultant Contracts,"
       Al Monitor (May 29, 2020), https://www.al-monitor.com/pulse/originals/2020/05/oman
       -contracts-spending-coronavirus-economy-oil-royal-court.html.
180.   *New Challenges Brought by Covid-19*, Jadwa Investment, Riyadh (June 2020), https://www
       .sustg.com/1-2-million-expat-workers-to-leave-saudi-arabia-in-2020-jadwa-estimates/.
181.   Fiona MacDonald, "Kuwait Doesn't Want to Be an Expat-Majority Nation Anymore,"
       Bloomberg (June 3, 2020), https://www.bloomberg.com/news/articles/2020-06-03/kuwait
       -needs-to-slash-expatriate-population-to-30-premier-says.
182.   Ahmed Al Omran and Andrew England, "Saudi Arabia: Why Jobs Overhaul Could
       Define MBS's Rule," *Financial Times* (February 28, 2019), https://www.ft.com/content
       /fc240c0e-29fb-11e9-88a4-c32129756dd8.
183.   Thompson, *Young, Male and Saudi*, 71–77.
184.   Marwa Rashad and Davide Barbuscia, "Saudi Foreign Reserves Fall at Fastest for Two
       Decades," *Reuters* (April 29, 2020), https://www.reuters.com/article/us-saudi-budget
       -idUSKCN22B0W5.
185.   *Foreign Merchandise Trade Statistics*, Planning and Statistics Authority, State of Qatar
       (April 2020).
186.   Fiona MacDonald, "Kuwait's Budget Crunch May Push It to Tap Fund for Life after Oil,"
       Bloomberg (July 6, 2020), https://tinyurl.com/y8bavjzv.
187.   "Gulf Countries to Experience Worst Economic Crisis in History—IIF," *Reuters*
       (June 2, 2020), https://uk.reuters.com/article/uk-gulf-economy-iif/gulf-countries-to
       -experience-worst-economic-crisis-in-history-iif-idUKKBN2390N6; Rory Fyfe, "GCC
       Deficit Could Reach $250bn with a 16 Percent Drop in Non-Oil Output," *MENA*
       Advisors (April 29, 2020), https://mena-advisors.com/2020/04/gcc-deficit-could-reach
       -250bn-with-a-16-drop-in-non-oil-output.
188.   Andrew England, "Middle East States Set for $1.3tn Oil Windfall, Says IMF," *Financial Times*
       (August 19, 2022), https://www.ft.com/content/94825404-e0a2-4a18-ab8d-2bc61fc7c1ab.
189.   Dominic Dudley, "World Bank Raises Questions about Gulf's Huge Public Sector Wage Bill,"
       Forbes (December 20, 2021), https://www.forbes.com/sites/dominicdudley/2021/12/20
       /world-bank-raises-questions-about-gulfs-huge-public-sector-wage-bill/.

190. Tarek Fadlallah, "The Puzzle of Profitless Growth in GCC Firms," *Middle East Institute* (August 31, 2021), https://www.mei.edu/publications/puzzle-profitless-growth-gcc-firms.

191. Karen E. Young, "The MBS Economy," *Foreign Affairs* (January 27, 2022), https://www.foreignaffairs.com/articles/saudi-arabia/2022-01-27/mbs-economy.

4. MILITARY SECURITY

1. Barry Buzan, Ole Wæver, and Jaap de Wilde, *Security: A New Framework for Analysis* (Boulder, CO: Lynne Rienner, 1998), 49.

2. H. H. Gerth and C. Wright Mills, *From Max Weber: Essays in Sociology* (New York: Oxford University Press, 1946), 77.

3. John Karlsrud, "Responsibility to Protect and Theorising Normative Change in International Organisations: From Weber to the Sociology of Professions," *Global Responsibility to Protect* 5, no. 1 (2013): 3–27.

4. Majid Khadduri, "The Role of the Military in Middle East Politics," *American Political Science Review* 47, no. 2 (June 1953): 517.

5. Joseph Kostiner, "On Instruments and Their Designers: The Ikhwan of Najd and the Emergence of the Saudi State," *Middle Eastern Studies* 21, no. 3 (1985): 298–322.

6. Daniel Silverfarb, "Great Britain, Iraq, and Saudi Arabia: The Revolt of the Ikhwan, 1927–1930," *International History Review* 4, no. 2 (1982): 228; and Ash Rossiter, "Survival of the Kuwaiti Statelet: Najd's Expansion and the Question of British Protection," *Middle Eastern Studies* 56, no. 3 (2020), 381–395, https://doi.org/10.1080/00263206.2020.1716339.

7. Silverfarb, "Great Britain, Iraq, and Saudi Arabia," 229–243.

8. Abdulaziz Al Fahad, "Raiders and Traders: A Poet's Lament on the End of the Bedouin Heroic Age," in *Saudi Arabia in Transition: Insights on Social, Political, Economic and Religious Change*, ed. Bernard Haykel, Thomas Hegghammer, and Stephane Lacroix (Cambridge: Cambridge University Press, 2015), 253.

9. Robert Lacey, *Inside the Kingdom* (London: Arrow, 2010), 16.

10. Nadav Safran, *Saudi Arabia: The Ceaseless Quest for Security* (Ithaca, NY: Cornell University Press, 1991), 54–55.

11. J. E. Peterson, *Defending Arabia* (Abingdon, UK: Routledge, 2017), 193.

12. Nigel Bromage, *A Soldier in Arabia* (London: Radcliffe, 2012), 128.

13. Bromage, *Soldier in Arabia*, 129–131.

14. Joseph Kraft, "Letter from Saudi Arabia," *New Yorker* (July 4, 1983), 124–126.

15. Safran, *Saudi Arabia*, 70.

16. Safran, *Saudi Arabia*, 68–69; and Peterson, *Defending Arabia*, 19–20.

17. On Lord Frederick Lugard and his concept of British indirect rule, see Bernard Porter, *The Lion's Share: A History of British Imperialism 1850 to the Present*, 5th ed. (Harlow, UK: Pearson, 2012), 159; and Frederick Lugard, *The Dual Mandate in British Tropical Africa* (Edinburgh and London: William Blackwood, 1922).

18. Ash Rossiter, *Britain and the Development of Professional Security Forces in the Gulf Arab States, 1921–71: Local Forces and Informal Empire* (PhD dissertation, Exeter University, 2014), 2.

19. Rosemarie Said Zahlan, *The Creation of Qatar* (London and New York: Croom Helm 1979), 59.

20. Derek Hopwood, *The Arabian Peninsula: Society and Politics* (Abingdon, UK: Routledge, 2005).

21. Rossiter, *Britain and the Development of Professional Security Forces*, 209–210.

22. John B. Kelly, "The Buraimi Oasis Dispute," *International Affairs (Royal Institute of International Affairs 1944-)* 32, no. 3 (1956): 318–326; and Tore Tingvold Petersen, "Anglo-American Rivalry in the Middle East: The Struggle for the Buraimi Oasis, 1952–1957," *International History Review* 14, no. 1 (1992): 71–91.

23. Peterson, *Defending Arabia*, 211; and Athol Yates, *The Evolution of the Armed Forces of the United Arab Emirates* (Warwick, UK: Helion, 2020), 323.

24. Rossiter, *Britain and the Development of Professional Security Forces*, 227.

25. James H. Noyes, *The Clouded Lens: Persian Gulf Security and U.S. Policy*, 2nd ed. (Stanford, CA: Hoover Institution, 1982), 39; and Rossiter, *Britain and the Development of Professional Security Forces*, 234.

26. Rossiter, *Britain and the Development of Professional Security Forces*, 241.

27. Yates, *The Evolution of the Armed Forces of the United Arab Emirates*, 322–325.

28. John E. Peterson, *Oman's Insurgencies: The Sultanate's Struggle for Supremacy* (London: Saqi, 2013), 465–466.

29. Rossiter, *Britain and the Development of Professional Security Forces*, 183–185.

30. This was suggested by Kristian Coates Ulrichsen, *The United Arab Emirates: Power, Politics, and Policymaking* (Oxford, UK: Routledge, 2017), 1614.

31. Rossiter, *Britain and the Development of Professional Security Forces*, 263.

32. David Wood, "The Middle East and the Arab World: The Military Context," *Adelphi Papers* 5, no. 20 (1965): 15; and Noyes, *The Clouded Lens*, 39.

33. Rossiter, *Britain and the Development of Professional Security Forces*, 164.

34. Quoted in Rossiter, *Britain and the Development of Professional Security Forces*, 266; and Ash Rossiter, "'Screening the Food from the Flies': Britain, Kuwait, and the Dilemma of Protection, 1961–1971," *Diplomacy and Statecraft* 28, no. 1 (2017): 85–109.

35. Rossiter, *Britain and the Development of Professional Security Forces*, 169, 269.

36. Rossiter, *Britain and the Development of Professional Security Forces*, 164.

37. Peterson, *Defending Arabia*, 103–105.

38. Peterson, *Defending Arabia*, 104.

39. Peterson, *Defending Arabia*, 104.

40. *Saudi Arabia and the United States: The New Context in an Evolving "Special Relationship,"* Subcommittee on Europe and the Middle East of the Committee on Foreign Affairs (Washington, DC: U.S. House of Representatives, 1981), 6–7.

41. "Defend Us Discretely," *The Economist* (June 6, 1981); and *Saudi Arabia and the United States*, 6–7.

42. *Memorandum from Secretary of State Rusk to President Kennedy*, U.S. State Department, Office of the Historian (June 12, 1963).

43. Laleh Khalili, "The Infrastructural Power of the Military: The Geoeconomic Role of the U.S. Army Corps of Engineers in the Arabian Peninsula," *European Journal*

of International Relations 24, no. 4 (2018): 911–933; Armistead I. Selden, *Memorandum from the Acting Assistant Secretary of Defense for International Security Affairs (Selden) to Secretary of Defense Laird*, U.S. State Department, Office of the Historian (November 10, 1971). For a detailed overview, see *Paper Prepared in the National Security Council*, "Middle East/Persian Gulf Arms Supply," U.S. State Department, Office of the Historian (January 19, 1977), https://history.state.gov/historicaldocuments/frus1969 -76ve09p2/d30.

44. Paul H. Nitze, *Memorandum from the Deputy Secretary of Defense (Nitze) to the Chairman of the Joint Chiefs of Staff (Wheeler)*, Office of the Secretary of Defense (Suitland, MD: Washington National Records Center, August 2, 1968).

45. "The Middle East and the Mediterranean," *Military Balance*, no. 1 (1973); and "The Middle East and the Mediterranean," *Military Balance*, no. 1 (1980).

46. Thomas L. McNaugher, *Arms and Oil: U.S. Military Strategy and the Persian Gulf* (Washington, DC: Brookings Institution, 1985), 137–138.

47. McNaugher, *Arms and Oil*, 137–138.

48. McNaugher, *Arms and Oil*, 136–137; and Zoltan Barany, *Military Officers in the Gulf: Career Trajectories and Determinants* (Washington, DC: Center for Strategic and International Studies, November 2019), 1–14, https://www.csis.org/analysis/military -officers-gulf-career-trajectories-and-determinants.

49. McNaugher, *Arms and Oil*, 136–137.

50. Anthony Pascal et al., *Man and Arms in the Middle East: The Human Factor in Military Modernization* (Santa Monica, CA: RAND Corporation, June 1979), 46–47.

51. McNaugher, *Arms and Oil*, 137–138; and Barany, *Military Officers in the Gulf*, 6–8.

52. Wood, "The Middle East and the Arab World," 10.

53. Laura Guazzone, "Gulf Co-Operation Council: The Security Policies," *Survival* 30, no. 2 (1988): 145.

54. Graham Boyce, *Scenarios for Possible Military Intervention in the Gulf*, Foreign and Commonwealth Office, London (August 7, 1986); and David Miers, *Confidential Letter*, Foreign and Commonwealth Office, London (July 15, 1986).

55. McNaugher, *Arms and Oil*, 138, 140–141.

56. *Future of: Royal Family. Probably Happenings on the Death of Ibn Saud*, Coll 6/16, India Office Records and Private Paper. British Library and Qatar Digital Library, https://www .qdl.qa/archive/81055/vdc_100000000555.0x00026c; and Florence Gaub, *Guardians of the Arab State: When Militaries Intervene in Politics, from Iraq to Mauritania* (London: Hurst, 2017), 156–158.

57. McNaugher, *Arms and Oil*, 138.

58. Richard L. Russell, "Future Gulf War," *Joint Forces Quarterly*, no. 55 (2009): 35–40.

59. Geraint Hughes, "A 'Model Campaign' Reappraised: The Counter-Insurgency War in Dhofar, Oman, 1965–1975," *Journal of Strategic Studies* 32, no. 2 (2009): 271–305; Walter C. Ladwig III, "Supporting Allies in Counterinsurgency: Britain and the Dhofar Rebellion," *Small Wars and Insurgencies* 19, no. 1 (2008): 62–88; and James F. Goode, "Assisting Our Brothers, Defending Ourselves: The Iranian Intervention in Oman, 1972–75," *Iranian Studies* 47, no. 3 (2014): 441–462.

60. Anthony H. Cordesman, "The Tanker War and the Lessons of Naval Conflict," in *The Lessons of Modern War, Volume 2: The Iran-Iraq War*, ed. Anthony H. Cordesman and Abraham R. Wagner (Washington DC: Center for Strategic and International Studies, 1990), 2–86, https://www.csis.org/analysis/lessons-modern-war-volume-ii-iran-iraq -war-%E2%80%93-chapter-14-tanker-war-and-lessons-naval.

61. The wider case will be developed further later in this chapter, but assessments by the likes of Michael Knights remain mostly extant. Michael Knights, *Troubled Waters: Future U.S. Security Assistance in the Persian Gulf* (Washington, DC: Washington Institute for Near East Policy, 2006), 121–163; Interview with anonymous former UAE-based military officer, June 12, 2019; Interview with anonymous former U.S. defense official, May 23, 2019.

62. *Egypt-Persian Gulf States: Mubarak's Security Agenda* (Washington, DC: CIA Library, January 13, 1988), https://www.cia.gov/library/readingroom/docs/DOC_0000189995.pdf.

63. "Who Guards the Gulf?," *The Economist* (September 7, 1991).

64. "Who Guards the Gulf?"

65. "Who Guards the Gulf?"

66. Tim Niblock, "Introduction," in *Social and Economic Development in the Arab Gulf*, ed. Tim Niblock (Abingdon, UK: Routledge, 2014), 11. There are exceptions to this rule, such as the series edited by Omar AlShehabi et al., starting in 2013: "الخلل الأمني بين النظام الاقتصادي والنظام السياسي" ("The Security Flaws between the Economic System and the Political System", in الخليج 2013: الثابت والمتحول (*Gulf 2013: Change and Transformation*) ed. Omar AlShehabi (Kuwait: مركز الخليج لسياسات التنمية [Gulf Centre for Development Policies], 2013).

67. Jane Kinninmont, *Future Trends in the Gulf* (London: Chatham House, 2015), 32–44, https://www.chathamhouse.org/sites/default/files/field/field_document/20150218 FutureTrendsGCCKinninmont.pdf.

68. Steffen Hertog, "Rentier Militaries in the Gulf States: The Price of Coup-Proofing," *International Journal of Middle East Studies* 43, no. 3 (2011): 400–402, http://dx.doi. org/10.1017/S0020743811000560; James T. Quinlivan, "Coup-Proofing: Its Practice and Consequences in the Middle East," *International Security* 24, no. 2 (1999): 131–165; Risa Brooks, "Civil Military Relations in the Middle East," in *The Future Security Environment in the Middle East: Conflict, Stability, and Political Change*, ed. Nora Bensahel and Daniel Byman (Santa Monica, CA: RAND Corporation, 2004), 136–138; and Caitlin Talmadge, *The Dictator's Army: Battlefield Effectiveness in Authoritarian Regimes* (Ithaca, NY and London: Cornell University Press, 2015), 19–20.

69. Gaub, *Guardians of the State*, 8–11.

70. Gaub, *Guardians of the State*, 12.

71. On the Saudi case, see Stephanie Cronin, *Armies and State Building in the Modern Middle East: Politics, Nationalism, and Military Reform* (London: I. B. Tauris, 2013), chapter 5.

72. McNaugher, *Arms and Oil*, 141–142; and Guazzone, "Gulf Co-Operation Council," 145.

73. See, for example, Anthony H. Cordesman, *Saudi Arabia Enters the Twenty-First Century, Volume 1* (Westport, CT and London: Praeger, 2003), 143, 284; Barry Rubin, "The Military in Contemporary Middle East Politics," *Middle East Review of International Affairs* 5, no. 1 (March 2001): 58–61; William Taylor, *Military Responses to the Arab Uprisings and*

the Future of Civil-Military Relations in the Middle East: Analysis from Egypt, Tunisia, Libya, and Syria (New York: Springer, 2014), 75, 129; Cronin, *Armies and State Building*, chapter 5; Daniel L. Byman and Jerrold D. Green, "The Enigma of Political Stability in the Persian Gulf Monarchies," *Middle East Review of International Affairs* 3, no. 3 (1999); and McNaugher, *Arms and Oil*, 141–142.

74. Brooks, "Civil Military Relations in the Middle East," 141–143.

75. Brooks, "Civil Military Relations in the Middle East," 143.

76. Andrew Dorman, Mike Lawrence Smith, and Matthew Uttley, "Jointery and Combined Operations in an Expeditionary Era: Defining the Issues," *Defense Analysis* 14, no. 1 (1998): 3.

77. McNaugher, *Arms and Oil*, 140.

78. *SIPRI Extended Military Expenditure Database, Beta Version*, Stockholm International Peace Research Institute (SIPRI) (2016).

79. *SIPRI Database*.

80. Anthony H. Cordesman, *The Gulf Military Balance, Volume I: The Conventional and Asymmetric Dimensions* (Lanham, MD: Rowman & Littlefield, 2014), 50.

81. Obtaining the explicit right to oversee the procurement or business relations in a given industry has long been a way for leaders to dispense largesse. One former Gulf minister of state for defense, for example, would give you his business card, on the back of which were the emblems for the dozen or more companies that he and his family owned that undertook the majority of the contracting in the state military. Zoltan Barany, *Arms Procurement and Corruption in the Gulf Monarchies* (Washington, DC: Center for Strategic and International Studies, May 11, 2020), https://www.csis.org/analysis /arms-procurement-and-corruption-gulf-monarchies.

82. Rubin, "The Military in Contemporary Middle East Politics."

83. Hertog, "Rentier Militaries in the Gulf"; David S. Sorenson, "Why the Saudi Arabian Defence Binge?," *Contemporary Security Policy* 35, no. 1 (2014): 116–137; Rubin, "The Military in Contemporary Middle East Politics," 49; Colum Lynch, "Arms Sales and the Militarization of the Middle East," *Foreign Policy* (October 22, 2013); and Christopher Davidson, *After the Sheikhs: The Coming Collapse of the Gulf Monarchies* (London: Hurst, 2012), 163–169.

84. David B. Roberts and Emile Hokayem, "Friends with Benefits: The Gulf States and the Perpetual Quest for Alliances," Century Foundation (January 2018), https://tcf.org /content/report/friends-with-benefits/.

85. For an example of the influence of politics on procurement, see Björn Hagelin and Peter Wallensteen, "Understanding Swedish Military Expenditures," *Cooperation and Conflict* 27, no. 4 (1992): 415–441.

86. "Qatar Seeks to Employ Jordanian Military Retirees," *Roya News* (September 22, 2019), https://en.royanews.tv/news/18738/Qatar%20seeks%20to%20employ%20Jordanian%20 military%20retirees.

87. Henry Jones, "Joint UK-Qatari Typhoon Squadron Stands Up," *UK Defence Journal* (July 25, 2018), https://ukdefencejournal.org.uk/joint-uk-qatari-typhoon-squadron -stands-up/.

88. David B. Roberts, "Lifting the 'Protection Curse': The Rise of New Military Powers in the Middle East," *Survival* 63, no. 2 (2021): 139–154.

89.   Sarah M. Brooks and Marcus J. Kurtz, "Oil and Democracy: Endogenous Natural Resources and the Political 'Resource Curse,'" *International Organization* 70, no. 2 (2016): 279–311.

90.   Brett V. Benson, *Constructing International Security: Alliances, Deterrence, and Moral Hazard* (New York: Cambridge University Press, 2012), 2–3.

91.   "Who Guards the Gulf?"

92.   On U.S. basing in the Gulf, see Geoffrey F. Gresh, *Gulf Security and the U.S. Military: Regime Survival and the Politics of Basing* (Stanford, CA: Stanford University Press, 2015), 74–91.

93.   Gregory Gause III, *Oil Monarchies: Domestic and Security Challenges in the Arab Gulf States* (New York: Council on Foreign Relations, 1994), 170–195.

94.   The overwhelming majority of the anti-mine capability in the Persian Gulf is located in the U.S. and the UK navies. Interview with Professor David Des Roches, London, June 2018. "For the Gulf States, Diplomacy Involves Buying Weapons They Don't Need," *The Economist* (March 1, 2018).

95.   Ahmad Ghaddar, "Strait of Hormuz: The World's Most Important Oil Artery," *Reuters* (July 5, 2018), https://www.reuters.com/article/us-iran-oil-factbox/strait-of-hormuz -the-worlds-most-important-oil-artery-idUSKBN1JV24O.

96.   For an overview and a useful timeline focusing on the Strait of Hormuz (and the roles and reactions of the Iranian and Gulf Arab sides), see "Strait of Hormuz," International Crisis Group, Brussels (March 22, 2019).

97.   Kenneth M. Pollack, *Armies of Sand: The Past, Present, and Future of Arab Military Effectiveness* (New York: Oxford University Press, 2019), ix; and Kenneth M. Pollack, *Arabs at War: Military Effectiveness, 1948–1991* (Lincoln: University of Nebraska Press, 2004), 574.

98.   Pollack, *Armies of Sand*, 368–393.

99.   Norville B. DeAtkine, "Western Influence on Arab Militaries: Pounding Square Pegs into Round Holes," *Middle East Review of International Affairs* 17, no. 1 (2013): 18–31; Norville B. DeAtkine, "Why Arabs Lose Wars," *Middle East Quarterly* 6, no. 4 (December 1999), https://www.meforum.org/441/why-arabs-lose-wars. The DeAtkine quote comes from David B. Roberts and Emile Hokayem, "The War in Yemen," *Survival* 58, no. 6 (2016): 159. See also the assessment of Glenn P. Kuffel, *The Gulf Cooperation Council's Peninsular Shield Force* (Newport, RI: U.S. Naval War College, 2000).

100.   David B. Roberts, "Bucking the Trend: The UAE and the Development of Military Capabilities in the Arab World," *Security Studies* 29, no. 2 (2020): 301–334.

101.   Roberts and Hokayem, "The War in Yemen," 157–186.

102.   The ability to undertake this kind of training and qualification with the U.S. military is unique to the UAE. See "UAE Military Pilots Conduct Landing Qualifications Aboard USS Lewis B. Puller," U.S. Central Command (May 22, 2020), https://www.centcom .mil/MEDIA/NEWS-ARTICLES/News-Article-View/Article/2195719/uae-military -pilots-conduct-landing-qualifications-aboard-uss-lewis-b-puller/; and Roberts, "Buck- ing the Trend," 303, 318–320.

103. Interview with senior Saudi military adviser, December 2, 2016. Interview with senior Gulf-based NATO military officer, September 19, 2015. Interview with Gulf-focused, UAE-based academic, October 26, 2016.

104. Ash Rossiter, "The Yemeni–Saudi Border from Boundary to Frontline," in *Yemen and the Gulf States: The Making of a Crisis*, ed. Helen Lackner and Daniel Martin Varisco (Berlin: Gerlach, 2018).

105. David Kirkpatrick et al., "Who Was behind the Saudi Oil Attack? What the Evidence Shows," *New York Times* (September 16, 2019), https://www.nytimes.com/interactive/2019/09/16/world/middleeast/trump-saudi-arabia-oil-attack.html.

106. Sandra Petersmann, "Tanker Attacks in the Gulf—Evidence or Warmongering?," *DW* (June 21, 2019), https://www.dw.com/en/top-stories/s-9097.

107. Gordon Lubold and Michael C. Bender, "U.S. to Remove Patriot Missile Batteries from Saudi Arabia," *Wall Street Journal* (May 7, 2020), https://www.wsj.com/articles/u-s-to-remove-patriot-missile-batteries-from-saudi-arabia-11588867916.

108. Mohammed Al Rumaihi, "الاستعداد الخليجي للتراجع الأميركي" ("Gulf Preparedness for the American Withdrawal"), *Al Arabiyya* (March 8, 2014), https://tinyurl.com/ydgjpa85; and David B. Roberts, "For Decades, Gulf Leaders Counted on U.S. Protection. Here's What Changed," *Washington Post* (January 30, 2020), https://www.washingtonpost.com/politics/2020/01/30/decades-gulf-leaders-counted-us-protection-heres-what-changed/.

109. Hammoud Abu Talib, "لا حليف لنا إلا نحن" ("We Have No Ally but Ourselves"), *Okaz* (September 18, 2019), https://www.okaz.com.sa/articles/na/1747015.

110. "Intel: How Saudi Arabia Is Looking Past the US for Arms," *Al Monitor* (November 8, 2018), https://www.al-monitor.com/pulse/originals/2018/11/intel-saudi-arabia-looking-past-us-arms-spain-south-africa.html; and Aniseh Bassiri Tabrizi and Justin Bronk, *Armed Drones in the Middle East: Proliferation and Norms in the Region* (London: Royal United Services Institute, 2018), https://rusi.org/explore-our-research/publications/occasional-papers/armed-drones-middle-east-proliferation-and-norms-region.

111. It remains unclear which facilities the UAE continues to operate. Certainly, the main base in Eritrea was a critical staging post for the war in Yemen, and it was downsized subsequently.

112. Neil Partrick, *Saudi Arabia's Elusive Defense Reform* (Washington, DC: Carnegie Endowment for International Peace, November 14, 2019), https://carnegieendowment.org/sada/80354.

113. Yasmine Farouk, *The Middle East Strategic Alliance Has a Long Way to Go* (Washington, DC: Carnegie Endowment for International Peace, February 8, 2019), https://carnegieendowment.org/2019/02/08/middle-east-strategic-alliance-has-long-way-to-go-pub-78317; and Abdul Hadi Habtoor, "الرياض مقرأ للقيادة الخليجية العسكرية الموحدة" ("Riyadh Is the Headquarters of the Unified Gulf Leadership"), *As Sharq Al Awsat* (December 23, 2019), https://tinyurl.com/yau9vjn6.

114. "New UK Military Base in Kuwait," *Arab Digest* (n.d.), https://arabdigest.org/visitors/sample-newsletters/new-uk-military-base-kuwait/.

5. ENVIRONMENTAL SECURITY

1. Barry Buzan, Ole Wæver, and Jaap de Wilde, *Security: A New Framework for Analysis* (Boulder, CO: Lynne Rienner, 1998), 74–75.

2. Marian R. Chertow, "The IPAT Equation and Its Variants," *Journal of Industrial Ecology* 4, no. 4 (2000): 13–20.

3. Buzan, Wæver, and Wilde, *Security*, 72–73.

4. Mari Luomi, *Environmental Security: Addressing Water and Climate Change Risks in the UAE*, Emirates Diplomatic Academy, Abu Dhabi (April 2019), 1–2.

5. Luomi, *Environmental Security*, 2.

6. Nico Stehr, "Man and His Environment: A General Perspective," *ARSP: Archiv für Rechts- und Sozialphilosophie/Archives for Philosophy of Law and Social Philosophy* 64, no. 1 (1978): 1–15.

7. Mari Luomi, *The Gulf Monarchies and Climate Change: Abu Dhabi and Qatar in an Era of Natural Unsustainability* (London: Hurst, 2012).

8. Luomi, *Gulf Monarchies and Climate Change*, 1–33.

9. Dan Smith and Florian Krampe, "Climate-Related Security Risks in the Middle East," in *Routledge Handbook on Middle East Security*, ed. Anders Jagerskog, Michael Schulz, and Ashok Swain (London: Routledge, 2019), 200.

10. Smith and Krampe, "Climate-Related Security Risks in the Middle East," 200.

11. Laurent A. Lambert and Hisham Bin Hashim, "A Century of Saudi-Qatari Food Insecurity: Paradigmatic Shifts in the Geopolitics, Economics and Sustainability of Gulf States Animal Agriculture," *Arab World Geographer* 20, no. 4 (2017): 263.

12. Lambert and Bin Hashim, "Saudi-Qatari Food Insecurity," 263.

13. Lambert and Bin Hashim, "Saudi-Qatari Food Insecurity," 263–264.

14. Sabrina Joseph, "Farming the Desert: Agriculture in the Oil Frontier, the Case of the United Arab Emirates, 1940s to 1990s," *British Journal of Middle Eastern Studies* 45, no. 5 (2018): 684.

15. Peter Sluglett, "Formal and Informal Empire in the Middle East," in *Historiography: The Oxford History of the British Empire*, ed. Robin W. Winks (Oxford: Oxford University Press, 1999), 419.

16. Frederick Lugard, *The Dual Mandate in British Tropical Africa* (Edinburgh and London: William Blackwood, 1922).

17. Omar Mohammed Al Qaraala and Ahmed Mohammed Tarawneh, "التنافس البريطاني العثماني على البحرين في النصف الثاني من القرن التاسع عشر الميلادي" ("British-Ottoman Rivalry over Bahrain in the Second Half of the Nineteenth Century"), العلوم الإنسانية والاجتماعية المجلد (*Humanities and Social Sciences Journal*) 1, no. 1 (2019); and Bernard Porter, *The Lion's Share: A History of British Imperialism 1850 to the Present*, 5th ed. (Harlow, UK: Pearson, 2012), 159.

18. Joseph, "Farming the Desert," 685.

19. Joseph, "Farming the Desert," 685.

20. J. B. Denson, *Trucial States Development*, Foreign and Commonwealth Office, London, FO 371/114656 (December 20, 1955).

21. Matthew MacLean, "Spatial Transformations and the Emergence of 'the National': Infra-structures and the Formation of the United Arab Emirates, 1950–1980" (Dissertation, New York University, 2017), 30.

22. MacLean, "Spatial Transformations," 33.

23. *Bahrain Letter: The Bahrain Agricultural Show, 1957*, Foreign and Commonwealth Office, London, FO 371/126957 (1957).

24. *Development of Agriculture in Trucial States*, Foreign and Commonwealth Office, London, FO 371/126956 (1957); *Agricultural Development in the Trucial States*, Foreign and Commonwealth Office, London, FO 371/114688 (1955); *Bahrain Letter*. Although there is nothing uniquely English about tent pegging (i.e., a specific form of equestrian showmanship), the similarities between these and other events undertaken in Bahrain and a traditionally conceived English summer fete are striking.

25. Joseph, "Farming the Desert," 688.

26. J. C. Eyre, *Financial and Technical Assistant for the Development of Agriculture in Muscat and Oman*, Foreign and Commonwealth Office, London, FO 371/140198 (March 18, 1959).

27. *Agricultural Development in Oman*, Foreign and Commonwealth Office, London, FCO 8/1686 (January 1–December 31, 1971); and Bernard A. Burrows, *Letter: Development of Agriculture in Oman: Agricultural Show in Bahrain*, Foreign and Commonwealth Office, London, FO 371/126957 (November 28, 1957).

28. Burrows, *Letter*.

29. *Agricultural Development in Oman*.

30. Denson, *Trucial States Development*.

31. *British "Spy" in Muscat*, Foreign and Commonwealth Office, London, FO 371/140198/75 - BA File 1282 (December 15, 1959).

32. Christian Koch, "Economics Trumps Politics in the United Arab Emirates," in *Political Change in the Arab Gulf States*, ed. Mary Ann Tetreault, Gwenn Okruhlik, and Andrzej Kapiszewski (London: Lynne Rienner, 2011), 666–681; and Robert J. Bazell, "Arid Land Agriculture: Shaikh up in Arizona Research," *Science* 171, no. 3975 (1971): 989–990, www .jstor.org/stable/1731297.

33. Paolo Caratelli, Maria Alessandra Misuri, and Mohamed El Amrousi, "Al-Ain's Cultural Landscape: Identity, Innovation and Sustainability in a Challenging Economy," *International Review for Spatial Planning and Sustainable Development* 7, no. 3 (2019): 45–62; and Luomi, *Gulf Monarchies and Climate Change*, 94–95.

34. It is also true, however, that this aspect of Zayed's legacy has been consistently burnished, emphasized, or perhaps even exaggerated after his death.

35. Diana K. Davis and Paul Robbins, "Ecologies of the Colonial Present: Pathological Forestry from the Taux De Boisement to Civilized Plantations," *Environment and Planning E: Nature and Space* 1, no. 4 (2018): 447.

36. Luomi, *Gulf Monarchies and Climate Change*, 94.

37. Joseph, "Farming the Desert," 690.

38. *Agriculture, Forestry, and Fishing, Value Added (% of GDP)* (2022), https://data .worldbank.org/indicator/NV.AGR.TOTL.ZS.

39. Lambert and Bin Hashim, "Saudi-Qatari Food Insecurity," 263–267.

40. Jones, *Desert Kingdom*, 5.

41. Joseph Kraft, "Letter from Saudi Arabia," *New Yorker* (July 4, 1983), 49.

42. Lambert and Bin Hashim, "Saudi-Qatari Food Insecurity," 263–274.

43. Jill Crystal, *Oil and Politics in the Gulf: Rulers and Merchants in Kuwait and Qatar* (Cambridge: Cambridge University Press, 1995), 155.

44. E. F. Henderson, *Industrialization in Qatar*, Foreign and Commonwealth Office, London, FCO 8/2296 (July 8, 1974).

45. *UK Co-Operation on Nuclear Energy with Gulf States*, Foreign and Commonwealth Office, London, FCO 8/2860 (January 1–December 31, 1977).

46. J. C. Kay, *Saudi Arabia: Technological Cooperation in Alternative Sources of Energy*, Foreign and Commonwealth Office, London, FCO 8/2592 (July 19, 1975); and *UK Co -Operation on Nuclear Energy with Gulf States*.

47. *UK Co-Operation on Nuclear Energy with Gulf States*.

48. C. T. W. Humfrey, *Middle East Contracts*, Foreign and Commonwealth Office, London, FCO 8/3820 (March 16, 1981); and *Oman Brief No 18 Non-Proliferation Treaty*, Foreign and Commonwealth Office, London, FCO 8/5848 (January 1985).

49. Reginald Hibbert, *President Giscard's Tour of the Gulf: Commercial and Economic Aspects*, Foreign and Commonwealth Office, London, FCO 8/3447/5 (March 17, 1980).

50. Hibbert, *President Giscard's Tour*.

51. For an overview of this and other contemporary environmental concerns in the Gulf, see Sabah Al Juneed et al., "البيئة والاستدامة في دول مجلس التعاون" ("The Environment and Sustainability in the [Gulf] Cooperation Council Countries"), in الاستدامة في الخليج :2020 الثابت والمتحول (*Change and Continuity 2020: Sustainability in the Gulf*), ed. Omar AlShehabi and Hamad Al Rayes (Kuwait: مركز الخليج لسياسات التنمية [Gulf Centre for Development Policies], 2020), 170–191.

52. Waleed Hamza and Mohiuddin Munawar, "Protecting and Managing the Arabian Gulf: Past, Present and Future," *Aquatic Ecosystem Health and Management* 12, no. 4 (2009): 435.

53. Hamza and Munawar, "Protecting and Managing the Arabian Gulf," 434–435.

54. Charles Sheppard et al., "The Gulf: A Young Sea in Decline," *Marine Pollution Bulletin* 60, no. 1 (2010): 26.

55. Sheppard et al., "The Gulf," 27; and *The Bahrain-Qatar Border Dispute: The World Court Decision, Part 1*, The Estimate (March 23, 2001).

56. John A. Burt, "The Environmental Costs of Coastal Urbanization in the Arabian Gulf," *City* 18, no. 6 (2014): 761.

57. Burt, "Environmental Costs," 765.

58. Bernhard Riegl, "Climate Change and Coral Reefs: Different Effects in Two High-Latitude Areas (Arabian Gulf, South Africa)," *Coral Reefs* 22, no. 4 (2003): 433.

59. Sheppard et al., "The Gulf," 22.

60. "The UAE National Framework Statement for Sustainable Fisheries (2019–2030)," Environment Agency Abu Dhabi and the Ministry of Climate Change and Environment (n.d.), 9, https://www.moccae.gov.ae/assets/download/749e9268/UAE%20National %20Framework%20Statement%20for%20Sustainable%20Fisheries%20(2019-2030) %20English.pdf.aspx; and Sheppard et al., "The Gulf," 23.

61. Humood A. Naser, "Assessment and Management of Heavy Metal Pollution in the Marine Environment of the Arabian Gulf: A Review," *Marine Pollution Bulletin* 72, no. 1 (2013): 6–13.

62. Burt, "Environmental Costs," 760.

63. Sheppard et al., "The Gulf," 15.

64. Mansour Almazroui, M. Nazrul Islam, Ramzah Dambul, and P. D. Jones, "Trends of Temperature Extremes in Saudi Arabia," *International Journal of Climatology* 34, no. 3 (2014): 808–826.

65. Mansour Almazroui et al., "Recent Climate Change in the Arabian Peninsula: Annual Rainfall and Temperature Analysis of Saudi Arabia for 1978–2009," *International Journal of Climatology* 32, no. 6 (2012): 954, 961, https://doi.org/10.1002/joc.3446.

66. David L. Chandler, "Study: Persian Gulf Could Experience Deadly Heat," *MIT News* (October 26, 2015), http://news.mit.edu/2015/study-persian-gulf-deadly-heat-1026.

67. Almazroui et al., "Recent Climate Change," 962.

68. Richard P. Jennings et al., "The Greening of Arabia: Multiple Opportunities for Human Occupation of the Arabian Peninsula During the Late Pleistocene Inferred from an Ensemble of Climate Model Simulations," *Quaternary International* 382 (2015): 183; and Almazroui et al., "Recent Climate Change," 956.

69. Jeremy S. Pal and Elfatih A. B. Eltahir, "Future Temperature in Southwest Asia Projected to Exceed a Threshold for Human Adaptability," *Nature Climate Change* 6, no. 2 (2016): 197–200.

70. Hadeel Banjar, "Motivating Sustainable Consumption Behaviour through Education, Incentive Programs, and Green Policies in Saudi Arabia," in *Sustainability in the Gulf: Challenges and Opportunities*, ed. Elie Azar and Mohamed Abdel Raouf (Abingdon, UK: Routledge, 2017), 249–273; and Jwen Fai Low, Maryam R. D. Al-Yammahi, and Andrea Schiffauerova, "The Gulf Region's Commitment to a Sustainable Lifestyle: A Bibliometric Study," in *Sustainability in the Gulf: Challenges and Opportunities*, ed. Elie Azar and Mohamed Abdel Raouf (Abingdon, UK: Routledge, 2017), 27.

71. Caline Malek, "Why Middle East Publics Have Mixed Views on Climate Change," *Arab News* (October 5, 2019), https://www.arabnews.com/node/1564706/middle-east.

72. See "Principles of the 50," https://www.uaeprinciples.ae/PrinciplesOf50-En.pdf (accessed December 22, 2021).

73. Abdullah Kaya et al., "Energy Consumption and Transition Dynamics to a Sustainable Future under a Rentier Economy: The Case of the GCC States," in *Sustainability in the Gulf: Challenges and Opportunities*, ed. Elie Azar and Mohamed Abdel Raouf (Abingdon, UK: Routledge, 2017), 200–207.

74. David Wallace-Wells, *The Uninhabitable Earth: Life after Warming* (London: Allen Lane, 2019), 167.

75. Michael McCormick et al., "Climate Change during and after the Roman Empire: Reconstructing the Past from Scientific and Historical Evidence," *Journal of Interdisciplinary History* 43, no. 2 (2012): 169–220; and Mari Luomi, "Environmental Change and Security," in *Facets of Security in the United Arab Emirates*, ed. Kristian Alexander and William Gueraiche (Abingdon, UK: Routledge, 2022), 37–49.

76. Anders Jägerskog, Michael Schulz, and Ashok Swain, "Contents," in *Routledge Handbook on Middle East Security*, ed. Anders Jägerskog, Michael Schulz, and Ashok Swain (Abingdon, UK: Routeldge, 2019), viii–ix.
77. Andy Spiess, "Food Security in the Gulf Cooperation Council (GCC) Economies (Working Paper)" (Hamburg: NDRD, 2011), http://www.ndrd.org/Spiess_-_Working _Paper_on_Food_Security_in_the_GCC.pdf.
78. For a discussion of definitional issues of food security, see Mark Gibson, "Food Security—a Commentary: What Is It and Why Is It So Complicated?," *Foods* 1, no. 1 (2012): 18–27, https://www.ncbi.nlm.nih.gov/pmc/articles/PMC5302220/.
79. Spiess, "Food Security in the Gulf Cooperation Council (GCC) Economies," 1–2.
80. Global Hunger Index, "The Concept of the Global Hunger Index," https://www.global hungerindex.org/about.html.
81. Jennifer Clapp, "Food Self-Sufficiency: Making Sense of It, and When It Makes Sense," *Food Policy* 66 (2017): 89.
82. Shira Efron et al., *Food Security in the Gulf Cooperation Council*, RAND Corporation and emerge85 (December 2018), 11.
83. Spiess, "Food Security in the Gulf Cooperation Council (GCC) Economies," 8.
84. Sara Fouad Almohamadi, "Qatar Dispute Exposes Regional Food-Security Failures," *IISS* (August 21, 2017), https://www.iiss.org/blogs/analysis/2017/08/qatar-food-insecurity.
85. "Food Production in Qatar Grows by 400 Percent since 2017," *The Peninsula* (March 13, 2019), https://tinyurl.com/d2rzcsbd.
86. "Milk Sheikhs: Why Qatar Is Raising Cows in the Desert," *The Economist* (May 17, 2018).
87. "Qatar Exceeds Set Target of 2019 in Achieving Food Self-Sufficiency," *The Peninsula* (January 9, 2020), https://thepeninsulaqatar.com/article/09/01/2020/Qatar-exceeds-set -target-of-2019-in-achieving-food-self-sufficiency.
88. Natalie Koch, "Agtech in Arabia: 'Spectacular Forgetting' and the Technopolitics of Greening the Desert," *Journal of Political Ecology* 26, no. 1 (2019): 667.
89. "Madagascar Leader Axes Land Deal," *BBC* (March 19, 2009), http://news.bbc.co.uk/1 /hi/world/africa/7952628.stm.
90. Adam Hanieh, *Money, Markets, and Monarchies: The Gulf Cooperation Council and the Political Economy of the Contemporary Middle East* (Cambridge: Cambridge University Press, 2018), 113.
91. Efron et al., *Food Security in the Gulf Cooperation Council*, 11–12.
92. George Odhiambo, "Water Scarcity in the Arabian Peninsula and Socio-Economic Implications," *Applied Water Science* 7 (2017): 2480–2481.
93. Martin Keulertz and Tony Allan, "The Water-Energy-Food Nexus in the MENA Region," in *Routledge Handbook on Middle East Security*, ed. Anders Jagerskog, Ashok Swain, and Michael Schulz (New York: Routledge, 2019), 158.
94. Keulertz and Allan, "Water-Energy-Food Nexus," 160.
95. Elie Elhadj, "Camels Don't Fly, Deserts Don't Bloom: An Assessment of Saudi Arabia's Experiment in Desert Agriculture," *SOAS Occasional Paper* 48 (2004): 4.
96. Elhadj, "Camels Don't Fly," 18.
97. Jones, *Desert Kingdom*, 230.

98. Elhadj, "Camels Don't Fly," 20; and Jones, *Desert Kingdom*, 230–231.

99. Food and Agriculture Organization (FAO)/International Food Policy Research Institute data from "The Middle East Needs Radical Agricultural Transformation," Castlereagh Associates, Surrey, UK (July 26, 2019), https://castlereagh.net/the-middle -east-needs-radical-agricultural-transformation/.

100. *Water Statistics in the State of Qatar 2017*, Planning and Statistics Authority (December 2019), https://www.psa.gov.qa/en/statistics/Statistical%20Releases/Environmental/Water /2017/Water-Statistics-2017-EN.pdf; and Sebastian Castelier, "Qatar's Agriculture Push Risks Further Groundwater Depletion," *Al Monitor* (August 26, 2019), https://www .al-monitor.com/pulse/originals/2019/08/qatar-agriculture-water-environmental -concerns.html.

101. Sachin Kumar, "IPO of Baladna Expected in Last Quarter of 2019," *The Peninsula* (May 26, 2019), https://thepeninsulaqatar.com/article/26/05/2019/IPO-of-Baladna-expected -in-last-quarter-of-2019.

102. Hassan Arafat, Toufic Mezher, and Omar Saif, "Water Security in the GCC Countries: Challenges and Opportunities," *Journal of Environmental Studies and Science* 4 (2014): 330.

103. Edward Jones et al., "The State of Desalination and Brine Production: A Global Outlook," *Science of the Total Environment* 657 (2018): 1348.

104. Tarik Bargal, "The Shifting Sands of Saudi Arabia's Water Plans," *Inframation News* (August 6, 2018); and "UAE to Get Largest Water Desalination Plant in the World," *Khaleej Times* (July 22, 2020), https://www.khaleejtimes.com/government/uae -to-get-largest-water-desalination-plant-in-the-world.

105. Ayhan Demirbas, Ayman A. Hashem, and Ahmed A. Bakhsh, "The Cost Analysis of Electric Power Generation in Saudi Arabia," *Energy Sources, Part B: Economics, Planning, and Policy* 12, no. 6 (2017): 591, 594.

106. Molly Walton, "Desalinated Water Affects the Energy Equation in the Middle East," *International Energy Administration* (January 21, 2019), https://www.iea.org/commentaries /desalinated-water-affects-the-energy-equation-in-the-middle-east.

107. Demirbas, Hashem, and Bakhsh, "Electric Power Generation," 594–595.

108. Jones et al., "The State of Desalination and Brine Production," 1350.

109. Arafat, Mezher, and Saif, "Water Security in the GCC Countries," 334; and Sheppard et al., "The Gulf," 28.

110. Sheppard et al., "The Gulf," 24–25.

111. *Vulnerability of Persian Gulf Desalination Systems: An Emerging Security Issue* (Washington, DC: Central Intelligence Agency, Directorate of Intelligence, October 1983).

112. David B. Roberts, "For Decades, Gulf Leaders Counted on U.S. Protection. Here's What Changed," *Washington Post* (January 30, 2020), https://www.washingtonpost.com /politics/2020/01/30/decades-gulf-leaders-counted-us-protection-heres-what-changed/.

113. Kamran Taremi, "The Role of Water Exports in Iranian Foreign Policy towards the GCC," *Iranian Studies* 28, no. 2 (June 2005): 323.

114. Gökçe Günel, "The Infinity of Water: Climate Change Adaptation in the Arabian Peninsula," *Public Culture* 28, no. 2 (2016): 291–315.

115. "World's First Climate-Controlled Raining Street Coming to Dubai," *Khaleej Times* (June 24, 2020), https://www.khaleejtimes.com/local-business/worlds-first-climate -controlled-raining-street-coming-to-dubai.

116. Günel, "The Infinity of Water," 292.

117. *Water for Prosperity and Development: Risks and Opportunities for the Gulf Cooperation Council Countries* (Washington, DC: World Bank Group, December 2017), 8, 15.

118. Günel, "The Infinity of Water," 300.

119. Kristian Coates Ulrichsen, *Qatar and the Arab Spring* (London: Hurst, 2014), 26; and Hamish R. Mackey, Huda Alkandari, and Gordon Mckay, "The Role of Tariffs in Reducing Residential Water Demand in Qatar," *Qatar Foundation Annual Research Conference Proceedings*, no. 1 (2018).

120. Glada Lahn, "Fuel, Food and Utilities Price Reforms in the GCC: A Wake-up Call for Business," Chatham House Research Paper (London: Royal Institute of International Affairs, 2016), 6.

121. Lahn, "Fuel, Food and Utilities Price Reforms in the GCC," 14.

122. Glen Carey and Zaid Sabah, "Saudi King Fires Water Minister after Complaints over Tariffs," *Bloomberg* (April 24, 2016), https://www.bloomberg.com/news/articles/2016-04-24 /saudi-king-fires-water-minister-after-complaints-over-tariffs.

123. Kristian Coates Ulrichsen, "Introduction," in *The Changing Security Dynamics of the Persian Gulf*, ed. Kristian Coates Ulrichsen (London: Hurst, 2017), 7–8.

124. Luomi, *Environmental Security*.

125. Z. A. Wendling et al., *2018 Environmental Performance Index* (New Haven, CT: Yale Center for Environmental Law and Policy, 2018).

126. Ben Halpern, Julia Stewart Lowndes, and Melanie Frazier, *Ocean Health Index* (2019), https://oceanhealthindex.org/.

127. J. Sachs et al., *Sustainable Development Report 2019* (New York: Bertelsmann Stiftung and Sustainable Development Solutions Network, 2019), 50–52.

CONCLUSION

1. Natalie Koch, "Agtech in Arabia: 'Spectacular Forgetting' and the Technopolitics of Greening the Desert," *Journal of Political Ecology* 26, no. 1 (2019): 680.

2. Christine Osborne, *The Gulf States and Oman* (Abingdon, UK: Routledge, 2017), 15, 97.

3. *Statistical Appendix*, International Monetary Fund (April 2019), https://www.imf.org /~/media/Files/Publications/REO/MCD-CCA/2019/April/English/Statistical-Appendix .ashx.

4. Friedrich August Hayek, "The Fatal Conceit: The Errors of Socialism," in *The Collected Works of F. A. Hayek*, ed. W. W. Bartley III (London: Routledge, 1992), 7.

5. F. Gregory Gause, "The Persistence of Monarchy in the Arabian Peninsula: A Comparative Analysis," in *Middle East Monarchies: The Challenge of Modernity*, ed. Joseph Kostiner (Boulder, CO: Lynne Rienner, 2000), 167–187.

6. Ernest Hemingway, *The Sun Also Rises* (eBook: Digital Fire, 2022), 181.

BIBLIOGRAPHY

Aarts, Paul, and Carolien Roelants. *Saudi Arabia: A Kingdom in Peril*. London: Hurst, 2015.

Abdo, Geneive. *The New Sectarianism: The Arab Uprisings and the Rebirth of the Shi'a-Sunni Divide*. New York: Oxford University Press, 2017.

Abousleiman, Issam. "Gender in the GCC—the Reform Agenda Continues." *Opinion: The World Bank*. February 24, 2021. https://www.worldbank.org/en/news/opinion/2021/02/24/gender -in-the-gcc-the-reform-agenda-continues.

"About the PIF." Accessed June 17, 2020. https://www.pif.gov.sa/en/Pages/About-PIF.aspx.

Abrahamian, Atossa Araxia. "Who Loses When a Country Puts Citizenship up for Sale?" *New York Times*. January 5, 2018. https://www.nytimes.com/2018/01/05/opinion/sunday /united-arab-emirates-comorans-citizenship.html.

Abu Talib, Hammoud "لا حليف لنا إلا نحن" ("We Have No Ally but Ourselves"). *Okaz*. September 18, 2019. Accessed June 20, 2020. https://www.okaz.com.sa/articles/na/1747015.

Agricultural Development in Oman. Foreign and Commonwealth Office, London, FCO 8/1686 (January 1–December 31, 1971).

Agricultural Development in the Trucial States. Foreign and Commonwealth Office, London, FO 371/114688 (1955).

Agriculture, Forestry, and Fishing, Value Added (% of GDP) (2022). https://data.worldbank.org /indicator/NV.AGR.TOTL.ZS.

Ahmed, Afshan. "The UAE's History Lesson." *The National*. November 8, 2011. https://www .thenationalnews.com/uae/the-uae-s-history-lesson-1.460608.

Al Alkim, Hassan Hamdan. *The GCC States in an Unstable World*. London: Saqi, 1994.

Al Ammari, B., and M. H. Romanowski. "The Impact of Globalization on Society and Culture in Qatar." *Pertanika Social Sciences and Humanities* 24, no. 4 (2016): 1535–1556.

Al Assaraj, Hussein Abdulmutallab. "اشكالية البطالة في دول مجلس التعاون الخليجي" ("The Paradox of Unemployment in the GCC Countries"). *Munich Personal RePEc Archive* 54600 (March 2014).

Al Awadhi, Hisham. تاريخ العبيد في الخليج العربي (*The History of Slaves in the Arabian Gulf*). Beirut and Cairo: دار التنوير للطباعة والنشر (House of Enlightnment for Printing and Publishing), 2021.

Albrecht, Holger, and Oliver Schlumberger. "'Waiting for Godot': Regime Change without Democratization in the Middle East." *International Political Science Review* 25, no. 4 (2004): 371–92.

Al Daaiji, Noora. "قراءة في تحولات الحركة النسوية السعودية: من الهامش إلى المركز" ("A Reading on the Saudi Feminist Movement from the Periphery to the Center"). In الثابت والمتحول 2018 : التنمية في هامش الخليج (*Change and Continuity 2018: Developments in the Margins of the Gulf*), edited by Omar AlShehabi, Esraa Al Muftah, and Khalil Buhazza. Kuwait: مركز الخليج لسياسات التنمية (Gulf Centre for Development Policies), 2018.

Al Dakhallah, Ayoob. التربية ومشكلات المجتمع في عصر العولمة (*Education and Societal Problems in the Age of Globalization*). Beirut: Dar Al Kotob Al Imiyah, 2015.

Al Dakhil, Khalid. *2003: Saudi Arabia's Year of Reform*. Sada. Washington, DC: Carnegie Endowment for International Peace, August 22, 2008.

Alebrahim, Abdulrahman. *Kuwait's Politics before Independence: The Role of the Balancing Powers*. Berlin: Gerlach, 2019.

Al Fahad, Abdulaziz. "Raiders and Traders: A Poet's Lament on the End of the Bedouin Heroic Age." In *Saudi Arabia in Transition: Insights on Social, Political, Economic and Religious Change*, edited by Bernard Haykel, Thomas Hegghammer, and Stephane Lacroix, 231–262. Cambridge: Cambridge University Press, 2015.

Al Fahad, Abdulaziz. "Rootless Trees: Genealogical Politics in Saudi Arabia." In *Saudi Arabia in Transition: Insights on Social, Political, Economic and Religious Change*, edited by Bernard Haykel, Thomas Hegghammer, and Stephane Lacroix, 263–291. Cambridge: Cambridge University Press, 2015.

Al Gergawi, Mishaal. "Death of the Khaliji." *Gulf News*. August 22, 2017. https://gulfnews.com /opinion/op-eds/death-of-the-khaliji-1.2078355.

Al Hakeem, Mariam. "Citizenship Restored to 5,266 Qataris." Gulf 2000 Archives. *Gulf News*. February 3, 2006. https://gulfnews.com/world/gulf/qatar/citizenship-restored-to-5266 -qataris-1.223912.

Al Hashemi, Saeed. "الحركات الإسلامية في عُمان قراءةٌ في معالم طريق غامض" ("Islamic Movements in Oman: Reading the Mysterious Milestones Along the Road"). In الحركات الاسلامية في الوطن العربي (*Islamic Movements in the Arab World*). Beirut: Centre for Arab Unity Studies, 2013.

Alhashmi, Thuraiya. "Cracking the Glass Ceiling: Gulf Women in Politics." Washington, DC: Arab Gulf States Institute Washington, July 6, 2018. https://agsiw.org/cracking-glass-ceiling -gulf-women-politics/.

Al Hussein, Eman. *Saudi First: How Hyper-Nationalism Is Transforming Saudi Arabia*. European Council on Foreign Relations (June 2019).

Al Hussein, Mira. "The Economic Contracts of New Gulf Citizenships." *Orient*. December 30, 2021. https://orientxxi.info/magazine/the-economic-contracts-of-new-gulf-citizenships,5265.

Al Juneed, Sabah, Ahmad Al Khouli, Nader Abdalhameed, and Ghadeer Kazem. "البيئة والاستدامة في دول مجلس التعاون" ("The Environment and Sustainability in the [Gulf] Cooperation Council Countries"). In الثابت والمتحول 2020: الاستدامة في الخليج (*Change and Continuity 2020: Sustainability in the Gulf*), edited by Omar AlShehabi and Hamad Al Rayes. Kuwait: مركز الخليج لسياسات التنمية (Gulf Centre for Development Policies), 2020.

Al Khatib, Anwar. "دراسة: 66% من القطريين يؤيدون استمرار العضوية في مجلس التعاون الخليجي" ("Study: 66 Percent of Qataris Support Continued Membership in the Gulf Cooperation Council"). *Al Arab*. February 26, 2018. Accessed June 10, 2020. https://tinyurl.com/y8cwpkt2.

Al-Kuwari, Ali Khalifah (ed.). الشعب يريد الإصلاح في قطر أيضا (*The People Want Reform in Qatar Too*). Beirut: The Knowledge Forum, 2012.

Allam, Nermin, and Magdalena Karolak. "Introduction." In *Gulf Cooperation Council Culture and Identities in the New Millennium*, edited by Nermin Allam and Magdalena Karolak, 1–12. Singapore: Palgrave MacMillan, 2020.

Allison, Graham. *Essence of Decision*. New York: Harper Collins, 1971.

Al Marri, Amna. "المستجدات في دولة قطر" ("New Developments in the State of Qatar"). In الثابت والمتحول 2020: الاستدامة في الخليج (*Change and Continuity 2020: Sustainability in the Gulf*), edited by Omar AlShehabi and Hamad Al Rayes. Kuwait: مركز الخليج لسياسات التنمية (Gulf Centre for Development Policies), 2020.

Al Marri, Amna, and Miriam Al Hajri. "المستجدات السياسية في دولة قطر" ("Political Developments in the State of Qatar"). In الثابت والمتحول 2018: التنمية يف هامش الخليج (*Change and Transformation: Development at the Margins of the Gulf*), edited by Omar AlShehabi, Ahmed Al Owfi, and Khalil Bohazza. Kuwait: مركز الخليج لسياسات التنمية (Gulf Centre for Development Policies), 2018.

Almazroui, Mansour, M. Nazrul Islam, Ramzah Dambul, and P. D. Jones. "Trends of Temperature Extremes in Saudi Arabia." *International Journal of Climatology* 34, no. 3 (2014): 808–826.

Almazroui, Mansour, M. Nazrul Islam, H. Athar, P. D. Jones, and M. Ashfaqur Rahman. "Recent Climate Change in the Arabian Peninsula: Annual Rainfall and Temperature Analysis of Saudi Arabia for 1978–2009." *International Journal of Climatology* 32, no. 6 (2012): 953–966. https://doi.org/10.1002/joc.3446.

Almezaini, Khalid S. *The UAE and Foreign Policy: Foreign Aid, Identities and Interests*. London: Routledge, 2012.

Almohamadi, Sara Fouad. "Qatar Dispute Exposes Regional Food-Security Failures." *IISS*. August 21, 2017. Accessed June 4, 2020. https://www.iiss.org/blogs/analysis/2017/08/qatar -food-insecurity.

Al Najjar, Ghanim. "Struggle over Parliament in Kuwait." Sada. Washington, DC: Carnegie Endowment for International Peace, August 18, 2008. Accessed June 24, 2019. https://carnegie endowment.org/sada/20845.

al-Nakeeb, Khaldoun Hassan, and L. M. Kenny (trans.). *Society and State in the Gulf and Arab Peninsula: A Different Perspective*. Routledge Library Editions. Abingdon, UK: Routledge (Arab Unity Studies), 2012.

Al-Nakib, Farah. *Kuwait Transformed: A History of Oil and Urban Life*. Stanford, CA: Stanford University Press, 2016.

Al-Nakib, Farah. "Revisiting Hadar and Badu in Kuwait: Citizenship, Housing, and the Construction of a Dichotomy." *International Journal of Middle East Studies* 46, no. 1 (2014): 5–30.

al-Naqeeb, Khaldoun Hasan. *Society and State in the Gulf and Arab Peninsula: A Different Perspective*. London: Routledge, 1990.

Al Omran, Ahmed. "Saudi Arabia's Sleepy City Offers Prince a Cautionary Tale." *Financial Times*. May 27, 2018. https://www.ft.com/content/ae48574c-58e6-11e8-bdb7-f6677d2e1ce8.

Al Omran, Ahmed, and Andrew England. "Saudi Arabia: Why Jobs Overhaul Could Define MBS's Rule." *Financial Times*. February 28, 2019. https://www.ft.com/content/fc240c0e-29fb -11e9-88a4-c32129756dd8.

Al Qaraala, Omar Mohammed, and Ahmed Mohammed Tarawneh. "الثاني من القرن التاسع عشر الميلادي التنافس البريطاني العثماني على البحرين في النصف" ("British-Ottoman Rivalry over Bahrain in the Second Half of the Nineteenth Century"). العلوم الإنسانية والاجتماعية المجلّد (*Humanities and Social Sciences Journal*) 1, no. 1 (2019).

al-Qasimi, Muhammad. *The Myth of Arab Piracy in the Gulf*. 2nd ed. London: Routledge, 1988.

Al-Ragam, Asseel. "'Denial of Coevalness': Discursive Practices in the Representation of Kuwaiti Urban Modernity." *Traditional Dwellings and Settlements Review* 28, no. 2 (2017): 7–20. www.jstor.org/stable/44779808.

Al Rasheed, Madawi. *A Most Masculine State: Gender, Politics and Religion in Saudi Arabia*. Cambridge: Cambridge University Press, 2013.

Al Rasheed, Madawi. "Caught between Religion and State: Women in Saudi Arabia." In *Saudi Arabia in Transition: Insights on Social, Political, Economic and Religious Change*, edited by Bernard Haykel, Thomas Hegghammer, and Stephane Lacroix, 292–313. Cambridge: Cambridge University Press, 2015.

Al Rasheed, Madawi. "Circles of Power: Royals and Saudi Society." In *Saudi Arabia in the Balance*, edited by Gerd Nonneman and Paul Aarts, 185–213. New York: New York University Press, 2005.

Al Rasheed, Madawi. *Muted Modernists: The Struggle over Divine Politics in Saudi Arabia*. London: Hurst, 2015.

Al Rasheed, Madawi. "Transnational Connections and National Identity: Zanzibari Omanis in Muscat." In *Monarchies and Nations: Globalization and Identity in the Arab States of the Gulf*, edited by Paul Dresch and James Piscatori, 96–113. New York: I. B. Tauris, 2013.

Al-Rashoud, Talal. "From Muscat to the Maghreb: Pan-Arab Networks, Anti-Colonial Groups, and Kuwait's Arab Scholarships (1953–1961)." *Arabian Humanities* 12, no. 12 (2019).

Al Rumaihi, Mohammed. "الاستعداد الخليجي للتراجع الأميري" ("Gulf Preparedness for the American Withdrawal"). *Al Arabiyya*. March 8, 2014. Accessed April 2, 2019. https://tinyurl.com/ydgjpa85.

Al Sarhan, Saud. "The Struggle for Authority: The Shaykhs of Jihadi-Salafism in Saudi Arabia, 1997–2003." In *Saudi Arabia in Transition: Insights on Social, Political, Economic and Religious Change*, edited by Bernard Haykel, Thomas Hegghammer, and Stephane Lacroix, 181–206. Cambridge: Cambridge University Press, 2015.

Al Sayed, Wafa. "Sawt Al-Bahrain: A Window onto the Gulf's Social and Political History." *LSE Blogs*. July 1, 2020. Accessed July 3, 2020. https://blogs.lse.ac.uk/mec/2020/07/01/sawt -al-bahrain-a-window-onto-the-gulfs-social-and-political-history/.

Alshawi, Hadi, and Andrew Gardner. "Tribalism, Identity and Citizenship in Contemporary Qatar." *Anthropology of the Middle East* 8, no. 2 (2013): 46–59.

AlShehabi, Ghassan. "حزب الله البحرين».. قصة متجذرة شائكة" ("Hezbollah Bahrain: A Deep Rooted Thorny Story"). *Al Majallah*. October 14, 2013. Accessed April 1, 2020. https://gulfpolicies.org/2019- 05-18-07-14-32/92-2019-06-25-12-45-40/765-2019-06-26-09-01-59.

AlShehabi, Omar. *Contested Modernity: Sectarianism, Nationalism, and Colonialism in Bahrain*. London: One World Academic, 2019.

AlShehabi, Omar. "تاريخه واسبابه ومعوقات مواجهته تفاقم الخلل السكاني في دول مجلس التعاون" ("The Population Imbalance in the GCC Countries: Its History and Its Causes and Impediments to Confronting It"). Paper presented at دول مجلس التعاون الخليجي في سياسات وآليات لمواجهة الخلل السكاني المتفاقم (Policies and Mechanisms to Address the Growing Population Imbalance in the Gulf Cooperation Council), 2013.

AlShehabi, Omar. تصدير الثروة واغتراب الإنسان: تاريخ الخلل الإنتاجي في دول الخليج العربية (Exporting Wealth and Alienating the Citizen: History of Production in the GCC). Beirut: Centre for Arab Unity Studies, 2018.

AlShehabi, Omar. "Show Us the Money: Oil Revenues, Undisclosed Allocations and Accountability in Budgets of the GCC States." LSE Research Online Documents on Economics 84521. London School of Economics and Political Science. LSE Library (2017).

AlShehabi, Omar, and Hamad Al Rayes. الثابت والمتحول 2020: الاستدامة في الخليج (Change and Continuity 2020: Sustainability in the Gulf). 8th ed. Kuwait: مركز الخليج لسياسات التنمية. (Gulf Centre for Development Policies), 2020.

Alterman, Jon B., and Margo Balboni. Citizens in Training: Conscription and Nation-Building in the United Arab Emirates. Doha, Qatar: Centre for International and Regional Studies, 2017. https://www.csis.org/analysis/citizens-training-conscription-and-nation-building -united-arab-emirates.

Al Zameea, Ali. "جدلية التنمية المستدامة وبنية الدولة وسياساتها العامة" ("The Dialectic of Sustainable Development, State Structure and Public Policies"). In الثابت والمتحول 2020: الاستدامة في الخليج (Change and Continuity 2020: Sustainability in the Gulf), edited by Omar AlShehabi and Hamad Al Rayes. Kuwait: مركز الخليج لسياسات التنمية (Gulf Centre for Development Policies), 2020.

@anhistorian (Abdullah Al Arian). "In Honor of Thomas Friedman's . . ." Twitter. November 24, 2017. Accessed August 6, 2018. https://twitter.com/anhistorian/status/934080718816399361.

Anderson, Lisa. "Absolutism and the Resilience of Monarchy in the Middle East." Political Science Quarterly 106, no. 1 (1991): 1–15.

Anderson, Lisa. "Arab Democracy: Dismal Prospects." World Policy Journal 18, no. 3 (2001): 53–60.

Anderson, Lisa. "Dynasts and Nationalists: Why Monarchies Survive." In Middle East Monarchies: The Challenge of Modernity, edited by Joseph Kostiner. Boulder, CO: Lynne Rienner, 2000.

Anderson, Richard, and Jawaher Al Bader. "Recent Kuwaiti Architecture: Revionalism vs. Globalization." Journal of Architectural and Planning Research 23, no. 2 (Summer 2006): 134–146.

Annual Statistics 2018. Saudi Arabian Monetary Authority. May 29, 2019. https://tinyurl.com /y7gzl783.

Arafat, Hassan, Toufic Mezher, and Omar Saif. "Water Security in the GCC Countries: Challenges and Opportunities." Journal of Environmental Studies and Science 4 (2014): 329–346.

Aras, Bülent, and Pınar Akpınar. "Turkish Foreign Policy and the Qatar Crisis." Istanbul Policy Center–Sabanci University–Stiftung Mercator Initiative (2017).

Ardemagni, Eleonora. Gulf Monarchies' Militarized Nationalism. Washington, DC: Carnegie Endowment for International Peace, February 28, 2019. https://carnegieendowment.org /sada/78472.

Ardemagni, Eleonora. "Icons of the Nation: The Military Factor in the UAE's Nation-Building." *LSE Blogs*. February 1, 2019. https://blogs.lse.ac.uk/mec/2019/02/01/icons-of-the-nation-the -military-factor-in-the-uaes-nation-building/.

Asfour, Gaber. "An Argument for Enhancing Arab Identity within Globalization." In *Globalization and the Gulf*, edited by John W. Fox, Nada Mourtada-Sabbah, and Mohammed Al Mutawa, 151–157. Abingdon, UK: Routledge, 2006.

Ayoob, Mohammed. "Defining Security: A Subaltern Realist Perspective." In *Critical Security Studies: Concepts and Cases*, edited by Keith Krause and Michael C. Williams, 145–170. London: Routledge, 1997.

Ayoob, Mohammed. "Political Islam: Image and Reality." *World Policy Journal* 21, no. 3 (2004): 1–14.

Babar, Zahra R. "The Cost of Belonging: Citizenship Construction in the State of Qatar." *Middle East Journal* 68, no. 3 (Summer 2014): 403–420.

Bahgat, Gawdat. "Sovereign Wealth Funds in the Gulf: An Assessment." In *The Transformation of the Gulf: Politics, Economics and the Global Order*, edited by David Held and Kristian Coates Ulrichsen, 218–236. London: Routledge, 2012.

The Bahrain-Qatar Border Dispute: The World Court Decision, Part 1. The Estimate. March 23, 2001.

Bahrain Letter: The Bahrain Agricultural Show, 1957. Foreign and Commonwealth Office, London, FO 371/126957 (1957).

"Bahrain/Kuwait: More Citizenships Revoked." *Gulf States Newsletter* 978. October 2, 2014.

"Bahrain/Qatar: Tribes' Mass Show of Allegiance." *Gulf States Newsletter* 1086. August 1, 2019.

Baldwin, David A. "The Concept of Security." *Review of International Studies* 23, no. 1 (1997): 5–26.

Baldwin, David A. "Security Studies and the End of the Cold War." *World Politics* 48, no. 1 (1995): 117–141.

Banjar, Hadeel. "Motivating Sustainable Consumption Behaviour through Education, Incentive Programs, and Green Policies in Saudi Arabia." In *Sustainability in the Gulf: Challenges and Opportunities*, edited by Elie Azar and Mohamed Abdel Raouf, 248–273. Abingdon, UK: Routledge, 2017.

Barany, Zoltan. *Arms Procurement and Corruption in the Gulf Monarchies*. Washington, DC: Center for Strategic and International Studies, May 11, 2020. https://www.csis.org/analysis /arms-procurement-and-corruption-gulf-monarchies.

Barany, Zoltan. *Military Officers in the Gulf: Career Trajectories and Determinants*. Washington, DC: Center for Strategic and International Studies, November 2019. https://www.csis.org /analysis/military-officers-gulf-career-trajectories-and-determinants.

Barari, Hassan A. "The Persistence of Autocracy: Jordan, Morocco and the Gulf." *Middle East Critique* 24, no. 1 (2015): 99–111.

Bargal, Tarik. "The Shifting Sands of Saudi Arabia's Water Plans." *Inframation News*. August 6, 2018.

Barnard, Anne, and Maria Abi-Habib. "Why Saad Hariri Had That Strange Sojourn in Saudi Arabia." *New York Times*. December 24, 2017. https://www.nytimes.com/2017/12/24/world /middleeast/saudi-arabia-saad-hariri-mohammed-bin-salman-lebanon.html.

Baskan, Birol, and Steven Wright. "Seeds of Change: Comparing State-Religion Relations in Qatar and Saudi Arabia." *Arab Studies Quarterly* 33, no. 2 (Spring 2011): 96–111.

"Bassiouni Commission Report Is Released." Economist Intelligence Unit, London. December 13, 2011. http://country.eiu.com/article.aspx?articleid=1838675968&Country=Bahrain&topic =Politics&subtopic=_6.

Bassiouni, Mahmoud Cherif, Nigel Rodley, Badria Al Awadhi, Philippe Kirsch, and Mahnoush H. Arsanjani. *Report of the Bahrain Independent Commission of Inquiry.* Manama, Bahrain: Bahrain Independent Commission of Inquiry, November 23, 2011. http://www.bici.org.bh /BICIreportEN.pdf.

Bazell, Robert J. "Arid Land Agriculture: Shaikh up in Arizona Research." *Science* 171, no. 3975 (1971): 989–90. www.jstor.org/stable/1731297.

Bazoobandi, Sara. *The Political Economy of the Gulf Sovereign Wealth Funds: A Case Study of Iran, Kuwait, Saudi Arabia and the United Arab Emirates.* Abingdon, UK: Routledge, 2013.

Bazoobandi, Sara, and Jeffrey B. Nugent. *Political Economy of Sovereign Wealth Funds in the Oil Exporting Countries of the Arab Region and Especially the Gulf.* Working Papers 1143, Economic Research Forum (2017).

Benson, Brett V. *Constructing International Security: Alliances, Deterrence, and Moral Hazard.* New York: Cambridge University Press, 2012.

Bianco, Cinzia. "Meet Oman's New Sultan. How Will He Navigate the Region's Turmoil?" *Washington Post.* January 15, 2020. https://www.washingtonpost.com/politics/2020/01/15 /meet-omans-new-sultan-how-will-he-navigate-regions-turmoil/.

Bilgin, Pinar. "Individual and Societal Dimensions of Security." *International Studies Review* 5, no. 2 (2003): 203–222.

Bishara, Fahad Ahmad, Bernard Haykel, Clive D. Holes, and James Onley. "The Economic Transformation of the Gulf." In *The Emergence of the Gulf States: Studies in Modern History*, edited by J. E. Peterson. London: Bloomsbury, 2016.

Boersma, Tim, and Steve Griffiths. *Reforming Energy Subsidies: Initial Lessons from the United Arab Emirates.* Brookings Institution and Masdar Institute. January 19, 2016. https://www.brookings .edu/research/reforming-energy-subsidies-initial-lessons-from-the-united-arab-emirates/.

Bostock, Bill. "Everything We Know About Neom, a 'Mega-City' Project in Saudi Arabia with Plans for Flying Cars and Robot Dinosaurs." *Business Insider.* September 23, 2019. Accessed June 13, 2020. https://www.businessinsider.in/miscellaneous/everything-we-know-about -neom-a-mega-city-project-in-saudi-arabia-with-plans-for-flying-cars-and-robot-dinosaurs /slidelist/71232419.cms.

Boyce, Graham. *Scenarios for Possible Military Intervention in the Gulf.* Foreign and Commonwealth Office, London (August 7, 1986).

BP Statistical Review of World Energy. London: British Petroleum, 2021.

BP Statistical Review of World Energy. London: British Petroleum, 2019.

Brant, Colin. *Valedictory from Qatar: A Land of Promise.* Foreign and Commonwealth Office, London (July 9, 1981).

Braunstein, Juergen. "Domestic Sources of Twenty-First-Century Geopolitics: Domestic Politics and Sovereign Wealth Funds in GCC Economies." *New Political Economy* 24, no. 2 (2019): 197–217.

British "Spy" in Muscat. Foreign and Commonwealth Office, London, FO 371/140198/75 - BA File 1282 (December 15, 1959).

Bromage, Nigel. *A Soldier in Arabia*. London: Radcliffe, 2012.

Brooks, Risa. "Civil Military Relations in the Middle East." In *The Future Security Environment in the Middle East: Conflict, Stability, and Political Change*, edited by Nora Bensahel and Daniel Byman, 129–162. Santa Monica, CA: RAND Corporation, 2004.

Brooks, Sarah M., and Marcus J. Kurtz. "Oil and Democracy: Endogenous Natural Resources and the Political 'Resource Curse.'" *International Organization* 70, no. 2 (2016): 279–311.

Brown, Nathan J. "The Remaking of the Saudi State." Washington, DC: Carnegie Endowment for International Peace, November 9, 2017. https://carnegieendowment.org/2017/11/09 /remaking-of-saudi-state-pub-74681.

Browning, Christopher S., and Pertti Joenniemi. "From Fratricide to Security Community: Re-Theorising Difference in the Constitution of Nordic Peace." *Journal of International Relations and Development* 16, no. 4 (2013): 483–513.

Brynen, Rex, Bahgat Korany, and Paul Noble (eds.). *Political Liberalization and Democratization in the Arab World: Theoretical Perspectives*, vol. 1. Boulder, CO: Lynne Rienner, 1995.

Bsheer, Rosie. "A Counter-Revolutionary State: Popular Movements and the Making of Saudi Arabia." *Past and Present* 238, no. 1 (2018): 233–277.

"Budget Deficit Drops by 60 Percent on Back of Higher Revenues." *Kuwait Times*. July 29, 2019. https://www.kuwaittimes.com/budget-deficit-drops-by-60-on-back-of-higher-revenues/.

Buller, Alicia. "Are You Paid According to Your Skin Colour?" *Gulf Business*. March 5, 2013. https://gulfbusiness.com/are-you-paid-according-to-your-skin-colour/.

Burdett, Anita L. P. (ed.). *British Resident E.F. Henderson, Doha, to JL Beaven Arabian Department, FCO London, "Qatar Internal" February 21, 1972*. Vol. IV: 1970–1971, Records of Qatar 1966–1971. Slough, UK: Archive Editions Limited, 2006.

Burke, Jason. *Al Qaeda: The True Story of Radical Islam*. London: I. B. Tauris, 2003.

Burrows, Bernard A. *Letter: Development of Agriculture in Oman: Agricultural Show in Bahrain*. Foreign and Commonwealth Office, London, FO 371/126957 (November 28, 1957).

Burt, John A. "The Environmental Costs of Coastal Urbanization in the Arabian Gulf." *City* 18, no. 6 (2014): 760–770.

Butterfield, Herbert. *The Whig Interpretation of History*. New York and London: W. W. Norton, 1965.

Buttorff, Gail, Bozena Welborne, and Nawra al-Lawati. "Measuring Female Labor Force Participation in the GCC." *Issue Brief* 1 (2018).

Buzan, Barry. *People, States and Fear: An Agenda for International Security Studies in the Post-Cold War Era*. 2nd ed. Colchester, UK: ECPR, 1991.

Buzan, Barry. *People, States and Fear: The National Security Problem in International Relations*. Brighton, UK: Wheatsheaf, 1983.

Buzan, Barry, and Lene Hansen. *The Evolution of International Security Studies*. Cambridge: Cambridge University Press, 2010.

Buzan, Barry, Ole Wæver, and Jaap de Wilde. *Security: A New Framework for Analysis*. Boulder, CO: Lynne Rienner, 1998.

Byman, Daniel L., and Jerrold D. Green. "The Enigma of Political Stability in the Persian Gulf Monarchies." *Middle East Review of International Affairs* 3, no. 3 (1999): 20–37.

Byrne, Malcolm. "CIA Confirms Role in 1953 Iran Coup." *National Security Archive Electronic Briefing Book* 435, no. 19 (2013). https://nsarchive2.gwu.edu/NSAEBB/NSAEBB435/.

Carapico, Sheila. "Arabia Incognita: An Invitation to Arabian Peninsula Studies." In *Counter-Narratives: History, Contemporary Society and Politics in Saudi Arabia and Yemen*, edited by Madawi Al Rasheed and Robert Vitalis, 11–33. New York: Palgrave Macmillan, 2004.

Caratelli, Paolo, Maria Alessandra Misuri, and Mohamed El Amrousi. "Al-Ain's Cultural Landscape: Identity, Innovation and Sustainability in a Challenging Economy." *International Review for Spatial Planning and Sustainable Development* 7, no. 3 (2019): 45–62.

Carey, Glen, and Zaid Sabah. "Saudi King Fires Water Minister after Complaints over Tariffs." *Bloomberg*. April 24, 2016. https://www.bloomberg.com/news/articles/2016-04-24/saudi-king-fires-water-minister-after-complaints-over-tariffs.

Carter, Robert. "The History and Prehistory of Pearling in the Persian Gulf." *Journal of the Economic and Social History of the Orient* 48, no. 2 (2005): 139–209.

Carvalho, Antonio, Jeff Youssef, and Nicolas Dunias. *Maximizing Employment of Nationals in the GCC*. Oliver Wyman, Marsh and McLennan (October 2018). https://www.oliverwyman.com/content/dam/oliver-wyman/v2/publications/2018/october/maximizing-employment-of-nationals-in-the-gcc.pdf.

Castelier, Sebastian. "Qatar's Agriculture Push Risks Further Groundwater Depletion." *Al Monitor*. August 26, 2019. https://www.al-monitor.com/pulse/originals/2019/08/qatar-agriculture-water-environmental-concerns.html.

Chalcraft, John. "Migration and Popular Protest in the Arabian Peninsula and the Gulf in the 1950s and 1960s." *International Labor and Working-Class History* 79, no. 1 (2011): 28–47.

Chalcraft, John. "Monarchy, Migration and Hegemony in the Arabian Peninsula." *Kuwait Programme on Development, Governance and Globalization in the Gulf States* 12 (2010).

Chandler, David L. "Study: Persian Gulf Could Experience Deadly Heat." *MIT News*. October 26, 2015. http://news.mit.edu/2015/study-persian-gulf-deadly-heat-1026.

"Changing Times for Saudi's Once Feared Morality Police." *France 24*. January 14, 2022. Accessed January 17, 2022. https://www.france24.com/en/live-news/20220114-changing-times-for-saudi-s-once-feared-morality-police?ref=tw.

Chertow, Marian R. "The IPAT Equation and Its Variants." *Journal of Industrial Ecology* 4, no. 4 (2000): 13–29.

Choucri, Nazli. "Asians in the Arab World: Labor Migration and Public Policy." *Middle Eastern Studies* 22, no. 2 (1986): 252–273.

"Citizenship Revoked to Stifle Dissent." *Gulf States Newsletter* 976. September 5, 2014. https://www.gsn-online.com/news-centre/article/citizenship-revoked-stifle-dissent.

Clapp, Jennifer. "Food Self-Sufficiency: Making Sense of It, and When It Makes Sense." *Food Policy* 66 (2017): 88–96.

Clawson, Patrick. "Sometimes the Grass Is Indeed Greener: The Successful Use of Energy Revenues." In *Beyond the Resource Curse*, edited by Brenda Shaffer and Taleh Ziyadov, 58–83. Philadelphia: University of Pennsylvania Press, 2011.

Coates Ulrichsen, Kristian. "Bahrain's Uprising: Domestic Implications and Regional and International Perspective." In *The New Middle East: Protest and Revolution in the Arab World*, edited by Fawaz A. Gerges, 332–352. New York: Cambridge University Press, 2014.

Coates Ulrichsen, Kristian. *Insecure Gulf*. London: Hurst, 2011.

Coates Ulrichsen, Kristian. "Introduction." In *The Changing Security Dynamics of the Persian Gulf*, edited by Kristian Coates Ulrichsen, 1–22. London: Hurst, 2017.

Coates Ulrichsen, Kristian. "Knowledge-Based Economies in the GCC." In *The Political Economy of the Persian Gulf*, edited by Mehran Kamrava. New York: Columbia University Press, 2012.

Coates Ulrichsen, Kristian. *Qatar and the Arab Spring*. London: Hurst, 2014.

Coates Ulrichsen, Kristian. *Qatar and the Gulf Crisis: A Study of Resilience*. New York: Oxford University Press, 2020.

Coates Ulrichsen, Kristian. *The United Arab Emirates: Power, Politics, and Policymaking*. Oxford, UK: Routledge, 2017.

Cole, Donald P. "Where Have the Bedouin Gone?" *Anthropological Quarterly* 76, no. 2 (Spring 2003): 235–267.

Cole, Donald P., and Soraya Altorki. "Was Arabia Tribal? A Reinterpretation of the Pre-Oil Society." *Journal of South Asian and Middle Eastern Studies* 15, no. 4 (Summer 1992).

Cole, Juan. "David and Goliath: How Qatar Defeated the Saudi and UAE Annexation Plot." *The Nation*. February 16, 2019. https://www.thenation.com/article/archive/david-and-goliath-how-qatar-defeated-the-saudi-and-uae-annexation-plot/.

Commins, David. *The Wahhabi Mission and Saudi Arabia*. London: I. B. Tauris, 2009.

Cooke, Miriam. *Tribal Modern: Branding New Nations in the Arab Gulf*. Berkeley: University of California Press, 2014.

Cordesman, Anthony H. *The Gulf Military Balance, Volume I: The Conventional and Asymmetric Dimensions*. Lanham, MD: Rowman & Littlefield, 2014.

Cordesman, Anthony H. *Saudi Arabia Enters the Twenty-First Century, Volume 1*. Westport, CT and London: Praeger, 2003.

Cordesman, Anthony H. "The Tanker War and the Lessons of Naval Conflict." In *The Lessons of Modern War, Volume 2: The Iran-Iraq War*, edited by Anthony H. Cordesman and Abraham R. Wagner, 2–86. Washington DC: Center for Strategic and International Studies, 1990. https://www.csis.org/analysis/lessons-modern-war-volume-ii-iran-iraq-war-%E2%80%93-chapter-14-tanker-war-and-lessons-naval.

"Country-Specific Updates—Gulf Cooperation Council (GCC)." *DLA Piper*. February 3, 2020. Accessed June 20, 2020. https://www.dlapiper.com/en/belgium/insights/publications/2020/01/vat-alert-january/country-specific-updates-gcc/#0.

Craig, Ben R. *The Souk Al-Manakh Crash*. Economic Commentary. Cleveland, OH: Federal Reserve Bank of Cleveland, 2019. https://www.clevelandfed.org/en/newsroom-and-events/publications/economic-commentary/2019-economic-commentaries/ec-201920-kuwait-souk-al-manakh.aspx.

Cronin, Stephanie. *Armies and State Building in the Modern Middle East: Politics, Nationalism, and Military Reform*. London: I. B. Tauris, 2013.

Crooks, Ed. "The Most Momentous Telegram of the 20th Century? Western Union Brings the News That Oil Has Been Found in Saudi Arabia, 80 Years Ago This Week, #CERAWeek18." Twitter. Accessed March 20, 2019. https://twitter.com/Ed_Crooks/status/971039511244361730.

"Crude Oil Production (Indicator)." Organization of Economic Co-operation and Development (2020). Accessed January 26, 2020. https://doi.org/10.1787/4747b431-en.

Crystal, Jill. "Coalitions in Oil Monarchies: Kuwait and Qatar." *Comparative Politics* 21, no. 4 (1989): 427–443.

Crystal, Jill. *Oil and Politics in the Gulf: Rulers and Merchants in Kuwait and Qatar*. Cambridge: Cambridge University Press, 1995.

Crystal, Jill. "Tribes and Patronage Networks in Qatar." In *Tribes and States in a Changing Middle East*, edited by Uzi Rabi, 37–56. New York: Oxford University Press, 2016.

Davidson, Christopher. *Abu Dhabi: Oil and Beyond*. New York: Columbia University Press, 2009.

Davidson, Christopher. *After the Sheikhs: The Coming Collapse of the Gulf Monarchies*. London: Hurst, 2012.

Davidson, Christopher. *The United Arab Emirates: A Study in Survival*. Boulder, CO: Lynne Rienner, 2005.

Davies, E. T. *Codewords under Operation Sodabread*. Manama: Foreign and Commonwealth Office, London (November 2, 1961).

Davis, Diana K., and Paul Robbins. "Ecologies of the Colonial Present: Pathological Forestry from the Taux De Boisement to Civilized Plantations." *Environment and Planning E: Nature and Space* 1, no. 4 (2018): 447–69.

Davis, Jeffrey, Rolando Ossowski, James A. Daniel, and Steven Barnett. "Stabilization and Savings Funds for Nonrenewable Resources: Experience and Fiscal Policy Implications." In *Fiscal Policy Formulation and Implementation in Oil-Producing Countries*, edited by J. M. Davis, R. Ossowski, and A. Fedelino, 273–315. Washington, DC: International Monetary Fund, 2001.

DeAtkine, Norville B. "Western Influence on Arab Militaries: Pounding Square Pegs into Round Holes." *Middle East Review of International Affairs* 17, no. 1 (2013).

DeAtkine, Norville B. "Why Arabs Lose Wars." *Middle East Quarterly* 6, no. 4 (December 1999). https://www.meforum.org/441/why-arabs-lose-wars.

"Defend Us Discretely." *The Economist*. June 6, 1981.

Demirbas, Ayhan, Ayman A. Hashem, and Ahmed A. Bakhsh. "The Cost Analysis of Electric Power Generation in Saudi Arabia." *Energy Sources, Part B: Economics, Planning, and Policy* 12, no. 6 (2017): 591–596.

Denson, J. B. *Trucial States Development*. Foreign and Commonwealth Office, London, FO 371/114656 (December 20, 1955).

Development of Agriculture in Trucial States. Foreign and Commonwealth Office, London, FO 371/126956 (1957).

Dewey, Caitlin, and Max Fisher. "Meet the World's Other 25 Royal Families." *Washington Post*. July 22, 2013. https://www.washingtonpost.com/news/worldviews/wp/2013/07/22/meet-the-worlds-other-25-royal-families/.

di Lampedusa, Giuseppe Tomasi. *The Leopard*. London: Vintage, 2007.

Diop, Abdoulaye, Kien Trung Le, Trevor Johnston, and Michael Ewers. "Citizens' Attitudes towards Migrant Workers in Qatar." *Migration and Development* 6, no. 1 (2017): 144–160.

DiPaola, Anthony. "Middle East's $2 Trillion Wealth Could Be Gone by 2034, IMF Says." *Bloomberg.* February 6, 2020. https://www.bloombergquint.com/technology/middle-east -s-2-trillion-wealth-could-be-gone-by-2034-imf-says.

Dorman, Andrew, Mike Lawrence Smith, and Matthew Uttley. "Jointery and Combined Operations in an Expeditionary Era: Defining the Issues." *Defense Analysis* 14, no. 1 (1998): 1–8.

Dresch, Paul. "Debates on Marriage and Nationality in the UAE." In *Monarchies and Nations: Globalization and Identity in the Arab States of the Gulf,* edited by Paul Dresch and James Piscatori, 136–157. New York: I. B. Tauris, 2013.

Dresch, Paul. "Introduction: Societies, Identities and Global Issues." In *Monarchies and Nations: Globalization and Identity in the Arab States of the Gulf,* edited by Paul Dresch and James Piscatori, 1–33. New York: I. B. Tauris, 2013.

Dresch, Paul. "The Place of Strangers in Gulf Society." In *Globalization and the Gulf,* edited by John W. Fox, Nada Mourtada-Sabbah, and Mohammed Al Mutawa, 210–232. Abingdon, UK: Routledge, 2006.

Dudley, Dominic. "Oman Sets up $18 Billion Sovereign Wealth Fund Even as Economy Shrinks." *Forbes.* June 5, 2020. https://www.forbes.com/sites/dominicdudley/2020/06/05/oman -sovereign-wealth-fund/.

Dudley, Dominic. "World Bank Raises Questions about Gulf's Huge Public Sector Wage Bill." *Forbes.* December 20, 2021. https://www.forbes.com/sites/dominicdudley/2021/12/20/world -bank-raises-questions-about-gulfs-huge-public-sector-wage-bill/.

Duke Anthony, John. "Aspects of Saudi Arabia's Relations with Other Gulf States." In *State, Society and Economy in Saudi Arabia,* edited by Tim Niblock, 148–170. Abingdon, UK: Routledge, 1982 (3rd ed. 2015).

Dutta, Soumitra, Bruno Lanvin, and Sacha Wunsch-Vincent. *Global Innovation Index 2019.* Ithaca, NY, Fontainebleu, France, and Geneva, Switzerland: Cornell University, INSTEAD, and World Intellectual Property Organization, 2019.

Economic Prospects and Policy Challenges for the GCC Countries. Internatioal Monetary Fund, Riyadh (October 26, 2016).

Edens, David G., and William P. Snavely. "Planning for Economic Development in Saudi Arabia." *Middle East Journal* 24, no. 1 (1970): 17.

Efron, Shira, Charles Fromm, Bill Gelfeld, Shanthi Nataraj, and Chase Sova. *Food Security in the Gulf Cooperation Council.* RAND Corporation and emerge85 (December 2018).

Egypt-Persian Gulf States: Mubarak's Security Agenda. Washington, DC: CIA Library, January 13, 1988. https://www.cia.gov/library/readingroom/docs/DOC_0000189995.pdf.

El Baghdadi, Iyad. "How the Saudis Made Jeff Bezos Public Enemy No. 1." *Daily Beast.* February 25, 2019. https://www.thedailybeast.com/how-the-saudis-made-jeff-bezos-public -enemy-1?source=twitter&via=desktop.

El Beblawi, Hazem. "Gulf Industrialization in Perspective." *Industrialization in the Gulf: A Socioeconomic Revolution* (2010): 185.

El Gomati, Anas. "The Libyan Revolution Undone—the Conversation Will Not Be Televised." In *Divided Gulf: The Anatomy of a Crisis*, edited by Andreas Krieg, 179–196. Singapore: Palgrave Macmillan, 2019.

El Haddad, Fathia. "مكتبة الرويح.. 100 عام من القراءة" ("Al Ruwaih Bookshop . . . 100 Years of Reading"). *Al Qabas*. July 8, 2020. https://www.alqabas.com/article/5785299.

Elhadj, Elie. "Camels Don't Fly, Deserts Don't Bloom: An Assessment of Saudi Arabia's Experiment in Desert Agriculture." *SOAS Occasional Paper* 48 (2004).

El Mallakh, Ragaei. *Qatar: Development of an Oil Economy*. London: Croom Helm, 1979.

Emmons, Alex. "Saudi Arabia Planned to Invade Qatar Last Summer." *The Intercept*. August 1, 2018. Accessed September 18, 2019. https://theintercept.com/2018/08/01/rex-tillerson-qatar-saudi-uae/.

England, Andrew. "Female Activists Swept up in Saudi Crackdown." *Financial Times*. August 1, 2018. https://www.ft.com/content/ef8fcaf2-959d-11e8-b747-fb1e803ee64e.

England, Andrew. "Middle East States Set for $1.3tn Oil Windfall, Says IMF." *Financial Times*. August 19, 2022. https://www.ft.com/content/94825404-e0a2-4a18-ab8d-2bc61fc7c1ab.

England, Andrew, and Simeon Kerr. "Saudi Foreign Reserves Fall as Sovereign Wealth Fund Spends Overseas." *Financial Times*. June 1, 2020. https://www.ft.com/content/6825366f-92db-4473-b5b2-cacda032d8ee.

England, Andrew, and Simeon Kerr. "US Sanctions Put Chill on Iranian Trade with UAE." *Financial Times*. July 26, 2019. https://www.ft.com/content/bbe3c99a-aee9-11e9-8030-530adfa879c2.

England, Andrew, and Arash Massoudi. "'Never Waste a Crisis': Inside Saudi Arabia's Shopping Spree." *Financial Times*. May 25, 2020. https://www.ft.com/content/af2deefd-2234-4e54-a08a-8dbb205f5378.

Exell, Karen, and Trinidad Rico. "'There Is No Heritage in Qatar': Orientalism, Colonialism and Other Problematic Histories." *World Archaeology* 45, no. 4 (2013): 670–685.

Eyre, J. C. *Financial and Technical Assistant for the Development of Agriculture in Muscat and Oman*. Foreign and Commonwealth Office, London, FO 371/140198 (March 18, 1959).

Fadlallah, Tarek. "The Puzzle of Profitless Growth in GCC Firms." *Middle East Institute*. August 31, 2021. https://www.mei.edu/publications/puzzle-profitless-growth-gcc-firms.

Faris, Ali. "المستجدات في مملكة البحرين" ("Developments in the Kingdom of Bahrain"). In في الخليج الثابت والمتحول 2020: الاستدامة في الخليج (*Change and Continuity 2020: Sustainability in the Gulf*), edited by Omar AlShehabi and Hamad Al Rayes. Kuwait: مركز الخليج لسياسات التنمية (Gulf Centre for Development Policies), 2020.

Farouk, Yasmine. *The Middle East Strategic Alliance Has a Long Way to Go*. Washington, DC: Carnegie Endowment for International Peace, February 8, 2019. https://carnegieendowment.org/2019/02/08/middle-east-strategic-alliance-has-long-way-to-go-pub-78317.

Faucon, Benoit, Jared Maslin, and Summer Said. "U.A.E. Backed Militia Leader's Bid to Take Control of Libyan Oil Exports." *Wall Street Journal*. July 13, 2018. https://www.wsj.com/articles/u-a-e-backed-militia-leaders-bid-to-take-control-of-libyan-oil-exports-1531474200.

Field, Michael. "Tree of the Al Attiyah." *Arabian Charts* (v.1). Accessed October 1, 2014. http://arabiancharts.wordpress.com/about/.

File 6/18 I, Arab and Persian Schools in Bahrain. Qatar Digital Library. https://www.qdl.qa/archive/81055/vdc_100034888669.0x000074.

File 35/3, the Divers' Riot of May 1932. British Library and Qatar Digital Library. https://www .qdl.qa/archive/81055/vdc_100025657940.0x00004f.

Florida, Richard, and Martin Kenney. "The New Age of Capitalism: Innovation-Mediated Production." *Futures* 25, no. 6 (1993): 637–651.

"Food Production in Qatar Grows by 400 Percent since 2017." *The Peninsula*. March 13, 2019. https://tinyurl.com/d2rzcsbd.

"For the Gulf States, Diplomacy Involves Buying Weapons They Don't Need." *The Economist*. March 1, 2018.

Foreign Merchandise Trade Statistics. Planning and Statistics Authority, State of Qatar (April 2020).

Fox, John W., Nada Mourtada-Sabbah, and Mohammed Al Mutawa. "The Arab Gulf Region." In *Globalization and the Gulf*, edited by John W. Fox, Nada Mourtada-Sabbah, and Mohammed Al Mutawa. Abingdon, UK: Routledge, 2006.

Freedman, Lawrence, and Efraim Karsh. *The Gulf Conflict, 1990–1991: Diplomacy and War in the New World Order*. London: Faber and Faber, 1993.

Freer, Courtney. *Challenges to Sunni Islamism in Bahrain since 2011*. Beirut: Carnegie Middle East Center, March 2019. https://carnegie-mec.org/2019/03/06/challenges-to-sunni -islamism-in-bahrain-since-2011-pub-78510.

Freer, Courtney. "The Changing Islamist Landscape of the Gulf Arab States." Washington, DC: Arab Gulf States Institute Washington, November 21, 2016. https://agsiw.org/wp-content /uploads/2016/11/Freer_ONLINE-1.pdf.

Freer, Courtney. *Rentier Islamism: The Influence of the Muslim Brotherhood in Gulf Monarchies*. New York: Oxford University Press, 2018.

Freer, Courtney. "Social Effects of the Qatar Crisis." *IndraStra Global* 10 (October 3, 2017). https://www.indrastra.com/2017/10/Social-Effects-of-Qatar-Crisis-003-10-2017-0013.html.

Freer, Courtney, and Andrew Leber. "The 'Tribal Advantage' in Kuwaiti Politics and the Future of the Opposition." *Brookings Institution*. April 19, 2021. https://www.brookings.edu /blog/order-from-chaos/2021/04/19/the-tribal-advantage-in-kuwaiti-politics-and-the-future -of-the-opposition/.

Friedman, Thomas. "Saudi Arabia's Arab Spring, at Last." *New York Times*. November 23, 2017. https://www.nytimes.com/2017/11/23/opinion/saudi-prince-mbs-arab-spring.html.

Fürtig, Henner. "Conflict and Cooperation in the Persian Gulf: The Interregional Order and US Policy." *Middle East Journal* 61, no. 4 (2007): 627–640.

Future of: Royal Family. Probable Happenings on the Death of Ibn Saud. Coll 6/16. India Office Records and Private Paper. British Library and Qatar Digital Library. https://www.qdl.qa /archive/81055/vdc_100000000555.0x00026c.

Fyfe, Rory. "GCC Deficit Could Reach $250bn with a 16 Percent Drop in Non-Oil Output." *MENA Advisors*. April 29, 2020. Accessed June 20, 2020. https://mena-advisors.com/2020/04/gcc -deficit-could-reach-250bn-with-a-16-drop-in-non-oil-output.

Gardner, Andrew M. "Gulf Migration and the Family." *Journal of Arabian Studies* 1, no. 1 (June 2011): 3–25.

Garfield, Leanna. "Saudi Arabia Is Building a $500 Billion Mega-City That's 33 Times the Size of New York City." *Business Insider*. February 22, 2018. https://www.businessinsider.com /saudi-arabia-mega-city-jordan-egypt-oil-2017-10.

Gaub, Florence. *Guardians of the Arab State: When Militaries Intervene in Politics, from Iraq to Mauritania.* London: Hurst, 2017.

Gause, F. Gregory. "The Persistence of Monarchy in the Arabian Peninsula: A Comparative Analysis." In *Middle East Monarchies: The Challenge of Modernity*, edited by Joseph Kostiner, 167–186. Boulder, CO: Lynne Rienner, 2000.

Gause, Gregory III. "Gulf Regional Politics: Revolution, War and Rivalry." In *The Dynamics of Regional Politics: Four Systems on the Indian Ocean Rim*, edited by W. Howard Wriggins. New York: Columbia University Press, 1992.

Gause, Gregory III. *The International Relations of the Persian Gulf.* New York: Cambridge University Press, 2010.

Gause, Gregory III. "Kings for All Seasons: How the Middle East's Monarchies Survived the Arab Spring." *Brookings Doha Center Analysis Paper* 8 (2013). https://www.brookings.edu/research /kings-for-all-seasons-how-the-middle-easts-monarchies-survived-the-arab-spring/.

Gause, Gregory III. *Oil Monarchies: Domestic and Security Challenges in the Arab Gulf States.* New York: Council on Foreign Relations, 1994.

Gause, Gregory III. "Understanding the Gulf States." *Democracy Journal*, no. 36 (Spring 2015).

Gengler, Justin. "Qatar's Ambivalent Democratization." *Foreign Policy*. November 1, 2011. Accessed February 15, 2013. http://mideast.foreignpolicy.com/posts/2011/11/01/qataris_lesson _in_revolution.

Gengler, Justin. "Society and State in Post-Blockade Qatar: Lessons for the Arab Gulf Region." *Journal of Arabian Studies* 10, no. 2 (2020): 238–255.

Gengler, Justin, and Majed Al Ansari. "Qatar's First Elections since 2017 Reveal Unexpected Impact of GCC Crisis." *Al Monitor.* April 24, 2019. https://www.al-monitor.com/originals /2019/04/qatar-first-elections-reveal-unexpected-impact-gcc-crisis.html.

Gerges, Fawaz A. (ed.). *The New Middle East: Protest and Revolution in the Arab World.* New York: Cambridge University Press, 2014.

Gerges, Fawaz A. "The Obama Approach to the Middle East: The End of America's Moment?" *International Affairs* 89, no. 2 (2013): 299–323.

Gerth, H. H., and C. Wright Mills. *From Max Weber: Essays in Sociology.* New York: Oxford University Press, 1946.

Ghabra, Shafeeq. النكبة ونشوء الشتات الفلسطيني في الكويت (*The Nakhba and the Emergence of the Palestinian Diaspora in Kuwait*). Doha, Qatar: Arab Centre for Research and Policy Studies, 2018.

Ghaddar, Ahmad. "Strait of Hormuz: The World's Most Important Oil Artery." *Reuters.* July 5, 2018. Accessed March 25, 2019. https://www.reuters.com/article/us-iran-oil-factbox/strait -of-hormuz-the-worlds-most-important-oil-artery-idUSKBN1JV24O.

Ghafar, Adel Abdel. "A New Kingdom of Saud?" *Cairo Review of International Affairs*, no. 45 (Winter 2018). https://www.thecairoreview.com/essays/a-new-kingdom-of-saud/.

Ghafar, Adel Abdel. "Saudi Arabia's McKinsey Reshuffle." Brookings Institution. May 11, 2016. https://www.brookings.edu/blog/markaz/2016/05/11/saudi-arabias-mckinsey-reshuffle/.

Ghobash, Mohammed Obaid. "الدولة الخليجية:خمسة مفاهيم للسلطة في الخليج - محمد عبيد غباش" ("Gulf States: Five Concepts of Power in the Gulf"). *Al Jazeera.* October 3, 2004. Accessed September 1, 2018. https://tinyurl.com/ya6jd9u9.

Gibson, Mark. "Food Security—a Commentary: What Is It and Why Is It So Complicated?" *Foods* 1, no. 1 (2012). https://www.ncbi.nlm.nih.gov/pmc/articles/PMC5302220/.

Glasser, Bradley L. "External Capital and Political Liberalizations: A Typology of Middle Eastern Development in the 1980s and 1990s." *Journal of International Affairs* 49, no.1 (1995): 45–73.

Glasze, Georg. "Segregation and Seclusion: The Case of Compounds for Western Expatriates in Saudi Arabia." *GeoJournal* 66 (2006): 84–88.

Glasze, Georg, and Abdallah Al Khayyal. "Gated Housing Estates in the Arab World: Case Studies in Lebanon and Riyadh." *Environment and Planning* 29, no. 3 (2002): 321–336.

Global Food Security Index. Economist Intelligence Unit, London (2019).

Global Hunger Index. "The Concept of the Global Hunger Index." https://www.globalhungerindex .org/about.html.

Goldberg, Jacob. *The Foreign Policy of Saudi Arabia: The Formative Years, 1902–1918.* Cambridge, MA: Harvard University Press, 1986.

Goode, James F. "Assisting Our Brothers, Defending Ourselves: The Iranian Intervention in Oman, 1972–75." *Iranian Studies* 47, no. 3 (2014): 441–462.

Gordon, R. D. *Qatar Investment in UK Property.* Foreign and Commonwealth Office, London (October 28, 1974).

Gräf, Bettina, and Jakob Skovgaard-Petersen. *Global Mufti: The Phenomenon of Yusuf Al-Qaradawi.* London: Hurst, 2009.

Grant, Bruce D. *U.S. Military Expertise for Sale: Private Military Consultants as a Tool of Foreign Policy.* USAWC Strategy Research Project. Pennsylvania: US Army War College, 1998. https:// citeseerx.ist.psu.edu/viewdoc/download?doi=10.1.1.466.5983&rep=rep1&type=pdf.

Gresh, Geoffrey F. *Gulf Security and the U.S. Military: Regime Survival and the Politics of Basing.* Stanford, CA: Stanford University Press, 2015.

Grethlein, Jonas. "'Future Past': Time and Teleology in (Ancient) Historiography." *History and Theory* 53 (October 2014): 309–330.

Guazzone, Laura. "Gulf Co-Operation Council: The Security Policies." *Survival* 30, no. 2 (1988): 134–148.

"Gulf Countries to Experience Worst Economic Crisis in History—IIF." *Reuters.* June 2, 2020. Accessed June 19, 2020. https://uk.reuters.com/article/uk-gulf-economy-iif/gulf-countries-to -experience-worst-economic-crisis-in-history-iif-idUKKBN2390N6.

"Gulf Economic Policy Tracker." American Enterprise Institute (2020). Accessed June 20, 2020. https://www.aei.org/multimedia/gulf-economic-policy-tracker/.

Günel, Gökçe. "The Infinity of Water: Climate Change Adaptation in the Arabian Peninsula." *Public Culture* 28, no. 2 (2016): 291–315.

Habtoor, Abdul Hadi. "الرياض مقرأ للقيادة العسكرية الخليجية الموحدة" ("Riyadh Is the Headquarters of the Unified Gulf Leadership"). *As Sharq Al Awsat.* December 23, 2019. Accessed June 20, 2020. https://tinyurl.com/yau9vjn6.

Hagelin, Björn, and Peter Wallensteen. "Understanding Swedish Military Expenditures." *Cooperation and Conflict* 27, no. 4 (1992): 415–441.

Halliday, Fred. *Arabia without Sultans.* 2nd ed. London: Saqi, 2002.

Halpern, Ben, Julia Stewart Lowndes, and Melanie Frazier. *Ocean Health Index* (2019). https:// oceanhealthindex.org/.

Hamid, Shadi. *Temptations of Power: Islamists and Illiberal Democracy in a New Middle East.* New York: Oxford University Press, 2014.

Hamid, Shadi. "The Tragedy of Egypt's Mohamed Morsi." *The Atlantic.* June 18, 2019. Accessed June 24, 2019. https://www.theatlantic.com/ideas/archive/2019/06/mohamed-morsi-and -end-egyptian-democracy/591982/.

Hamza, Waleed, and Mohiuddin Munawar. "Protecting and Managing the Arabian Gulf: Past, Present and Future." *Aquatic Ecosystem Health and Management* 12, no. 4 (2009): 429–439.

Hanieh, Adam. *Money, Markets, and Monarchies: The Gulf Cooperation Council and the Political Economy of the Contemporary Middle East.* Cambridge: Cambridge University Press, 2018.

Hansen, Lene. "The Little Mermaid's Silent Security Dilemma and the Absence of Gender in the Copenhagen School." *Millennium Journal of International Studies* 29 (2000): 285–306.

Harris, Jerry. "Statist Globalization in China, Russia and the Gulf States." In *The Nation in the Global Era*, edited by Jerry Harris, 29–53. Leiden, Netherlands: Brill, 2009.

Hashimoto, Kohei, Jareer Elass, and Stacy Eller. "Liquefied Natural Gas from Qatar: The Qatargas Project." Baker Institute Energy Forum, Rice University (Stanford, CA: December 2004).

Hassan, Hassan. "The 'Conscious Uncoupling' of Wahhabism and Saudi Arabia." *New Lines Magazine.* February 22, 2022. https://newlinesmag.com/argument/the-conscious-uncoupling -of-wahhabism-and-saudi-arabia/.

Hayek, Friedrich August. "The Fatal Conceit: The Errors of Socialism." In *The Collected Works of F. A. Hayek*, edited by W. W. Bartley III. London: Routledge, 1992.

Heard-Bay, Frauke. "The United Arab Emirates: Statehood and Nation-Building in a Traditional Society." *Middle East Journal* 59, no. 3 (2005): 357–375.

Heeg, Jennifer Carol. *Seeing Security: Societal Securitization in Qatar.* PhD dissertation, Georgetown University, 2010.

Held, David, and Kristian Coates Ulrichsen. "Introduction: The Transformation of the Gulf." In *The Transformation of the Gulf: Politics, Economics, and the Global Order*, edited by David Held and Kristian Coates Ulrichsen. Abingdon, UK: Routledge, 2012.

Hemingway, Ernest. *The Sun Also Rises.* eBook: Digital Fire, 2022.

Henderson, E. F. *Industrialization in Qatar.* Foreign and Commonwealth Office, London, FCO 8/2296 (July 8, 1974).

Henderson, Simon. *A Fifty-Year Reign? MBS and the Future of Saudi Arabia.* Washington: DC, Washington Institute for Near East Policy, April 2019.

Henderson, Simon, and Kristian Coates Ulrichsen. *Kuwait: A Changing System under Stress.* Washington, DC: Washington Institute for Near East Policy, October 2019. https://www .washingtoninstitute.org/policy-analysis/kuwait-changing-system-under-stress-sudden -succession-essay-series.

Herb, Michael. *All in the Family.* Albany: State University of New York, 1999.

Herb, Michael. "A Nation of Bureaucrats: Political Participation and Economic Diversification in Kuwait and the United Arab Emirates." *International Journal of Middle East Studies* 41, no. 3 (2009): 375–95.

Herb, Michael. *The Wages of Oil: Parliaments and Economic Development in Kuwait and the UAE.* Ithaca, NY: Cornell University Press, 2014.

Hermann, Margaret G., and Joe D. Hagan. "International Decision Making: Leadership Matters." *Foreign Policy*, no. 110 (1998): 124–137.

Hertog, Steffen. "The Costs of Counter-Revolution in the GCC." *Foreign Policy*. May 31, 2011. Accessed November 1, 2015. http://foreignpolicy.com/2011/05/31/the-costs-of-counter-revolution-in-the-gcc/.

Hertog, Steffen. *Princes, Brokers, and Bureaucrats: Oil and the State in Saudi Arabia*. Ithaca, NY: Cornell University Press, 2011.

Hertog, Steffen. "Rentier Militaries in the Gulf States: The Price of Coup-Proofing." *International Journal of Middle East Studies* 43, no. 3 (2011): 400–402. http://dx.doi.org/10.1017/S0020743811000560.

Hibbert, Reginald. *President Giscard's Tour of the Gulf: Commercial and Economic Aspects*. Foreign and Commonwealth Office, London, FCO 8/3447/5 (March 17, 1980).

Hinnebusch, Raymond. "Foreign Policy in the Middle East." In *The Foreign Policies of Middle East States*, edited by Raymond Hinnebusch and Anoushiravan Ehteshami. Boulder, CO: Lynne Rienner, 2014.

Hinnebusch, Raymond. "The Politics of Identity in Middle East International Relations." In *International Relations of the Middle East*, edited by Louise Fawcett. Oxford: Oxford University Press, 2016.

HM Government Policy in Persian Gulf. Foreign and Commonwealth Office, London (January 1–December 31, 1971).

Hobsbawm, Eric, and Terence Ranger. *The Invention of Tradition*. Cambridge: Cambridge University Press, 2010.

Holes, Clive D. "Language and Identity in the Arabian Gulf." *Journal of Arabian Studies* 1, no. 2 (2011): 129–145.

Hopwood, Derek. *The Arabian Peninsula: Society and Politics*. Abingdon, UK: Routledge, 2005.

Hubbard, Ben. "One Year on, Shadow of Khashoggi's Killing Stalks Saudi Prince." *New York Times*. October 2, 2019. https://www.nytimes.com/2019/10/02/world/middleeast/khashoggi-killing-mbs-anniversary.html.

Hubbard, Ben. "Saudi Arabia Agrees to Let Women Drive." *New York Times*. September 26, 2017. https://www.nytimes.com/2017/09/26/world/middleeast/saudi-arabia-women-drive.html.

Hubbard, Ben. "Saudi Arabia Lightens up, Building Entertainment Industry from Scratch." *New York Times*. March 17, 2018. https://www.nytimes.com/2018/03/17/world/middleeast/saudi-arabia-entertainment-economy.html.

Hubbard, Ben. "Saudi Arabia Says Detainees Handed over More Than $100 Billion." *New York Times*. January 30, 2018. https://www.nytimes.com/2018/01/30/world/middleeast/saudi-arabia-corruption.html.

Hubbard, Ben. "Saudi King Unleashes a Torrent of Money as Bonuses Flow to the Masses." *New York Times*. February 19, 2019. https://www.nytimes.com/2015/02/20/world/middleeast/saudi-king-unleashes-a-torrent-as-bonuses-flow-to-the-masses.html.

Hubbard, Ben. "Why Spy on Twitter? For Saudi Arabia, It's the Town Square." *New York Times*. November 7, 2019. https://www.nytimes.com/2019/11/07/world/middleeast/saudi-arabia-twitter-arrests.html.

Hubbard, Ben, and Vivian Yee. "Saudi Arabia Extends New Rights to Women in Blow to Oppressive System." *New York Times*. August 2, 2019. https://www.nytimes.com/2019/08/02/world/middleeast/saudi-arabia-guardianship.html.

Hudson, Michael C. "After the Gulf War: Prospects for Democratization in the Arab World." *Middle East Journal* 45, no. 3 (1991): 407–426.

Hughes, Geraint. "A 'Model Campaign' Reappraised: The Counter-Insurgency War in Dhofar, Oman, 1965–1975." *Journal of Strategic Studies* 32, no. 2 (2009): 271–305.

Human Development Report 2010. United Nations Development Programme. Basingstoke, UK: Palgrave Macmillan, November 2010.

Humfrey, C. T. W. *Middle East Contracts*. Foreign and Commonwealth Office, London, FCO 8/3820 (March 16, 1981).

Huntington, Samuel P. "Democracy's Third Wave." *Journal of Democracy* 2, no. 2 (1991): 12–34.

Huntington, Samuel P. *Political Order in Changing Societies*. New Haven, CT and London: Yale University Press, 1968.

Huysmans, Jef. "Revisiting Copenhagen: Or, on the Creative Development of a Security Studies Agenda in Europe." *European Journal of International Relations* 4, no. 4 (1998): 479–505.

Hvidt, Martin. "The Dubai Model: An Outline of Key Development-Process Elements in Dubai." *International Journal of Middle East Studies* 41, no. 3 (2009): 397–418. https://doi.org/doi:10.1017/S0020743809091120.

Hvidt, Martin. *Economic Diversification in GCC Countries: Past Record and Future Trends*. London School of Economics (January 2013).

Hvidt, Martin. "Planning for Development in the GCC States: A Content Analysis of Current Development Plans." *Journal of Arabian Studies* 2, no. 2 (2012): 189–207.

Hvidt, Martin. "The Role of 'Lavish Construction Schemes' in 'Late-Late-Late' Developing Societies: The Case of the Arab Gulf States." In *Under Construction: Logics of Urbanism in the Gulf Region*, edited by Steffen Wippel, Katrin Bromber, Christian Steiner, and Birgit Krawietz, 55–68. Farnham, UK: Ashgate, 2014.

Hvidt, Martin. "The State and the Knowledge Economy in the Gulf: Structural and Motivational Challenges." *Muslim World* 105, no. 1 (2015): 24–45.

Ilias, Shayerah. *Iran's Economic Conditions: U.S. Policy Issues*. Washington, DC: Congressional Research Service, June 15, 2009.

The Impact of the Blockade on Families in Qatar. Doha, Qatar: Hamad bin Khalifah University Press, 2018. https://www.difi.org.qa/wp-content/uploads/2018/07/Blockade-English-FINAL.pdf.

"In Latest Spending Cut, Oman Not Renewing Majority of Foreign Consultant Contracts." *Al Monitor*. May 29, 2020. Accessed June 20, 2020. https://www.al-monitor.com/pulse/originals/2020/05/oman-contracts-spending-coronavirus-economy-oil-royal-court.html.

"Intel: How Saudi Arabia Is Looking Past the US for Arms." *Al Monitor*. November 8, 2018. https://www.al-monitor.com/pulse/originals/2018/11/intel-saudi-arabia-looking-past-us-arms-spain-south-africa.html.

Jabbari, Alexander. "The Ancient Word Linking Oman, Thailand and Aboriginal Australia." *The National* (n.d.). Accessed October 21, 2021. https://www.thenationalnews.com/opinion/comment/the-ancient-word-linking-oman-thailand-and-aboriginal-australia-1.1247153.

Jägerskog, Anders, Michael Schulz, and Ashok Swain. "Contents." In *Routledge Handbook on Middle East Security*, edited by Anders Jägerskog, Michael Schulz, and Ashok Swain. Abingdon, UK: Routledge, 2019.

Janis, Irving L. *Victims of Groupthink: A Psychological Study of Foreign-Policy Decisions and Fiascoes.* Boston: Houghton Mifflin, 1972.

Jennings, Richard P., Joy Singarayer, Emma J. Stone, Uta Krebs-Kanzow, Vyacheslav Khon, Kerim H. Nisancioglu, Madlene Pfeiffer, et al. "The Greening of Arabia: Multiple Opportunities for Human Occupation of the Arabian Peninsula During the Late Pleistocene Inferred from an Ensemble of Climate Model Simulations." *Quaternary International* 382 (2015): 181–99.

The Jobs Agenda for the Gulf Cooperation Council Countries. Washington, DC: World Bank Group, 2018.

Jones, Calvert W. "Adviser to the King: Experts Rationalization, and Legitimacy." *World Politics* 71, no. 1 (2019): 1–43.

Jones, Calvert W. *Bedouins into Bourgeois: Remaking Citizens for Globalization.* Cambridge: Cambridge University Press, 2017.

Jones, Edward, Manzoor Qadir, Michelle van Vliet, Vladimir Smakhtin, and Seong-mu Kang. "The State of Desalination and Brine Production: A Global Outlook." *Science of the Total Environment* 657 (2018).

Jones, Henry. "Joint UK-Qatari Typhoon Squadron Stands Up." *UK Defence Journal.* July 25, 2018. https://ukdefencejournal.org.uk/joint-uk-qatari-typhoon-squadron-stands-up/.

Jones, Jeremy, and Nicholas Ridout. *A History of Modern Oman.* New York: Cambridge University Press, 2015.

Jones, Marc Owen. *Political Repression in Bahrain.* Cambridge: Cambridge University Press, 2020.

Jones, Toby. *Desert Kingdom: How Oil and Water Forged Modern Saudi Arabia.* Cambridge, MA: Harvard University Press, 2010.

Joseph, Sabrina. "Farming the Desert: Agriculture in the Oil Frontier, the Case of the United Arab Emirates, 1940s to 1990s." *British Journal of Middle Eastern Studies* 45, no. 5 (2018): 678–694.

Kablan, Marwan. "سياسة قطر الخارجية: النخبة في مواجهة الجغرافيا" ("Qatari Foreign Policy: Elites Versus Geography"). *Siyasat Arabiya,* no. 28 (September 2017). https://www.dohainstitute.org/ar/Lists/ACRPS-PDFDocumentLibrary/Siyassat28_kablan_Qatar%27s_Foreign_Policy_Elite_Versus_Geography.pdf.

Kamrava, Mehran. "The Arab Spring and the Saudi-Led Counterrevolution." *Orbis* 56, no. 1 (2012): 96–104.

Kamrava, Mehran. "The Political Economy of Rentierism in the Persian Gulf." In *Political Economy of the Persian Gulf,* edited by Mehran Kamrava. New York: Columbia University Press, 2012.

Kamrava, Mehran. *Qatar: Small State, Big Politics.* Ithaca, NY: Cornell University Press, 2013.

Kamrava, Mehran. *Troubled Waters: Insecurity in the Persian Gulf.* Ithaca, NY: Cornell University Press, 2018.

Kapiszewski, Andrzej. "Arab Labor Migration to the GCC States." In *Arab Migration in a Globalized World.* Geneva: International Organization for Migration, 2004, 115–133.

Kapiszewski, Andrzej. "Elections and Parliamentary Activity in the GCC States: Broadening Political Participation in the Gulf Monarchies." In *Constitutional Reform and Political Participation in the Gulf*, edited by Abdulhadi Khalaf and Giacomo Luciani, 88–133. Dubai: Gulf Research Center, 2006.

Karlsrud, John. "Responsibility to Protect and Theorising Normative Change in International Organisations: From Weber to the Sociology of Professions." *Global Responsibility to Protect* 5, no. 1 (2013): 3–27.

Katzman, Kenneth. *Oman: Politics, Security, and U.S. Policy*. Congressional Research Service (June 17, 2020).

Kay, J. C. *Saudi Arabia: Technological Cooperation in Alternative Sources of Energy*. Foreign and Commonwealth Office, London, FCO 8/2592 (July 19, 1975).

Kaya, Abdullah, Nazli Choucri, I-Tsung Tsai, and Toufic Mezher. "Energy Consumption and Transition Dynamics to a Sustainable Future under a Rentier Economy: The Case of the GCC States." In *Sustainability in the Gulf: Challenges and Opportunities*, edited by Elie Azar and Mohamed Abdel Raouf, 197–209. Abingdon, UK: Routledge, 2017.

Kelly, J. B. *Eastern Arabian Frontiers*. London: Frederick A. Praeger, 1964.

Kelly, John B. "The Buraimi Oasis Dispute." *International Affairs (Royal Institute of International Affairs 1944-)* 32, no. 3 (1956): 318–26.

Kepel, Gilles. *The War for Muslim Minds*. Cambridge, MA: Harvard University Press, 2006.

Kerr, Simeon. "DP World Profits Rise by a Tenth despite 'Geopolitical Challenges.'" *Financial Times*. March 14, 2019. https://www.ft.com/content/2f339cfc-4628-11e9-a965-23d669740bfb.

Kerr, Simeon. "Dubai Fears the End of Its 'Build It and They Will Come' Model." *Financial Times*. April 1, 2019. https://www.ft.com/content/4d169d0c-4be4-11e9-8b7f-d49067e0f50d.

Kerr, Simeon. "New Monarch and Yemen Offensive Spark Wave of Saudi Nationalism." *Financial Times*. May 24, 2015. https://www.ft.com/content/3b9358b4-feee-11e4-84b2-00144feabdc0.

Kerr, Simeon. "Oman Swears in New Sultan Following Death of Qaboos." *Financial Times*. January 11, 2020. https://www.ft.com/content/b274993a-3444-11ea-a6d3-9a26f8c3cba4.

Kerr, Simeon. "Saudi Investors Check out after Hotel Turned into Luxury Prison." *Financial Times*. November 17, 2017. https://www.ft.com/content/4cb6a472-caf5-11e7-ab18-7a9fb7d6163e.

Kerr, Simeon. "Saudi King Stamps His Authority with Staff Shake-up and Handouts." *Financial Times*. January 30, 2015. https://www.ft.com/content/8045e3e0-a850-11e4-bd17-00144feab7de.

Kerr, Simeon. "UAE Pushes Merchant Families to Open up to Competition." *Financial Times*. December 26, 2021. https://www.ft.com/content/116b083a-1811-4501-ad9b-2f6a3183db3e.

Keulertz, Martin, and Tony Allan. "The Water-Energy-Food Nexus in the MENA Region." In *Routledge Handbook on Middle East Security*, edited by Anders Jagerskog, Ashok Swain, and Michael Schulz. New York: Routledge, 2019.

Khadduri, Majid. "The Role of the Military in Middle East Politics." *American Political Science Review* 47, no. 2 (June 1953): 511–524.

Khalaf, Abdulhadi. *Bahrain's Parliament: The Quest for a Role*. Sada. Washington, DC: Carnegie Endowment for Middle East Peace, 2004. https://carnegieendowment.org/sada/21282.

Khalaf, Sulayman. "The Evolution of the Gulf City Type, Oil, and Globalization." In *Globalization and the Gulf*, edited by John W. Fox, Nada Mourtada-Sabbah, and Mohammed Al Mutawa, 254–275. Abingdon, UK: Routledge, 2006.

Khalili, Laleh. "The Infrastructural Power of the Military: The Geoeconomic Role of the U.S. Army Corps of Engineers in the Arabian Peninsula." *European Journal of International Relations* 24, no. 4 (2018): 911–933.

"The King's Risky Move." *The Economist*. November 26, 2011. https://www.economist.com /middle-east-and-africa/2011/11/26/the-kings-risky-move.

"Kingdom of Saudi Arabia Budget Report 2019." *KPMG*. December 21, 2018. https://home .kpmg/sa/en/home/insights/2018/12/kingdom-of-saudi-arabia-budget-report.html.

Kinninmont, Jane. "Bahrain." In *Power and Politics in the Persian Gulf Monarchies*, edited by Christopher Davidson. London: Hurst, 2011.

Kinninmont, Jane. "Citizenship in the Gulf." In *The Gulf States and the Arab Uprisings*, edited by Ana Echagüe, 47–58. Spain: FRIDE, 2013.

Kinninmont, Jane. *Future Trends in the Gulf*. London: Chatham House, 2015. https://www .chathamhouse.org/sites/default/files/field/field_document/20150218FutureTrends GCCKinninmont.pdf.

Kinnvall, Catarina. *Globalization and Religious Nationalism in India: The Search for Ontological Security*. London: Routledge, 2007.

Kirkpatrick, David D. "Saudis End Purge That Began with Hundreds Locked in the Ritz-Carlton." *New York Times*. January 31, 2019. https://www.nytimes.com/2019/01/31/world/middleeast /saudi-arabia-corruption-purge.html.

Kirkpatrick, David, Christoph Koettl, Allison McCann, Eric Schmitt, Anjali Singhvi, and Gus Wezerek. "Who Was behind the Saudi Oil Attack? What the Evidence Shows." *New York Times*. September 16, 2019. https://www.nytimes.com/interactive/2019/09/16/world /middleeast/trump-saudi-arabia-oil-attack.html.

Knights, Michael. *Troubled Waters: Future U.S. Security Assistance in the Persian Gulf*. Washington, DC: Washington Institute for Near East Policy, 2006.

Koch, Christian. "Economics Trumps Politics in the United Arab Emirates." In *Political Change in the Arab Gulf States*, edited by Mary Ann Tetreault, Gwenn Okruhlik, and Andrzej Kapiszewski, 167–189. London: Lynne Rienner, 2011.

Koch, Natalie. "Agtech in Arabia: 'Spectacular Forgetting' and the Technopolitics of Greening the Desert." *Journal of Political Ecology* 26, no. 1 (2019): 666–86.

Kolodziej, Edward A. "Renaissance in Security Studies? Caveat Lector!" *International Studies Quarterly* 36, no. 4 (1992): 421–438.

Kolodziej, Edward A. *Security and International Relations*. New York: Cambridge University Press, 2005.

Kostiner, Joseph. "On Instruments and Their Designers: The Ikhwan of Najd and the Emergence of the Saudi State." *Middle Eastern Studies* 21, no. 3 (1985): 298–323.

Kraft, Joseph. "Letter from Saudi Arabia." *New Yorker*. July 4, 1983.

Kraft, Joseph. "Letter from Saudi Arabia." *New Yorker*. October 20, 1975.

Krane, Jim. *Energy Kingdoms*. New York: Columbia University Press, 2019.

Krause, Keith, and Michael Charles Williams. "From Strategy to Security: Foundations of Critical Security Studies." In *Critical Security Studies*, edited by Keith Krause and Michael Charles Williams, 33–59. Minneapolis: University of Minnesota Press, 1997.

Krause, Wanda. "Gender and Participation in the Arab Gulf." In *The Transformation of the Gulf: Politics, Economics, and the Global Order*, edited by David Held and Kristian Coates Ulrichsen. Abingdon, UK: Routledge, 2012.

Kuffel, Glenn P. *The Gulf Cooperation Council's Peninsular Shield Force*. Newport, RI: U.S. Naval War College, 2000.

Kulish, Nicholas, and Mark Mazzetti. "Saudi Royal Family Is Still Spending in an Age of Austerity." *New York Times*. December 27, 2016. https://www.nytimes.com/2016/12/27/world /middleeast/saudi-royal-family-money.html.

Kumar, Sachin. "IPO of Baladna Expected in Last Quarter of 2019." *The Peninsula*. May 26, 2019. https://thepeninsulaqatar.com/article/26/05/2019/IPO-of-Baladna-expected-in-last -quarter-of-2019.

Kuwait Selected Issues. Washington, DC: International Monetary Fund, January 2018.

"Kuwaiti Islamists Take a Hit in Parliament." *Arab Weekly*. March 24, 2019. Accessed July 2, 2020. https://thearabweekly.com/kuwaiti-islamists-take-hit-parliament.

"Kuwaiti Succession Gets Clearer, but Disappoints Next Generation." *Gulf States Newsletter* 775. February 10, 2006. https://www.gsn-online.com/downloadable/2084.

LaBianca, Oystein S., and Sandra Arnold Scham. *Connectivity in Antiquity: Globalization as a Long-Term Historical Process*. Abingdon, UK: Routledge, 2016.

Labor Market Reforms to Boost Employment and Productivity in the GCC—an Update. Washington, DC: International Monetary Fund, October 25, 2014.

Lacey, Robert. *Inside the Kingdom*. London: Arrow, 2010.

Lackner, Helen. *A House Built on Sand*. London: Ithaca, 1978.

Lacroix, Stephane. "Saudi Arabia Finally Let Women Drive. Don't Mistake It for Democratic Reform." *Washington Post*. October 5, 2017. https://www.washingtonpost.com/news/monkey -cage/wp/2017/10/05/saudi-arabia-finally-let-women-drive-dont-mistake-it-for-democratic -reform/.

Lacroix, Stephane. "Understanding Stability and Dissent in the Kingdom." In *Saudi Arabia in Transition: Insights on Social, Political, Economic and Religious Change*, edited by Bernard Haykel, Thomas Hegghammer, and Stephane Lacroix, 167–180. Cambridge: Cambridge University Press, 2015.

Lacroix, Stephane, and George Holoch (trans.). *Awakening Islam*. Cambridge, MA: Harvard University Press, 2011.

Ladwig, Walter C. III. "Supporting Allies in Counterinsurgency: Britain and the Dhofar Rebellion." *Small Wars and Insurgencies* 19, no. 1 (2008): 62–88.

Lahn, Glada. "Fuel, Food and Utilities Price Reforms in the GCC: A Wake-up Call for Business." Chatham House Research Paper. London: Royal Institute of International Affairs, 2016.

Lahn, Glada, and Paul Stevens. *Burning Oil to Keep Cool: The Hidden Energy Crisis in Saudi Arabia*. Chatham House Research Paper. London: Royal Institute of International Affairs, 2011. https://www.chathamhouse.org/sites/default/files/public/Research/Energy,%20Environment %20and%20Development/1211pr_lahn_stevens.pdf.

Lamb, A. T. *First Impressions of Kuwait*. Kuwait: Foreign and Commonwealth Office (August 1, 1974).

Lambert, Laurent A., and Hisham Bin Hashim. "A Century of Saudi-Qatari Food Insecurity: Paradigmatic Shifts in the Geopolitics, Economics and Sustainability of Gulf States Animal Agriculture." *Arab World Geographer* 20, no. 4 (2017): 261–281.

Leber, Andrew. "@Mckinsey Advising #Saudi on Gov't Reform Way Back in 1980. Cc @Adelaghafar." Twitter. June 21, 2016. https://twitter.com/AndrewMLeber/status/745337286758379520.

Leber, Andrew Michael, and Charlotte Lysa. "Onwards and Upwards with Women in the Gulf." *Middle East Report.* January 11, 2018. https://merip.org/2018/01/onwards-and-upwards-with -women-in-the-gulf/.

Leigh, David, and Rob Evans. "Secrets of Yamamah." *The Guardian.* Accessed July 30, 2017. https://www.theguardian.com/baefiles/page/0,,2095831,00.html.

Le Renard, Amélie. *A Society of Young Women: Opportunities of Place, Power, and Reform in Saudi Arabia.* Stanford, CA: Stanford University Press, 2014.

Le Renard, Amélie. *Western Privilege: Work, Intimacy, and Postcolonial Hierarchies in Dubai.* Stanford, CA: Stanford University Press, 2021.

Lesch, Ann M. "Osama Bin Laden: Embedded in the Middle East Crises." *Middle East Policy* 9, no. 2 (2002): 82–91.

Longva, Anh Nga. "Nationalism in Pre-Modern Guise: The Discourse on Hadhar and Badu in Kuwait." *International Journal of Middle East Studies* 38 (2006): 171–187.

Looney, Robert E. "Review: The Arab World's Uncomfortable Experience with Globalization." *Middle East Journal* 61, no. 1 (Spring 2007): 341–345.

Low, Jwen Fai, Maryam R. D. Al-Yammahi, and Andrea Schiffauerova. "The Gulf Region's Commitment to a Sustainable Lifestyle: A Bibliometric Study." In *Sustainability in the Gulf: Challenges and Opportunities,* edited by Elie Azar and Mohamed Abdel Raouf, 7–30. Abingdon, UK: Routledge, 2017.

Lubold, Gordon, and Michael C. Bender. "U.S. to Remove Patriot Missile Batteries from Saudi Arabia." *Wall Street Journal.* May 7, 2020. https://www.wsj.com/articles/u-s-to-remove -patriot-missile-batteries-from-saudi-arabia-11588867916.

Lucas, Russell E. "Monarchical Authoritarianism: Survival and Political Liberalization in a Middle Eastern Regime Type." *International Journal of Middle East Studies* 36, no. 1 (2004): 103–119.

Lugard, Frederick. *The Dual Mandate in British Tropical Africa.* Edinburgh and London: William Blackwood, 1922.

Luomi, Mari. "Environmental Change and Security." In *Facets of Security in the United Arab Emirates,* edited by Kristian Alexander and William Gueraiche. Abingdon, UK: Routledge, 2022.

Luomi, Mari. *Environmental Security: Addressing Water and Climate Change Risks in the UAE.* Emirates Diplomatic Academy, Abu Dhabi (April 2019).

Luomi, Mari. *The Gulf Monarchies and Climate Change: Abu Dhabi and Qatar in an Era of Natural Unsustainability.* London: Hurst, 2012.

Lynch, Colum. "Arms Sales and the Militarization of the Middle East." *Foreign Policy.* October 22, 2013.

Mabon, Simon. "Sovereignty, Bare Life and the Arab Uprisings." *Third World Quarterly* 38, no. 8 (2017): 1782–99.

MacDonald, Fiona. "Kuwait's Budget Crunch May Push It to Tap Fund for Life after Oil." *Bloomberg*. July 6, 2020. Accessed July 7, 2020. https://tinyurl.com/y8bavjzv.

MacDonald, Fiona. "Kuwait Doesn't Want to Be an Expat-Majority Nation Anymore." *Bloomberg*. June 3, 2020. https://www.bloomberg.com/news/articles/2020-06-03/kuwait-needs-to-slash -expatriate-population-to-30-premier-says.

Mackey, Hamish R., Huda Alkandari, and Gordon Mckay. "The Role of Tariffs in Reducing Residential Water Demand in Qatar." *Qatar Foundation Annual Research Conference Proceedings*, no. 1 (2018).

MacLean, Matthew. "Spatial Transformations and the Emergence of 'the National': Infrastructures and the Formation of the United Arab Emirates, 1950–1980." Dissertation, New York University, 2017.

"Madagascar Leader Axes Land Deal." *BBC*. March 19, 2009. http://news.bbc.co.uk/1/hi/world /africa/7952628.stm.

Maierbrugger, Arno. "Domain Grabber Registers Burj Khalifa's Web Address." *Gulf News*. January 6, 2010. https://gulfnews.com/business/domain-grabber-registers-burj-khalifas-web -address-1.563400.

Malbrunot, Georges. "Oman: La Succession de l'inamovible Sultan Qabus Plane Sur Le Pays" ("Oman: The Succession of the Irremovable Sultan Qabus Hovers Over the Country"). *Le Figaro*. March 19, 2019. https://www.lefigaro.fr/international/2019/03/18/01003-20190318 ARTFIG00164-oman-la-succession-de-l-inamovible-sultan-qabus-plane-sur-le-pays.php.

Malek, Caline. "Why Middle East Publics Have Mixed Views on Climate Change." *Arab News*. October 5, 2019. https://www.arabnews.com/node/1564706/middle-east.

Malik, Adeel. *The Political Economy of Macroeconomic Policy in Arab Resource-Rich Countries*. Working Papers 1117. Economic Research Forum. Revised June 7, 2017.

Marcel, Valeris. "National Oil Companies in the Middle East." In *Oil Titans*, edited by Valeris Marcel. Washington, DC: Brookings, 2005.

"Marmore: Gulf Cooperation Council (GCC) Sovereign Wealth Funds Experience Asset Growth." *Sovereign Wealth Fund Institute*. June 4, 2019. https://www.swfinstitute.org/news /73342/marmore-gulf-cooperation-council-gcc-sovereign-wealth-funds-dominate-in-asset -growth.

Matthews, C. D. "Bedouin Life in Contemporary Arabia: Preliminary Remarks." *Rivista Degli Studi Orientali* 35 (1960): 31–61.

Matthiesen, Toby. "Red Arabia: Anti-Colonialism, the Cold War, and the Long Sixties in the Gulf States." In *Routledge Handbook of the Global Sixties*, 94–105. London: Routledge, 2018.

Matthiesen, Toby. "Sectarianization as Securitization: Identity Politics and Counter-Revolution in Bahrain." In *Sectarianization: Mapping the New Politics of the Middle East*, edited by Nader Hashemi and Danny Postel. London: Hurst, 2017.

Mazzetti, Mark, Ben Hubbard, Walt Bogdanich, and Michael Forsythe. "Consulting Firms Keep Lucrative Saudi Alliance, Shaping Crown Prince's Vision." *New York Times*. November 4, 2018. https://www.nytimes.com/2018/11/04/world/middleeast/mckinsey-bcg-booz-allen-saudi -khashoggi.html.

McCormick, Michael, Ulf Büntgen, Mark A. Cane, Edward R. Cook, Kyle Harper, Peter Huybers, Thomas Litt, et al. "Climate Change during and after the Roman Empire: Reconstructing the

Past from Scientific and Historical Evidence." *Journal of Interdisciplinary History* 43, no. 2 (2012): 169–220.

McDonald, Matt. "Securitization and the Construction of Security." *European Journal of International Relations* 14, no. 4 (2008): 563–587.

McFarland, Victor. *Oil Powers: A History of the U.S.-Saudi Alliance.* New York: Columbia University Press, 2020.

McNaugher, Thomas L. *Arms and Oil: U.S. Military Strategy and the Persian Gulf.* Washington, DC: Brookings Institution, 1985.

McSweeney, Bill. "Identity and Security: Buzan and the Copenhagen School." *Review of International Studies* 22, no. 1 (1996): 81–93.

Melikian, Levon H. "Gulf Reactions to Western Cultural Pressures." In *The Arab Gulf and the West*, edited by B. R. Pridham, 203–218. Beckenham, UK: Croom Helm, 1985.

Memorandum from Secretary of State Rusk to President Kennedy. U.S. State Department. Office of the Historian (June 12, 1963).

Menaldo, Victor. "The Middle East and North Africa's Resilient Monarchs." *Journal of Politics* 74, no. 3 (2012): 707–722.

Menoret, Pascal. "Cities in the Arabian Peninsula: Introduction" *City* 18, no. 6 (2013): 698–700.

Menoret, Pascal. *Joyriding in Riyadh: Oil, Urbanism, and Road Revolt.* New York: Cambridge University Press, 2014.

"The Middle East and the Mediterranean." *Military Balance*, no. 1 (1980).

"The Middle East and the Mediterranean." *Military Balance*, no. 1 (1973).

"The Middle East Needs Radical Agricultural Transformation." Castlereagh Associates, Surrey, UK. July 26, 2019. Accessed June 2, 2020. https://castlereagh.net/the-middle-east-needs -radical-agricultural-transformation/.

Miers, David. *Confidential Letter.* Foreign and Commonwealth Office, London (July 15, 1986).

Milhench, Claire. "Global Sovereign Fund Assets Jump to $7.45 Trillion—Preqin." *Reuters.* April 12, 2018. Accessed June 20, 2020. https://tinyurl.com/yb2rbfvf.

"Milk Sheikhs: Why Qatar Is Raising Cows in the Desert." *The Economist.* May 17, 2018.

Miller, Judith. "Creating Modern Oman: An Interview with Sultan Qabus." *Foreign Affairs* 76 (May/June 1997): 13. https://www.foreignaffairs.com/articles/oman/1997-05-01/creating -modern-oman-interview-sultan-qabus.

Miller, Rory. *Desert Kingdoms to Global Powers.* London: Yale University Press, 2016.

Mirgani, Suzi. "Consumer Citizenship: National Identity and Museum Merchandise in Qatar." *Middle East Journal* 73, no. 4 (2019): 555–572.

Mirza, Hussein Ismail. "أسباب العزوف عن المشاركة السياسية في الإنتخابات في الكويت: دراسة مسحية" ("Reasons for Not Participating in Political Elections in Kuwait: A Survey"). المركز الديمقراطي العربي (Arab Democratic Centre) (May 2017).

Mirzoev, Tokhir N., Ling Zhu, Yang Yang, Tian Zhang, Erik Roos, Andrea Pescatori, and Akito Matsumoto. *The Future of Oil and Fiscal Sustainability in the GCC Region.* Departmental Paper. Washington, DC: International Monetary Fund, 2020. https://www.imf.org /en/Publications/Departmental-Papers-Policy-Papers/Issues/2020/01/31/The-Future-of -Oil-and-Fiscal-Sustainability-in-the-GCC-Region-48934.

Mitchell, Jocelyn Sage, and Justin J. Gengler. "What Money Can't Buy: Wealth, Inequality, and Economic Satisfaction in the Rentier State." *Political Research Quarterly* 72, no. 1 (2019): 75–89. https://doi.org/10.1177/1065912918776128.

Mitchell, Timothy. *Carbon Democracy: Political Power in the Age of Oil.* London: Verso, 2011.

Moini, Joy S., Tora K. Bikson, Richard Neu, and Laura DeSisto. *The Reform of Qatar University.* Santa Monica, CA: RAND Corporation, 2009.

Moore-Gilbert, Kylie. "Sectarian Divide and Rule in Bahrain: A Self-Fulfilling Prophecy?" *Middle East Institute.* January 19, 2016. https://www.mei.edu/publications/sectarian-divide -and-rule-bahrain-self-fulfilling-prophecy.

Moritz, Jessie. "Reformers and the Rentier State: Re-Evaluating the Co-Optation Mechanism in Rentier State Theory." *Journal of Arabian Studies* 8, no. 1 (2018): 46–64. https://doi.org/10.1080 /21534764.2018.1546933.

Moser, Sarah, Marian Swain, and Mohammed H. Alkhabbaz. "King Abdullah Economic City: Engineering Saudi Arabia's Post-Oil Future." *Cities* 45 (2015): 71–80.

Mouline, Nabil. "Enforcing and Reinforcing the State's Islam." In *Saudi Arabia in Transition: Insights on Social, Political, Economic and Religious Change*, edited by Bernard Haykel, Thomas Hegghammer, and Stephane Lacroix, 44–68. Cambridge: Cambridge University Press, 2015.

"Moving Saudi Arabia's Economy Beyond Oil." *Mckinsey.* December 1, 2015. https://www .mckinsey.com/featured-insights/employment-and-growth/moving-saudi-arabias -economy-beyond-oil.

Murad, Imad. "عرضة أهل قطر.. الحصار يلمّ شمل القبائل" ("The Dance of the Qatari People . . . the Siege Unifies the Tribes"). December 18, 2018. Accessed May 1, 2020. https://tinyurl.com/y7hd7sss.

Murphy, Emma C. "Institutions, Islam and Democracy Promotion: Explaining the Resilience of the Authoritarian State." *Mediterranean Politics* 13, no. 3 (2008): 459–466.

"Museum to Commemorate UAE's Martyrs to Be Built." *The National.* September 7, 2015. https://www.thenationalnews.com/uae/government/museum-to-commemorate-uae-s -martyrs-to-be-built-1.132202.

Nakhleh, Emile A. *Bahrain.* New York: DC Heath, 1976.

Nakhleh, Emile A. "Could Bahrain's New Prime Minister Chart a New Path toward Reform?" *Responsible Statecraft.* November 19, 2020. Accessed December 28, 2021. https://responsible statecraft.org/2020/11/19/could-bahrains-new-prime-minister-chart-a-new-path-toward-reform/.

Naser, Humood A. "Assessment and Management of Heavy Metal Pollution in the Marine Environment of the Arabian Gulf: A Review." *Marine Pollution Bulletin* 72, no. 1 (2013): 6–13.

Nehme, Michel G. "Saudi Arabia 1950–80: Between Nationalism and Religion." *Middle Eastern Studies* 30, no. 4 (1994): 930–943.

Nemeth, Bence. *How to Achieve Defence Cooperation in Europe? The Subregional Approach.* Bristol, UK: Bristol University Press, 2022.

Neo, Ric. "Religious Securitisation and Institutionalised Sectarianism in Saudi Arabia." *Critical Studies on Security* 8, no. 3 (2020): 1–20.

Neumann, Ronald. "Bahrain's Rulers Last Chance to Save Their Country." *National Interest.* June 20, 2019. https://nationalinterest.org/feature/bahrains-rulers-last-chance-save-their-country -63532.

New Challenges Brought by Covid-19. Jadwa Investment, Riyadh (June 2020). https://www.sustg .com/1-2-million-expat-workers-to-leave-saudi-arabia-in-2020-jadwa-estimates/.

"New UK Military Base in Kuwait." *Arab Digest* (n.d.). Accessed June 20, 2020. https://arabdigest .org/visitors/sample-newsletters/new-uk-military-base-kuwait/.

Niblock, Tim. "Introduction." In *Social and Economic Development in the Arab Gulf*, edited by Tim Niblock. Abingdon, UK: Routledge, 2014.

Niblock, Timothy. *Saudi Arabia: Power, Legitimacy and Survival.* London: Routledge, 2006.

Nin-Pratt, Alejandro, et al. *Agriculture and Economic Transformation in the Middle East and North Africa: A Review of the Past with Lessons for the Future.* International Food Policy Research Institute (2018).

Nitze, Paul H. *Memorandum from the Deputy Secretary of Defense (Nitze) to the Chairman of the Joint Chiefs of Staff (Wheeler).* Office of the Secretary of Defense. Suitland, MD: Washington National Records Center, August 2, 1968.

Nonneman, Gerd. "Analyzing Middle East Foreign Policies: A Conceptual Framework." In *Analyzing Middle East Foreign Policies and the Relationship with Europe*, edited by Gerd Nonneman, 188–130. Abingdon, UK: Routledge, 2005.

Nonneman, Gerd. "European Policies towards the Gulf: Patterns, Dynamics, Evolution, and the Case of the Qatar Blockade." *Journal of Arabian Studies* 10, no. 2 (2020): 278–304.

Nonneman, Gerd. *Political Reform in the Gulf Monarchies: From Liberalisation to Democratization.* Sir William Luce Fellowship Paper. Durham, UK: University of Durham, Institute for Middle Eastern and Islamic Studies, 2006.

Nonneman, Gerd. "Political Reform in the Gulf Monarchies: From Liberalization to Democratization? A Comparative Perspective." In *Reform in the Middle East Oil Monarchies*, edited by Anoushiravan Eteshami and Steven Wright. Reading, UK: Ithaca, 2011.

Norton, Augustus Richard (ed.). *Civil Society in the Middle East.* Leiden, Netherlands: Brill, 1996.

Noyes, James H. *The Clouded Lens: Persian Gulf Security and U.S. Policy.* 2nd ed. Stanford, CA: Hoover Institution, 1982.

Nye, Joseph S., and Sean M. Lynn-Jones. "International Security Studies: A Report of a Conference on the State of the Field." *International Security* 12, no. 4 (1988): 5–27.

Odhiambo, George. "Water Scarcity in the Arabian Peninsula and Socio-Economic Implications." *Applied Water Science* 7 (2017): 2479–2492.

Oman Brief No 18 Non-Proliferation Treaty. Foreign and Commonwealth Office, London, FCO 8/5848 (January 1985).

Oman: Domestic Forces and the Succession. Washington, DC: Central Intelligence Agency, March 1985.

"One Hundred Ports 2021." *Lloyds List.* https://lloydslist.maritimeintelligence.informa .com/-/media/lloyds-list/images/top-100-ports-2021/top-100-ports-2021-digital-edition .pdf.

One Year Later: Assessing Bahrain's Implementation of the BICI Report. Project on Middle East Democracy, November 2012. https://pomed.org/one-year-later-assessing-bahrains -implementation-of-the-bici-report/.

Osborne, Christine. *The Gulf States and Oman.* Abingdon, UK: Routledge, 2017.

Ottaway, Marina, and Michele Dunne. *Incumbent Regimes and the "King's Dilemma" in the Arab World: Promise and Threat of Managed Reform*. Washington, DC: Carnegie Endowment for International Peace, 2007. https://carnegieendowment.org/2007/12/10/incumbent-regimes -and-king-s-dilemma-in-arab-world-promise-and-threat-of-managed-reform-pub-19759.

Outlook for Producer Economies 2018. International Energy Agency, Paris (2018).

Pal, Jeremy S., and Elfatih A. B. Eltahir. "Future Temperature in Southwest Asia Projected to Exceed a Threshold for Human Adaptability." *Nature Climate Change* 6, no. 2 (2016): 197–200.

Paper Prepared in the National Security Council. "Middle East/Persian Gulf Arms Supply." U.S. State Department. Office of the Historian (January 19, 1977). https://history.state.gov /historicaldocuments/frus1969-76ve09p2/d30.

Parry, Ian, Simon Black, and Nate Vernon. *Still Not Getting Energy Prices Right: A Global and Country Update of Fossil Fuel Subsidies*. Working Paper. Washington, DC: International Monetary Fund, 2021. https://www.imf.org/en/Publications/WP/Issues/2021/09/23/Still -Not-Getting-Energy-Prices-Right-A-Global-and-Country-Update-of-Fossil-Fuel-Subsidies -466004.

Partrick, Neil. "Nationalism in the Gulf States." In *The Transformation of the Gulf: Politics, Economics, and the Global Order*, edited by David Held and Kristian Coates Ulrichsen. Abingdon, UK: Routledge, 2012.

Partrick, Neil. *Saudi Arabia's Elusive Defense Reform*. Washington, DC: Carnegie Endowment for International Peace, November 14, 2019. https://carnegieendowment.org/sada/80354.

Pascal, Anthony, et al. *Man and Arms in the Middle East: The Human Factor in Military Modernization*. Santa Monica, CA: RAND Corporation, June 1979.

Passmore, K. J. *Visit to the UAE and Kuwait by Puss Transport*. Ministerial Visit from the UK to the Persian Gulf, General. Foreign and Commonwealth Office, London (December 15, 1981).

Past and Present Problems of Iraq's Boundaries with Kuwait and Saudi Arabia. Washington: DC: Central Intelligence Agency, August 1975. https://www.cia.gov/readingroom/document/cia -rdp86t00608r000600140013-8.

Perry, John Curtis. *Singapore: Unlikely Power*. New York: Oxford University Press, 2017.

Petersen, Tore Tingvold. "Anglo-American Rivalry in the Middle East: The Struggle for the Buraimi Oasis, 1952–1957." *International History Review* 14, no. 1 (1992): 71–91.

Petersmann, Sandra. "Tanker Attacks in the Gulf—Evidence or Warmongering?" *DW*. June 21, 2019. Accessed May 19, 2020. https://www.dw.com/en/top-stories/s-9097.

Peterson, J. E. "The Arabian Peninsula in Modern Times: A Historiographical Survey." *American Historical Review* 96, no. 5 (1991): 1435–49. http://www.jstor.org/stable/2165280.

Peterson, J. E. "Change and Continuity in Arab Gulf Society." In *After the War: Iraq, Iran and the Arab Gulf*, edited by Charles Davies. Chichester, UK: Carden, 1990.

Peterson, J. E. *Defending Arabia*. Abingdon, UK: Routledge, 2017.

Peterson, J. E. "Review: Christopher M. Davidson. After the Sheikhs." *Asian Affairs* 45, no 1 (2014).

Peterson, J. E. "Tribes and Politics in Eastern Arabia." *Middle East Journal* 31, no. 3 (Summer 1977): 297–312.

Peterson, John E. *Oman's Insurgencies: The Sultanate's Struggle for Supremacy*. London: Saqi, 2013.

Peterson, John E. "Oman: Three and a Half Decades of Change and Development." *Middle East Policy* 11, no. 2 (2004): 125.

Phillips, Sarah G., and Jennifer S. Hunt. "'Without Sultan Qaboos, We Would Be Yemen': The Renaissance Narrative and the Political Settlement in Oman." *Journal of International Development* 29, no. 5 (2017): 645–660.

Piscatori, James. "Managing God's Guests: The Pilgrimage, Saudi Arabia and the Politics of Legitimacy." In *Monarchies and Nations: Globalization and Identity in the Arab States of the Gulf*, edited by Paul Dresch and James Piscatori, 140–177. New York: I. B. Tauris, 2013.

Policy Challenges in the Gulf Cooperation Council Countries. Washington, DC: International Monetary Fund, May 1996.

Pollack, Kenneth M. *Arabs at War: Military Effectiveness, 1948–1991.* Lincoln: University of Nebraska Press, 2004.

Pollack, Kenneth M. *Armies of Sand: The Past, Present, and Future of Arab Military Effectiveness.* New York: Oxford University Press, 2019.

Porter, Bernard. *The Lion's Share: A History of British Imperialism 1850 to the Present.* 5th ed. Harlow, UK: Pearson, 2012.

Porter, Michael E. "Clusters and the New Economics of Competition." Harvard Business Review (November–December 1998). https://hbr.org/1998/11/clusters-and-the-new-economics -of-competition.

"Principles of the 50." Accessed December 22, 2021. https://www.uaeprinciples.ae/Principles Of50-En.pdf.

Pyne-Jones, Louise. *Thousands of Al Ghofran Tribesmen Stripped of Their Qatari Citizenship Fight for Their Rights.* London: International Observatory of Human Rights, May 13, 2019.

"Qaboos Bequeaths a Smooth Succession as Haitham Bin Tariq Takes over in Oman." *Gulf States Newsletter* 1096. January 23, 2020. https://www.gsn-online.com/news-centre/article /qaboos-bequeaths-smooth-succession-haitham-bin-tariq-takes.

"Qatar: Al-Murrah Return, 'Seeking Mercy.'" *Gulf States Newsletter* 1078. April 4, 2019.

"Qatar Exceeds Set Target of 2019 in Achieving Food Self-Sufficiency." *The Peninsula.* January 9, 2020. https://thepeninsulaqatar.com/article/09/01/2020/Qatar-exceeds-set-target -of-2019-in-achieving-food-self-sufficiency.

"Qatar 'Fake News' Law Signals 'Worrying Regression': Rights Group." *Al Jazeera.* January 24, 2020. Accessed May 2, 2020. https://www.aljazeera.com/news/2020/01/qatar-fake-news-law -signals-worrying-regression-rights-group-200122071721600.html.

"Qatar to Invest $15 Billion in Turkey: Source Says Banks the Focus." *Reuters.* August 15, 2018. Accessed June 20, 2020. https://uk.reuters.com/article/us-turkey-currency-qatar-investments /qatar-to-invest-15-billion-in-turkey-source-says-banks-the-focus-idUKKBN1L01P7.

"Qatar Seeks to Employ Jordanian Military Retirees." *Roya News.* September 22, 2019. Accessed June 20, 2020. https://en.royanews.tv/news/18738/Qatar%20seeks%20to%20employ%20Jordanian %20military%20retirees.

Quinlivan, James T. "Coup-Proofing: Its Practice and Consequences in the Middle East." *International Security* 24, no. 2 (1999): 131–165.

Ramos, Stephen J. *Dubai Amplified: The Engineering of a Port Geography.* Farnham, UK: Ashgate, 2010.

Rashad, Marwa, and Davide Barbuscia. "Saudi Foreign Reserves Fall at Fastest for Two Decades." *Reuters.* April 29, 2020. Accessed June 20, 2020. https://www.reuters.com/article/us-saudi-budget-idUSKCN22B0W5.

Raval, Anjli. "Saudi Aramco Sticks by $75bn Dividend despite Sharp Profit Fall." *Financial Times.* March 21, 2021. https://www.ft.com/content/b91097a9-c554-4e5c-9b89-a8abec354a55.

Raval, Anjli. "Saudi Aramco Stretches away as Top IPO after Extra Sale." *Financial Times.* January 12, 2020. https://www.ft.com/content/6ecc8978-3524-11ea-a6d3-9a26f8c3cba4.

Raval, Anjli, and Neil Hume. "Saudi Aramco Listing Presents Challenge for Investors." *Financial Times.* January 10, 2016. https://www.ft.com/content/0f331bde-b784-11e5-b151-8e15c9a029fb.

Resident, Political. *Secret Telegram from the Political Resident to the Secretary of State for India.* August 30, 1935.

Richmond, J. C. B. *Despatch No. 42.* Kuwait: Foreign and Commonwealth Office, London (August 14, 1960). https://www.agda.ae/en/catalogue/tna/fo/371/148912/n/4.

Richmond, Sir John. *An Evaluation of Kuwait as a Welfare State.* Foreign and Commonwealth Office (June 16, 1963). https://www.agda.ae/en/catalogue/tna/fo/371/168780/n/4.

Riedel, Bruce. "The Prince of Counter-Terrorism." *Brookings Essay.* September 29, 2015. Accessed November 1, 2015. http://www.brookings.edu/research/essays/2015/the-prince-of-counterterrorism.

Riegl, Bernhard. "Climate Change and Coral Reefs: Different Effects in Two High-Latitude Areas (Arabian Gulf, South Africa)." *Coral Reefs* 22, no. 4 (2003): 433–446.

Roberts, David B. "Breaking the Saudi Rules of Succession." *Washington Post.* May 27, 2015. https://www.washingtonpost.com/news/monkey-cage/wp/2015/05/27/breaking-the-saudi-rules-of-succession/.

Roberts, David B. "Bucking the Trend: The UAE and the Development of Military Capabilities in the Arab World." *Security Studies* 29, no. 2 (2020): 301–334.

Roberts, David B. "A Dustup in the Gulf." *Foreign Affairs.* June 13, 2017. Accessed August 8, 2017. https://www.foreignaffairs.com/articles/middle-east/2017-06-13/dustup-gulf.

Roberts, David B. "For Decades, Gulf Leaders Counted on U.S. Protection. Here's What Changed." *Washington Post.* January 30, 2020. https://www.washingtonpost.com/politics/2020/01/30/decades-gulf-leaders-counted-us-protection-heres-what-changed/.

Roberts, David B. "Is Qatar Bringing the Nusra Front in from the Cold?" *BBC.* March 6, 2015. Accessed June 6, 2015. http://www.bbc.co.uk/news/world-middle-east-31764114.

Roberts, David B. "Kuwait." In *Power and Politics in the Persian Gulf Monarchies*, edited by Christopher Davidson. London: Hurst, 2011.

Roberts, David B. "Lifting the 'Protection Curse': The Rise of New Military Powers in the Middle East." *Survival* 63, no. 2 (2021): 139–154.

Roberts, David B. "Mosque and State: The United Arab Emirates' Secular Foreign Policy." *Foreign Affairs.* March 18, 2016. Accessed May 5, 2016. https://www.foreignaffairs.com/articles/united-arab-emirates/2016-03-18/mosque-and-state.

Roberts, David B. "News from Qatar Protest." *TheGulfBlog.com.* March 16, 2011. Accessed December 4, 2014. http://thegulfblog.com/2011/03/16/news-from-qatar-protest/.

Roberts, David B. "Ontological Security and the Gulf Crisis." *Journal of Arabian Studies* 10, no. 2 (2021): 221–237.

Roberts, David B. "Qatar and the Muslim Brotherhood: Pragmatism or Preference?" *Middle East Policy* 21, no. 3 (2014): 84–94.

Roberts, David B. "Qatar and the UAE: Exploring Divergent Responses to the Arab Spring." *Middle East Journal* 71, no. 4 (2017): 544–562.

Roberts, David B. "Qatar Shuffles Back to the Future." Washington, DC: Arab Gulf States Institute Washington, December 13, 2018. Accessed June 17, 2020. https://agsiw.org/qatar-shuffles-back-to-the-future/.

Roberts, David B. *Qatar: Securing the Global Ambitions of a City-State*. London: Hurst, 2017.

Roberts, David B. "Qatar's Shura Council Elections: Incrementally Strengthening Local Politics." Washington, DC: Arab Gulf States Institute Washington, October 7, 2021. https://agsiw.org/qatars-shura-council-elections-incrementally-strengthening-local-politics/.

Roberts, David B. *Securing the Qatari State*. Washington, DC: Arab Gulf States Institute Washington, June 2017.

Roberts, David B., and Emile Hokayem. "Friends with Benefits: The Gulf States and the Perpetual Quest for Alliances." Century Foundation (January 2018). https://tcf.org/content/report/friends-with-benefits/.

Roberts, David B., and Emile Hokayem. "The War in Yemen." *Survival* 58, no. 6 (2016): 157–186.

Roll, Stephan. "Aramco's IPO and Bin Salman's Fiscal Takeover." Sada. Washington, DC: Carnegie Endowment for International Peace, December 2, 2019. https://carnegieendowment.org/sada/80463.

Roll, Stephan. "A Sovereign Wealth Fund for the Prince: Economic Reforms and Power Consolidation in Saudi Arabia." Research Paper, 8. Berlin: Stiftung Wissenschaft und Politik, 2019.

Rossiter, Ash. *Britain and the Development of Professional Security Forces in the Gulf Arab States, 1921–71: Local Forces and Informal Empire*. PhD dissertation, Exeter University, 2014.

Rossiter, Ash. " 'Screening the Food from the Flies': Britain, Kuwait, and the Dilemma of Protection, 1961–1971." *Diplomacy and Statecraft* 28, no. 1 (2017): 85–109.

Rossiter, Ash. "Survival of the Kuwaiti Statelet: Najd's Expansion and the Question of British Protection." *Middle Eastern Studies* 56, no. 3 (2020): 381–395. https://doi.org/10.1080/00263206.2020.1716339.

Rossiter, Ash. "The Yemeni–Saudi Border from Boundary to Frontline." In *Yemen and the Gulf States: The Making of a Crisis*, edited by Helen Lackner and Daniel Martin Varisco, 29–44. Berlin: Gerlach, 2018.

Rothschild, Emma. "What Is Security?" *Daedalus* 124, no. 3 (1995): 53–98.

Rubin, Barry. "The Military in Contemporary Middle East Politics." *Middle East Review of International Affairs* 5, no. 1 (March 2001).

Rugh, Andrea B. "Backgammon or Chess? The State of Tribalism and Tribal Leadership in the United Arab Emirates." In *Tribes and States in a Changing Middle East*, edited by Uzi Rabi, 57–77. New York: Oxford University Press, 2016.

Russell, Richard L. "Future Gulf War." *Joint Forces Quarterly*, no. 55 (2009).

Russell, Sharon Stanton. "Politics and Ideology in Migration Policy Formulation: The Case of Kuwait." *International Migration Review* 21, no. 1 (1989): 24–47.

Ruthven, Malise. "The Saudi Trillions." *London Review of Books* 39, no. 17 (September 7, 2017). https://www.lrb.co.uk/the-paper/v39/n17/malise-ruthven/the-saudi-trillions.

Rutledge, Emilie J. "Labor Markets in the Gulf and the South Asian Migration." In *South Asian Migration in the Gulf*, edited by Mehdi Chowdhury and S. Irudaya Rajan. Cham, Switzerland: Palgrave Macmillan, 2018.

"Sabah Takes over as Kuwaiti Parliament Shows Its Muscle." *Gulf States Newsletter* 774. January 27, 2006. https://www.gsn-online.com/downloadable/1203.

Sachs, J., G. Schmidt-Traub, C. Kroll, G. Lafortune, and G. Fuller. *Sustainable Development Report 2019*. New York: Bertelsmann Stiftung and Sustainable Development Solutions Network, 2019.

Safran, Nadav. *Saudi Arabia: The Ceaseless Quest for Security*. Ithaca, NY: Cornell University Press, 1991.

Saif, Salem. "When Consultants Reign." *Jacobin*. May 9, 2016. Accessed August 21, 2019. https://www.jacobinmag.com/2016/05/saudi-arabia-aramco-salman-mckinsey-privatization/.

Sakr, Naomi. "Channels of Interaction: The Role of Gulf-Owned Media Firms in Globalization." In *Monarchies and Nations: Globalization and Identity in the Arab States of the Gulf*, edited by Paul Dresch and James Piscatori, 34–51. New York: I. B. Tauris, 2013.

Salame, Ghassan (ed.). *Democracy without Democrats? The Renewal of Politics in the Muslim World*. London and New York: I. B. Tauris, 1994.

Salamey, Imad. "Middle Eastern Exceptionalism: Globalization and the Balance of Power." *Democracy and Security* 5, no. 3 (2009): 249–260.

Salim, Reem. "طي الكتمان: اتجاهات الفقر في دول مجلس التعاون الخليجي" ("Untold: Trends in Poverty in the GCC"). مركز البديل للتخطيط والدراسات الاستراتيجية (*Al Badeel Centre for Planning and Strategic Studies*). Accessed June 20, 2020. https://tinyurl.com/y9cd6tut.

Sanger, David. "Under Pressure, Dubai Company Drops Port Deal." *New York Times*. March 10, 2006. https://www.nytimes.com/2006/03/10/politics/under-pressure-dubai-company-drops-port-deal.html.

Saudi Arabia's Economic Cities. Saudi Arabian General Investment Authority (n.d.). https://www.oecd.org/mena/competitiveness/38906206.pdf.

"Saudi Arabia: MBS Promises 'Giga-Projects.'" *Gulf States Newsletter*. November 2, 2017.

"Saudi Arabia Sets Itself up for a Fall with Ambitious Economic Reform Plan." *Gulf States Newsletter* 40, 1014. May 5, 2016.

Saudi Arabia and the United States: The New Context in an Evolving "Special Relationship." Subcommittee on Europe and the Middle East of the Committee on Foreign Affairs. Washington, DC: U.S. House of Representatives, 1981.

"Saudi Aramco to Be Separated from the Oil Ministry." Economist Intelligence Unit, London (May 4, 2015). http://country.eiu.com/article.aspx?articleid=583135242.

"Saudi Aramco Reports Strong 2019 Results despite Difficult Macro Environment." *Saudi Aramco*. March 15, 2020. Accessed June 17, 2020. https://www.saudiaramco.com/en/news-media/news/2020/saudi-aramco-full-year-2019-results#:~:text=Total%20dividend%20payments%20were%20%2473.2,%2C%20through%20December%2031%2C%202019.

"Saudi Aramco's Public Debut Is a Hollow Victory." *Financial Times*. December 12, 2019. https://www.ft.com/content/db9cb912-1cf4-11ea-9186-7348c2f183af.

The Saudi Economy in 2019. Jadwa Investment, Riyadh (February 2019).

"Saudi Finance Minister Says No Need to Create Sovereign Wealth Fund." *Reuters.* December 26, 2014. Accessed June 18, 2020. https://www.reuters.com/article/us-saudi-sovereign-funds /saudi-finance-minister-says-no-need-to-create-sovereign-wealth-fund-idUSKBN0 K40A820141226.

"Saudi Royal Wealth: Where Do They Get All That Money?" *Wikileaks.* November 30, 1996. Accessed July 31, 2019. https://www.aftenposten.no/norge/i/LAvE9/30111996saudi-royal-wealth -where-do-they-get-all-that-money.

Schlesinger, Arthur M. Jr. *The Cycles of American History.* New York: Mariner Books, 1990.

Seccombe, Ian J. "Labour Migration to the Arabian Gulf: Evolution and Characteristics 1920–1950." *British Journal of Middle Eastern Studies* 10, no. 1 (1983): 3–20.

Segal, Eran. "Political Participation in Kuwait: Dīwāniyya, Majlis and Parliament." *Journal of Arabian Studies* 2, no. 2 (2012): 127–141.

Seikaly, May. "Kuwait and Bahrain: The Appeal of Globalization and Internal Constraints." In *Iran, Iraq, and the Arab Gulf States,* edited by Joseph A. Kechichian, 177–192. New York: Palgrave, 2001.

Selden, Armistead I. *Memorandum from the Acting Assistant Secretary of Defense for International Security Affairs (Selden) to Secretary of Defense Laird.* U.S. State Department. Office of the Historian (November 10, 1971).

Shambayati, Hootan. "The Rentier State, Interest Groups, and the Paradox of Autonomy: State and Business in Turkey and Iran." *Comparative Politics* 26, no. 3 (1994): 307–331. www.jstor .org/stable/422114.

Shams, Wadha. "المستجدات في سلطنة عمان" ("Developments in the Sultanate of Oman"). In الثابت واملتحول املواطنة يف تيارات الخليج :2019 (*Change and Continuity 2019: Citizenship Currents in the Gulf*), edited by Omar AlShehabi and Khalil Buhazza. Kuwait: مركز الخليج لسياسات التنمية (Gulf Centre for Development Policies), 2019.

Sheppard, Charles, et al. "The Gulf: A Young Sea in Decline." *Marine Pollution Bulletin* 60, no. 1 (2010): 13–38.

Sick, Gary. "The Siege of Doha." *LobeLog.* June 16, 2017. Accessed June 27, 2019. https://lobelog .com/the-siege-of-doha/.

Silverfarb, Daniel. "Great Britain, Iraq, and Saudi Arabia: The Revolt of the Ikhwan, 1927–1930." *International History Review* 4, no. 2 (1982): 222–248.

Simpson, Colin. "Good Salary, Depending on Where You're Coming From." *The National.* April 26, 2012. https://www.thenationalnews.com/uae/good-salary-depending-on-where -you-re-coming-from-1.574113.

SIPRI Extended Military Expenditure Database, Beta Version. Stockholm International Peace Research Institute (SIPRI) (2016).

Slater, A. H. K. *United Kingdom/United Arab Emirates (UAE) Joint Committee.* Foreign and Commonwealth Office, London. FCO 8/3143 (October 3, 1978). https://www.agda.ae/en /catalogue/tna/fco/8/3142.

Slater, J. F. *Mr Barratt's Visit to Qatar.* Foreign and Commonwealth Office, London (November 27, 1974).

Sluglett, Peter. "Formal and Informal Empire in the Middle East." In *Historiography: The Oxford History of the British Empire*, edited by Robin W. Winks. Oxford: Oxford University Press, 1999.

Smith, Cooper. "These Are the Most Twitter-Crazy Countries in the World, Starting with Saudi Arabia (!?)." *Business Insider*. November 7, 2013. Accessed June 3, 2020. https://www.business insider.com/the-top-twitter-markets-in-the-world-2013-11?r=US&IR=T.

Smith, Dan, and Florian Krampe. "Climate-Related Security Risks in the Middle East." In *Routledge Handbook on Middle East Security*, edited by Anders Jagerskog, Michael Schulz, and Ashok Swain, 199–210. London: Routledge, 2019.

Smith Diwan, Kristin. "Divided Government in Kuwait: The Politics of Parliament since the Gulf War." *Domes* 8, no. 1 (1999): 1–18.

Smith Diwan, Kristin. "Who Is Sunni? Chechnya Islamic Conference Opens Window on Intra -Faith Rivalry." Washington, DC: Arab Gulf States Institute Washington, September 16, 2016. Accessed June 2, 2020. https://agsiw.org/who-is-a-sunni-chechnya-islamic-conference-opens -window-on-intra-faith-rivalry/.

Smith, Keith. "Realist Foreign Policy Analysis with a Twist: The Persian Gulf Security Complex and the Rise and Fall of Dual Containment." *Foreign Policy Analysis* 12, no. 3 (2016): 315–333.

Smith, Steve. "The Increasing Insecurity of Security Studies: Conceptualizing Security in the Last Twenty Years." *Contemporary Security Policy* 20, no. 3 (1999): 72–101.

Snider, Lewis W. "Comparing the Strength of Nations: The Arab Gulf States and Political Change." *Comparative Politics* 20, no. 4 (1988): 461–484.

Sorenson, David S. "Why the Saudi Arabian Defence Binge?" *Contemporary Security Policy* 35, no. 1 (2014): 116–137.

Sorkin, Andrew Ross. "In the Saudi Desert, World's Business Leaders Follow the Money." *New York Times*. October 23, 2017. https://www.nytimes.com/2017/10/23/business/dealbook/in -the-saudi-desert-worlds-business-leaders-follow-the-money.html.

Spiess, Andy. "Food Security in the Gulf Cooperation Council (GCC) Economies (Working Paper)." Hamburg: NDRD, 2011. http://www.ndrd.org/Spiess_-_Working_Paper_on_Food _Security_in_the_GCC.pdf.

Springborg, Robert, and Clement Moore Henry. *Globalization and the Politics of Development in the Middle East*. Cambridge: Cambridge University Press, 2010.

Stam, Allan C. *Win, Lose, or Draw: Domestic Politics and the Crucible of War*. Ann Arbor: University of Michigan Press, 1999.

Statistical Appendix. International Monetary Fund (April 2019). https://www.imf.org/~/media /Files/Publications/REO/MCD-CCA/2019/April/English/Statistical-Appendix.ashx.

Stehr, Nico. "Man and His Environment: A General Perspective." *ARSP: Archiv für Rechts- und Sozialphilosophie/Archives for Philosophy of Law and Social Philosophy* 64, no. 1 (1978).

Steinberg, Guido. *Leading the Counter-Revolution: Saudi Arabia and the Arab Spring*. Berlin: German Institute for International and Security Affairs, 2014. https://www.swp-berlin.org /publications/products/research_papers/2014_RP07_sbg.pdf.

Stenslie, Stig. "Salman's Succession: Challenges to Stability in Saudi Arabia." *Washington Quarterly* 39, no. 2 (2016): 117–138.

Steps Taken by the Government of Bahrain to Implement the Recommendations in the 2011 Report of the Bahrain Independent Commission of Inquiry. Washington, DC: U.S. Department of State, June 21, 2016.

Stiglitz, Joseph. "Public Policy for a Knowledge Economy." *Remarks at the Department for Trade and Industry and Center for Economic Policy Research* 27, no. 3 (1999): 3–6.

Stock, Wolfgang G., Julia Barth, and Julia Gremm. "The Era after Oil: Knowledge-Intensive Cities on the Arabian Gulf." In *Knowledge-Intensive Economies and Opportunities for Social, Organizational, and Technological Growth*, edited by Miltiadis Lytras, Linda Daniela, and Anna Visvizi, 63–88. Hershey, PA: IGI Global, 2019.

"Strait of Hormuz." International Crisis Group, Brussels. March 22, 2019.

Strayer, Robert. "Decolonization, Democratization, and Communist Reform: The Soviet Collapse in Comparative Perspective." *Journal of World History* 12, no. 2 (2001): 375–406.

Strobl, Staci. "Progressive or Neo-Traditional? Policewomen in Gulf Cooperation Council (GCC) Countries." *Feminist Formations* 22, no. 3 (2010): 51–74.

Suliman, Abubakr M., and Rehana Hayat. "Leadership in the UAE." In *Leadership Development in the Middle East*, edited by Beverly Dawn Matcalfe and Fouad Mimouni. Cheltenham, UK: Edward Elgar, 2012.

A Survey of Global Terrorism and Terrorist Financing. Washington, DC: U.S. Government, April 22, 2015. https://www.govinfo.gov/content/pkg/CHRG-114hhrg95059/html/CHRG -114hhrg95059.htm.

Tabrizi, Aniseh Bassiri, and Justin Bronk. *Armed Drones in the Middle East: Proliferation and Norms in the Region*. London: Royal United Services Institute, 2018. https://rusi.org/explore -our-research/publications/occasional-papers/armed-drones-middle-east-proliferation -and-norms-region.

Tadros, Mahfouz E. "The Arab Gulf States and the Knowledge Economy: Challenges and Opportunities." Washington, DC: Arab Gulf States Institute Washington, 2015. https://agsiw .org/wp-content/uploads/2015/07/Tadros_Knowledge-Economy_Rev1.pdf.

Talmadge, Caitlin. *The Dictator's Army: Battlefield Effectiveness in Authoritarian Regimes*. Ithaca, NY and London: Cornell University Press, 2015.

Tamirisa, Natalia, and Christoph Duenwald. *Public Wage Bills in the Middle East and Central Asia*. Washington, DC: International Monetary Fund, 2018.

Taremi, Kamran. "The Role of Water Exports in Iranian Foreign Policy towards the GCC." *Iranian Studies* 28, no. 2 (June 2005): 311–328.

Tariq Alhasan, Hasan. "The Role of Iran in the Failed Coup of 1981: The IFLB in Bahrain." *Middle East Journal* 65, no. 4 (2011): 603–617.

Taryam, Abdullah Omran. *The Establishment of the United Arab Emirates*. Abingdon, UK: Routledge, 1987.

Taylor, Adam. "The Once Flourishing Iranian Community in Dubai Faces Pressure amid Persian Gulf Tensions." *Washington Post*. August 13, 2019. https://www.washingtonpost.com/world /middle_east/the-once-flourishing-iranian-community-in-dubai-faces-pressure-amid -gulf-tensions/2019/08/12/450dfb88-afa7-11e9-9411-a608f9d0c2d3_story.html.

Taylor, William. *Military Responses to the Arab Uprisings and the Future of Civil-Military Relations in the Middle East: Analysis from Egypt, Tunisia, Libya, and Syria*. New York: Springer, 2014.

Thompson, E. P. *The Making of the English Working Class*. New York: Penguin, 2013 (orig. 1963).

Thompson, Mark C. *Being Young, Male and Saudi: Identity and Politics in a Globalized Kingdom*. Cambridge: Cambridge University Press, 2019.

Tisdall, Simon. "Sudan: How Arab Autocrats Conspired to Thwart Reformists' Hopes." *The Guardian*. June 3, 2019. https://www.theguardian.com/world/2019/jun/03/sudanese -crackdown-comes-after-talks-with-egypt-and-saudis.

Toth, Anthony B. "Tribes and Tribulations: Bedouin Losses in the Saudi and Iraqi Struggles over Kuwait's Frontiers, 1921–1943." *British Journal of Middle Eastern Studies* 32, no. 2 (2005): 145–167.

Toumi, Habib. "Qatari Plots against Bahrain Revealed." *Gulf News*. August 22, 2017. https:// gulfnews.com/world/gulf/qatar/qatari-plots-against-bahrain-revealed-1.2078073.

Trenwith, Courtney. "Kuwait's New PPP Law Is 'Selling' the Country, Says MPS." *Arabian Business*. July 1, 2014. Accessed August 21, 2019. https://www.arabianbusiness.com/kuwait-s -new-ppp-law-is-selling—country-says-mps-556260.html.

Trofimov, Yaroslav. *The Siege of Mecca*. London: Penguin, 2007.

U.S. Interests in and Policy toward the Persian Gulf. U.S. House of Representatives (1972).

"UAE Military Pilots Conduct Landing Qualifications Aboard USS Lewis B. Puller." U.S. Central Command. May 22, 2020. https://www.centcom.mil/MEDIA/NEWS-ARTICLES/News-Article -View/Article/2195719/uae-military-pilots-conduct-landing-qualifications-aboard-uss-lewis -b-puller/.

"The UAE National Framework Statement for Sustainable Fisheries (2019–2030)." Environment Agency Abu Dhabi and the Ministry of Climate Change and Environment (n.d.). https://www.moccae.gov.ae/assets/download/749e9268/UAE%20National%20Framework %20Statement%20for%20Sustainable%20Fisheries%20(2019-2030)%20English.pdf.aspx.

"UAE to Get Largest Water Desalination Plant in the World." *Khaleej Times*. July 22, 2020. https:// www.khaleejtimes.com/government/uae-to-get-largest-water-desalination-plant-in-the-world.

UK Co-Operation on Nuclear Energy with Gulf States. Foreign and Commonwealth Office, London, FCO 8/2860 (January 1–December 31, 1977).

Untermeyer, Chase. "Qatar: Update on Nationality Issue." *Wikileaks*. Doha, Qatar, May 10, 2005. https://wikileaks.org/plusd/cables/05DOHA845_a.html.

Valeri, Marc. "Liberalization from Above: Political Reforms and Sultanism in Oman." In *Constitutional Reform and Political Participation in the Gulf*, edited by Abdulhadi Khalaf and Giacomo Luciani, 187–210. Dubai: Gulf Research Center, 2006.

Valeri, Marc. "Oman." In *Power and Politics in the Persian Gulf Monarchies*, edited by Christopher Davidson. London: Hurst, 2011.

Valeri, Marc. *Oman: Politics and Society in the Qaboos State*. London: Hurst, 2017.

Van Pelt, Mary Cubberly. "The Sheikhdom of Kuwait." *Middle East Journal* (1950): 12–26.

Verhoeven, Harry. "The Gulf and the Horn: Changing Geographies of Security Interdependence and Competing Visions of Regional Order." *Civil Wars* 20, no. 3 (2018): 333–357.

Vitalis, Robert. *Oilcraft: The Myths of Scarcity and Security That Haunt U.S. Energy Policy*. Stanford, CA: Stanford University Press, 2020.

Vulnerability of Persian Gulf Desalination Systems: An Emerging Security Issue. Washington, DC: Central Intelligence Agency, Directorate of Intelligence, October 1983.

Wæver, Ole. *Aberystwyth, Paris, Copenhagen: New "Schools" in Security Theory and Their Origins between Core and Periphery.* Presented at the annual meeting of the International Studies Association. Montreal, March 17–20, 2004.

Wæver, Ole. "The History and Social Structure of Security Studies as a Practico-Academic Field." In *Security Expertise: Practice, Power, Responsibility,* edited by Trine Villumsen Berling and Christian Bueger, 76–106. Oxford, UK: Routledge, 2015.

Wald, Ellen. *Saudi Inc.: The Arabian Kingdom's Pursuit of Profit and Power.* New York and London: Pegasus, 2018.

Wallace-Wells, David. *The Uninhabitable Earth: Life after Warming.* London: Allen Lane, 2019.

Walt, Stephen M. "The Renaissance of Security Studies." *International Studies Quarterly* 35, no. 2 (1991): 211–239.

Walton, Molly. "Desalinated Water Affects the Energy Equation in the Middle East." *International Energy Administration.* January 21, 2019. Accessed June 4, 2020. https://www.iea.org /commentaries/desalinated-water-affects-the-energy-equation-in-the-middle-east.

Warren, David H. *Rivals in the Gulf: Yusuf Al-Qaradawi, Abdullah Bin Bayyah, and the Qatar-UAE Contest over the Arab Spring and the Gulf Crisis.* Abingdon, UK: Routledge, 2021.

Water for Prosperity and Development: Risks and Opportunities for the Gulf Cooperation Council Countries. Washington, DC: World Bank Group, December 2017.

Water Statistics in the State of Qatar 2017. Planning and Statistics Authority (December 2019). https://www.psa.gov.qa/en/statistics/Statistical%20Releases/Environmental/Water/2017 /Water-Statistics-2017-EN.pdf.

Wehrey, Frederic. *The Burning Shores: Inside the Battle for the New Libya.* New York: Farrar, Straus and Giroux, 2018.

Wendling, Z. A., J. W. Emerson, D. C. Esty, M. A. Levy, and A. de Sherbinin. *2018 Environmental Performance Index.* New Haven, CT: Yale Center for Environmental Law and Policy, 2018.

"When Kings and Princes Grow Old." *The Economist.* July 15, 2010. https://www.economist.com /briefing/2010/07/15/when-kings-and-princes-grow-old.

"Who Guards the Gulf?" *The Economist.* September 7, 1991.

Wilkinson, John C. "Traditional Concepts of Territory in South East Arabia." *Geographical Journal* 149, no. 3 (1983): 301–15. http://www.jstor.org/stable/634004.

Williams, Michael. *Culture and Security: Symbolic Power and the Politics of International Security.* London: Routledge, 2007.

Willoughby, John. "Segmented Feminization and the Decline of Neopatriarchy in GCC Countries of the Persian Gulf." *Comparative Studies of South Asia, Africa and the Middle East* 28, no. 1 (2008): 184–199.

Wolfers, Arnold. " 'National Security' as an Ambiguous Symbol." *Political Science Quarterly* 67, no. 4 (1952): 481–502.

"Women Apply in Their Thousands to Drive Trains in Saudi Arabia." *The Guardian.* February 17, 2022. https://www.theguardian.com/world/2022/feb/17/women-apply-in-their-thousands-to -drive-trains-in-saudi-arabia.

Wood, David. "The Middle East and the Arab World: The Military Context." *Adelphi Papers* 5, no. 20 (1965): 3–22.

"World's First Climate-Controlled Raining Street Coming to Dubai." *Khaleej Times*. June 24, 2020. https://www.khaleejtimes.com/local-business/worlds-first-climate-controlled-raining -street-coming-to-dubai.

World Energy Prices: An Overview. International Energy Agency Statistics (2019). https:// iea.blob.core.windows.net/assets/567bac7c-5b6f-4aab-8e88-90af3e464d97/World_Energy _Prices_2019_Overview.pdf.

Worth, Robert F. "Leftward Shift by Conservative Cleric Leaves Saudis Perplexed." *New York Times*. April 4, 2014. https://www.nytimes.com/2014/04/05/world/middleeast/conservative-saudi -cleric-salman-al-awda.html.

Worth, Robert F. "Mohammed Bin Zayed's Dark Vision of the Middle East's Future." *New York Times*. January 2, 2020. https://www.nytimes.com/2020/01/09/magazine/united-arab-emirates -mohammed-bin-zayed.html.

Yamani, Mai. *Changed Identities: The Challenge of the New Generation in Saudi Arabia*. London: Royal Institute of International Affairs, 2000.

Yates, Athol. *The Evolution of the Armed Forces of the United Arab Emirates*. Warwick, UK: Helion, 2020.

Yergin, Daniel. *The Prize: The Epic Quest for Oil, Money and Power*. New York: Simon and Schuster, 2011.

Yizraeli, Sarah. "Al Sa'ud: An Ambivalent Approach to Tribalism." In *Tribes and States in a Changing Middle East*, edited by Uzi Rabi, 95–110. New York: Oxford University Press, 2016.

Yom, Sean. "Understanding the Durability of Authoritarianism in the Middle East." *Arab Studies Journal* 13/14, no. 2/1 (Fall 2005/Spring 2006): 227–233.

Young, Karen E. "The MBS Economy." *Foreign Affairs*. January 27, 2022. https://www.foreignaffairs .com/articles/saudi-arabia/2022-01-27/mbs-economy.

Young, Karen E. "Sovereign Risk: Gulf Sovereign Wealth Funds as Engines of Growth and Political Resource." *British Journal of Middle Eastern Studies* 47, no. 1 (2020): 96–116.

Zahlan, Rosemarie Said. *The Creation of Qatar*. London and New York: Croom Helm, 1979.

Zahlan, Rosemarie Said. *The Making of the Modern Gulf States: Kuwait, Bahrain, Qatar, the United Arab Emirates and Oman*. Reading, UK: Ithaca, 1998.

Zahlan, Rosemarie Said. *The Making of the Modern Gulf States: Kuwait, Bahrain, Qatar, the United Arab Emirates and Oman*. Abingdon, UK: Routledge, 1989.

Zakaria, Fareed. *The Future of Freedom: Illiberal Democracy at Home and Abroad*. New York: W. W. Norton, 2007.

Zellman, Gail L., Gery W. Ryan, Louay Constant, Charles A. Goldman, Dominic J. Brewer, Catherine H. Augustine, and Cathleen Stasz. *Education for a New Era: Design and Implementation of K-12 Education Reform in Qatar*. Santa Monica, CA: RAND Corporation, 2007.

Ziadah, Rafeef. "Constructing a Logistics Space: Perspectives from the Gulf Cooperation Council." *Environment and Planning D: Society and Space* 36, no. 4 (2018): 666–682.

Zoepf, Katherine. "Talk of Women's Rights Divides Saudi Arabia." *New York Times*. May 31, 2010. https://www.nytimes.com/2010/06/01/world/middleeast/01iht-saudi.html.

"عشيرة الغفران 'تشكو قطر إلى مجلس حقوق الإنسان'" ("Al-Ghafran Clan Complains About Qatar to Human Rights Council"). *BBC Arabic*. March 9, 2018. Accessed July 6, 2019. http://www.bbc.com /arabic/middleeast-43342736.

"عام / أمر ملكي: يكون يوم (22 فبراير) من كل عام يوماً لذكرى تأسيس الدولة السعودية باسم (يوم التأسيس) ويصبح إجازة رسمية" ("General/Royal Decree: The Day [February 22] of Each Year Shall Be a Day to Commemorate the Founding of the Saudi State under the Name [Foundation/Founders Day] and It Becomes an Official Holiday"). *Saudi Press Agency*. January 27, 2022. Accessed February 1, 2022. https://www.spa.gov.sa/2324646.

"أنا قطر وقبيلتي قطرية" شعار القبائل في عرضة هل قطر" ("I Am Qatar and My Tribe Is Qatari: The Slogan of Tribes 'Welcome Qatar'"). *Al Sharq*. December 18, 2017. Accessed February 4, 2019. https://tinyurl .com/y7klj9g4.

"محمد بن سلمان على جبهة الحرب" ("Mohammed Bin Salman on the War Front"). *Elaph*. July 10, 2015. Accessed January 24, 2020. https://elaph.com/Web/News/2015/7/1025189.html.

"المستجدات السياسية في دولة الإمارات" ("Political Developments in the UAE"). In الثابت والمتحول 2017: الخليج والإصلاح الاقتصادي في زمن الأزمة النفطية (*Change and Continuity 2017: The Gulf and Economic Reform in a Time of Oil Crisis*), edited by Omar AlShehabi, Ahmed Al Owfi, and Khalil Bohazza. Kuwait: مركز الخليج لسياسات التنمية (Gulf Centre for Development Policies), 2017.

"الخلل الأمني بين النظام الاقتصادي والنظام السياسي" ("The Security Flaws between the Economic System and the Political System"). In الخليج 2013: الثابت والمتحول (*Gulf 2013: Change and Transformation*), edited by Omar AlShehabi. Kuwait: مركز الخليج لسياسات التنمية (Gulf Centre for Development Policies), 2013.

"النظام الأساسي" ("The Statute"). Gulf Cooperation Council. Accessed February 19, 2018. http://www .gcc-sg.org/ar-sa/AboutGCC/Pages/Primarylaw.aspx.

INDEX

Abd Al Karim Qasim, 35

Abe, Shinzo, 57

Abu Dhabi: contemporary history of, 75; Dubai and, 59, 122, 124; FPPMS in, 88; Investment Authority, 118; leadership in, 68; Martyr's Day in, 60; Muslim Brotherhood to, 42–43; power of, 58–59; Qatar and, 32; Saadiyat Island, 168; UAE and, 29–30, 58–64, 143; UK and, 123; water in, 170

Afghanistan, 85–86, 153–154, 158

Africa. *See* Middle East and North Africa

agriculture: in Arab world, 163–165; economics of, 63; FAO, 176, 180; subsidies for, 168–169; water and, 167–168, *175*, *175–184*, *178*, *179*, *183*. *See also* environmental politics

Ajman, 30, 34, 58, 105, 143–144

Al Alaywat, Abdul Ali, 82

Albania, 68

Aliens' Residence Law, 74

Allison, Graham, 67

Alshehabi, Omar, 29–30

Al Amoudi, Mohammed, 51

Anderson, Lisa, 16

Anthony, John Duke, 83

Arab Cold War, 84

Arab League, 16, 80

Arab revolt, 73

Arab Spring: in Bahrain, 201n23; diplomacy in, 44–45; elitism in, 40–41; for Gulf States, 40–44, 63–66; for monarchies, 8, 20; politics of, 82, 87–88, 122, 150, 157–158; society after, 101

Arab world: agriculture in, 163–165; Asia and, 68; Bedouin tribes in, 32; Britain in, 6–7; climate change in, 3, 14, 163–165; contemporary history of, 15, 187–197; democratization of, 8; desalination in, 169–173, 180–181, 185–186; diplomacy in, 20–21, 50, 150–151, 154–155; diversity in, 76; economics of, 3, 3–4; education in, 131; energy consumption in, 172–174, *173*; Europe in, 146; expatriates in, 74; foreign politics in, 85; history of, 11, 79–80; industry in, 243n81; IPOs in, 116; monarchies in, 65; nationalism in, 78, 149; NATO in, 155, 159; Ottoman Empire in, 194–195; politics of, 43; postcolonialism in, 69–70; religion in, 100–101; RSC concept in, 12–13; scholarship on, 1–2; sedentarization in, 80; society of, 5–6, 93–94; Sunni Muslims in, 82–83; UK in, 6–7, 143–144, 221n53; U.S. in, 7, 157–158;

COVID crisis, 6, 117, 121, 134, 194

CPSA. *See* Council for Political and Security Affairs

Cuban missile crisis, 67

dairy industry, 63, 169, 180

Darfur, 164

De Atkine, Novell, 155

defense. *See* military

democratization: in Arab Spring, 87; of Arab world, 8; in Cold War, 101; globalization of, 37–38; of government, 98–99; in Gulf War, 39; in Kuwait, 201n20; politics of, 42; in Qatar, 40; scholarship on, 7

desalination, 169–173, 180–181, 185–186

Desert Shield/Storm, 37–38, 48, 86, 147

detribalization, 80–81

development: diversification and, 112–122, *113*, *119*; in Dubai, 123–124, 168; in Gulf States, 112–122, *113*, *119*; Human Development Index, 2; research and, 131–132, *132*; in UAE, 129

Dhofar rebellion, 18

diplomacy: in Arab Spring, 44–45; in Arab world, 20–21, 50, 150–151, 154–155; blockades in, 60, 62–63, 65, 67; economics and, 52–53; to GCC, 159; geopolitics of, 67–68; with Gulf States, 18; with Kuwait, 35–36, 150, 160; with Mubarak, 157–158; politics of, 30–31; Saudi Arabia in, 63, 149–150, 156–157; with Trucial States, 166; with U.S., 40, 146–147

diversification: development and, 112–122, *113*, *119*; economics of, 4, 14, 109, 127, 135, 177; politics of, 103–104, 158, 169, 191; with SWF, 191; with technology, 185–186

diversity, 76, 92–93

Doha, 34, 43, 57, 62, 88

Dubai: Abu Dhabi and, 59, 122, 124; development in, 123–124, 168; in globalization, 2; history of, 73; Iran and, 59; military, 30; oil in, 236n151; Qatar and, 171; reform in, 21–22; U.S. and, 121; water tariffs in, 182. *See also* Arab world; Gulf States

economics: of agriculture, 63; of Arab world, 3, 3–4; budget deficits, 121–122, 127, 134; in China, 152; during COVID crisis, 6, 117, 121, 134, 194; of defense, 41; diplomacy and, 52–53; of diversification, 4, 14, 109, 127, 135, 177; economic vision/plans, 50, 53, 103–104, 112–117, 122–130, *126*, 191; Economist Intelligence Unit, 178, *178*; of energy, 191–192; of environmental politics, 32, 166–169; of expansion, 36–37; in globalization, 117; in Gulf States, 102–104, 125–126, 135–137; knowledge economies, 130–135, *132*; in Kuwait, 22, 136; of LNG, 1–2; local, 78–79; of military, 67–68; of oil, 75, 106–108, *107–108*, 189–190; of PIF, 50; politics and, 56–57, 102–104; of rent, 104–113, *107*, *108*; in Saudi Arabia, 57, 76–77, 122; in Souq Al Manakh, 126–127; of subsidies, 168–170, 179–183, 186, 191, 197; of SWF, *113*, 113–122, *119*; in UAE, 236n151; visions in, 122–130, *126*; of Western powers, 188

ecosystems, 163, 165, 170–174, *173*, 184

education, 21, 48, 84, 109, 125, 131, 191

Egypt: government of, 23; Iran and, 21; Iraq and, 84; Islam in, 87–88; leadership in, 150; Lebanon and, 77; Muscat and, 168; Palestine and, 74; protests in, 39; Qatar and, 23; Saudi Arabia and, 146, 170; Syria and, 71; Tunisia and, 8; UAE and, 122; U.S. and, 41, 157–158; Yemen and, 17–18

electricity, 181–182

elitism, 23, 27, 38–44, 55–56, 93, 135–136, 196

Elizabeth, II (queen), 124

energy: consumption, 172–174, *173*; economics of, 191–192; electricity, 181–182; to IMF, 134–135; nuclear, 158, 169–170; politics, 109–111, 177–178, 182–184, *183*; in Qatar, 181–182; subsidies, 172, *173*. *See also* oil

England. *See* United Kingdom

environmental politics: economics of, 32, 166–169; in Gulf States, 163–165, 171–174, *173*, 184–186; risk in, 174–184, *175*, *178*, *179*, *183*

Essence of Decision (Allison), 67

Europe, 9, 57–58, 66, 92, 120, 134–135, 146

GPSR Authorized Representative: Easy Access System Europe, Mustamäe tee 50, 10621 Tallinn, Estonia, gpsr.requests@easproject.com

www.ingramcontent.com/pod-product-compliance
Lightning Source LLC
Chambersburg PA
CBHW022138020426
42334CB00015B/954